D0399214

Models of Capitalism

Growth and Stagnation in the Modern Era

David Coates

Polity Press

First published in 2000 by Polity Press in association with Blackwell Publishers Ltd

Reprinted 2001

Editorial office:
Polity Press
65 Bridge Street
Cambridge CB2 1UR, UK

Marketing and production:
Blackwell Publishers Ltd
108 Cowley Road
Oxford OX4 1JF, UK

Published in the USA by
Blackwell Publishers Inc.
Commerce Place
350 Main Street
Malden, MA 02148, USA

A catalogue record for this book is available from the British Library.

Library of Congress Cataloging-in-Publication Data

Coates, David.
    Models of capitalism: growth and stagnation in the modern era
/ David Coates.
      p.   cm.
    Includes bibliographical references and index.
    ISBN 0-7456-2058-2
    ISBN 0-7456-2059-0 (pbk.)
    1. Capitalism.   I. Title.
    HB501   .C63   2000
    330.12'2 – dc21
                              99–32965
                                 CIP

Typeset in 10.5 on 12 pt Ehrhardt
by Best-set Typesetter Ltd., Hong Kong
Printed in Great Britain by TJ International, Padstow, Cornwall

This book is printed on acid-free paper.

Contents

Acknowledgements

Table 1.1 is reproduced by kind permission of the Social Market Foundation; tables 1.2, 1.3, 1.6, 6.1 and 8.1 by kind permission of the National Institute of Economic and Social Research; table 8.2 by kind permission of the editors of *Competition and Change*; figure 1.1 by kind permission of the Controller of Her Majesty's Stationery Office; figure 5.1 by kind permission of Nicholas Brealey Publishing Company; figure 7.1 with the permission of the publisher, Stanford University Press, © 1989 by the Board of Trustees of the Leland Stanford Junior University. The extract from W. Streeck's *Social Institutions and Economic Performance* is reproduced with the permission of Sage Publications. An earlier version of chapter 4 appeared in L. Panitch and C. Leys (eds), *The Socialist Register 1999* (Merlin Press); and a fuller version of the Appendix is to be found in *New Political Economy*, volume 4, number 1.

Preface

By the time a broad comparative study of this kind is completed, whole new sets of debts have necessarily been accumulated: debts to scholars on whose detailed labours the general analysis rests; debts to colleagues who have provided the climate and space in which to read and reflect upon that scholarship; and debts to friends who have read or discussed parts or all of the results of that reading and reflection. The references cited at the end of this volume stand as testimony to the scale of that first debt. Here I would simply like to record my thanks to a smaller group of colleagues and friends.

My understandings of the issues discussed in this volume have benefited enormously from conversations down the years with Leo Panitch, Greg Albo, Peter Nolan and Jeff Henderson. Individual parts of the argument developed here were strengthened by listening to and taking advice from (among others) Andreas Bieler, Phil Cerny, Tony Elger, Diane Elson, Richard Higgott, Colin Leys, Steve Ludlam, David Marsh, Stan Metcalfe, Jamie Peck, Hugo Radice, Gareth Api Richards, Ngai-Ling Sum, Matthew Watson, Rorden Wilkinson and Karel Williams; and the whole manuscript was read (and improved immensely) by Colin Hay, in a characteristic act of generosity and rigour which went far beyond the call of duty. None of them bear any responsibility, of course, for any deficiencies that remain, but each has helped in his or her different way to keep those deficiencies to manageable proportions: and I thank them for that.

Three other sets of acknowledgements are necessary and appropriate. One is to the economic journalists writing for the *Financial Times*, and in particular to Robert Taylor, for the sheer quality of the reporting on which so many of us now depend. The second is to my former colleagues in the Government Department of the University of Manchester, without whose support and comradeship this whole exercise could never have been completed. And the third, by far the most important, is to both my immediate and my extended family. The writing of this book has been a pleasure because my family have been a pleasure: in the UK most centrally Eileen and Jonathan, but also Edward and Thomas, Anna, Ben, Emma and now Megan, and in the US Mary Jane, Pete and Loran, Mike and Donna, Chris and Carol, Steve and Jo. As Eileen, Jonathan and I now switch locations, from one side of our Atlantic family to the other, it is an appropriate moment to record publicly the extent of my private debt to them all. It is impossible not to believe in the potentiality of the human spirit when surrounded by a family of such quality and love.

Guide to Country Story Lines

The following table indicates the main blocks of material on particular countries.

Chapter	US	UK	Sweden	West Germany	Japan
1	2–6	2–6	2–6	2–6	2–6
2	24–43	43–53	–	–	–
3	–	–	72–4	64–72	54–64
4	–	86–94	94–101	–	–
5	–	135–41	–	–	127–35
6	149–57	–	–	167–77	177–90
7	201–10	193–201	–	210–13	213–23
8	248–50	244–7	239–44	239–44	234–9

1

Capitalist Models and Economic Growth

Amid the optimism of a new century, the legacies of the past still lie like a nightmare on the brain of the living. Communism may have fallen (in Europe at least) but in the policy-making circles of the advanced capitalist world three quite enormous issues of economic policy remain to be resolved. In a capitalist economy, is the achievement of economic growth best left to the market, or should its orchestration be a central task of government? Do old ways of governing capitalist economies need now to be replaced by new ones? And should we be in pursuit of the one 'right way' of ordering economic and social life in the pursuit of economic growth, or do we still face a range of viable capitalist models?

These questions have all been around for a very long time, but they have gathered new urgency and force of late, as the pattern of economic performance among advanced capitalist economies has altered sharply. In the 1980s, in both the US and the UK, the policy debate was dominated by questions of economic decline, power was held by advocates of market-based capitalism, and the majority of their critics were pressing strongly for a managed economy of the seemingly more successful German or Japanese variety. By the late 1990s, in contrast, it was the German and Japanese economies that were widely perceived to be in difficulties, governmental power in both Washington and London had been captured by centre-left parties, and it was the advocates of unregulated capitalism who now offered sceptical opposition to the new 'third way' in politics. Suddenly, in the context of increasing globalization, old certainties have been replaced by new doubts; and the search is on again for solutions to problems of economic growth which, only a decade ago, appeared to have clear, definite, but varied solutions. In the face of such uncertainties, students of contemporary politics need rapidly to familiarize themselves with things hitherto of concern only to academic specialists: the causes of the various postwar economic 'miracles', the meaning and significance of globalization, the virtues and vices of flexible labour markets, the difference between first, second and third 'ways' in economic management, the nature of different capitalist models, and so on. The purpose of this volume is to facilitate that process of rapid learning.

The pattern of postwar economic growth

Economic growth is not the easiest thing to measure. On the contrary, the empirical and conceptual complexities of economic measurement are so contentious (and the implications of different modes of measurement for the results generated so vast) that 'measuring the wealth of nations' is now the subject of a vast technical literature (see in particular Maddison, 1995a; Shaikh and Tonak, 1994; Coates, 1995a). But that literature notwithstanding, it is clear that, even among advanced capitalist economies, patterns of economic performance have varied significantly over the postwar period as a whole, and that they have varied no matter how that performance is measured. Whether we use discrete indicators (such as output growth, the productivity of capital or labour, trade share, investment, or living standards) or simply competitive league tables, the picture remains broadly the same. It is a picture of initial postwar US economic supremacy (a supremacy shared in the late 1940s by the UK as the capitalist bloc's second major economic power); it is a picture of subsequent convergence and catch-up by a select group of northern European and Asian economies; and it is a picture of recent unexpected economic turbulence.

If we take the figures in table 1.1 as our starting point, they confirm that per capita income in the US in 1950 was significantly higher than elsewhere in the world system, and that in 1950 at least, living standards in the UK were only rarely exceeded in Western Europe, and then only just. They also show that forty years later average per capita income in the US was still higher than elsewhere (although the margin of difference was much less), that living standards in Japan were by then close to North American standards, and that those in the UK had slipped well behind average levels in most of northern Europe. The figures also show that what links the two dates are spectacularly different overall growth performances: an increase of per capita income in the US and UK of 230 per cent compared with a change in GDP per head of more than 900 per cent in Japan and Taiwan and of around 500 per cent in West Germany and Italy.

Statistics are, of course, highly malleable, and in consequence have to be approached with a developed sensitivity to the manner of their construction and to their framework of underpinning assumptions. In table 1.1 the choice of 1950 as the base year is critical: it was a time when the former Axis powers were still suffering extreme postwar dislocation and the Allies

Table 1.1 Real GDP per person, 1950–1994 (international dollars at 1990 values)

	1950		1973		1994[a]	
1	USA	9,573	Switzerland	17,903	USA	22,569
2	Switzerland	8,939	USA	16,607	Switzerland	20,830
3	New Zealand	8,495	Canada	13,644	Hong Kong	19,592
4	Australia	7,218	Sweden	13,494	Japan	19,505
5	Canada	7,047	Denmark	13,416	Denmark	19,305
6	UK	6,847	Germany	13,152	Germany	19,097
7	Sweden	6,738	France	12,940	Singapore	18,797
8	Denmark	6,683	Netherlands	12,763	Norway	18,372
9	Netherlands	5,850	New Zealand	12,575	Canada	18,350
10	Belgium	5,346	Australia	12,485	France	17,968
11	France	5,221	UK	11,992	Austria	17,285
12	Norway	4,969	Belgium	11,905	Belgium	17,225
13	Germany	4,281	Austria	11,308	Netherlands	17,152
14	Finland	4,131	Japan	11,017	Australia	17,107
15	Austria	3,731	Finland	10,768	Sweden	16,710
16	Ireland	3,518	Italy	10,409	Italy	16,404
17	Italy	3,425	Norway	10,229	UK	16,371
18	Spain	2,397	Spain	8,739	New Zealand	15,085
19	Portugal	2,132	Greece	7,779	Finland	14,779
20	Singapore	2,038	Portugal	7,568	Taiwan	12,985
21	Hong Kong	1,962	Ireland	7,023	Ireland	12,624
22	Greece	1,951	Hong Kong	6,768	Spain	12,544
23	Japan	1,873	Singapore	5,412	South Korea	11,235
24	Taiwan	922	Taiwan	3,669	Portugal	11,083
25	South Korea	876	South Korea	2,840	Greece	10,165

Source: Crafts, 1997a: 15

[a] Provisional calculations on the 1997 data suggest further movement still, with Japan slipping to 6th place, Germany to 13th, Sweden to 17th and even the USA to 2nd (behind Singapore). Of our five key economies, only the UK improved its ranking between 1994 and 1997, moving to 14th. I am grateful to Gareth Api Richards for this information.

were enjoying a brief period of unchallenged world supremacy. The choice of end year (1994) is also significant, marking the moment when the Japanese economy had settled firmly into its first major postwar recession and the US and UK economies had begun their prolonged 1990s period of growth and job creation. The choice of *base level* is equally important: spectacular growth rates are much easier to achieve if the starting point is low (as it was with Japan in 1950), if economies are at different points in their own growth histories (as was visibly the case with South Korea), and if economies lie ahead with superior technologies that can be copied and with markets that can be raided (as did the US and the UK). There is a dimension – actually a very large dimension – of simple 'catch up and convergence' tucked away in the figures of table 1.1 (whose importance and significance we shall discuss fully in chapter 6); but there are real changes tucked away there too, changes that cannot be simply explained – and explained away – in such a fashion. Three sets of such changes deserve our particular attention.

1   The first is the significant weakening in the relative positions of both the US and the UK economies over the period as a whole, the gap between levels of performance in the US economy and those in other leading capitalist economies diminishing over time, and the UK economy slipping down a variety of league tables on such things as output, productivity, investment and living standards, particularly before 1979.

2   The second is the remarkable surge of growth in a number of northern European economies (including the German, Benelux and Scandinavian economies) in the 1950s and 1960s, the more prolonged growth of the Japanese economy and the recent growth surge of the Asian Tiger economies – a surge that has effectively added a new regional grouping of major capitalist industrial economies to the regional groupings in north America and northern Europe laid down before 1945.

3   The third (hinted at in table 1.1, but clearly evident in table 1.2) is the revival of the post-1979 UK economy relative initially to the German and recently even to the Japanese economies, and the revival too of the US economy's capacity to generate growth and employment. In fact, by as early as 1994 the US had replaced Japan as the world's 'most competitive nation' in the league tables produced by the Geneva-based World Economic Forum, Japan having occupied the top position for the previous seven years (*Financial Times*, 6 September 1995). All this before the more provisional statistical data covering the second half of the 1990s began to document the scale of the post-1992 Japanese recession, the post-1997 East Asian economic 'crisis' and the slowing down of productivity, growth and employment rates in most (although by no means all) of the northern European economies. These were all developments that restored some degree of international competitiveness to some economies (the UK's perhaps, the US more certainly), which had been widely seen before 1980 as weakening (and even as potentially terminally flawed).

Indeed each of the major capitalist economies has a slightly different postwar growth story to tell, as table 1.4 attempts to indicate. The best decades for the West German economy, in terms of economic growth, were definitely those before 1973. After the first oil crisis, West German growth rates settled back to nearer the average for the OECD as a whole. The Swedish economy also had its best decades before 1973; but it then settled into a growth rate that was lower than the OECD average. The Japanese

Table 1.2 Annual percentage change in GDP, 1992–1997

Country	1992	1993	1994	1995	1996	1997
US	2.7	2.3	3.5	2.0	2.8	3.8
UK	−0.5	2.1	4.3	2.7	2.2	3.3
Germany	1.9	−1.2	2.8	1.9	1.4	2.3
Japan	1.0	0.3	0.7	1.4	4.1	0.8
South Korea	6.2	4.8	6.3	4.5	4.9	4.4

Source: National Institute Economic Review, 3/98: 121

Table 1.3 Rates of unemployment, 1992–1997 (seasonally adjusted per cent of total labour force, by national definition)

Country	1992	1993	1994	1995	1996	1997
US	7.5	6.9	6 1	5.6	5.4	4.9
UK	9.9	10.5	9 5	8.3	7.6	5.7
Germany	7.8	9.1	9 6	9.5	10.5	11.5
Japan	2.2	2.5	2 9	3.2	3.3	3.4

Source: National Institute Economic Review, 3/98: 121

Table 1.4 Real GDP growth, 1950–1990 (average annual percentage change)[a]

	1950–1960	1960–1973	1973–1980	1980–1990
US	3.3	4.0	2.1	3.0
UK	2.8	3.1	0.9	2.7
Germany	8.2	4.4	2.2	1.9
Sweden	3.4	4.6	1.7[b]	1.7
Japan	8.8	9.6	3.7	4.2
South Korea[c]	1.3	6.5	7.4	6.8

[a] OECD rates: 1950–73, 4.7%; 1973–87, 2.4%.
[b] the Swedish figure is an average for 1970–92.
[c] the South Korean figures are GDP per head.
Sources: Giersch et al., 1992: 4; Pilat, 1994: 8; Henrekson et al., 1996: 243–4; Henderson, 1990: 276, 279

economy, by contrast, sustained its high-growth performance relative to that average right up to 1992, although in its case also the years of truly spectacular rates of growth were over by 1973. The 'Asian growth miracle' after 1973 occurred elsewhere, in places such as South Korea. By contrast, the growth performance of both the US and the UK economies was more sluggish throughout, and was particularly dire in the years between the first oil crisis and the second (1973–1979). In comparative terms, the best growth decade for those economies was the 1990s. Certainly the UK economy then managed to pull itself out of the long recession into which it had settled between 1989 and 1992, to perform its own small 'catch up' operation on its main European rivals; both it and the US economy spent most of the 1990s lowering their officially recorded levels of unemployment as unemployment *rose* both in the newly united Germany and in Japan.

The question of capitalist models

It is with the origins and determinants of these key features of the postwar economic growth story that the text which follows is primarily concerned; and it is so for at least three distinguishable sets of reasons. The first is that the causes of that growth pattern are academically contentious, and that those academic disputes trigger very different bodies of advice for politicians and civil servants committed to the pursuit of growth. Which explanation is correct, therefore, is of immense political (and not just academic) interest. The second is that behind these academic debates and policy recommendations lie real disagreements about the viability of particular models of capitalist organization and their associated political projects, and hence real issues about desirable and attainable futures. The rights of workers in particular rise and fall with the viability of these underlying models. And the third is that economic growth touches so many aspects of social life, and does so regardless of the political projects within which it occurs, that its achievement is a prerequisite for the protection of so much that is of importance to us all, workers or not.

At the core of the contemporary debate on why growth rates differ stands a *neo-liberal* economic orthodoxy. In that dominant paradigm, economic growth is explained as a consequence of the freeing of market forces and the associated development of appropriate factors of production; and differences in growth performance are explained as by-products of the degree of market freedom achieved and of the resulting differences in factor quantity and quality. As is explained in more detail in the Appendix, neo-liberalism has both an 'old' and a 'new' face, but in both these forms neo-liberal explanations of economic performance have never been entirely without challenge. To their right has long stood a *conservative* strand of argument uneasy with the social consequences of untrammelled markets, an unease normally articulated without the support of a complete and distinctive theory of how capitalist economies grow, and one prone to emphasize the pivotal role of non-market factors (cf trust and culture) in explaining different patterns of economic growth. To their left have long stood both *centre-left* and *Marxist* explanations of how capitalist economies perform: explanations of different growth rates that either emphasize discrete non-market-based factors as key shapers of the way markets operate or point to the manner in which market-based interactions are qualitatively transformed by their insertion into different capitalist-based class systems and the resulting social structures of accumulation. There was a time (throughout the 1960s, and in certain circles well into the 1970s) when centre-left arguments were the dominant ones, pushing liberal views of markets off centre-stage; but since the 'crisis of Keynesianism' in the 1970s liberalism has returned apace – and economic policy now is shaped by a much narrower and more right-wing range of views than was conventional two decades ago.

As we shall see in more detail as the argument unfolds, there is a close affinity between the policy packages adopted in the pursuit of economic growth and wider bodies of economic theory. Advocates of market-based capitalism tend to draw on the arguments of neo-classical economics in defence of their case. Advocates of 'third way' packages tend to empathize with 'new growth theory' (as was once famously admitted by Gordon Brown, Chancellor of the Exchequer in the UK's New Labour Government after 1997). Certain conservative-inspired popularizers of more trust-based forms of capitalism (Fukuyama in particular) tend to treat neo-classical economics as essentially correct but limited, and to talk of 'a missing twenty per cent of human behaviour about which neo-classical economics can give only a poor account' (Fukuyama, 1995: 13). And more centre-left advocates of German and Japanese modes of capitalist organization tend, as we shall see, to mobilize Schumpeterian or post-Keynesian understandings of the growth process to sustain their preference for cartelized forms of corporate organization and proactive government spending. These particular economic theories are therefore yet another 'academic specialism' with which the general student of politics now needs to be familiar. (They are surveyed briefly in the Appendix, to assist those readers whose knowledge of economic theory is currently limited.)

For it is hard to overstate the contemporary political importance of the current academic debate on why growth rates differ, or to overestimate the centrality of the 'labour question' to that debate. As we shall see later, both 'old' and 'new' versions of neo-liberal growth theory ultimately subscribe to the view that growth depends on competitiveness, and that competitiveness depends in large part on the control of labour costs. 'Old growth theory' points the finger of responsibility for labour costs at 'inflexibilities' created by trade union organization and power. 'New growth theory' tends to shift the focus of responsibility away from trade unionism towards issues of labour skills and training, and even on occasions dabbles sympathetically with the more conventional centre-left argument that the key to labour-market flexibility is a set of trust-based industrial relationships guaranteed by extensive worker rights and trade union powers. Yet within that entire policy spectrum – from those who would achieve economic growth by cutting trade union powers to those who would achieve economic growth by increasing them – the relationship of labour power to international competitiveness is still seen as central. More radical voices still problematize other social actors and processes, as we shall see. The nature of *capital*, the force of *culture*, the capacities of the *state* – these too have a presence in the contemporary debate on why growth rates differ. But the central preoccupation of most academic commentators and contemporary policy-makers is with questions of labour power. In most policy-making circles these days, labour power and international competitiveness are invariably seen as incompatible, and policy is inexorably directed at reducing the first in order to enhance the second.

This is why one of the main research questions underpinning this study is whether 'flexible' labour markets are a necessary condition for successful capital accumulation: whether they were in the immediate past, and whether the new conditions of intensified global competition now make the erosion of trade union rights and levels of labour remuneration even more vital to the achievement and retention of international competitiveness. We need to know whether it was always necessary in the past, and is always necessary now, to cut wages, intensify work routines and reduce workers' and trade union rights, if the economic growth of a particular economy is to be sustained in the face of competition from companies based abroad. As we shall see in more detail in chapter 4, that was certainly the thrust of the neo-liberal project developed in the UK by Margaret Thatcher in the 1980s; and even now, when UK politics is dominated by the 'third way' thinking of New Labour, it remains conventional to argue both that UK labour markets have to *remain flexible* if competitiveness is to be sustained and that European labour markets have to *become more flexible* if unemployment is to be reduced. The Thatcherite solution to the diminished competitiveness of European welfare capitalism was to dismantle welfare rights. The Blairites talk only of reforming those rights: but in practice the direction of policy is similar. Because it is, particularly the European-based debate about how to encourage economic growth in the new millennium is in essence a debate about the viability of a particular capitalist model. It is a debate about the future of welfare capitalism, as that has been understood and lived by northern European labour movements since 1945.

Ultimately this should not surprise us, for in fact each of the major positions in the contemporary debate on why growth rates differ among advanced capitalist economies has historically been associated with a distinct set of attitudes to the viability or otherwise of discrete *models* of capitalism. Indeed the varying fortunes of economies thought to exemplify those models have shaped (and continue to shape) the popular (and to a degree even the academic) discussion of contemporary growth strategies in important ways, the confidence of their advocates ebbing and flowing as their particular exemplars prosper and decline. So enthusiasts for market-led capitalisms lost ground to their opponents as the United States' competitive advantage was eroded – first by Western-European-based companies and then by Japanese-based ones – in the 1970s and 1980s; and in the same manner critics of market-led models had their confidence shaken by the growing sclerosis of Western European economies in the 1990s and by the 'crisis of the Asian model' which broke in the summer of 1997. For there can be no doubting the close fit that exists between different theories of economic growth and the institutional arrangements characteristic of different capitalist models. Broadly speaking, neo-liberal scholarship tends to favour Anglo-American practices, in which neither the state nor the unions have a significant economic role or voice. Conservative scholarship tends to favour developmental models of the East Asian kind, or occasionally the French kind, in which political institutions work closely with private capital in the pursuit of growth (Barnett, 1986; Albert, 1993; Fukuyama, 1995). Centre-left scholarship invariably has a penchant for consensual models of a Scandinavian or German hue, in which trade unions figure as a junior governing partner, and extensive welfare rights underpin private economic relationships, while Marxist scholarship, which in the West has long eschewed centrally planned economic models of Soviet derivation, tends predictably to see deep and irresolvable contradictions in capitalism however organized, and therefore calls down a plague on all these houses.

In the broadest sense the choice of model in that clash of political projects can be (and should be) reduced to one of three: to a choice between a *market-led* form of capitalism and two differing forms of capitalist organization which are often presented by their advocates as more *trust-based* than market-led, one in which state power is of central importance to local capital accumulation, and one built around an explicit compact between capital, labour and the state. It should be said, in passing, that the relevant academic literature is more profligate than that (for a full survey, see Coates, 1999b). It is replete with models differentiated either by geographical location (the 'Scandinavian model', the 'Asian model' and the like) or by institutional variation (bank-based systems versus credit-based, 'individualistic' versus 'communitarian' value systems, 'coordinated' versus 'non co-ordinated' forms of labour market regulation, and so on). It is also replete with schemas that differentiate capitalism into a wide range of polar types. Sometimes capitalism comes in two types (Albert, 1993), sometimes in four (Scott, 1997: 16–18), but quite often, as here, in three (Thurow, 1992; Hart, 1992a; 1992b; Marquand, 1988). For there is a broad recognition in the work of scholars now often referred to in the professional literature on political science as the 'new institutionalists' that over the postwar period as a whole it has been possible to discern in the debate about the growth performance of advanced capitalist economies the presence of a number of ideal types of capitalist organization, of at least the following kind.

- *Market-led* capitalisms, in which accumulation decisions lie overwhelmingly with private companies, which are left free to pursue their own short-term profit motives and to raise their capital in open financial markets. In such capitalisms, workers enjoy only limited statutory industrial and social rights, and earn only what they can extract from their employers in largely unregulated labour markets. State involvement in economic management is limited largely to the creation and protection of markets; and the dominant understandings of politics and morality in the society as a whole tend to be individualistic and liberal in form. The USA is conventionally treated as the quintessential example of a market-led capitalism, although the UK has often also been included, in its 1979–1997 Thatcherite form – hence the general label 'neo-American' or 'Anglo-Saxon' capitalism often attached to this generic model (Albert, 1993). In this text they will be referred to as 'liberal capitalisms'.

- *State-led* capitalisms, in which, by contrast, accumulation decisions are again primarily seen as the right and responsibility of private companies, but in which those decisions are invariably taken only after close liaison with public agencies, and are often indirectly determined through administrative guidance and bank leadership. In such capitalisms, labour movements still tend to lack strong political and social rights; but there is space for forms of labour relations that tie some workers to private corporations through company-based welfare provision. The dominant cultural forms in such capitalisms are likely to be conservative-nationalist in content. The Japanese economy in the immediate postwar period and the South Korean economy more recently have often been cited as the prime examples of state-led capitalisms: hence the tendency to label this model either 'Asian capitalism' or the 'developmental state' form.

- *Negotiated or consensual* capitalisms, in which the degree of direct state regulation of capital accumulation may still be small, but the political system entrenches a set of strong worker rights and welfare provision which give organized labour a powerful market presence and the ability to participate directly in industrial decision-making. The dominant cultural networks in these capitalisms tend to be either social democratic or Christian democratic ones. The postwar Scandinavian and West German economies have often been offered as exemplars of this capitalist type: hence the label 'European welfare capitalism' or even the 'Rhine model' (Albert, 1993).

The academic debate on why growth rates differ, and on the associated desirability of particular capitalist models, has therefore been (and remains) simultaneously a technical and a political debate. It remains a technical debate in the sense that each position embodies a different assessment of the relation of the market to the state (both in the past and in the future) in successful cases of economic growth. For some, the state is a vital economic actor. For others, states help economies best by leaving things to the market. But since in a capitalist economy leaving things to the market means leaving things to private capital, techrical assessments of appropriate state–market relations necessarily and quickly slide into political assessments of which set of private interests are most compatible with interests of a more general kind. So each argument on how states and markets did or should interact quickly transmutes itself into a judgement about the extent to which economic growth was or is best attained. Should it be by leaving accumulation to the owners of private capital, free of regulation and constraint, or by supplementing (even, in extreme cases, replacing) their role with that of others – political agencies, like the state, or social agencies, like trade unions? And that in its turn means that what ultimately is central to the debate on why growth rates differ is the question of social power and privilege: who governs, who is rewarded, who pays the price, whose economic and political interests should take precedence and why? The debate on why growth rates differ is thus in part an arena for the pursuit of technical disagreements, but it is also an arena for the pursuit of interests and values.

The parameters of the study

If we are to examine the causes of the postwar growth performance of advanced capitalist economies and assess the past and future viability of a range of capitalist models as routes to growth, we need to set down at the outset a number of parameters: on how we shall measure economic performance, at what level of economic activity we shall measure it, and with which economies we shall be centrally concerned.

(1) *The measurement of economic performance* As we noted at the outset, there are genuine problems of conceptualization and measurement to be settled before growth rates can be adequately compared and their significance assessed. At the simplest level we need to be aware that there are problems of reliability and signification. Conventionally, when the performance of national economies is being examined, the data available for use are organized under such indices as gross national product, rate of inflation, level of unemployment, the state of the balance of payments, the level and growth of labour and the scale and quality of investment. It is not always easy, even with these indices, to gather data that can safely be compared either over time or between countries (on this, Hart, 1992a: 204–10; Levitas and Guy, 1996); and even when we can, the choice of time frame and countries of reference remains critical for the shape of the resulting argument. We have seen that already in the construction of the first set of tables. To slice time up, to show one economy growing rapidly and another not, and to imply thereby that the first has structural strengths denied to the second, may be to misread the position each occupies in two linked sequences: their position in the sequence of catch-up and convergence, and their position on their own growth trajectory from 'under-development' to 'maturity' – a tra-

jectory along which, according to many writers, growth rates necessarily vary over time (Rostow, 1960; Kaldor, 1966; Porter, 1990). All we can do in relation to this set of legitimate concerns is attempt to control or allow for both catch-up and trajectory (on this, see chapter 6), while extending the time frame of analysis to a period which allows us to treat different growth paths within it as genuinely indicative of underlying differences in economic strength.

Yet the selection of indicators to locate underlying economic strength is itself highly contentious, and dependent on prior positions in a number of fiercely contested debates. One concerns the proper weighting of economic and social variables in the calculation of economic growth. Not all commentators on relative competitive performance are content with indicators that rest on economic indicators alone (of the kind which underlay table 1.1), some preferring instead to use what they term a 'misery index': 'the sum of the inflation rate and the standardised unemployment rate' (Crafts, 1993b: 328–9). Indeed of late even the United Nations has taken to producing a more socially sensitive indicator – a Human Development Index (HDI) – 'based on three elements – life expectancy at birth, knowledge measured by a weighted average of literacy and school enrolment, and income which is discounted heavily above some threshold' (Crafts, 1997b: 77; also Crafts, 1997c). That index, as table 1.5 shows, leaves the position of the US, Japan, Germany and the UK largely unaltered in world league tables of performance; but it does reposition a number of the Asian 'tiger economies' in a quite dramatic way. And if, in addition, instead of measuring simply GDP per head, we include a measure of hours worked (and thereby GDP per hour worked), that repositioning becomes more dramatic still. Table 1.5 suggests that the impact of making such adjustments is both to indicate the greater leisure time enjoyed by European and (until recently) North American workers and to raise European growth rates while depressing Asian ones. Japan in particular drops from third place in GDP per person to eighteenth in GDP per hour. The overall result, as Crafts suggests, is that 'conventional rankings of economic performance based on real GDP/person underplay European success' such that when measuring living standards at least, 'comparison should not be confined to levels or growth rates of real GDP/person' (1997b: 81, 83). The full significance of the dramatic shift in the position of the Japanese economy in such tables will be discussed more fully, first in chapter 5, then in chapter 8.

A second point of contention surrounding the measurement of economic performance concerns the supposedly special importance of manufacturing industry as the 'engine of growth' in modern economies, and hence the use of indices of *de-industrialization* as measures of underperformance. There are certainly political economists committed to the view that 'manufacturing matters' (Cohen and Zysman, 1987), for whom the strengths and weaknesses of an economy's industrial base are vital to its growth. But there are others, probably more plentiful, who see service-sector growth as

Table 1.5   Rankings for 1992

	GDP per person	GDP per hour	HDI
US	1	9	1
Switzerland	2	6	2
Japan	3	18	3
West Germany	4	4	5
Hong Kong	5	19	13
Denmark	6	11	8
Canada	7	7	4
France	8	2	6
Norway	9	5	7
Belgium	10	1	10 =
Austria	11	8	12
Sweden	12	10	10 =
Netherlands	13	3	9
Australia	14	12	14
Italy	15	14	15
Singapore	16	21	18
UK	17	15	17
Finland	18	17	16
Spain	19	13	19
Ireland	20	16	20
Taiwan	21	23	22
Portugal	22	22	23
Greece	23	20	21
South Korea	24	24	24

Source: Crafts, 1997o: 81

inevitable in a mature economy and a sign of its general health, for whom measures of manufacturing's contribution to GDP and employment do not, of themselves, say anything of particular significance. For our purposes, the resolution of this important disagreement lies in a sensitivity to the distinction between positive and negative de-industrialization (Rowthorn and Wells, 1987). The contribution of the manufacturing sector to employment can decline for one of two reasons. It can decline because the manufacturing sector is highly productive and competitive, able to shed labour into service employment without generating inflation or trade deficits; or it can decline for lack of competitiveness, when labour is shed either into unemployment or into service employment, which then sucks in large volumes of manufactured goods. It is the first (positive) form of de-industrialization that indicates economic strength, the second (negative) that indicates weakness. The distinction between the two therefore points to the value of retaining, for our purposes here, the test of economic growth established by A.J. Singh two decades ago: that in a strong economy, the manufacturing sector should be able to satisfy 'the demands of consumers at home [and] also to sell enough of its product abroad to pay for the nation's import requirements' and to do so 'at socially acceptable levels of output, employment and the exchange rate' (Singh, 1977: 128). It is a test echoed elsewhere in the growth literature, not least by the President's Commission on Industrial Competitiveness in the United States, which in 1985 set as 'the industry standard' 'the degree to which a nation can, under free and fair market conditions, produce goods and services that meet the test of international markets while simultaneously maintaining or expanding the real income of its citizens' (cited in Cohen, 1995: 22; see also Tyson, 1992: 1). It is also a test which puts a very large question mark over the adequacy of the UK's postwar economic performance, as the data captured so starkly in figure 1.1 indicates.

Indeed there is much to be gained from differentiating 'growth performance' from 'trade performance', because although the two are obviously

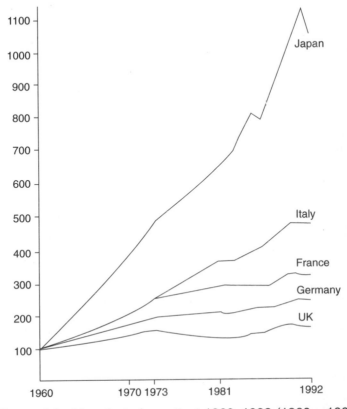

Figure 1.1   Manufacturing output 1960–1992 (1960 = 100)
Source: Select Committee on Trade and Industry, 1994: 16

Table 1.6 Current balance of payments (US$ billions)

	1989	1990	1991	1992	1993	1994	1995	1996	1997
US	−104	−92	−4	−51	−86	−124	−115	−135	−155
UK	−37	−33	−14	−18	−15	−2	−6	−3	7
Germany	57	49	−15	−19	−15	−21	−23	−14	−2
Japan	59	36	71	112	132	131	111	66	94

Source: National Institute Economic Review, 3/98 123

related, they do not necessarily coincide in time. The Japanese 'growth miracle', for example, slowed after 1973; yet it was after 1973 that the penetration of US markets for cars and consumer electronics by Japanese-based producers became so marked, and so politically significant. In fact, as table 1.6 shows, the US and UK economies continued to run large deficits on their balance of payments throughout most of the 1990s, even as their growth performance improved. Those deficits were lower at the end of the 1990s than they were at their peak in the mid and late 1980s; but they remain in place none the less. Japan, by contrast, ended the century still in possession of a large surplus in its overseas accounts, even though by then its growth performance had seriously declined.

Such a linking of growth performance and trade performance places the emphasis of attention on questions of competitiveness, and privileges the strengths and weaknesses of those sectors of a modern economy producing commodities that are traded across national borders. Not everyone, however, feels such a focus is in any way desirable or legitimate. Paul Krugman, for example, is on record as seeing such an 'obsession with competitiveness as both wrong and dangerous' (1994a: 44), because – in his view – world trade is not a zero-sum game, and 'it is simply not the case that the world's leading nations are to any important degree in competition with each other, or that any of their major economic problems can be attributed to failures to compete on world markets' (ibid.: 30). While seeing the force of his underlying concern with productivity rather than with competitiveness, such a level of scepticism is still hard to square with the constraints on growth and investment experienced by those postwar economies, not least the UK's, whose manufacturing sectors progressively failed to meet Singh's test. It seems safer to go along with the larger number of economists who have pointed to the importance, for long-term sustainable growth, of the achievement by nationally based firms of competitiveness in its various forms: price competitiveness, non-price competitiveness (the two together being what Pfaller and his colleagues term 'performing competitiveness'), and a more general form of competitiveness (which they term 'structural competitiveness'). This last is particularly important for our purposes here (Pfaller et al., 1991).

By 'performing competitiveness' Pfaller, Therborn and Gough mean the ability of nationally based firms to compete in open markets at home and abroad, something usually measured by market share. By 'structural competitiveness' they mean the ability of national economies to provide high and growing per capita incomes while exposed to foreign competition, something best measured, in their view, by growth in productivity. The distinction between the two forms of competitiveness is important because the notion of structural competitiveness inserts into the analysis, from the outset, concerns with the *consequences* of economic growth, and in particular with its impact on the people caught up in it. Performing competitiveness alone does not do that. Performing competitiveness is obviously a prerequisite for structural competitiveness, but it can be achieved (and often is achieved) by the use of devices (low wages and competitive devaluations among others) which erode long-term structural strength. The distinction between the two forms of competitiveness then leaves us in a position to judge the social desirability of different routes to economic growth, and locks into the analysis from its inception indicators of performance which are social and economic rather than merely financial and economic – indicators such as income levels, leisure time, the provision of welfare and job security as well as those charting output growth, inflation rates and exchange rate stability.

The distinction between the two forms of competitiveness also points to the manner in which the general performance of an economy (its structural competitiveness) is necessarily the product of the performing competitiveness of its constituent parts, and thus raises for us another issue on which prior clarification is required – the appropriate level of analysis at which studies of international competitiveness and economic growth ought properly to be pitched.

(2)   *Whose economic performance?* Normally, in discussions on economic growth and international competitiveness, the main unit of analysis adopted is the 'national economy', and the main question asked is why some national economies out-perform others in both output growth and trade share. That question has never precluded other questions being put as well: questions about the competitiveness of firms or industries across national boundaries, and questions about the competitiveness of regional blocs containing more than one national economy. But until recently at least, in most of the relevant academic literature (and in the associated popular commentary), sectoral and regional concerns have normally been subordinated to, or subsumed within, national ones, partly because most of the easily accessible statistical material was (and still is) generated by national bodies and organized in national categories, and partly because in the past national economies have visibly operated as reasonably self-contained units, interacting with each other only at the margin. Recently, however, the appropriateness of this focus on competing *national* economies has been seriously challenged as being – in a critical sense – 'yesterday's problem', one ren-

dered anachronistic by economic developments at both the supra-national and sub-national levels.

This study's concern with national economic performance sits in tension with the arguments of those who feel that to focus on the national economy is now to *undershoot* – that national economies have become too small, and too penetrated by global processes of trade, production and communication, to be any longer the appropriate focus of analysis. The argument here is that, when the largest private corporations have sales only just below the entire GDP of economies as substantial as Sweden and Indonesia, we now find ourselves in an age of 'the borderless economy', in which 'nation states are no longer meaningful units in which to think about economic activity. In a borderless world, they combine things at the wrong level of aggregation' (Ohmae, 1995: vii, 131).

And this study's concern with national economies also sits uneasily with the arguments of those who feel that to focus on the national economy is to *overshoot* – that 'macro national-level analysis is too generalised, too gross and too deterministic' (Wilks and Wright, 1991: 18); that a national economy is really a sum of regional economies or industrial clusters, such that the analysis of the competitiveness of whole economies ought properly to be reset as the analysis of the competitiveness of its parts. Michael Porter is a case in point; he argues that:

> No nation can be competitive in everything. So to seek to explain competitiveness at the national level is to ask the wrong question. . . . To find answers, we must focus not on the economy as a whole, but on specific industries and industry segments. While efforts to explain aggregate productivity growth in entire economies have illuminated the importance of the quality of a nation's human resources and the need for improving technology, an examination at this level must by necessity focus on very broad and general determinants that are not sufficiently complete and operational to guide company strategy or public policy. It cannot address the central issue [of] why and how meaningful and commercially viable skills and technology are created. This can only be understood fully at the level of particular industries. *(Porter, 1990: 8)*

Porter and others are quite right to point to the different roles played by particular industries in different economies, and hence to the importance of explaining why particular sectors are more successful than others within one national economy. There certainly can be no disagreement with the argument that, to be fully understood, economies need to be disaggregated; and indeed such disaggregation will occur in many of the chapters that follow. But what is also true is that to be fully understood economies also need to be put back together. For if the injunction from Porter were one that would have us study economic growth and international competitiveness *only* at the level of particular industries, then it would arbitrarily and illegitimately shut down an important analytical space. In particular it would preclude any exploration of the impact of broader social, cultural and political forces on the competitiveness of particular industries (broader forces that are invariably rooted in discrete and distinct national histories and institutions); and in so doing, it would preclude any examination of at least one of the major explanatory systems available to us as we explore why growth rates differ – the argument that social systems of accumulation differ between national economies in economically significant ways – an explanatory framework for which (as we shall see repeatedly throughout this volume) strong supporting research evidence already exists (Whitley, 1992a; 1992b; Costello, 1993; Hollingsworth and Boyer, 1997; Freeman and Soete, 1997: 36–7). Fortunately however, this is not the force of Porter's injunction, for he too possesses 'a strong conviction that the national environment . . . play[s] a central role in the competitive success of firms' and recognizes that 'some national environments seem more stimulating to advancement and progress than others' (Porter, 1990: xii). Set in that context therefore, Porter's earlier injunction is less a barrier to scholarship than a guide to action. It helps to reset the central research question to which this study ought properly to be addressed, moving it from the blunt concern with 'why is one national economy more successful than another?' to the more complex conundrum of 'why . . . a nation become[s] the home base for successful international competitors in an industry. . . . And why is one nation often the home for so many of an industry's world leaders?' (Porter, 1990: 1).

Yet this re-specification of the text's central problem still keeps the focus of study very much on the national, and hence some distance from Ohmae's enthusiasm for 'borderless economies'. So why are we not to go the whole globalization gamut from the outset, and put aside any concern with national economic performance? The answer is partly a technical and pragmatic one. Most of the easily accessible data 'comes in the form of national time series' (Lucas, 1988: 37), which are easier to organize around a sub-set drawn from, at most, 200 national units than from '5.5 billion individual economic agents, several million firms [and] several thousand regions' (Maddison, 1995a: 91). But pragmatism is ultimately not the main issue here. A full immersion in the current enthusiasm for globalization needs also to be resisted on the grounds of evidence and values. For it remains the case that the bulk of economic life is still lived and organized nationally. Historically that was certainly so for *all* the key institutions and forces of a capitalist society; and it remains so – at least for workers if not always, these days, for the owners and senior executives of large corporations. Both the state and labour are still overwhelmingly nationally anchored (except for any degree of international labour migration). It is only sections of capital that are not; and even then, the most transnational of corporations still has to 'embed' itself in local social institutions and operate under local political regulation. Labour may now be increasingly internationally structured by the emergence of new forms of global capital: the globalization of labour processes may indeed be one crucial element in the erosion of national difference, national autonomy and the space for national action. But the impact of such global structuring still has to articulate with more nationally and locally based processes of social and political determination; and its effects (and the effects of its articulation) are still lived and experienced primarily at the national and sub-national level. *To stay on the terrain of the national is therefore to stay on the terrain of labour and the state*, and to stay close to what will be our central concerns throughout this study: namely the viability of nationally based commercial concerns, in so far as they contribute to the enhancement of the work experiences, job security and social prospects of national labour forces.

Moreover, much of this pressure to abandon national levels of analysis in the current academic preoccupation with globalization is highly charged politically: it is, after all, a key part of the current ideological onslaught of neo-liberalism. As David Marquand has it, 'the fashionable notion that a mysterious process known as globalization has dissolved national frontiers and made national governments powerless prevents serious thought about the role of the state and cripples social-democratic policy-making' (Marquand, 1996). It may be the case, of course, that the space for the effective social democratic management of national economies *is* indeed closing, and that in consequence an analysis of 'national' routes to economic competitiveness is increasingly anachronistic. That is the key question which this study must ultimately answer. But such a closure should not be assumed from the outset by the choice of level of analysis; and it particularly should not be so assumed by those of us with leftward-leaning value positions and intellectual frameworks. For in truth global interconnections between economies have characterized capitalism as a world system from the outset; and if the scale and character of those global linkages are now qualitatively different, it is still the case that any new form of globalization is less a fact than a question (Hirst and Thompson, 1996; Radice, 1999). And as a question – as a process in dispute – globalization is still best approached from the viewpoint of the national economies subject to it. It is still best defined initially in a simple way, as a matter of capital export and import by transnational corporations across national boundaries, not least because such a definition helps to clarify both the social forces and institutions that are directing it (and benefiting from it) and the central political issue it then raises – how (and to what degree) nationally based and democratically grounded forces and institutions can shape or control global capital to produce socially desirable forms of economic growth. By focusing this study on national economies, there is no desire to ignore questions of globalization. Rather the choice of a national entry level of analysis is designed to establish a clear capacity to examine systematically the precise impact of global processes on national levels of decision-making at the start of the new millennium.

The shape of the answer

In line with this view that the impact of globalization on the autonomy and viability of capitalist models is best approached through a firm grounding in the detail of individual national cases, the study that follows is built around the examination of a series of economies which have been chosen for the key position they occupy in the debate about capitalist models. Four such economies will centrally concern us: the US and UK, as exemplars of liberal capitalism, West Germany, as an exemplar of a negotiated or consensual capitalist model and Japan, as an exemplar of a more statist or developmental capitalist type. Since the West German model sat in (and that of the united Germany remains locked within) a wider set of arguments about the desirability and viability of corporatist forms of capitalist organization, of a type most fully developed in postwar Scandinavia, the study will (where appropriate) widen out to examine the Swedish economy; and by the same token, the discussion of postwar Japanese economic growth will periodically be informed by data and observations from the literature on the East Asian tiger economies, with whom Japanese growth has recently been so intimately linked. But the main focus of the study will be on the four economies that are central to the English-language-based literature on capitalist models: and its data sets will be drawn exclusively from material written in (or translated into) English.

Part I is a survey of the main arguments deployed to explain the postwar growth patterns of the four economies, and is so organized as to throw into sharp relief the conflicting claims made for the contribution (positive and negative) to growth performance of four commonly mentioned variables: the power of labour movements, the dominant forms of education, training and culture, the structure of business organization and the role of the state. The research data available on the impact of each of those variables on the postwar growth performance of the four main economies will then be surveyed in part II, in order to leave us able, in chapter 8, to evaluate the various explanations on offer, and to use that evaluation to consider the viability of particular forms of capitalist organization in the globalized economy of the twenty-first century.

Part I

Capitalist Models:
The Arguments

2

Liberal Capitalism:
Retreat and Revival?

Surveying (and indeed living through) the postwar pattern of differential economic growth from within the UK may not have been as materially pleasant as surveying it from the safe haven of a more successful capitalist economy, but at least it awakened early a strong awareness that more successful capitalisms did exist elsewhere. Indeed for the last forty years at least, anyone following the public debate on economic performance in the UK was bound to know that capitalism came in a number of national 'models', and that the enhancement of economic performance required realignment behind a superior model of some kind. But capitalist modelling was not (and is not) just a UK disease. It is a tendency triggered everywhere by economic underperformance. So as the US economy lost world market share in the 1970s and 1980s, first to the leading European economies and then to the Japanese, a whole American literature emerged concerned with the 'coming battle' between differently organized economic blocs (Thurow, 1992) and preoccupied with the 'weaknesses' of liberal capitalist growth models. The parallel vulnerability of European economies to first American and later Asian competition had a similar effect on the volume of academic and public discussion in continental Europe, although there the main preoccupation lay with the commensurate competitive 'weaknesses' of more consensual or negotiated forms of capitalist organization (Albert, 1993; Lindbeck, 1985). Then, as we noted in chapter 1, as rising unemployment in the Swedish and German economies was joined by unexpected East Asian economic turmoil in 1997, more 'statist' forms of capitalism came under the critical hammer too, to enable the advocates of liberal models of capitalism of the US and UK kind to rekindle their confidence. In the process the strengths and weaknesses of particular models of capitalism became major political issues across the entire advanced capitalist world, and whole literatures emerged on the causes of economic underperformance in particular national contexts. It is with certain of those literatures that this and the next chapter are centrally concerned.

The erosion of the American dream?

The first economy with which any discussion of the rise and fall of postwar capitalist models has to deal is the US; and the first question it must address is the degree to which (if at all) it is still legitimate to talk of the US way of organizing economic life as being in any sense 'in decline'. As we shall see later (both briefly in this chapter and more fully in chapter 8), that debate has been put largely off limits in the 1990s, marginalized for the bulk of the US policy-community by eight years of sustained American economic growth after 1991. But it was definitely not off limits in the US in the 1980s, when, on the contrary, texts on the nature and consequences of US economic decline abounded: best-selling volumes with titles like *America: what went wrong?*, *The American Disease*, *The End of Affluence*, *The Pooring of America* and *The End of the American Century* (respectively Bartlett and Steele, 1992; Lodge, 1986; Madrick, 1995; Batra, 1993; Schlossstein, 1989). Since those texts set in motion themes which still resonate through the contemporary debate on capitalist models, it is with the substance of the 1980s 'industrial policy debate' in the US that we need here to begin.

Certainly among the white middle-class US electorate to whom Bill Clinton addressed his presidential campaign in 1992, there appeared to be a strong sense that the current generation of white American workers did not enjoy the sense of job security, and access to steadily rising living standards, that their parents had known a generation before. The cohort of white Americans born either side of the Second World War then looked to have been the fortunate ones, enjoying in postwar suburban America a standard of living without US historical precedent or European/Asian contemporary equivalence. At the start of the 1990s they appeared to have become the unique beneficiaries of the prodigious productivity of the postwar US economy, enjoying, as a generational cohort, unprecedented general levels of consumption, even in old age. The children and grandchildren who grew up in their shadow, with their experience as an important cultural landmark, still retained their faith in the attainability of the 'American dream' (Lipset, 1996: 287). Economic life in the US in the 1980s had not dented that, even though by then these next generations of white Americans – 'baby boomers' and their offspring – were experiencing (as they continue to experience) much higher degrees of both intra- and inter-generational *downward* mobility than had their parents: because, unlike them, they have been (and remain) heavily exposed to the twin processes of corporate 'downsizing' and stagnant real wages that beset the US economy after 1973. White Americans who are under 50 at century's end simply have to make far greater personal efforts than did their parents – in terms of hours worked and number of jobs held – to retain their place on the roller-coaster of middle-class American affluence (an affluence, of course, which even at the peak of its distribution across the US population as a whole never extended to large sections of America's black and Hispanic populations). For the moment in the US, this generational shortfall in economic performance seems still largely to be understood as a matter of personal failing; but as Newman has it, there are many commentators for whom it is actually 'symptomatic of far-reaching, structural disorders in the US economy' (Newman, 1994: 341–2).

For those commentators, the US economic record through to 1991 provided significant volumes of both internal and external supporting evidence. Internally, that evidence was at its starkest in the spheres of consumption, employment and earnings. Externally, it was most visible in relative US levels of investment, productivity and performance in world trade.

Considering consumption, the evidence of 'structural disorder' was at its most marked in the scale of poverty that persisted amid US affluence, and in the diminished capacity of even the new generation of affluent Americans to buy their own homes and cars. 'A joint study by the Labour and Commerce departments concluded in 1994', for example, 'that the distribution of income in America [was now] the most unequal among developed countries' (Madrick, 1995: 138): with the top 5 per cent of income earners receiving more than the bottom 40 per cent and with intensifying inequality of income between ethnic groups throughout the 1980s (Bowles et al., 1990: 140–1). By the same token, the median age of first-time house buyers, which had been 27 in 1980, rose to 35 by 1991 (Newman, 1994: 339); and the age of the average US family car was by then greater than at any time since 1948 – one car in three on American roads being more than 10 years old (the figure in the early 1970s was one in ten) (Madrick, 1995: 140). Yet none of this was necessarily surprising when set in the context of hours worked and pay earned in the US after the Vietnam War. US pay rates for non-supervisory workers (some 80 per cent of the labour force) fell in real terms by 15 per cent in the two decades after 1973, and by as much as 25 per cent for workers aged 25–35 (Maddick, 1995: 16); and commensurately the hours worked by that labour force actually grew.

Quite against the trend in advanced capitalist economies, US workers in the 1990s worked *more* hours than their parents had a generation before, spending on average an additional 163 hours a year at work in 1990 compared with 1970, losing leisure time, as Schor put it, to 'the equivalent of an extra month a year' (Schor, 1992: 29), and doing so increasingly in service rather than in manufacturing employment. In the 1950s one American worker in three was employed in manufacturing. By 1990 that figure had fallen to 17 in 100 (Bartlett and Steele, 1992: 18); and by then, a record 7 million workers in the US were regularly working two jobs in an attempt to maintain their living standards. Yet in spite of all their extra effort, throughout the 1980s 'the standard of living by and large fell, stagnated or grew very slowly for most Americans, even though [they] were working longer and harder' (Madrick, 1995: 128–9) with the result that US labour lost its decisive international advantage as consumers, by then earning no more than 'workers did in Germany, France or Norway, and only a little more than workers earned in a wide range of other nations' (ibid.: 82). And significantly for our purposes, the revival of the US economy in the 1990s did not quickly reverse these trends. On the contrary, as the 1996–7 survey of *The State of Working America* recorded,

> the problem of deteriorating wages, which was responsible for the slow growth of incomes and widening inequality in the past, has not only continued in the 1990s, but it has also pulled down new groups of workers. After more than a decade of wage growth for most women, the bottom two-thirds of women in the workforce saw their wages decline between 1985 and 1995. In the 1980s, families compensated for stagnant and declining male wages by working longer and sending more family members to work, a trend that appears to have reached its maximum capacity. As a result, the incomes of middle class families have stagnated and fallen in the 1990s. At the same time jobs have become less secure and less likely to offer health and pension benefits . . . [such that in spite of low inflation and unemployment] the typical American family is worse off in the mid 1990s than it was at the end of the 1970s. *(Mishel, Bernstein and Schmitt, 1997: 3–4)*

By the same token, rates of investment in US-based plant and equipment in the 1970s and 1980s were generally low when compared with those prevalent in the more rapidly growing sections of the advanced capitalist world. The result, by 1990, Thurow estimated, was that 'plant and equipment investment per member of the labour force [in the US was at best only] half that of Germany, one third that of Japan' (Thurow, 1992: 254). Baumol had similar figures: with net fixed investment as a percentage of GNP in the 1970s running at 7 per cent in the US, but 12–13 per cent in Germany and France and 20 per cent in Japan (Baumol et al., 1994: 3). Between 1960 and 1989 'the US share[d] with the UK the distinction of having the lowest rate of investment among all the OECD countries' (Britton, 1992: 4: see also table 6.1, p. 159). Moreover, even before the redistribution of labour into low productivity service employment got fully under way, rates of growth of labour productivity in the US economy were – by leading international standards – already unimpressive. GDP per hour worked grew in the US by 2.5 per cent per annum between 1950 and 1973, and by just 1 per cent per annum between 1973 and 1987. The equivalent figures for Germany were 5.9 and 2.6 per cent, for France 5 and 3.2 per cent, and for Japan 7.6 and 3.5 per cent. And in the 1980s the US trade deficit with those other industrial economies became large and seemingly permanent, emerging for the first time this century (at $1.5 billion) in 1971, touching $30 billion in 1978 and $38 billion in 1982, then peaking for the 1980s at $152 billion in 1987, and by the 1990s habitually running at well over $100 billion. The US began the 1990s with its share of world trade in manufactured goods having been equalled by the German economy and passed by the Japanese (Spulber, 1995: 22); and then throughout the 1990s it ran a series of payments deficits (of between 1.9 and 2.5 per cent of GDP) sufficiently large to trigger warnings from the IMF, among others, of likely adverse consequences for stock markets and interest rates in the US at the century's end (*Financial Times*, 14 April 1998: 1).

To many UK-based observers well used to such a constellation of long hours, stagnating wages, low productivity and diminishing international competitiveness, the signs seemed obvious: the US economy had moved (or was moving) into its period of post-imperial decline, tail-spinning after that of the UK down the international league tables of economic performance. However things were not quite as straightforward as that, for the issue of whether the US economy is in tail-spin was (and remains) a fiercely contested one. In fact, scholarship has stretched here – in Cohen's apt phrase – from the Cassandras to the Pollyannas (Cohen, 1995:11) in a debate which has turned partly on the adequacy and appropriateness of particular measures of economic performance, and partly on how those measures ought properly to be read or understood. The Cassandras saw in the US economy in the 1980s 'a deeply rooted, multifaceted competitiveness problem' (ibid.: 29), either with the world in general or just with Japan; and they tended to measure or indicate that problem (as we have begun to do here) by reference to 'trade deficits, slowly measured productivity growth, job-loss and de-industrialisation' (Galbraith and Calman, 1994: 161). The Pollyannas, by contrast, 'flatly den[ied] that the United States [had] a competitiveness problem of any significance' (Cohen, 1995: 29) at all, and pointed to such things as emerging technologies, strong aggregate growth and continuing immigration in support of their bullish view of US prospects. In dispute between them in the 1980s was the significance of the diminishing *gap* in performance between the US economy and the rest of the advanced capitalist world, and in the 1990s the status and character of the US economy's recovery from 1991. It was a dispute about whether the US cup of economic growth, which visibly overflowed in the golden years of the long postwar boom, was now best seen as half full or half empty; and it was a dispute replete with policy implications, one fought out around the linked issues of trade deficits, de-industrialization and comparative productivity performance.

In that dispute the Pollyannas had a point, but only to a degree. They were certainly right to treat with scepticism the more outlandish of the claims made in the 'declinist' literature about the long-term significance of current US performance on trade, competitiveness and industrial structure.

It is true, for example, that the US share of world trade has fallen quite dramatically since the 1950s. The US's share of world GNP in 1950 stood at 40 per cent and its share of world trade at 20 per cent; by 1980 those percentages had halved. But as we noted in chapter 1, 1950 was a very unusual year. If the base year for comparison is shifted, say to the 1970s, the trajectory of the contemporary US economy looks far more secure. If US trade performance is then examined simply for the 1990s, it looks more secure still; and if trade with Japan is excluded from the figures, the US trade deficit (certainly in high technology goods) largely disappears. And in any case, trade deficits are not an automatic guide to international standing for an economy whose internal market is of the US's scale (and where in consequence trade across its borders constitutes only a small percentage of its GDP). Nor are they in any way a guide to the profitability of US-owned companies, when the export of US capital is so marked a feature of the world system. And indeed the growth of trade is, in essence, a positive sum game (Omerod, 1996: 123). Economies may lose a particular *share* of that trade, but if world trade is growing in total they need not also lose *volume*. Goods manufactured in the US may now make up a smaller share of global trade flows than in the 1950s – in fact by the mid 1990s they were roughly back to their 1970 level (Nau, 1990: x) – but the volume of US exports continues to grow. The financing of those flows may indeed affect long-term economic performance – the question of international debt is something to which we shall need to return – but that is quite different from the question of shares in world trade; and shares are, at best, only a blunt indicator of international performance.

Then there is the question of whether trade matters, of whether competitiveness has not become – to follow Krugman – a misleading 'obsession'. Krugman, as we noted in chapter 1, has pointed to the central importance, for living standards, of general labour productivity, and to the limited proportion of US economic activity that enters world trade; and he has used both arguments to stress the importance of productivity gains in non-tradable economic sectors (particularly services) as a guide to economic health. He clearly has a point: the international competitiveness of whole national economies is not the sole determinant (and ultimately not the major determinant) of the well-being of their populations. Internal labour productivity is that determinant. But as we have already observed, it may be that he claims too much, even for the US, where the 1950s experience of limited involvement in world trade (relative to the massive size of its internal market) has given way to a more normal capitalist pattern, with 17 per cent of US manufactured goods exported by 1980 and 21 per cent of all goods sold in the US made abroad (Magaziner and Reich, 1982: 31). With such an emerging scale of involvement in world trade – Magaziner and Reich estimated that, as early as 1982, maybe 70 per cent of all US-produced goods were operating in potentially international markets (ibid.: 32) – the Tyson definition of economic competitiveness against which Krugman argued gathers greater force: the 'ability to produce goods and services that meet the test of international markets while . . . citizens enjoy a standard of living that is both rising and sustainable' (Tyson, 1992: 1). By that definition, which is entirely appropriate for any industrial economy in which mass consumption of manufactured goods persists, regardless of their place of production, US international competitiveness has weakened over the postwar period as a whole; and US trade statistics are both an index of that weakening and a potential constraint on future US-generated employment and consumption.

However it is simply not the case, as the fiercer critics of US de-industrialization initially had it (Bluestone and Harrison, 1982), that the US economy is becoming one focused on 'information, hamburgers and dress shops' (Weidenbaum and Athey, 1984: 117) alone. US employment *is* increasingly service-provided and service-based, with consequent adverse impacts on overall labour productivity and real wages; but US output still contains an enormous manufacturing and trading sector, whose real contribution to US GDP remains virtually unchanged (Lawrence, 1987: 28; Baumol et al., 1991: 121). The US economy is indeed de-industrializing – in the sense of redistributing labour from manufacturing employment to service employment – but it is not doing so at a faster rate, or on a greater scale, than other advanced capitalist economies. Indeed its degree of service employment growth is, in comparative terms, rather slow (Baumol et al., 1991: 119–21). In fact, between 1973 and 1980, when employment growth in manufacturing was approaching its postwar peak, the US actually 'increased its employment in manufacturing at a faster rate than any other major industrial country, including Japan' (Lawrence, 1987: 33). And if there is a problem here, it seems to lie less in the distribution of employment between manufacturing and services than in the distribution of employment *within* the service sector itself, in that 'the US labour force has been absorbed increasingly not just by services generally, but predominantly by their stagnant sub-sector' (ibid.: 126). It is not the loss of manufacturing employment that is currently threatening US living standards so much as the concentration of those displaced workers in low productivity service provision.

This is not to deny that the 1980s saw serious job losses in a number of once dominant US manufacturing industries: in the car industry, in steel, in textiles and in electronics. Nor is it to deny that these industries have, historically, been the US's largest industrial employers. It is just that this pattern of sectorally and regionally restricted de-industrialization can be read in more than one way, and can be treated just as easily as part of a process of structural adjustment as it can as part of a process of economic decline. Certainly economists and commentators close to the Republican Party were reluctant in the 1980s to treat the problems of the auto industry as representative of some broader US industrial malaise, preferring instead to see the shedding of labour from the older industries of the US north-east and mid-west as part of a redistribution of US industrial capital into new areas of comparative advantage, as older areas of US industrial dominance were colonized by less sophisticated competitors; and they later found (and offered) comfort in the subsequent ability of US car producers to 'bounce back', in the apparent ability of the broad mass of US manufacturers to 'hold their own while adjusting to the business cycle' (Weidenbaum and Athey, 1984: 118), and in what they understand to be the continued – even enhanced – competitive superiority of US-based corporations in more high-tech, high-value-added products (Lawrence, 1984: 3). And certainly the American mid-west did experience a significant revival in growth and employment in the 1990s: the 1997 growth rate of the eight states around Chicago, for example, was 3.8 per cent and their unemployment level only 4.2 per cent (*Financial Times*, 22 May 1998: 2). Unemployment in the rust belt had been over 10 per cent a decade before; and this spectacular improvement in regional performance was in line with that more general improvement in overall US growth rates since April 1991 which gave the economy its most sustained period of unbroken growth since the 1960s. Indeed as late as 1998 the absolute lead of US manufacturing in labour productivity, which the US had enjoyed throughout the postwar period, remained intact; and at the top of the business cycle (in 1996 and 1997) rates of growth of labour productivity in the US grew briefly at 2 per cent per annum, well above the 0.6 per cent per annum average of the 1986–95 period, and back to at least 1970 levels.

So if the US economy was in decline in the 1980s, as many on the US centre-left argued it was, that decline was visibly not terminal; and in fact, because it was not, in many ways this centre-left 'declinism' simply paved the way to a renewed 'triumphalism' of neo-liberalism in US business circles in the 1990s, as the doom-laden prophecies of unstoppable Japanese industrial dominance visibly came unstuck (see Spulber, 1995: 145, 250). But such triumphalism has itself to be guarded against. For what the Pollyannaish reading of the contemporary US left unnoted and unresolved were two important features of recent US economic history that might still indicate seeds of longer-term decline. The first is why US dominance in certain mass-production consumer goods – for so long *the* motif of American economic superiority – was so eroded in the 1980s. The second is the potential relationship between the sources of that loss of dominance and the ability of US-based companies to retain competitive advantage in the new high-tech industries into which US capital is increasingly moving.

For visibly the US economy lost competitive advantage in a number of particularly important manufacturing sectors in the 1980s, mainly sectors based on medium-level technology and servicing mass markets at home and abroad. Michael Porter provided the following report of US competitive strength and weakness for 1985:

- strong in agriculture, defence, aerospace, transportation (aircraft), computers and software (though weakening in semi-conductors), health-care related products, consumer packaged goods, consumer and business services;
- weak/weakening in 'transportation-related goods and services, machinery of many types, machine tools, office products and equipment other than computers, consumer electronics, consumer durables of all types, apparel and related products, steel and other materials, and telecommunications equipment (except large central office switches and fibre optics, which are areas of strength)'. *(Porter, 1990: 519)*

Porter noted that the US's greatest loss of competitiveness from the early 1970s had been in steel, automobiles, machine tools, consumer electronics and office equipment, and that his research teams had found a more generally 'declining competitive advantage . . . in many' (ibid.: 519) of the industries studied by them. This general weakening of competitive edge was noted too by the MIT team undertaking a similar exercise alongside Porter, with significant diminutions of US-based competitive advantage throughout the 1980s in US industries as diverse as semiconductors, commercial aircraft, consumer electronics, steel, chemicals, textiles, automobiles, machine tools and even education and training (Dertouzos et al., 1989: see Cuomo, 1992: 8–9 for a similar list). In fact, consumer electronics, automobiles and textiles in particular felt the impact, within the US internal market throughout the 1980s, of strong and effective foreign competition, particularly from Japanese-based producers; and it was their loss of competitive edge that coloured the entire debate on US economic futures in presidential campaigns from Reagan in 1980 to Clinton in 1992.

And so it should have: for these industries were not (and are not) economically insignificant. On the contrary, US industry from 1970 to 1992 lost market share in the big-volume products consumed by the American middle class, and was unable to compensate for these enhanced import flows of consumer goods by any equivalent increase in the volume and value of high-tech sales abroad. And this shortfall occurred for more than price reasons. Part of the US loss of market share *was* due to the rise of low wage, predominantly Asian competition, and to the strength of the US dollar. By 1990, according to Madrick, 'about 36 per cent of [US] imports were from nations whose wages were 50 per cent or less than [those in the US] compared with only about 25 per cent from such nations in 1978' (Madrick, 1995: 71). But wage differentials did not explain the superiority of Japanese-based producers, who by the 1980s had established significant productivity leads over US-based producers in steel, automobiles, electrical machinery and the production of precision equipment (Pfaller, 1991: 54) and in a string of what van Ark called 'investment industries' (van Ark, 1992: 65). Indeed as early as 1983 'only a quarter of the Japanese cost advantage over American-made small cars was owed to lower wages' (Pfaller, 1991: 75). Nor in any case was price the only element in competitiveness. The MIT study found clear signs that 'in such areas as product quality, service to customers, and speed of product development, American companies [were] no longer perceived as world leaders, even by American consumers'. They also found evidence that 'technological innovations [were] being incorporated into practice more quickly abroad, and [that] the pace of invention and discovery in the United States may be slowing'; and they followed the President's 1985 Commission on Industrial Competitiveness in questioning what they termed the 'productive performance' of US-based manufacturing industry on such dimensions as 'quality, timeliness of service, flexibility, speed of innovation, and command of strategic technologies' (Dertouzos et al., 1989: 26, 33).

Against such a background, it is still possible to be Pollyannaish – to put the emphasis on the recent resurgence of US industry, its ability to pull back some of the lost ground. Nau for one does that: emphasizing the revival of US manufacturing productivity in the second half of the 1980s, and the rapid growth of US exports as the dollar weakened (Nau, 1990: x). So too do Spulber (1995) and Lipset (1996: 59). But it seems more sensible at least to ask the Porter question: 'how could a position of such consistent strength in sophisticated high productivity fields turn into one where competitive advantage was eroding in so many advanced industries' and where, in consequence 'per capita income growth was the slowest of any of the nations ... studied in the postwar period'? (Porter, 1990: 519). Porter put the US case study report in his *The Competitive Advantage of Nations* alongside a section on 'the slide of Britain'. Mainstream US manufacturing industry slid out of its position of world dominance in the quarter century after the oil crisis of 1973. We need to explore why.

Debating US underperformance

Factors in decline

One characteristic response to that question emerged over the years from the doyen of growth accounting, Edward Denison, whose whole work had focused on locating the sources of US economic growth. The early Denison treated the diminution of the US productivity lead as primarily a question of convergence, as European economies 'concentrated upon learning what the United States is already doing' in research and development, and added 'substantial increments to their growth rates by imitating and adopting American practices' (Denison, 1967: 344, 283). Even in 1967, however, Denison had been aware that 'the performance of the US economy [was] not ... all that it might be', particularly in the area of 'investment in non-residential structures and equipment and inventories' (ibid.: 345, 343); and certainly two decades later it was that sense of unease – that 'darker picture of deterioration of productivity growth' (Denison, 1985: 2) – that by then was shaping the entire Denison corpus. By the mid 1980s, Denison had his own list of factors that in his view had been unfavourable to US growth since 1973. These included changes in the composition of the labour force by age and sex, costs to business of regulations to abate pollution and to protect employees' health and safety, and the costs of crime to business; but on his own calculations these left nearly two-thirds of the growth slowdown unexplained. The whole Denison method of factor disaggregation then predisposed him to doubt whether 'any one output determinant was responsible for the decline in the growth rate of residual productivity after 1973', and left him with the impression that the decline was 'more likely to have resulted from small to moderate adverse changes in many of the immeasurable output determinants' (ibid.: 56). It also predisposed him (and to a degree actually equipped him) to discount some of the more popular explanations of economic underperformance. Importantly, he found no evidence that the blame lay with labour – that inadequate work effort explained the shortfall (ibid.: 47). Nor by then did he think – counter to his Appendix to the 1964 study and to the majority of growth accountants – that inadequate investment levels were at 'the heart of the problem'; and he set his face firmly against interventionist industrial policy as its cure (ibid.: 59). Instead he tentatively aligned himself with those who linked recent US economic decline to the inadequate performance of American management (ibid.: 44), and in particular to their general abdication of what Hayes and Abernathy called 'their strategic responsibilities' (1980: 68).

This is not to imply that growth accounting did not have a more ambitious set of insights to offer on the determinants of economic performance. For, as Abramovitz noted in the early 1960s, the whole logic of the Denison approach privileged certain variables as vital to growth, including the rate of growth of the labour force, its level of education, the proportion of GDP devoted to capital formation and the potential of research and development (Abramovitz, 1962). Denison might in the end have decided to emphasize inadequacies in the management of these factors of production as the key to underperformance, rather than inadequacies in factor supply *per se*: but others using his or similar accounting techniques remained truer to the view that the quantity of factor inputs was a critical element in the postwar US growth story. Baumol and McLennan, for example, took this line: arguing strongly in the mid 1980s that 'insufficient investment [was] one of the major causes of the US productivity slowdown', that 'for the private business sector as a whole, lack of capital investment account[ed] for over 20 per cent of the decline during the 1970s', and that 'among the other major sources of the slowdown ... [were] low outlays for research and development, the rise in the direct and indirect costs of regulation, and the increase in energy prices' (Baumol and McLennan, 1985: 9). They conceded some ground to the qualitative dimensions of factor-use to which Denison alluded: not simply management quality but, in relation to Japan in particular, cultural differences and differences in worker–management institutions. But for them, these aspects of growth performance were elusive because they were non-quantifiable (ibid.: 52); and they were in any case, at best, marginal to the story. According to Baumol and McLennan's reading of the bulk of the growth-accounting literature comparing Japan with the US after 1973, 'a primary source of the disparity [lay] in the inferior US performance in terms of saving and investment', such that 'most of the differences in manufacturing productivity [were] explainable by the fact that Japanese workers use[d] more plant and equipment than their American counterparts' (ibid.: 17). It was not that gross investment in manufacturing plant and equipment failed to rise in the US in the 1970s and early 1980s; it was simply that it did not rise fast enough to keep pace with the growth in the labour force, and so pulled per capita investment down, and productivity with it.

The Baumol and McLennan analysis then pointed in a particular policy direction: towards the stimulation of research and development, the encouragement of saving and investment and the removal of 'impediments to freedom of resource allocation by the market mechanism' (ibid.: 232). But not all growth accountancy pointed in that direction. Nor did the 1980s arguments of all the major figures in the history of classical growth theory, from which the tradition of growth accounting emerged. For in that decade there was at least one major study, associated with Robert Solow, that was uneasy with explanations privileging low US levels of savings and investment: the 1989 MIT study *Made in America*. In that study, Solow and his co-authors distanced themselves from explanations that relied primarily on macro-economic variables, focusing instead on a set of institutional factors which they claimed were undermining growth performance: 'outdated strategies, short time horizons, technological weaknesses in development and production, neglect of human resources, failure of co-operation' and 'government and industry at cross purposes' (Dertouzos et al., 1989: 43, 44). From their study of a string of case studies across the US economy, the MIT team decided that:

> the causes of this problem go well beyond macro-economic explanations of high capital costs and inadequate savings to the attitudinal and organisational weaknesses that pervade America's production system. These weaknesses are deep rooted. They affect the way people and organisations interact with one another and with long-term technological and market risks; and they affect the way business, government, and educational institutions go about the task of developing the nation's most precious asset, its human resources. They introduce rigidities into the nation's production system at a time of extraordinarily rapid change in the international economic environment. *(Dertouzos et al., 1989: 166)*

For the MIT team, as for many commentators on US economic underperformance in the 1980s, there was a pattern to the weaknesses in industrial performance, which their detailed case work persistently uncovered; and it was this pattern that was said to hold the key to the vulnerability of US-based producers to overseas competition. There were key elements in that pattern. One was *education and training* – investment in human capital – serious inadequacies in what Porter termed 'factor creation' and which the MIT study thought had been dangerously neglected (Dertouzos et al., 1989: 36). Another was *capital formation and supply*: for some (including Krugman) a low national savings rate, for others (like Porter) a deeply entrenched 'short-termism' in the US banking system similar to that emphasized by Hutton in his analysis of UK industrial weakness. A third was (as Denison emphasized) inadequacies in the quality, character and drive of contemporary US *management* (with resulting defects in the quality of products produced and in the trajectory of product development). A fourth, often cited, was *attitudes, values and ideologies*: in a spectrum from the too complacent to the too liberal. And for some commentators, although not for all, deficien-

cies in US macro-economic and industrial *policy* also then figured: indeed
(as we have already noted) the debate over the need for industrial policy was
the axis around which this whole literature developed in the 1980s, with
fiercely held views on either side (in favour, Magaziner and Reich, 1982;
Johnson, 1982; Scott and Lodge, 1986; against, Lawrence, 1984; Baumol
and McLennan, 1989; for an overview, Johnson, 1984; Thompson, 1989;
Graham, 1992; Froud et al., 1996). But whether government policy was in
or out as a contributory causal element, there was a striking range of agreement across a tranche of predominantly centre-left studies of the US
economy in the 1980s, that the causal patterns here were strongly interre-
lated and deeply entrenched, and that they were mutually interacting to
unravel – to use Porter's imagery – the US growth diamond.

Porter's own specification of how that diamond was beginning to unravel
in the 1980s was representative of much of that analysis. The Porter explanation of weakening US competitiveness emphasized:

- *poor faction creation*: especially 'the eroding quality of human
  resources relative to other nations' (Porter, 1990: 522) triggered by
  inadequacies in the US education system and inadequate training
  systems; but also the low and declining rate of household savings and
  large federal budgets, which sent interest rates from the lowest of the
  advanced capitalist nations in the 1950s to among the highest in the
  1980s; and slow wage growth and generous labour supply, which
  reduced the pressure on employers to innovate and invest in training;
- *the weakening of demand conditions*: especially the loss of the postwar
  US international position as the home of the world's most affluent
  and demanding consumers; plus the emergence in the US and elsewhere of highly sophisticated and segmented markets not easily serviced by US-style standardized mass production;
- *the thinning of industrial clusters*: particularly in machinery and specialized inputs, as the normal US arms-length relationship between
  buyers and suppliers, and between industries and universities,
  became increasingly dysfunctional, and as eroding US productive
  performance induced buyers of specialist goods to redirect their
  demand abroad;
- *changes in firms' strategy, structure and rivalry*: primarily changes in
  the quality motivations and recruitment of US corporate managers,
  which sapped the rate of innovation and upgrading, the diminishing
  number of managers with technical backgrounds, the diversion of
  top talent away from industry, the short-termism of institutional
  investors, the US corporate propensity for mergers and alliances, the
  ebbing of domestic rivalry, and the dependence of senior managers
  on high short-term dividends for their own bonuses and career
  development;
- *government indifference to the need for educational reform*: its under-
  utilization of antitrust laws, its massive budget deficits, its relaxation

of environmental and safety standards and its propensity largely to ignore the needs of the civilian industrial sector in favour of national security and the social agenda; as Porter had it, 'American policy was based on the assumption that US industry had a commanding position. Today, for often self-inflicted reasons, that assumption is a shaky one' (ibid.: 531–2).

Paradigm choice

The MIT study, for its part, did more than simply list a general set of institutional factors eroding US competitive performance. It also conducted a series of detailed case studies, and claimed to have found in them two general forms of US corporate organization and practice. It found, and criticized, a prevalent form, one in which it noted 'the preferences of American firms for organising production hierarchically, their tendency to institutionalise arms-length relationships between firms and finance, thus perpetuating narrow planning horizons, their inability to develop effective collective structures for technological development, and their systematic neglect of human resources' (Lindberg and Campbell, 1991: 392). But it also found a minority of strong US firms in each of the sectors it examined in detail, and attributed their success to an equally interlinked set of attributes: '(1) a focus on simultaneous improvements in cost, quality and delivery; (2) closer links to customers; (3) closer relationships with suppliers; (4) the effective use of technology for strategic advantage; (5) less hierarchical and less-compartmentalized organizations for greater flexibility; and (6) human-resource policies that promote continuous learning, teamwork, participation, and flexibility' (Dertouzos et al., 1989: 118).

In so doing, the MIT study positioned itself alongside those who were arguing the need for a paradigm shift in corporate organization and managerial practice to restore US economic competitiveness, a paradigm shift apparently already made by Japanese companies and supposedly the prime source of their recent economic success. The case for such a paradigm change was regularly laid before the general US reading public in the 1980s and early 1990s in a series of popular texts (from Lodge, 1986, through Thurow, 1992, to Best, 1990, Hart, 1994 and Fukuyama, 1995), and it was also widely reproduced in the academic literature, not least through the centre-left writings of Robert Reich and the more explicitly Schumpeterian enthusiasms of William Lazonick.

Robert Reich (Clinton's first Secretary of State for Labour) had been among the first to develop the paradigm argument, arguing as early as 1983 that 'the industries that will sustain the next stage of America's economic evolution will necessarily be based on a skilled, adaptable and innovative labour force and on a more flexible, less hierarchical organisation of work' (1983: 13). Reich saw how 'ill prepared for adaptation' the US economy currently was, and thought that 'America [had] a choice: it [could] adapt itself

to the new economic realities by altering its organisations, or it [could] fail
to adapt and thereby continue its present decline' (ibid.: 14, 21). What Reich
then added to this widely held view was a dash of social democratic optimism, a belief that the needs of corporate America and the agenda of the
progressive Left were being brought into harmony by paradigmatic change.
Thus:

> in advanced capitalist countries, productivity and economic growth are
> coming to depend not so much on the overall level of investment as on how
> investment is used. . . . Put simply, the organisation of an advanced economy
> can either encourage productivity – by providing people with skills and
> knowledge and by inspiring high morale and motivation in the work force –
> or discourage productivity by doing just the opposite . . . The way people are
> organised is becoming a crucial determinant of productivity . . . When we use
> unemployment to battle inflation, we do not recognise the toll it takes on
> America's future productivity. When we trim our collective expenditures on
> education, training, health, nutrition, and similar intangibles, we do not see
> its cost in terms of America's future economic growth. Policies that spread
> the benefits and burdens of economic change more equitably among our
> citizens are superior to those that widen the gap between rich and poor. . . .
> America's place in the evolving world economy will increasingly depend on
> its workers' skills, vigour, initiative, and capacity for collaboration and adap-
> tation. The kinds of policies we need may be termed social justice or invest-
> ments in America's future: regardless of the label, they represent the next
> stage of America's economic and social advance. *(Reich, 1983: 19–20)*

This, of course, was a call for trust capitalism with a vengeance; and where
Reich took the debate, others then followed. In fact the role of paradigms
in explaining economic underperformance was given its fullest and most
pristine formulation not in his writings, but in those of William Lazonick.
The central Lazonick argument was that the history of industrial capitalism had to be periodized, since the forms of corporate organization and
managerial practices vital to dominance in one period invariably acted as a
barrier to dominance in the next, and so shifted centres of economic leadership. They did so because (and to the degree that) 'institutional rigidities'
slowed the capacity of leading economies to adapt to new corporate requirements as competitive and technological conditions altered. Lazonick argued
that successful forms of economic organization in one period always became
embedded. They drew to themselves strong institutional supports, sectional
interests and ways of thought and action, and were cushioned for a time
from the need to change by their ability to live off the surpluses of the past.
They became (in Schumpeterian terms) 'adaptive' rather than 'innovative';
and because they did, their rapid re-alignment to new forms of corporate
activity became extremely difficult to trigger. So, according to Lazonick, the
UK went into early-twentieth-century economic decline because its leading
industrial companies remained too long wedded to forms of 'proprietary
capitalism' no longer appropriate to the new age of scientific management
and mass production; and the US industrial sector spent the 1980s losing

market dominance because its leading corporations were still too immersed in forms of organization and ways of managing that worked well in the period of 'managerial capitalism' but less well in technological and market conditions requiring a more 'collective capitalist' form of response.

Thus for Lazonick, past US strengths and current US weaknesses were two sides of the same coin. US forms of managerial capitalism had spent the first six decades of the twentieth century sweeping all before them. They certainly had seen off the British: but down-wind of that success, and in the world transformed by the rise and dissemination of US-initiated methods of mass production and scientific management, the strengths of US corporate structure and practice were turning into weaknesses. Two very important Achilles heels were emerging. One was the nature of the relationship established in the US between capital and labour in the period of managerial capitalism, the other the relationship emerging between US industrial and financial institutions, and between US industrial institutions themselves, towards the end of that same period.

According to Lazonick, on this side of the Third Industrial Revolution it was not enough to have managerial structures capable of coordinating specialized divisions of labour and maintaining control over the main labour processes. Those were the organizational priorities released by the Second Industrial Revolution, which had served the US well. But organizational priorities had now shifted: from control to commitment, and from the management of an alienated labour force to the establishment of trust relationships between all the participants in the productive process. The key to competitive success in the wake of the Third Industrial Revolution, according to Lazonick, was policies to 'educate the labour force, mobilise committed financial resources, and co-ordinate inter-dependent innovative efforts' (Lazonick, 1991a: 57). These were policies readily attainable in economies with strong networks of companies, close long-term relations between industry and finance and high levels of job security and job satisfaction at all levels of the industrial hierarchy. But they were not readily attainable in economies of the US type. They were simply not the dominant features of the industrial landscape in the liberal model of modern capitalism; and because they were not, economies which adhered to the liberal model (particularly the US economy) were now beginning to lose their international place.

So, in the sphere of labour relations, and in comparison particularly with the Japanese, US corporate management and US labour unions had settled into patterns after the war which traded high wages for full managerial control. This settlement then enhanced an already evident propensity among US managers to 'take skills and initiative off the shop floor' (Lazonick, 1994a: 181) and to treat their blue-collar workers as easily expendable commodities; and it had left no space for the consolidation of relationships of commitment and trust between the company and its workforce. In consequence the organization of work on the shop-floor became, according to Lazonick:

the Achilles heel of US manufacturing . . . With its managerial structures in place, American industry may have entered the second half of the twentieth century in the forefront of the development of productive resources. But its weakness lay in the utilisation of productive resources-manufacturing processes in which large numbers of shop-floor workers had to interact with costly plant and equipment. . . . the major industrial enterprises did not give these blue-collar workers substantive training. Nor . . . did they make explicit, and hence more secure, the long-term attachment of the hourly employee to the enterprise. Without this commitment of the organisation to the individual, one could not expect the commitment of the individual to the organisation that might have enabled US mass producers to respond quickly and effectively to the Japanese challenge. *(Lazonick, 1994a: 188)*

Likewise, on the organization of capital itself, what had worked well once now no longer did, as the balance of forces within the US economy shifted from the ascendancy of 'value creating forces' to the ascendancy of 'value extracting ones' (Lazonick, 1994b: 82). The key value extractors, for Lazonick, were the financial institutions which were deregulated in the 1970s and which were overwhelmingly preoccupied with the quarterly 'bottom line', and the senior executives of industrial companies who, by rewarding themselves with generous stock options, had separated their own interests from those of even the rest of the managerial structure. The control exercised in the 1980s by these two groups over productive activity in the US – what elsewhere Lazonick referred to as the shift from 'venture capitalists to vulture capitalists' (Lazonick, 1992: 159) – had introduced a corrosive 'short-termism' into US corporate practice, privileging 'adaptive' over 'innovative' investment, and inducing 'enterprises that engaged in innovative investment strategies in the past [to] turn to adaptive strategies that merely live off their prior successes' (ibid.: 80). Under such leadership, too many US companies were said to be no longer making 'the types of investments that were required to remain competitive on global markets' (ibid.: 101, 102), indulging instead in a potentially lethal 'down-sizing' of technically competent personnel. The result, we were told, was 'a serious erosion of organisational capabilities within the enterprise without any guarantee that the reduction in investment in human capabilities and the reconstitution of comparable organisational capabilities will occur elsewhere in the economy' (ibid.: 104).

According to Lazonick, that is, adversarial industrial relations blocked the capacity of US-based corporations fully to exploit the productive potential released by the Third Industrial Revolution; and inadequacies in ownership structure and practice threatened any long-term capacity 'to get the American system of capital allocation back on track' (ibid.: 112). He took the impaired performance of the US economy after 1973 as evidence that the US possessed the *wrong kind of capitalism*, such that if it was to recapture its earlier productive potential it had to move to a new – more trust-based – form of industrial organization and corporate practice. 'Proprietary capitalism has long since vanished, and managerial capitalism can no longer compete' (Lazonick, 1992: 159). To survive as a major economic player, the US 'must grasp the enormous, and apparently growing, economic power of collective capitalism' (ibid.: 160) and strengthen the value-creating forces in the US economy and society. Its public bodies must invest in education at all levels. Its private corporations must invest in research and development, and in the development of the capacities of all levels of the corporate labour force. It must reset its pattern of industrial relations from an adversarial to a participatory or partnership form; it must shift power from value extractors to value creators; and it must undergo an 'ideological revolution', by making a major cultural move away from its commitment to 'the myth of the market economy' and its associated faith in (and preoccupation with) stock market values (ibid.: 109). It must do, that is, a lot of very important things.

Contradictions of dominance

Such a programme of root and branch reform aligned Lazonick, in his turn, with some of the most radical explanations of (and commentaries upon) the competitive performance of US capitalism in the 1980s. Among these were analyses which (like Lazonick's) singled out particular features of US corporate capital as the barrier to sustained employment and growth: particularly the division between finance and industry, and the short-sightedness of senior US management (Pollin, 1996: 270). But there were also analyses which emphasized the deleterious impact on economic performance of US military expenditure, the industrial role of the Pentagon and the global political concerns of the US state; and there were analyses which saw US economic decline as inexorably linked to the disintegration of the particular settlement underpinning postwar global capitalist growth, and to entirely unavoidable contradictions between factions of the US ruling class and between it and US labour. In the main, these were all forms of analysis which shared Lazonick's critique of US corporate practice while avoiding his enthusiasm for its Japanese equivalent.

One line of argument here was that it was the burden of military expenditure carried by the US economy that held the key to its underperformance in the 1980s. A number of leading centre-left commentators included such an argument in their overall explanatory portfolios: Thurow (1992: 19–21) with his sense of the potential conflict between military and economic superiority; Johnson (1982: 4) with his characterization of the Pentagon as the US's equivalent to MITI; and even Reich (1983: 189–93) with his castigation of the Pentagon's industrial policy as a source of conservatism and backwardness in the US manufacturing economy. But the argument was at its sharpest in the writings of Dumas (1982) and of Markusen and Yudken (1992). High military expenditure, as they saw it, eventually created high inflation and unemployment in the postwar US. It did so because Pentagon contracts cushioned manufacturing industry from competitive pressures to innovate and change and distorted the distribution of US research personnel and product development. It did so because US military expenditures abroad more than offset US trade balances even in the golden years of the long boom, and generated few valuable spin offs from military production to the civilian industrial sector, and it did so because a weakening civilian industrial sector was then left exposed to the arrival of foreign competition nurtured in the security created by the US military presence in South-east Asia, at the cost of US jobs, living standards and rates of economic growth.

Arguments of this kind also featured in the writings of a group of US radical scholars who developed their own distinctive 'take' on the nature of the postwar US settlement by using the notion of 'social structures of accumulation' to explain US economic and social difficulties in the 1980s (Bowles et al., 1984; 1990; Bowles and Edwardes, 1993; Kotz et al., 1994). These SSA analysts explained the decline of US economic power not as the product of 'institutional inertia' in the face of a new paradigm of industrial organization, as Lazonick had it, but as the product of emerging class contradictions within an economic and social order which, even if orchestrated by postwar US institutional power, was quintessentially capitalist in character. The fall of US economic dominance was linked by these theorists to the working out of a set of necessary contradictions within that capitalist order: contradictions within the US capitalist class, and between it and other industrial and financial bourgeoisies, and contradictions between US capital and the American proletariat organized both as workers and as citizens. The result was a particular way of telling the postwar US story, broadly as follows:

- Externally, the success of 'Pax Americana', which had created a world market for US exports, began to unravel from the mid 1960s, as the reconstruction of competitor capitalisms under the US nuclear umbrella eroded the American productivity advantage and the associated world demand for US goods, and as 'the military role of the United States ... indispensable in helping to police the postwar international system ... [came to] constitute an enormous drain on the productive capacity of the United States and to stimulate a series of powerful Third World challenges to American imperialism' (Gordon, 1994: 52). Here the weight of the analysis was focused not so much on the emergence of new forms of capitalist organization in Japan, as in 'paradigm choice' arguments, as on the burdens borne by US capital as the price of successful world leadership.
- Internally, postwar American growth was also undermined by success over time: by the success of those initially excluded from the limited capital–labour accord in winning social and political benefits by organizing themselves militantly as citizens, and by the shift in class power from management to labour that came to the white male working class in the postwar US as the consequence of full employ-

ment and strong labour contracts. Here the weight of the analysis was less on the way that the adversarial character of postwar US labour relations eroded the capacity of management to trigger commitment and loyalty from American workers – as Lazonick had it – and more on the costs of social provision and on the inability of US managers to intensify the rate of labour exploitation.

In arguing in this way, SSA analysts positioned themselves close to regulation theory, and drew heavily on Marxist political economy in their analyses of crisis (Kotz, 1994: 85). In their hands, Lazonick's 'paradigm choice' became one between qualitatively different social structures of accumulation; and they were much concerned with the disintegration of what regulation theories would call Fordism. But even in their writings there was a strong echo of Lazonick's argument that a new and competitively stronger form of capitalism was emerging to which US capitalism needed to respond. So Bowles, Gordon and Weisskopf, for example, argued almost in passing that 'an outmoded hierarchical and conflictual system of industrial relations [lay] at the root of the continuing inability of the United States to solve the productivity problem' and that 'during the 1980s, the United States was consistently outpaced on the productivity front by nations that have adopted more meaningful forms of worker participation in decision-making, job security, and collective bargaining' (1990: 156; similarly, Bowles and Edwardes, 1993: 255). And the same notion of a paradigm choice was evident in other radical scholarship on US economic underperformance which was influenced by regulation theory in the 1980s (Piore and Sabel, 1984; Best, 1990; Lash and Urry, 1987; 1994; Lipietz, 1989). Time and again we were told by such theorists that capitalism, whose postwar golden age had been organized on the basis of Fordist mass production, was now shifting to a new paradigm of organization variously labelled 'flexible specialization', the 'new competition', 'disorganized capitalism', 'reflexive accumulation' or 'post Fordism'. The US had been economically dominant under Fordism, but was slipping now because it could not easily adjust to the disintegration of its previously dominant regulatory mode.

So the terminology of the most radical scholarship produced on US decline in the 1980s tended to differ from that used by Lazonick; but the explanation of US economic underperformance it was used to develop quite often did not. What actually differed was the greater sense, in the literature more influenced by Marxism than in that influenced by Schumpeterian growth theory, of the *precarious* nature of the new paradigm, its susceptibility to its own internal contradictions, and the associated absence of any likelihood of prolonged Japanese dominance over the US. The future was foreshadowed differently the more radical the theoretical framework deployed. Where centre-left scholarship anticipated a secure future for US capitalism (and its workers) if a stronger capitalist model was adopted, the Marxist literature anticipated a future of generalized instability. Indeed in the finest of that Marxist scholarship, Giovanni Arrighi made that particularly clear, by situating the SSA argument in a grand sweep of world history stretching back over five centuries. In a series of publications from 1982 to 1994 Arrighi followed Bowles, Gordon and Weisskopf in linking the diminishing competitiveness of US-based manufacturing firms in the 1980s to a wider account of the rise and fall of the postwar international settlement, one in which contradictions between US-based industry and the US state played an important role, and in which certain East Asian economies in particular used the deepening markets of Pax Americana to catch up and overtake indigenous US producers. But unlike the SSA theorists, Arrighi did not leave that story unanchored in time and space. Instead he treated US economic underperformance as merely the latest example of the way in which contradictions of dominance within world capitalism necessarily undermine hegemonic centres of capitalist power, as were first Genoa, then Holland and finally Britain in the past. US economic decline after 1973, for Arrighi, could be fully understood only as part of this larger, inexorable pattern of systemically rooted contradictions. Hegemonic powers in a world capitalist system always have 'terminal crises'. The US regime of accumulation was simply experiencing its.

The UK in retreat

If the US economy did spend the 1980s hitting its 'hegemonic wall', it would not be the first dominant power to do so. Where the US economy perhaps walked then, the UK had definitely trodden before. For UK world economic dominance was of course a nineteenth-century, not a twentieth-century phenomenon; and so there is no contemporary UK equivalent to the current US dispute about whether the national economy has been (or is) in long-term decline. That decline is generally recognized across both the academic and the political spectrums. Where controversy rages is over the causes of that decline and, by association, over whether at least some of those causes were laid to rest by the Thatcherite 'policy revolution' of the 1980s.

The data on UK economic performance

The data on UK economic data performance before 1980 are relatively uncontroversial, and also plentiful (Matthews, Feinstein and Odling-Smee, 1982; Crafts, 1991; 1993b). They show that the UK economy lost its position of global pre-eminence in the production and export of manufactured goods from the 1890s, and that, although UK-based exporters of manufactured goods were then given a fresh lease of life by the temporary dislocation of their main European competitors in the decade after 1945, they lost ground to them (and to Japanese manufacturing firms) steadily from the 1960s. For 'from the 1870s to the 1970s the growth of output and productivity in the UK was low by the standards of other advanced economies' with 'the growth gap . . . particularly pronounced in the Golden Age from 1950 to 1973 when the British growth rate was only about half the OECD average' (Crafts, 1993b: 331). It was in those first two postwar decades that 'British manufacturing levels were overtaken by France and Germany' (ibid.), and in the next two that the output of goods from UK-based manufacturing firms levelled out. Alone among the major industrial powers, the UK's manufacturing output failed to grow on any scale after the oil crisis of the early 1970s (see figure 1.1 for confirmation); indeed 'not until 1988 did UK manufacturing output recover its level in the peak year of 1973, and (as late as 1992) it was less than 1% higher than in 1973, whereas output increased by 27% in France, 25% in Germany, 85% in Italy and 119% in Japan during the same period' (Select Committee on Trade and Industry, 1994: 16). In 1983 an economy that had once been the 'workshop of the world' became a net importer of manufactured goods for the first time in peacetime in 200 years, and spent the 1980s as a net exporter of capital and in possession of a large and apparently irreducible balance of payments deficit. With such a competitive slippage, it is little wonder that as late as 1985 a committee of leading parliamentarians could worry about the 'grave threat' posed by manufacturing failure, not simply to the standard of living but 'to the economic and social stability of the nation' (House of Lords Select Committee, 1985: 83) as a whole.

The House of Lords Report that year bemoaned Treasury complacency and public 'unawareness of the seriousness of its predicament' (ibid.: 56); and well it might. For from the 1960s, and possibly from even earlier, the rate of investment in manufacturing plant and equipment in the UK settled at a level well below that common in more successful economies abroad. In fact, between 1960 and 1993 investment in machinery and equipment only averaged 8.4 per cent of GDP. This was higher than the US's 7.6 per cent (as the US began its own slippage back into the pack of chasing competitor economies); but it was less than the figures for West Germany (8.7 per cent), France (8.9 per cent), and Italy (9.8 per cent), and way behind the figure for Japan (12.4 per cent) (*Financial Times*, 12 July 1996). In real terms, net manufacturing investment in the UK settled between 1979 and 1989 at a level just one-sixth of that achieved in the decade immediately before the oil crisis, as the manufacturing sector moved from an investment level equivalent to 4 per cent of its output in the 1960s to one equivalent to a mere 0.6 per cent in the 1980s (Kitson and Michie, 1995: 2). The associated rate of growth of labour productivity in the UK also settled below that of US labour, Japanese labour and labour across northern Europe. The value added per worker hour in UK manufacturing in 1987 was only 58 per cent of that added in the US (van Ark, 1992: 68); and output per worker hour in German manufacturing that year was a clear 22 per cent higher than in the UK (O'Mahoney, 1992: 46). Against such a background, the share of world trade captured by UK-based manufacturing firms inevitably diminished, down from 16.3 per cent of total global exports in 1960 to just 8.4

per cent by 1990. Employment in UK-based manufacturing also collapsed, 3.5 million full-time manufacturing jobs (40 per cent of the original total) going in the two decades after 1973 (Employment Policy Institute, 1993: 1); and real wages in the UK (and associated living standards) dropped from northern Europe's highest in the late 1950s to its second lowest by the late 1980s. The UK economy in the first three decades of the postwar period became 'the sick man of Europe', and was widely recognized as such.

Most of those indicators of economic underperformance persist. The UK remains a net importer of manufactured goods with a stubborn deficit on its balance of payments. Its investment and productivity levels remain below those of its major industrial competitors, serious skills shortages are still evident, and the record of major UK-based companies on R&D spending (as a percentage of sales) is still lower than that of major companies in any of the other G7 economies in every industrial sector except pharmaceuticals (*Financial Times*, 26 June 1997). But the 1990s did witness a diminution in the UK's 'productivity gap' – if not primarily with Japan and the US, then certainly with continental Europe (Lansbury and Mayes, 1996: 21, 30); and this was definitely enough to stop (and even slightly to reverse) the UK's hitherto apparently headlong flight down all the international economic league tables. So, for example, O'Mahoney and Wagner found that 'in 1973 German aggregate manufacturing had a clear productivity level advantage and this showed a dramatic increase between 1973 and 1979. The reversal of the productivity trends in the following decade' then 'led to a productivity gap in 1989 which was lower than in the early 1970s' and which left labour productivity in 23 sectors of German industry greater than in the UK, whereas in 1979 that number had been 27 (O'Mahoney and Wagner, 1996: 145). Similarly Oulton's figures for output per person employed in manufacturing show the UK increasing on average 4.6 per cent per annum from 1979 to 1992, with Japan increasing at only 3.6%, the US at 2.4% and Germany easily the lowest at 1.8%, a differential large enough to improve the UK's unit labour cost performance (a measure influenced also by changes in wages and exchange rates) over both Germany and Japan, if not over the US (Oulton, 1994: 57). Certainly a number of key economic sectors actually strengthened their world competitive position from the 1980s (most notably financial services and aerospace, but also car manufacture and retailing), and overall the UK economy (like its US counterpart) experienced a sustained period of unbroken economic growth in the second half of the 1990s. In the process the UK attracted the lion's share of East Asian foreign direct investment into Europe before 1996, investment which (among other things) helped to trigger improvements in productivity in the key automobile industry. That five-year growth run also brought unemployment down – indeed by 1998 to a low (of around 5%) not seen in the UK since the deep recession of the early 1980s – and in so doing ran against the wider European trend of rising unemployment in the 1990s.

Yet even here performance was patchy and frail. The 1980s narrowing of the productivity gap with continental Europe was an achievement largely based on contraction, on a fall in manufacturing output of 14% between 1979 and 1981 and a rise of only 12% thereafter. 'Output per worker did increase, but primarily because there were fewer workers, rather than because Britain was producing more goods' (Kitson and Michie, 1996c). The employment figures themselves mask a significant shift in the UK after 1979 from full-time, secure and high-paid employment to part-time, insecure and low-paid employment. The total number of full-time jobs in the UK economy actually *fell* (by over 3 million) during the Tories' tenure of office; and as late as 1998 only 50% of the new jobs then being created were full-time and secure (Employment Policy Institute, 1998: 8). And by 1998 the UK manufacturing sector had officially moved back into recession, recording falls in output in two successive quarters for the first time since 1992. Even in its growth period in the 1990s, UK-based manufacturing industry managed to combine its new-found productivity with its long-established stagnation of output. The 'recovery' of 1993 and 1994 turned out to be yet another blip, leaving 'the total increase in manufactured output between 1973 and 1992 as a derisory 1.3 per cent' (Wolf, 1996a: 18). No wonder then that, even after five years of growth, a tranche of concerned institutions (from the OECD and the CBI to the new Labour Government) remain convinced that – as the CBI had it – 'on a range of competitiveness measures – including training and innovation – the majority of companies measured by the CBI's competitiveness data bank ranked either as poor or only fair' (*Guardian*, 23 September 1997), or that, as the McKinsey management consultancy firm controversially told the Labour Government, 'output per head – stripping out health, education and the civil service – is [still] 40 per cent lower than in the US and 20 per cent below that in western Germany' (*Guardian*, 15 May 1998). The 'productivity gap' recorded between exporting companies based in the UK and particularly their European competitors may have narrowed; but that narrowing was as much the product of their underperformance as of any major renaissance of general UK competitiveness – a consequence, it would appear, more of the generalized spread of 'the British disease' abroad than of its systematic eradication in the UK itself (Wolf, 1996b: 11).

The debate on the UK's decline

Such an economic record has long invited a literature on the nature and causes of economic decline. That literature has been surveyed elsewhere (Coates, 1983b; 1994; 1995b; 1996), so will not be covered in detail in this chapter. Instead, we must note two features of the debate about the UK's economic underperformance that will inform our later discussion on the strengths and weaknesses of particular capitalist models. One is the persistence of that debate well into the 1990s, in both official policy circles and in academic and popular discussion. The second is the strong parallels between at least part of that debate and the US equivalent which we have just explored at length.

The contemporary upsurge in official, academic and popular discussion of economic performance in the UK need not delay us long. But what is remarkable about it is the width of agreement evident in much of the official material produced on this topic in the 1990s. The Select Committee on Trade and Industry produced its report in 1994. The then Conservative government produced three white papers on competitiveness between 1994 and 1996 (Conservative Government, 1994; 1995; 1996). The Labour Party indirectly triggered the IPPR report *Promoting Prosperity* in 1997. In all of them the focus of criticism was broadly consistent, and largely in line with the MIT Commission findings for the US that the UK economy suffered, as the IPPR had it, from 'too many inefficient and poorly run companies, too many underachieving people, too little investment in research, innovation and physical capital, and too frequent shifts in government policy' (IPPR, 1997: 1–2). There were more radical outriders to this consensus (Will Hutton in particular, as we shall see in a minute); but in general the official consensus prevalent in UK policy-making circles by the late 1990s was that described by Nick Crafts: 'low levels of investment, inadequate management, inappropriate education and training standards and industrial relations systems' (Crafts, 1993b: 331). Even Michael Heseltine, the Major Government's most senior industry minister, is on record as criticizing the quality of investment in UK industry – particularly its lack of concentration on R&D spending and on the training and re-skilling of labour (Heseltine, 1996: 22).

In the wider academic debate on the causes of the UK's economic underperformance, however, consensus is harder to find; and for our purposes here, four lines of argument are worthy of note, three of which have clear US parallels, and one of which does not. There are clear US parallels within the UK debate (as we shall see) around issues of paradigm choice, contradictions of dominance, and the need for pro-active state policy. Where the UK debate extends the US one, however is on the question of UK labour.

As we saw earlier, for some analysts at least the US labour movement did play an important f subordinate role in the social structure of accumulation underpinning postwar US prosperity; but in general, explanations of US prosperity and decline in the 1980s left 'the labour question' largely on one side. The equivalent UK debate did (and does) not. It particularly did not in the 1970s, when a series of neo-liberal economists (and, more significantly, a series of leading Conservative politicians) singled out trade union power as the chief source of UK economic decline (see Coates, 1994: 27–40). Trade unions found themselves blamed for low investment in UK manufacturing industry, for the low utilization (and therefore low productivity) of existing investment and even for the high taxation and borrowing levels of postwar UK governments. Indeed the Conservatives entered office in 1979 convinced that 'solving the union problem [was] the key to Britain's recovery' (Joseph, 1979), that the competitiveness of UK-based exporting industries had been undermined directly by excessive trade union industrial power and indirectly by trade union political power. They accordingly spent the next 18 years systematically eroding both the legal rights of trade unions and the effective capacity of workers and their representatives to block the ability of UK managers to manage. And as they did so, they helped to put in place a powerful new orthodoxy linking economic underperformance directly and primarily to inflexibility in labour markets, and linking that inflexibility to trade union industrial power.

The validity or otherwise of that set of linkages will be a major concern of chapter 4. What concerns us here is the legacy of these Thatcherite claims in the literature, which emerged *after* 1979 in response to the Conservative Government's systematic erosion of trade union power. For in that literature we can see both a minor and a major voice. The minor voice (with definite US links and parallels) drew on Harvard-based arguments about the potentially beneficial effects of strong trade unionism to argue that weakening the trade unions only made UK economic performance worse, by locking the economy onto a low-wage, low-value-added growth trajectory that left the UK as a screwdriver and warehouse economy on the edge of a more prosperous and more corporatist Europe (see in particular Nolan, 1995; Coates, 1994). But the major voice ran entirely counter to that, conceding retrospectively the force of the Thatcherite argument against trade union power in the 1970s by linking the rise in productivity evident in the UK economy in the 1980s and 1990s either directly or indirectly to trade union 'reform' – to what Crafts referred to as 'the Thatcher shock' (Crafts, 1992: 25).

Much of the 'new growth theory' literature and the associated recent growth accounting material on UK economic performance in the past two decades has linked 'the productivity surge experienced by British manufacturing in the 1980s . . . largely' to 'reductions in over-manning and restrictive practices particularly in industries subject to adverse employment shocks and notably in unionised firms and where competition increased' (ibid.). Their studies have either addressed the issue of industrial relations reform directly, and asserted its positive contribution to recent economic growth (Oulton, 1995: 67) or included such reforms in a longer set of improvements lying behind the narrowing of the UK productivity gap (Crafts, 1993a: 50, 75). Such new growth theorists have not by that process of reasoning been persuaded of the entire adequacy of the Thatcherite project. On the contrary, many of them have criticized it for its failure to supplement trade union reform with adequate investment in human capital and R&D (Crafts, 1992: 33). But they were (and presumably remain) convinced that 'weaker trade unions and a major shake-out of inefficiencies' were vital prerequisites for economic recovery, such that by achieving them 'obstacles to "catch up" in Britain were reduced and relative economic decline was ended for the time being' (Crafts, 1993b: 345). And by arguing in that way, of course, new growth theorists of the Crafts variety have given a very powerful reinforcement to the neo-liberal view that trade union power was a major barrier to successful UK economic performance in the past.

It is, however, a feature of much writing of this kind that it also concedes the possibility that 'the UK's relative economic decline was due to some quite different cause . . . to factor X' (Oulton, 1995: 67) which it has not yet managed to identify and measure, and that the 'industrial relations hypotheses' which Crafts and others have developed are only one of a set of conflicting explanations of the 1980s productivity surge, a set which also includes a whole series of hypotheses about the size, distribution and age of the UK's *capital* stock. Some economists have emphasized the impact on overall productivity levels of the closure of inefficient or unprofitable firms and plants during the 1980–2 recession. Others have pointed to the scrapping of old machinery in that recession, yet others to the way the intensification of international competition in the 1980s triggered a diffusion of technologies and forms of work organization that enabled UK productivity rates suddenly to close the gap on more advanced economies elsewhere (Lansbury and Mayes, 1996: 21–2). In fact the recent debate between economists on why investment levels in UK manufacturing industry have been so low has generated what Andrew Britton has correctly labelled as:

> two broad alternative answers. First the supply of capital to industry has been low. According to this view industry in the UK has had no shortage of investment opportunities but has lacked an adequate supply of finance at a reasonable price. The reasons for this could be 'short termism' in financial markets, credit rationing by banks or other such imperfections. . . . Second the demand for capital has been too low. Here the problem lies with the underlying structure of the economy rather than its financial system. For some reason there is a lack of profitable investment opportunities in the UK: it could be that trade unions are too powerful, government economic policy is too unstable or that there are too few incentives to enterprise. *(Britton, 1992: 3)*

What neither side in that debate denies is that the level of investment in UK manufacturing industry has been (and remains) too low.

Beyond the boundaries of conventional economics, other hypotheses have emerged too, concerned with variables of a more institutional and political kind which growth accounting has difficulty in measuring. There exists, for example a body of mainly Marxist-inspired material that replicates the critique of military spending and imperialism with which we closed the section on US decline (on this, see Coates, 1994: 190–200), and to which we shall return in chapter 7. There is also a more Weberian-inspired body of writing linking twentieth-century UK economic underperformance to a prolonged cultural malaise (a loss of 'the industrial spirit') occasioned by the incomplete nature of the UK's nineteenth-century bourgeois revolution (for this, see pp. 135–41). But these are not the most widely known counter-arguments to neo-liberal theses on UK decline. That accolade more properly falls to Schumpeterian- and Keynesian-inspired arguments, including those on 'paradigm shifts' developed by Lazonick. The UK's long twentieth-century decline, in this view, owed little to trade union

power, except to the degree that a certain kind of craft unionism and decentralized collective bargaining have been part of the long legacy of the socio-
economic paradigm (of 'proprietary capitalism' in Lazonick's terminology)
into which UK industrial capital settled in the nineteenth century, and from
which it never adequately broke. As we have now seen, the general
Lazonick thesis was that economic decline is triggered by 'institutional
rigidities', by a set of institutional arrangements which, though successful
in the past, become outmoded over time, but which have a capacity to persist
and become sources of underperformance. Central to the Lazonick view of
the UK was its early establishment of small-scale family-based industrial
units which possessed no professional managerial strata or developed internal R&D capacities, no close links (either horizontal or vertical) with suppliers and customers and no organic connections to local financial
institutions. Such a form of corporate organization, he has argued, was
enough to provide a brief moment of world manufacturing leadership in the
mid-nineteenth century, but was insufficient to protect and deepen that
position of leadership as the scale of markets grew, as the nature of dominant technologies developed, and as forms of corporate capitalism emerged.

   If Lazonick is correct, twentieth-century UK economic underperformance is to be understood as the product of 'entrenched institutional structures – including the structures of industrial relations' but also 'industrial
organisation, educational systems, financial intermediation, international
trade, and state-enterprise relations' which collectively 'constrained the
ability of individuals, groups, or corporate entities to transform the productive system' (Elbaum and Lazonick, 1984: 569). In fact, according to
Lazonick, the UK's economic dominance in the twentieth century has been
hit not once, but twice. Its inability to modernize its corporate structures
and associated social, cultural and political systems left it vulnerable to
decline after the second industrial revolution at the start of the twentieth
century, when it lost out primarily to the competitive power of US-based
corporate/managerial capitalist concerns (which left it, that is, as a weak
and subordinate version of the then dominant liberal capitalist model). But
similarly rooted institutional rigidities and inertia left the UK economy
vulnerable again at the end of the twentieth century, when a third wave of
technological developments left even US managerial capitalism vulnerable
to competition from more consensual/trust-based capitalist models of first
a German but then a Japanese kind. As we shall see in more detail in chapter
3, Lazonick is an enthusiastic advocate of Japanese 'collective capitalism'
over the US 'managerial capitalism'. His argument on the UK is that it has
historically lacked the modernizing institutions to catch up effectively with
either of them.

   Such a neo-Schumpeterian view of the broad institutional barriers to
the UK achievement of high rates of economic growth not only acts as a
powerful theoretical counter-weight to neo-liberal theses on UK economic
decline; it also sits easily alongside a more post-Keynesian understanding of
the roots of that underperformance. At the heart of that post-Keynesian

reading is an emphasis on the importance of the manufacturing sector as the 'engine of growth', and a sharp critique of UK financial institutions as inadequate suppliers of investment and leadership to that manufacturing base. The key popular text here in the 1990s was Will Hutton's widely read *The State We're In* (Hutton, 1994).

The Hutton rebuttal of Thatcherite neo-liberalism rested on a sustained critique of what he (following Cain and Hopkins, 1993a, 1993b) termed 'gentlemanly capitalism', on a condemnation of the unwillingness of an aristocratically dominated UK financial sector to establish close, long-term relations with local manufacturing industry. The Hutton explanation of the UK's economic underperformance hardly mentioned the unions at all. It pointed instead to an 'endemic' short-termism in the investment habits of UK financial institutions, and linked that – as John Zysman had earlier done (Zysman, 1983) – to the dependence of large UK companies on the stock market rather than the banking sector for investment funds. The UK economy was (and is) in decline, according to Hutton, because the core relationship between its various sectors – between what in Marxist terms would be understood as industrial and financial capital – is too driven by immediate private interests, by ease of 'exit' from company ownership and by unregulated market imperatives, and is commensurately insufficiently mediated by long-term relationships of mutual interest, 'voice' and trust. Add to that an excessive commitment to liberal ideas, particularly in government, and the absence of a written constitution to constrain the application of unbridled liberalism by Thatcherite governments between 1979 and 1997, and you end up – according to Hutton – with a UK economy seeking economic salvation in the wrong direction – trying in the 1980s to rid itself of any social democratic constraints on the construction of a liberal model of capitalism, just at the moment when more trust-based capitalist models (which for Hutton were in any case socially and morally preferable) were demonstrating their competitive superiority. In fact you end up, according to Hutton, doubly disadvantaged:

> in trying to copy the US, the British have ended up with the worst of both worlds. We have neither the dynamism of the US or of East Asia, nor European institutions of social cohesion and long term investment. Britain has imported the mechanisms by which risk and insecurity are increased for those least able to bear it, while retaining a financial system that combines demand for high returns with minimal acceptance of risk. With European levels of unemployment and American levels of working poor, Britain has unleashed the processes that have hollowed out US manufacturing without any compensating dynamics. *(Hutton, 1994: 19)*

So the debate on the UK's economic underperformance, no less than that on the recent state of the US economy, is (and throughout has been) informed by distinct differences of theoretical view and different attitudes to the strengths and weaknesses of particular capitalist models. In the broadest sense, analysts sympathetic to neo-classical growth theory (in either its old or its new form) have bought into at least part of the Thatcher project, understanding the problem of underperformance as ultimately a question of barriers to the full workings of markets (and particularly labour markets) while disputing between themselves (old growth theorists against new) on the necessity or desirability of limited state action to improve the quality (or even the magnitude) of investment in human capital, technology and innovation. Analysts of a more Schumpeterian or Keynesian persuasion have found that faith in markets either too static or too misplaced (and the resulting policy debate too narrow and too union/labour focused. They have looked instead to the sources of dynamism released by the various forms of corporate governance in which the range of potent stakeholders is wider than is conventional in shareholder-based capitalisms, and have in consequence seen inadequacies in market-based capitalist models which separate company from company, industry from finance, and even manager from worker. For them, the US and UK economies have lost elements of their previous competitive dominance because of the inability of liberal modes of capitalist organization to tap into (and to harness) sources of economic adaptability and change rooted in competitive relationships which are mediated through relationships of cooperation and trust.* It is at economies which have managed what Hutton called 'a fusion of competition and co-operation' (Hutton, 1994: 255) while enjoying high rates of economic growth that they recommend we look; and in so doing they take us away from the UK and the US into the debates that surround economic performance in East Asia and continental Western Europe.

---

*   Nor have they been alone on the Left in making that argument. This is Robert Brenner's recent view of why Japanese and German capitalism outstripped US capitalism for a large chunk of the postwar period.

> The constellation of leading social forces that emerged to shape the post-war German and Japanese economies were the converse of those found in the US. The advantages possessed by German and Japanese manufacturers by virtue of their later development . . . went beyond those that were bound to be exhausted over time – cheap labour recruited from the countryside, access to the latest techniques by borrowing from the US, and the benefits of a particular position in the product cycle. Their advantages came to include more permanent politico-institutional factors which had a longer term impact, making for the maintenance of favourable conditions for capital accumulation. Because German, and especially Japanese, manufacturing firms were able to embed themselves within advanced institutional forms for organizing intra-manufacturing, finance-manufacturing, and capital-labour relations which had no counterpart in the US, as well as secure state support of a kind unavailable in the US, these firms were able to achieve a level and quality of investment and a capacity to control costs inexplicable in purely market terms. These political and economico-institutional arrangements allowed manufacturers access to cheaper capital, increased socialization of risk, greater protection (even if partial and temporary) from international competition, longer time horizons for returns on investment, more favourable opportunities to invest in human capital, and greater investments in socially necessary, but individually unprofitable endeavours, particularly infrastructure, education, and research. (Brenner, 1998: 44)

3

Trust-based Capitalism: Revival and Retreat

As I write, early in 1999, news is dominated by the East Asian economic crisis: by South Korean debt, internal industrial restructuring and labour protests, by Indonesian and Malaysian political turmoil and by Japanese recession. It is also dominated by a series of visits to East Asia by leading Western European politicians and international bankers – in 1998 most notably the head of the IMF and the UK Chancellor of the Exchequer (on behalf of the European Union) – offering advice to the Japanese and South Korean governments on how to transform their economies into liberal capitalist ones. But it was not always so. On the contrary, in the Western media until as late as 1997, and in more informed circles until at least 1992, the pattern of advice and modelling ran largely in the other direction. For until the 1990s the growth rates achieved by the postwar Japanese economy were by far the highest in the advanced capitalist world: and Japan was widely perceived (and copied) as capitalism's miracle economy. But the wheels rather came off that miracle in the 1990s, as the Japanese economy then ran into six years of relatively stagnant growth, and did so at precisely the moment that US and UK growth rates were unexpectedly quickening; and the decade ended in a major and more general crisis of the East Asian tiger economies that had flourished in Japan's wake, a crisis which then raised serious and widely articulated doubts about the adequacy of Japanese economic institutions and the quality of Japanese economic management.

The causes, consequences and significance of the 1990s downturn in Japanese economic fortunes will be a major theme of chapters 6–8. The task of the first half of this chapter is to lay out explanations (most of which were produced before 1992) of the spectacular growth rates achieved by the Japanese economy in the first four postwar decades. As in chapter 2, what follows here is an exercise in exposition. Evaluation will come later.

The rise of the Japanese economy

Particularly among those commentators who were convinced that what the US faced by the century's end was a fundamental paradigm choice, US economic weaknesses in the 1980s were primarily defined against perceived Japanese strengths. As we have just seen, it was their view that in the old production paradigm – the one on which US postwar success had been built – 'success was based on access to natural resources, pools of labour, [and] scientific knowledge'. The new paradigm, by contrast (as Michael Porter told the incoming President Clinton), privileged dynamism, innovation, research and development, training and supplier relationships (Clinton, 1993: 41). In the new paradigm, after what Lazonick termed 'the third industrial revolution . . . far from prosperity requiring a perfection of the market mechanism . . . the wealth of different nations [had] become increasingly dependent on the planned co-ordination that [took] place within business organizations' and, in consequence, the only economies to flourish would be those able to reduce the economic uncertainty necessarily associated with innovative investment by 'means of policies that educate[d] the work force, mobilise[d] committed financial resources, and co-ordinate[d] interdependent innovative efforts' (Lazonick, 1991a: 13, 57). According to the commentators who in the 1980s wanted US capitalism to make this paradigm shift, it was Japanese social and industrial practices that constituted the appropriate model for this future competitiveness: Japanese attitudes and ideology (Lodge, 1986: 14), Japanese ways of linking industry and finance (Thurow, 1992: 34), Japanese worker–manager relations (Lazonick, 1991a: 44), even Japanese state practices (Zysman and Cohen, 1986: 42–4).

Yet the advocates of paradigm change were not alone in their careful scrutiny of the sources of postwar Japanese economic success. Growth accountants too poured over the appropriate Japanese data with immense care. Edward Denison, for example, was an early player in the rising American literature on what in the 1970s was still described as 'Asia's New Giant' (Patrick and Rosovsky, 1976). His 1976 study located the Japanese margin of growth over other leading capitalist economies between 1953 and 1971 (at 8.8 per cent per annum, an average margin of 4.6%) as resting on a better Japanese performance on all growth factors. As he put it, 'the answer is not to be found in any single determinant of growth. Rather, changes in almost all important determinants were highly favourable in comparison with other countries, and in none was the change particularly unfavourable'. So he found labour supply responsible for 0.9% out of the 4.6% margin of Japanese superiority, investment in new equipment responsible for 1.2%, applications of new knowledge for 1.0%, and redistribution away from agriculture to industry for 0.3%. The Denison emphasis in his 1976 study settled ultimately on Japan's massive increase in the size of the capital stock – increasing, he noted, 'at a pace quite outside the range observed in other advanced countries' (Denison and Chung, 1976: 63) – and in Japan's capacity to absorb and exploit new ideas with the minimum of delay and worker resistance. But he was characteristically cautious – as others, as we shall see, habitually were not – on the possible *cultural* origins of this distinctly Japanese capacity to gain economic advantages from additions to knowledge at a rate that exceeded the growth rate of world knowledge in total, saying only that 'attitudes and practices that may have helped Japan can be suggested' but whether they 'led to better decisions we cannot judge' (ibid.: 82–3).

Arguments of this kind then helped to sustain a conventional neo-liberal explanation of postwar Japanese economic growth – one emphasizing the role of market forces and the mobilization of new economic resources. Later (pp. 153–4) we shall meet the important and widely discussed Krugman argument that there was nothing particularly miraculous about postwar Japanese growth, that it rested on the mobilization of hitherto unused factors of production – capital certainly, but especially labour – and not on any dramatic increase in the productivity of the factors mobilized, and that as such it was a once-and-for-all catch-up operation that was bound eventually to slow down, and which did not therefore constitute a qualitatively novel growth path or experience (Krugman, 1994b). But for the moment it is enough to note the earlier arguments of Patrick and Rosovsky in *Asia's New Giant* as typical of that general approach. Against those impressed by Japanese uniqueness, they 'gently suggest[ed as early as 1976] that Japanese growth was not miraculous' and that it could 'be reasonably well understood and explained by ordinary economic causes' (1976: 6). In particular, postwar Japan possessed a highly educated and skilled labour force – 'in a sense overeducated relative to the static needs of the economy' (ibid.: 12), great differences in pay and productivity between economic sectors, 'substantial managerial, organizational, scientific, and engineering skills capable of rapidly absorbing and adapting the best foreign technology' (ibid.: 12) and a government supportive of Japanese big business. Their view was that 'while the government [had] certainly provided a favourable environment, the main impetus to growth has been private–business investment demand, private saving, and industrious and skilled labour operating in a market-oriented environment of relative prices' (ibid.: 48). Japanese postwar economic success, that is, was best understood as simply the successful working through of a 'market-oriented, private enterprise economic system' (ibid.: 43) and did not require – to be understood – any additional ingredient of a specially Japanese kind, be that 'government policy or leadership, labor-management practices and institutions, or more vaguely defined cultural attributes' (ibid.: 6; see also Miwa, 1996: 27).

However, the bulk of the specialist literature on Japanese postwar economic success has not taken this line. On the contrary, it has gone in entirely the opposite direction, emphasizing the economic consequences of the unique social, political, institutional and cultural settings surrounding Japanese capital accumulation. It has used the postwar Japanese growth story to argue against neo-liberal orthodoxies in conventional economics, presenting postwar Japanese 'success' as a vindication of either a post-Keynesian enthusiasm for state action or a neo-Schumpeterian enthusiasm for the competitive dynamism of large corporations. In most of the recent relevant literature, that is, Japan has been treated as evidence *against* the neo-liberal enthusiasm for market-based liberal capitalism. Its institutional structures and social arrangements have been paraded as quintessential elements of a 'trust-based' alternative whose success originated in those structural differences from the liberal model: differences of culture, industrial relations, corporate organization and politics. To grasp the depth and complexity of this argument on (and advocacy of) 'trust-based capitalism', it is necessary to examine each of these supposed differences in turn.

(1)   *The uniqueness of Japanese culture*   The argument on Japanese culture has come in a variety of forms – some simplistic (even racist) in character, others sophisticated and nuanced attempts to integrate ideational analysis with more easily quantifiable forms of social explanation. It is the latter, of course, that concern us here, particularly those sensitive to the fact that, while the range of behavioural predispositions in Japan and other advanced capitalist economies is large and does overlap – so that we are not talking here of absolute cultural differences – none the less the centres of gravity of each range, what Dore called their 'central tendencies' (Dore, 1993: 76), do settle at different points in different societies. We are concerned, that is, with those prepared to argue that there are real and discernible cultural differences in play in advanced capitalist economies, and that those cultural differences do help to explain differences in economic performance.

    In material of this quality and sophistication, it is generally recognized that dominant cultural systems have their own complex histories and have to be understood as deriving from those histories (on this, see in particular Dore, 1987: 92). On some occasions, the main emphasis is placed on recent triggers to cultural change, as when Lodge, for example, emphasized the impact of wartime defeat on the uniquely consensual nature of postwar Japanese society and thinking (Lodge, 1986: 16). But more normally, the central theme of those histories is the long-term impact of Confucianism, and particularly of Japanese rather than Chinese Confucianism, with its greater emphasis on loyalty and nationalism (Morishima, 1982: 9, 15; Fukuyama, 1995: 178–82). In the culturalist literature on Japan, Confucianism is said to encourage particular forms of economic activity, and to shift the centre of gravity of economic understandings away from those prevalent in the predominantly Protestant Christian West. A Confucian society – we are told – is not like a society informed by a Protestant ethic. It is still a society which prizes achievement and innovation. Indeed, even more than the modern West, it 'is a kind of *diploma society* in which people are distinguished by their educational attainments' (Morishima,

1982: 17) and in which, in consequence, highly meritocratic forms of schooling are likely to emerge (Dore, 1985: 211). But it is one in which attitudes to authority and leadership, on the one hand, and to social status and social distance, on the other, are likely to be quite different from those prevalent in societies whose pre-capitalist ideational systems were largely Christian in character. Dore thought it 'obvious that Japan is a society in which hierarchical ranking permeates personal interactions more than most' (ibid.: 197). He also thought that in Britain, by contrast, 'authority is generally much more problematic than in Japan: its legitimacy is always closer to being questioned' (ibid.: 203–4), and neither age nor rank attract as much automatic respect. According to Dore, cultures infused with Confucian values are likely to leave people 'much more willing to foreclose their options by making long-term commitments' and to hold 'diffuse obligations to promote the welfare of others' (Dore, 1993: 76–7). 'People born and brought up in Japanese society do not much like openly adversarial bargaining relationships, which are inevitably low-trust relationships, because information is hoarded for bargaining advantage and each tries to manipulate the responses of the other in his own interest. Poker is not a favourite Japanese game' (Dore, 1988: 96). As he later observed, 'in Japan, producing goods and services which enhance the lives of others is good. Spending one's life in the speculative purchase and sale of financial claims is bad' (Dore, 1993: 77). It is not that such a 'productionist ethic' is entirely missing from capitalisms with a Christian background – of course not; it is rather that Anglo-Saxon individualism tends to encourage a 'property' view of companies and a more limited view of corporate responsibilities, whereas the less individualist culture inherited by, say, contemporary Japanese economic actors is said to encourage them to hold a wider 'entity or community' view of the corporation and its responsibilities (Dore, 1993: 67).

The result, we are told, is a qualitatively different pattern of labour turnover (high in the US, low in Japan) and managerial loyalty (high in Japan, low in the US), a qualitatively different attitude to shareholders and their short-term concerns (dominant in the US, tempered by long-term thinking and responsibility to employees in Japan) and an associated greater willingness among Japanese managers to build relationships of trust between themselves and those they manage. Precisely because authority relationships and generational respect are so entrenched, so the argument runs, Japanese managers are far less prone to establish sharp social barriers between themselves and subordinates than is normal in the UK, are more tolerant of criticism from below, do not maintain so great a set of income differentials between themselves and those they manage and feel powerful obligations to take cuts in their own living standards if forced by circumstances to impose them on the workers they employ (Dore, 1985: 203–6). 'Perhaps the crucial element facilitating trust in a Japanese firm', according to Dore, 'is the fact that the contractual nature of the employment relationship is obscured or replaced by a sense of common membership in a corporate entity which has objectives which can be shared by all its

members' (ibid.: 212). In such a firm, 'the Confucian emphasis on industrious productiveness . . . both reaffirms the precedence given to employees
over shareholders and provides grounds for workers to think of their skill
as something to take pride in, rather than just a commodity to be sold as
dearly as possible' (ibid.: 214). It is not that inherited ideas entirely drown
out trends and problems common to capitalism wherever it is located. It is
just, so the argument runs, that dominant ideas shape the way those trends
and problems are defined, understood and acted upon in different national
settings, and in this way act as an important *additional* source of international competitiveness. As Dore put it: 'there is nothing really which is so
very culturally specific about what I have called the "Confucian recipe for
industrial success". It is, basically, about the conditions for establishing trust
in authority. And in modern societies, trust comes expensive; expensive, particularly, in terms of managerial effort and abstention from privilege' (ibid.:
217).

(2)   *Industrial relations*   Such cultural forces help to explain, for those persuaded of them, certain key social underpinnings of Japanese economic life.
They help to explain the ferocity and seriousness of Japanese education,
with near-universal school participation to 18, 40% attendance at tertiary
institutions, fierce examination pressure and typically 20–30 per cent more
hours spent at school than in the UK (Dore, 1985: 199). They help to
explain the high level of personal saving in Japan; and they are said to hold
the key to Japan's uniquely consensual system of industrial relations.

'The [Japanese] communitarian business firm', Thurow has written, 'has
a very different set of stakeholders' from an American or British firm, 'who
must be consulted when its strategies are being set'. US and UK investment
decisions are primarily shareholder-driven and dividend-led. Not so in
Japan. 'In Japanese business firms', according to Thurow, 'employees are
seen as the number one stakeholder, customers number two, and the share-
holders a distant number three' (Thurow, 1992: 33); and because of this
ordering of priorities, Japanese companies are much more willing than their
major Anglo-Saxon rivals to guarantee job security and welfare provision to
their employees, and to open corporate decision-making to worker involvement. They are also more willing to invest in the skills of their workers,
treating them not as a 'factor of production to be rented when it is needed
and laid off when it is not' (ibid.: 33) but as core members of the corporate
team. The management literature in English on Japan is replete with examples of this style of labour management – 'the firm as a surrogate family'
(Eccleston, 1989: 69) – including the famous case of the Mazda reorganization of 1974–5, when production workers were transferred to 'marketing
jobs, including door-to-door selling' to 'avoid the damage to company status
that would have accompanied widespread redundancies' (ibid.: 45). The literature is also replete with examples of the trust shown by senior Japanese
managers in their subordinates, and of their willingness to countenance the
collective 'self-monitoring' of the labour process by work teams and quality

circles. Decentralization of decision-making is thus a marked feature, we
are told, of Japanese labour management, such that – if Lash and Urry are
to be believed – 'in directly comparable cases similar decisions were taken
on average one step lower in firm hierarchies in Japan than in the USA'
(Lash and Urry, 1994: 71).

For Lazonick and many other commentators on US–Japan economic
relations, labour relations are the principal factor in Japanese success in US
markets. They hold the key both to the quality of Japanese goods (through
the skill levels of Japanese workers) and to the propensity of Japanese industry for innovation and change. UK industry cuts (segments in Lazonick's
phrase) the hierarchical triangle of generalist managers, specialist technicians and routine operatives just below the generalist managers with their
'quest for elite status'. US companies characteristically segment the hierarchy further down, dividing managers and specialists on the one side from
operatives on the other, so integrating line and staff managers while refus-
ing to treat blue-collar workers as part of the company in any meaningful
sense. The Japanese cut is said to be lower still, slicing through the company
work-force only at the bottom level of the operative grade (Lazonick, 1991a:
44–5); this enables Japanese industry to 'build on communities of interest
within the enterprise by extending membership in the community not only
to managers but also to non-managerial personnel' (Lazonick, 1994a: 182).
From his own studies of competitive advantage on the shop-floor,
Lazonick claimed to have detected qualitatively different labour management styles at work in UK, US and Japanese capitalism. 'Whereas UK
employers simply *left skills on* the shop floor', he wrote, 'and American
employers sought to *take skills off* the shop floor, Japanese employers have
put skills on the shop floor by investing in the development of the capabilities of their shop-floor workers' (Lazonick, 1995: 90); and in doing so,
Japanese employers won the competitive edge. Lazonick again:

> Through the organizational commitments inherent in permanent employ-
> ment, the skills and efforts of male blue-collar workers have been made inte-
> gral to the organizational capabilities of their companies, thus enabling the
> Japanese to take the lead in innovative production systems such as just-in-
> time inventory control, statistical quality control, and flexible manufacturing.
> Critical to the functioning of these production systems is the willingness of
> Japanese managers to leave skills and initiative on the shop floor. Indeed, the
> recent success of Japanese mass producers in introducing flexible manufac-
> turing owes much to the fact that, for decades before the introduction of the
> new automated technologies, blue-collar workers were granted considerable
> discretion to monitor and adjust the flow and quality of work on the shop
> floor. *(Lazonick, 1991a: 42–3)*

(3)   *Corporate organization*   This argument on the Japanese style of labour
management is just part of a wider set of claims about the unique internal
configuration of the Japanese firm. At its most extreme, that set of claims
presents the postwar Japanese form of economic organization as 'a new eco-

nomic system of historic importance . . . neither capitalism nor socialism'
but rather 'human capitalism or the "human enterprise system"' (Ozaki,
1991: 1). On this argument, whereas 'in capitalism . . . capital is valued most
among all factors of production . . . under the Japanese system this capital
orientation is largely replaced by people orientation', by anchoring industrial
sovereignty in the hands of the 'managers and workers who produce the
firm's output' and by embracing 'a humanistic economic philosophy' (ibid.:
9–10). That philosophy is then said to give the Japanese human enterprise
system three distinguishing characteristics, which both set it apart from
liberal models of capitalism and give it a world competitive edge. These three
distinguishing characteristics are its commitment to consensual industrial
relations (of the kind we have just discussed), to joint worker–manager sovereignty, and to a high degree of inter-firm cooperation.

Because the 'human enterprise system' is predicated on the recognition
of the supreme importance of human resources as factors of production,
and on the view that those human resources work best if motivated well and
trained to their full capacity, Japanese companies – we are told – conceive
of their existing labour force as their own internal labour market (their own
internal pool of human capital). Because Japanese companies expect their
workers to remain with them over a sustained period of time, they are consequently prepared to invest systematically in their training, moving workers
between jobs as technological change and shifting market conditions
require, and providing job-specific in-house training as they do so.
Japanese companies encourage their workers to operate as teams, tying
individual rewards to team performance, and encouraging the sharing of
knowledge and ideas between senior and junior members of each team.
There is, we are told, a particular 'Japanese-style management system'
(JSMS) built around lifetime employment, seniority-based wages and enterprise unionism for between 25 and 30 per cent of the best-trained Japanese
workers 'in the large, most technologically advanced firms operating in the
strategically important sectors of the Japanese economy' (Ozaki, 1991:
97); it is a management system in which most managers are recruited
internally, in which managerial salaries (and salary differentials) are low by
North American standards, and in which both workers and managers share
equally in corporate success and failure. This team working and JSMS
are said to combine then to trigger high levels of corporate innovation and
cost-efficiency.

The capacity of workers and managers to cooperate so closely in this way
in the Japanese 'human enterprise system' is said to derive in part from the
structures of ownership and control surrounding the Japanese firm. In an
American company, ownership is clear: it lies with stock-holders, to whose
interests senior managers have necessarily to be attentive and to whom
regular and substantial dividend payments have to be made. In a typical
Japanese firm, by contrast, 'thanks to inter-firm mutual stockholding and a
relatively heavy reliance on debt financing, the role of [such external] capitalists is reduced to a point of insignificance', and 'management, in effect,
is almost completely free' to 'disdain dividends as unwelcome costs to the

firm that are not, like interest, tax deductible' (Ozaki, 1991: 15). Most large US firms stand alone, reliant for capital on retained profits and equity flotations. They are linked to even their major suppliers and corporate customers by unmediated market relationships. The typical Japanese firm, by contrast, sits in the midst of an interlocking web of linked corporations – bound into long-term relationships of trust and support between suppliers and manufacturers, and between industrial groups and their key banking units. In both the US and Japan, stock-holders, bankers, managers and workers necessarily interact: but under the Japanese system of 'human capitalism . . . they play different roles, so that the distribution of power among them becomes quite another matter' (ibid.: 15). Where American corporate relationships are mediated externally through markets and internally through hierarchies, the Japanese system of human capitalism mixes the two, surrounding the internally integrated firm with 'a close network of semi-integrated subcontracting relations with smaller firms in the context of an organised market', while bedding the large firm itself into 'wider circles of corporate grouping – enterprise groups'. As Ozaki accurately puts it, that 'representative enterprise grouping' has no obvious US parallel, consisting as it does of 'a major city bank, a major trading company, and a major manufacturing firm as the central core of the group' plus 'several large manufacturing firms in different product lines, below which lie pyramids of affiliated smaller subcontracting firms' (ibid.: 53). These enterprise groupings, according to Lazonick, 'permit the core companies to enjoy the advantages that the vertical integration of production and distribution creates for the borrowing of technology and the implementation of process and product innovation, without enduring the disadvantages of unmanageable bureaucracies that stifle technological and organisational change' (Lazonick, 1994a: 178).

The result, we are told, is that what Fruin has called 'the Japanese enterprise system' is qualitatively different in both character and performance from enterprise systems elsewhere in the advanced capitalist world. 'Based on the strategic interaction and alignment of three basic forms of industrial organisation – factory, firm and inter-firm network', the Japanese enterprise system is said to be particularly generative of 'high productivity, functional specialisation and manufacturing adaptability' (Fruin, 1992: 3). The claims made for this enterprise system by its overseas admirers are very large indeed. They like the way in which the large Japanese firm at its core 'trains and retrains its workers [and] offers them a measure of social security' (Hutton, 1994: 274). They like the way the large Japanese firm meets the Schumpeterian requirements of 'the new competition', competing strategically, and acting as 'a learning organisation that is continuously creating new productive services by teamwork and experience' (Best, 1990: 166). They like the way the core firms within each enterprise grouping 'seek neither high yields nor capital gains on their equity positions' but 'hold the shares for the sake of ensuring reinvestment in industry in general, which over the long term generates more business for the companies in the activities in which their competitive advantage lies' (Lazonick, 1994a: 178). They like the way in which the enterprise grouping as a whole generates 'lifelong, rather than highly mobile employment relationships . . . long-term, obligated, rather than auction-market mobile, supplier relations . . . [and] patient, long-term committed, rather than short-term, returns-sensitive, equity capital and the consequent absence of takeovers' (Dore, 1997: 26). They like what Dore calls the way the enterprise grouping combines 'integration by "institutional interlock" and integration by "motivational congruity"' into a system of what he terms 'relational contracting' (Dore, 1993: 75); and in particular they like the quite different patterns of enterprise behaviour it sustains. Dore again:

> there are some good reasons for thinking that it might be because of, not in spite of, relational contracting that Japan has a better growth performance than the rest of us. There is undoubtedly a loss of allocative efficiency. But the countervailing forces that more than outweigh that loss can also be traced to relational contracting. Those countervailing forces are those that are conducive not to allocative efficiency but to what Harvey Leibenstein calls X-efficiency – the abilities to plan and program, to co-operate without bitchiness in production, to avoid waste of time or materials – capacities which Leibenstein tries systematically to resolve into the constituent elements of selective degrees of rationality and of effort. *(Dore: 1988: 97)*

(4)   *State practices*   The final player in the conventional explanation of postwar Japanese success is the state itself, and particularly its prestigious industry ministry MITI. The key text in English on postwar industrial policy in Japan is Chalmers Johnson's *MITI and the Japanese Miracle* (1983), in which the Japanese state is presented as a 'developmental state', both geared to and equipped for the orchestrated stimulation of private-sector economic growth. Johnson positions Japan as a 'late industrialiser' and the Japanese state as a 'capitalist developmental state' (Johnson, 1995: 67), emphasizing (in contradistinction to conventional neo-liberal understandings of the role of the state) that, in economies seeking to make up lost ground on already existing capitalist powers, it was quite common to find that 'the state itself led the industrialisation drive, that is, it took on *developmental* functions' (Johnson, 1982: 19). Neo-classical economics tends to operate with a highly static notion of economic efficiency. The advocates of (or enthusiasts for) industrial policy tend to be more Schumpeterian in their predilections, measuring 'the allocation of resources according to their effects on the pace and direction of technological change' (Johnson et al., 1989: xvii). The case they put is that Japan is now at 'the forefront of a new technological trajectory' because Japanese industry has been the long-term beneficiary of a postwar 'interventionist targeting strategy' by the Japanese state 'that gradually but definitely guided Japan's industrial structure towards those sectors with the greatest growth and technological potential'. The claim is that 'policy affected where and how much investment occurred, what kinds of skills and technological learning took place, and by its influence on the production profile of the economy, policy ultimately affected the pace and direction of

technological innovation and diffusion' (ibid.). It was not just that the postwar Japanese economy was blessed with companies capable of exploiting the 'new competition'. It was also that Japan possessed an established tradition of state action and an associated set of state institutions, able and willing to coordinate those companies in a national pattern of industrial and economic reconstruction based on the institutionalization of technological innovation and diffusion. 'In the Japanese variant of capitalism', so the argument goes, 'markets have been emphasised as a source of growth rather than as a source of short-run efficiency, and a primary role of government has been to supply incentives to promote growth through markets' (ibid.: 32).

So in a powerful argument for an active industrial policy – an argument primarily directed towards the American centre-left – we are informed that the postwar Japanese state played both a 'gatekeeper' and a 'developmental' role to turn the Japanese economy into a major force in the international economy (Zysman and Cohen, 1986: 42), and may now indeed be playing the role of a 'catalyst state' to the internationalization of Japanese capital in a new era of global capital (Weiss, 1997: 20; 1998: 209–11). The state, we are told, acted as a national economic gate-keeper until at least 1970, controlling the entry of capital, technology and manufactured goods, effectively preventing the Japanese domestic market from being colonized by foreign companies bent on export-penetration. The result, as Zysman and Cohen have reported, was that 'in almost all cases, neither money nor technology could in itself allow outsiders to buy or bully their way into a permanent position in the Japanese market' (Zysman and Cohen, 1986: 42). At the same time, MITI used its influence over the Japanese Development Bank and other public financial agencies, and its powerful battery of administrative controls (over subsidies, import licences, and the provision of industrial parks and transport facilities) to 'guide' postwar Japanese companies into industries and technologies it thought desirable. The postwar Japanese state did not replace the force of market competition but rather orchestrated it, using 'intense but controlled domestic competition' as a substitute for 'the pressures of the international market to force development' (ibid.: 43). MITI initially steered Japanese private capital out of low wage textile production into heavy industries such as steel, chemicals, shipbuilding and cars. More recently it shifted its preferences towards more 'knowledge-intensive' industries such as semi-conductors, computers, tele-communications, high-definition television, biotechnology and aerospace (Kenworthy, 1995: 101; Johnson et al., 1989 25; for a detailed summary, Lazonick, 1994a: 177). And although MITI's influence over Japanese companies changed in character (and waned in potency) as those companies flourished, there are still academics prepared to emphasize that MITI and other Japanese economic agencies have now found a new role for the Japanese state, as the orchestrator of the export of Japanese capital Where MITI once closed trade borders to foreign entry, it now – we are told – provides (via Japanese overseas development aid) 'a wide array of incentives to finance overseas investment, promote technology alliances between national and foreign firms, and encourage regional relocation of production networks' (Weiss, 1997: 20–1) in order to ensure the continued competitiveness and world impact of Japanese corporate capital. And if this is so, then 'in the light of the East Asian experience, it appears that state capacity for industrial transformation is alive and well, at least in those countries where postwar development has occurred under the aegis of so-called developmental states' (ibid.: 23).*

The quiet strength of West German capitalism

As we first observed in chapter 1, the West German economy is commonly linked with the Japanese in the debates on comparative economic performance and the strength of alternative capitalist models. Those who make that link tend to argue three related things: that since 1945 West German capitalism has been organized in a distinctly consensual way (in a model which some treat as unique, and others as part of a more general European social consensus model); that the performance of this model has been superior to that of liberal capitalist models in the postwar period; and that this superior growth performance has been a consequence of the distinctive features of the model itself.

The crucial variable at play here – as with the argument on Japan – is invariably the capacity of the institutional structures surrounding West German capitalism to generate 'trust relationships' between key economic actors – so facilitating long-term industrial restructuring and a full utilization of existing industrial technologies. Depending on the politics of the analyst, which are normally centre-left in some form (although not exclusively – there is a Gaullist voice in the debate (Albert, 1993; even Barnett, 1986)) those trust relationships are anchored either in *intra-capital* relationships (with the emphasis on cooperation between large German companies, between German industry and German banks, and between small and large German capital) or in *capital–labour* relations (in a sweep of enthusiasm which moves from advocates of social market economies to enthusi-

---

* In passing it should be noted that this view of the Japanese state as a key economic actor is often subsumed into a wider set of arguments on development strategies, with similar arguments being put for the Taiwanese and South Korean states. Robert Wade, for example, has argued that

> the governments of Taiwan, Republic of Korea and Japan have an unusually well developed capacity for selective intervention; and that this capacity rests upon (a) a powerful set of policy instruments, and (b) a certain kind of organisation of the state, and of its links with other major economic institutions in the society. The East Asian three show striking similarities with respect to both instruments and institutions. They also, of course, show striking similarities with respect to (c) superior economic performance – notably with respect to rapid restructuring of the economy towards higher technology production' *(Wade, 1988: 130–1)*.

It should be noted however that Wade is scrupulous in insisting that 'we do not know . . . what are the causal connections between (a), (b) and (c)' (ibid.: 131).

asts for the 'beneficial constraints' imposed on German capital by strong labour unions). Those emphasizing capital–capital accords tend to collapse Germany and Japan together. Those emphasizing capital–labour accords tend to collapse or relate Germany and Sweden. The first open up an anti-liberal argument on the role of state–capital relations in industrial restructuring. The second open up an anti-liberal argument on labour power and international competitiveness. Germany therefore stands at the cross-roads of the two main thrusts of the anti-liberal case; and many opponents of liberal market forms of capitalism manage to combine an enthusiasm for both lines of argument at one and the same time, so extolling both Japan and Germany as superior capitalist models. Hutton's 'stakeholding' argument is a classic case in point (Hutton, 1994: 257–84; see also, more cautiously, Soskice, 1991).

As in the Japanese case, however, there is a neo-liberal presence in the debate on postwar West German economic performance, a strand of argument that is critical of West German 'social market' modelling, that downplays the longevity and degree of postwar West German superiority, and that makes much of recent difficulties in the German economy. Such neo-liberal analyses tend to specify the West German 'economic miracle' as a phenomenon of the 1950s, to see the trade union role in West German industrial politics after that as a drag on economic performance, and to collapse the West German loss of productivity edge in the last two decades into their more general critique of European welfare (Giersch et al., 1992). Their case is not without support in the broad empirical data. The 1950s were West Germany's miracle decade – with an average annual growth rate for GDP of 8.2%. Rates of GDP growth thereafter did slow: to 4.4% per annum on average between 1960 and 1973, 2.2% per annum 1973–1980 and 1.9% 1980–1990; and of course in the 1990s unemployment in the united Germany did rise to unprecedented postwar levels.

However for our purposes here, this neo-liberal argument is very much the minority voice, not least because advocates of the German model have been (and remain) able credibly to emphasize the underlying strength and tenacity of German social market institutions and the continued capacity of those institutions to handle the internal adjustment problems necessitated by intensified global competition and by post-Cold-War German unification (see, for example, Carling and Soskice, 1997). Across the full run of post-Keynesian, Schumpeterian and Marxist literatures on differential growth patterns, West Germany continues to figure strongly in arguments about the necessity of sinking capitalist accumulation into specific social settings. So, for example, both Hutton and Albert have argued strongly for the economic *and* social superiority of the German model (Hutton, 1994: 262; Albert, 1993: 14⁻); and Porter has stressed the persisting width and depth of German industrial clusters in sophisticated engineering, chemicals, pharmaceuticals and metals and metal working (Porter, 1990: 356–7). Even Fukuyama presented West Germany as 'the country displaying the highest degree of spontaneous sociability . . . after Japan' (1995: 207); however, it should be noted that in the more specifically German-focused literature his favoured cultural variables are invariably pushed into a minor place, relegated in favour of an emphasis on institutional relationships between (and within) broad social classes. This, for example, is Christel Lane's view of the German model.

> The German model of production-oriented capitalism, implying both a greater concern with, and a closer integration of management and labour around productive tasks, is the expression of an industrial order in which economic actors adhere to a limited communitarianism. Both the productivist bias and the greater collectivity orientation are dependent on a mode of finance provision which allows the development of long-term horizons in developing strategy for both individual firms and whole industries. It is further reinforced by a system of education and training which puts a strong emphasis on skill development at all levels and responsiveness to industrial needs. These orientations are supported by strong and dense associational networks and by both local and national state organizations. *(Lane, 1995: 3)*

(1)   *Corporate organization*   What the latter approach signals is the importance that many commentators attach, as a source of continuing German industrial strength, to Germany's high level of internal organization, by which they mean the persistence in Germany, behind a façade of liberal economics, of 'a degree of industrial concentration and inter-firm co-operation that . . . often goes relatively unnoticed' (Allen, 1989: 266). This 'organized' nature of German capitalism has long attracted academic comment. Andrew Shonfield noted it (and praised it) in the mid 1960s (Shonfield, 1965: 242, 260). Alfred Chandler documented it extensively in the 1980s (Chandler, 1990: 395). Lash and Urry, Porter and a host of others followed suit, linking the internal organization of German capitalism to Gershenkron-inspired arguments about late industrialization, and noting the speed with which late-nineteenth-century German capital followed US capital in making Chandler's 'three pronged investment in manufacturing, marketing and management'. Chandler in particular developed a distinctive argument on both the similarities and differences between US and German capital. He saw them both as becoming 'first movers in many of the new capital-intensive industries' of the Second Industrial Revolution (and as such well equipped to take out UK-based competition and to recover rapidly from wartime dislocation); but he also saw them differing markedly in their areas of competitive strength and internal organization. For Chandler, whereas US firms emerged strongly in both consumer and producer goods industries, in Germany successful firms were heavily concentrated in the production and distribution of producer goods (nearly two-thirds of the 200 largest German companies in 1929 were clustered in metals, chemicals and the three machinery groups). Especially in chemicals and heavy machinery industries, German firms prospered by exploiting economies of scope rather than scale; and in the process they retained more of a family management element than was normal in the US. More significantly still for Chandler,

German and US companies differed (and continue to differ) in their inter-firm and intra-firm relations. According to his data, there was (and there remains) a much higher level of cooperation in Germany between big firms than was (and is) the case in the US. In Germany, that is, the historian finds a higher tolerance of cartels, and a greater corporate propensity to pay close attention to the needs and welfare of their employees. In Germany, the historian finds what Chandler himself wanted to term 'a larger system . . . *organized capitalism*' (Chandler, 1990: 395).

(2) *The special role of German banks* At the heart of that system, for many commentators, stand the German banks. Of late, Hutton in particular has been quite adamant about this. According to him,

> the German banks are uniquely powerful, holding shares themselves and on behalf of others in the major German companies, making long-term loans, acting as information clearing houses and assessing industrial and commercial prospects in partnership with their borrowers. They are the stable backers of German industry and loyal long-term shareholders. They know the companies they finance, sit on their boards and can more accurately assess their risks. The system is orderly because its financial components give it the time and space it needs. *(Hutton, 1994: 264)*

West German universal banks are thus said to have played two key roles in postwar German reconstruction: providing the bulk of investment funds for German industry, and monitoring firms closely, restructuring them and their management where necessary (Edwardes and Fischer, 1994: 7–11). (German banks are said to have played a powerful shaping role in early German industrialization too, thus avoiding the industry–finance gap which progressively opened up in the UK in the last quarter of the nineteenth century.) They are said to be closely involved with their firms in the modern era because every borrowing firm has a house bank, and the bank sits on that firm's supervisory board (because of the bank's own share-holdings and as proxy for other share-holders who have deposited their shares with the bank). This is then said to give German banks better information about industrial conditions and needs, and to induce better lending rates than, say, in the UK, where bank–industry links are not so formalized or intimate. It is also said to induce a long-term relationship between the bank and the individual industrial or commercial firm, since in return for house-bank status, the bank has a built-in propensity to stay with the firm from cradle to grave. Among other things, this gives greater continuity to supervisory board membership, and reduces the short-termism endemic to managerial practice in more stock-market-based systems – where senior managers have to use high dividends to keep share-holders happy and predators at bay (Pollin, 1995). It is also claimed, by those enamoured of German banking practices, that West Germany's crucial SME sector is particularly protected by the presence of this bank-based system, given the flotation costs and loss of ownership control associated with stock-market-type funding. The exis-

tence of locally-based savings and cooperative banks and a specific industry
bank (all without UK equivalents) are supposedly critical to the health of
the SME sector. That at least was Hutton's view: 'the strength of the famous
Mittelstand – the medium size business sector that is . . . the backbone of
German industry' resulted in part from the manner in which smaller companies could attract 'long term committed finance from the regional state
banks' (1994: 266).

(3) *State practices*   State power is also given an explanatory role in West
German economic success by those commentators unimpressed by neo-
liberal growth theory, although even by them a role that is less central and
direct than was that of Japan's MITI in its prime. Officially, of course, the
West German model is a 'social market' one in which the state has only
limited competencies and the private sector is officially unregulated and
unprotected. However, the claim by analysts like Linda Weiss (1998:
119–37) is that behind the façade of non-intervention, the German state has
and does play a critical economic role: that 'Germany's industrial strength
owes much to the capabilities of a developmental state which – like that
of Japan and the NIC's – has emphasized production rather than
consumption-based objectives, and to a state-informed system of private co-
ordination which has ensured constant industrial upgrading' (ibid.: 119).
The argument on the economic role and contribution of the German state
takes one or both of two characteristic forms. One strand emphasizes (in
the manner of Gerschenkron) that late industrializers like Germany relied
from the beginning on a more active state than did either the UK or even
the US (for protectionism, state direction of investment, development of
education and R&D, and possibly welfare protection), consolidating in the
process a state tradition of active industrial policy and a set of associated
attitudes in the governing and employing classes (a conservative statism)
that were equally absent in the US and UK cases. The second element in
the argument asserts that this left a particular postwar legacy vital to the
recent West German success story: a degree of active state involvement
behind the façade of social market economics, and a willingness (even
enthusiasm) for concertation and corporatism (a willingness to enshrine in
law the welfare provisions and rights of workers and trade unions of West
Germany's negotiated compromise).

     Weiss in particular has argued that the postwar West German state
merely submerged its transformative role rather than dismantled it (a policy
of state denial made necessary by geo-political factors), and operated
through a particular system of private-sector governance in which trade
associations and cartels also played a critical role. She has argued that the
resulting West German postwar system of industrial governance was
capable of slowly adapting to new technologies, while retaining a vital capacity to innovate and transform (particularly by state deployment of technology policy and industrial finance). The postwar German state, in her eyes,
is a more distributive, less developmental state than was Japan's; but it is

still one whose role was vital to postwar German economic success. What both the pre- and postwar German states did, so the claim runs, was help create a system of organized capitalism: not just by tariff protection and welfarism, but also by underwriting the banks and encouraging long-term investment relations (Weiss, 1998: 122). In the inter-war years, fascism played a critical role in restructuring German mass production (Reich, 1990: 305–6); and in the postwar period the new Bonn-based government demonstrated 'a willingness and ability to provide strategic economic guidance' (Weiss, 1998: 126) – especially in the reconstruction period up to and around the Korean War – not least by encouraging a high investment, low consumption regime through its direction of Marshall Aid funds to basic materials and heavy goods industries. Weiss admitted that Bonn lacks a MITI (ibid.: 128) but insisted that even so the postwar years were 'not an era of state retreat. Quite the contrary: throughout the 1950s and again from the mid 1960s', she wrote, 'state agencies pursued an active policy of targeting and subsidizing strategic sectors of industry including aeronautics, coal, computers and nuclear energy' (Weiss' 1998: 128).

(4) *Organized labour in the West German story*   The postwar West German state also underwrote a particular capital–labour accord; and it is this feature of the West German trust-based form of capitalism which is said by many of its adherents to differentiate it most starkly, as a model of capitalist organization, not simply from the liberal capitalist model but also from the Japanese. For the final ingredient in most explanations of postwar West German success is its welfarist and corporatist underpinnings. Not all intellectual and political currents are equally at ease with this ingredient, of course. For liberal scholarship in particular, as we have already noted, the rights of German labour are now a (even the) major source of economic underperformance, and Schumpeterians like Porter seem more comfortable with issues of labour skilling (as sources of economic strength) than with welfare rights and trade union powers; but even conservative trust-theorists like Fukuyama and certainly centre-left advocates of negotiated capitalisms (from Hutton and Crouch to Soskice and Streeck) do see union strength as an important 'positive constraint' on German economic development.

They at least make three very powerful arguments. They insist that labour skilling in West Germany was a critical element in the postwar success story. They insist that West Germany's generous system of welfare provision consolidated trust-relationships and associated labour market flexibility. And, most novel of all, they insist that strong unions blocked off sweat-shop short-termist economic policies, that strong labour rights acted as a set of 'beneficial constraints' on West German capital. Whether labour power can be so beneficial to capital accumulation will be discussed at length in chapters 4 and 5. What we need to do here, to close this exposition of the debate about the West German version of trust capitalism, is establish the flavour and details of the claims made about the character and regulation of West German labour markets.

Many commentators have been impressed by the quality of the West German education and training systems. Porter in particular has treated this as vital, insisting that 'more significant than the available pool of factors is the quality and sheer depth of mechanisms in Germany for creating advanced and specialized factors . . . schooling, technical colleges, universities . . .' and that 'another factor-creating mechanism in Germany whose importance is hard to over-estimate is a well-developed and distinctive apprenticeship system' (Porter, 1990: 368–9). He has claimed that, in consequence, German workers are better trained and have a better theoretical grasp than 'workers in most countries' (ibid.: 369); and he is not alone in that view. The literature abounds with claims that 'the constant supply of skilled workers has made German productivity levels the highest in Europe' (Hutton, 1994: 265: see also Wever and Berg, 1993; Prais, 1995). Christel Lane has gone further, arguing that the German system of vocational training is more than just an up-skilling mechanism: that it also sets up a 'virtuous circle' of 'behavioural and attitudinal patterns' which trigger product change and labour market flexibility (1990: 248). Her enthusiastic endorsement of the West German model is worth citing at length.

> The strengths of German manufacturing enterprises are widely seen to emanate from two core institutional complexes – the system of vocational education and training and the system of industrial relations. The first not only creates high levels of technical skill throughout the industrial enterprise but also engenders a homogeneity of skills at all levels of the hierarchy, as well as fostering certain orientations to the work task and the work community. These characteristics, in turn, structure organizational relations, influence communication and cooperation along both horizontal and vertical lines and encourage labour deployment in accordance with the principle of responsible autonomy. The craft ethos permeates the whole of the organization and creates a common focus and identity for management and production workers, although not necessarily a community of interests. The co-operative works culture, fostered by the training system, is further reinforced by the system of industrial relations, particularly by the works council. *(Lane, 1989: 298)*

In that assessment of the labour dimension of the West German model, Lane touched too on the importance of power sharing in West German industry between management and workers, something singled out as of particular importance for West German postwar economic success not simply by Lane but also by advocates of wider 'stakeholding' in modern industry (Perkin, 1997; Soskice, 1997; Hutton, 1994) and by more conservative advocates of trust-based 'institutional reciprocity' (Fukuyama, 1995: 217). At its strongest, this enthusiasm for codetermination becomes an argument about the beneficial impact on German industrial performance of a strong set of worker rights – rights to employment security, to training and to high wages – rights which combine to oblige German employers to compete on the basis of innovation and quality rather than on price, to compete, that is, on the basis of what Wolfgang Streeck has termed 'diversified quality production' (Streeck, 1992). Streeck has been (with David Soskice) among the most articulate advocates of what Soskice calls 'co-ordinated market economies' or 'flexibly co-ordinated systems' (1991: 48), listing at least five sets of worker rights that act as 'an interactive pattern of mutual reinforcement and causation'. The Streeck argument carries us to the absolute heart of the centre-left rejection of neo-liberal attitudes to unregulated labour markets; and because it does it is vital to reproduce it here in as full a form as possible. According to Streeck, strong worker rights impose 'beneficial constraints' on West German capitalism through five different mechanisms:

1 A system of 'rigid' wage determination, operated by strong and well-established trade unions and employers' associations, that keeps wages higher, and variation between wages lower, than the labor market would determine. Unless employers are willing to move production elsewhere, this forces them to adapt their product range to non-price-competitive markets capable of sustaining a high wage level. A high and even wage level also makes employers more willing to invest in training and re-training as a way of matching workers' productivity to the externally fixed, high costs of labor. . . .

2 A policy of employment protection that compels employers to keep more employees on their payroll for a longer time than many might on their own be inclined to. Large German firms are subject to effective limitations on their ability to access the external labor market. High employment stability is imposed on firms through collective agreements, co-determination and legislation. To compensate for such external rigidities, firms have to increase their internal flexibility. By forcing firms to adjust through the internal labor market by redeployment, employment protection thus further encourages employer investment in training and retraining. Moreover, high employment security and the resulting identification of workers with the firm not only make for comparatively easy acceptance of technological change but also help create and support the co-operative attitudes among workers that are necessary for flexible organizational decentralization of competence and responsibility. . . .

3 A set of binding rules that obliges employers to consult with their work forces and seek their consent above and beyond what many or most would on their own find expedient. . . Having an assured 'voice' in the management of the enterprise makes it possible for work forces to forego short-term advantages for larger, longer-term benefits, without having to fear that they may not be around to collect those when they materialize. This, in turn, enables managements to invest more in longer-term projects. Co-determination thus insulates both management and labor from opportunistic pressures. . . .

4 A training regime that is capable of obliging employers to train more workers and afford them broader skills than required by immediate product or labor market pressures. The result is an excess pool of

'flexible', polyvalent workers and skills that constitutes an important advantage in periods of fast technological change. . . .

5   A system of rules regarding the organization of work, created by trade union or government intervention and obliging employers to design jobs more broadly than many of them would feel necessary. . . . While the results are often less than satisfactory from the position of workers' representatives, together they amount to further pressure for 'de-Taylorization' of work through longer work cycles and job enrichment. . . . In combination with high and even wages, high employment security, co-determination and training, the imposition on employers of non-Taylorist work rules thus impedes the use of new technology for 'rationalization' purposes and encourages a 'modernization' strategy of industrial adjustment that is highly conducive to diversified quality production. *(Streeck, 1992: 32–4)*

In defence of corporatism

The West German model, so described, points up the central importance of labour and labour power in the establishment of international competitiveness. At the heart of the argument of the advocates of negotiated capitalisms is the view that economies (even when privately owned) function best if the workers within them feel secure, and if the distribution of rewards and power with which they are associated is equitable and just. The thrust of the case being made in defence of 'trust-based' capitalisms of the German variety is that the liberal model of capitalism, with its commitment to labour market flexibility through job insecurity, its large differentials of pay and conditions and its heavy concentration of industrial decision-making in its managerial and ownership strata, is actually *less* likely than other models to flourish in conditions of intensified competition and rapid technological change. To an audience immersed – as most UK and US audiences are – in a popular culture infused with neo-liberal attitudes to the superiority of unregulated markets, such claims must sound intuitively false; yet beyond the UK and US shores there is a vast literature – both scholarly and popular – which makes precisely this defence of Western European corporatism against its liberal detractors. As a last stage in our survey of debates on capitalist models, therefore, this more general defence of corporatism also needs to be put in place.

Much of the research literature concerned with corporatism and economic competitiveness focuses on the relative performance of different advanced economies after the first oil crisis of 1973. The general thrust of this literature is that corporatist economies coped with the strains of intensified competition after 1973 *better* than non-corporatist economies, that, in spite of neo-liberal claims about market competition and optimal factor distribution, 'paradoxically . . . the Walrasian ideal of full employment with approximately equal wages seem[ed] to have been best achieved

in the social corporatist countries' (Pekkarinen et al., 1992: 4). Quite
what the data claims to show depends in part on how corporatism is defined
and which economies are therefore labelled as corporatist, which periods and
performance indicators are chosen, and which sets of countries are included
in the survey; but it is certainly not uncommon in the corporatist-focused
research literature to meet versions of the claim that 'where the Left was
politically strong, and the trade union movement was centralized and unified,
[economies] performed somewhat better than where those conditions were
less prevalent' (Garrett and Lange, 1936≥>: 517; see also Cameron,
1984; Lange, 1984; Lange and Garrett, 1985; Katzenstein, 1985). The case
for a positive relationship between corporatism and competitiveness is normally built around one or both of two related propositions: on the impact
of strong ('encompassing') trade unions on wage levels and employment;
and on the impact of generalized welfare provision on labour market flexibility and investment in human capital.

The general case on wage moderation (and associated industrial costs) on
offer in much of this literature is that high levels of economic performance
can be expected from political systems at both ends of the capitalist spectrum, from fully marketized economies and from strongly corporatist ones,
but not from economies caught half-way between these polar alternatives. To
take one much cited example from a number of similar theses, Garrett and
Lange, in their study of economic growth between 1960 and 1973 and
between 1974 and 1983, argued for the ability of 'countries with symmetri-
cal or coherent political structures – in which labour was strong both organizationally and politically (corporatist cases), or in which labour was very
weak on both dimensions (approximating market economies) – . . . to adjust
to the post–1974 international crisis better than the mixed cases in which the
political economies were less coherent (politically strong and organizationally weak, or vice versa)' (1986: 531–2). The reason for this, so the argument
runs, is that the protection and enhancement of national competitiveness
after 1973 required substantial structural adjustments which *either* untrammelled markets *or* strongly regulated ones were able to deliver: the first
because of the impact of unemployment on wage rates, the second because
'strongly co-ordinated union movements are prone to wage moderation
rather than militancy' (Kenworthy, 1995: 127) and/or because 'a high degree
of social solidarity on the part of those with secure jobs' (Glyn, 1992: 133)
allowed state employment and reductions in working time to soften the
impact of private-sector restructuring on general levels of unemployment.
Even neo-liberal-based arguments of the type famously developed by
Mancur Olson (1982) allowed for the possibility that broadly based trade
unions might transcend their sectionalism for a greater collective good; but
only, Garrett and Lange argued, if they could be certain that the restraint of
militancy would indeed generate collective gains for their members. Garrett
and Lange suggested that 'two political conditions would seem most likely to
meet these requirements and thus promote union restraint: an historically
strong political Left, and prospects for direct control of government by a

party of the Left closely linked to the union movement' (Lange and Garrett, 1985: 798; also Alvarez et al., 1991; Garrett, 1998).

A second and related line of argument on corporatism is that, contrary to neo-liberal expectations and policy proposals, the welfare states sustained by strong trade unionism can and do compete with economies carrying fewer and lower social overheads. At its most modest, the claim has been simply that when the welfare state is under attack as a burden on competitiveness and growth the case for the prosecution remains unproven (Korpi, 1985; Gough, 1996: 219; Corry and Glyn, 1994: 212) and that for the defence remains 'plausible' (Atkinson, 1995: 730). Slightly more self-confident, there is also the claim that the record of welfare capitalisms on competitiveness and growth is mixed rather than uniformly poor, and that the negative impact of welfare expenditure is minor and exaggerated (Kenworthy, 1995). Such a defence of welfare expenditure has then been turned, by people like Pfaller, Therborn and Gough, into a nuanced advocacy of welfare systems, via the reassertion of the positive impact of strong welfare rights on investment in human capital and the orientation of national economies to 'high productivity and high quality production' (Pfaller et al., 1991: 296). The balance of weakness and strength has been tipped even more in corporatism's favour in the writings of David Soskice, where coordinated market economies (his preferred term for corporatism) flourish competitively because (and to the degree that) strong trade unionism is embedded in a wider set of institutional structures at all levels of the economy and society (Soskice, 1990); and a similar sensitivity to the need to judge welfare states by the institutions into which they are embedded (particularly the character of the surrounding industrial relations systems) can be found also in recent writings on the impact of welfare states on the economy by Esping Andersen (1994: 725–6). By this stage in the literature, of course, it is the *superiority* of welfare-based capitalisms over market-based capitalisms which emerges as the argument's central motif: that what we need to do, if we are to understand the proper relationship between social democratic corporation and economic growth, is 'reverse dramatically . . . the anti-Left and anti-union implications' of conventional growth theory, and recognize instead that 'organizationally and governmentally, strong labour movements may emerge as major benefactors, as purveyors of relatively rapid income growth, and also of somewhat more equal distribution of income' (Hicks, 1988: 700).

So as we turn now to explore the determinants of postwar growth paths, against the background of an economics profession (and a policy debate) largely set up in neo-liberal terms, it is important to remember the scale and strength of the literatures defending 'trust-based' models of capitalist organization. For they, particularly those focused on Western European corporatism, treat the pro-union regulation of labour markets by sympathetic governments as a *source* of growth rather than as a *barrier* to growth; and because they do, it is with the question of labour power that part II of this study needs properly to begin.

Part II

Capitalist Models: The Evidence

4

The Power of Organized Labour

If we are fully to grasp the impact of labour on the international competitiveness of advanced capitalist economies in the postwar period, we need to be clear about the agenda released by the use of the term 'labour' itself. For some commentators on capitalist economic performance, to isolate the labour dimension of competitiveness is to focus on the way labour is organized in the work process, and on the manner in which changes in dominant forms of organizing work aid or hinder the capacity of particular firms or industries to protect or enhance their market shares. For others, it is to focus on the question of the capacities possessed by particular national labour forces and to explore the ability of particular political and social systems to trigger skill renewal and upgrading at a rate commensurate with that achieved by their major economic competitors. For yet others, it is to concentrate on the industrial and political impact of labour-based institutions, to establish the extent to which trade unions and left-wing political parties adopt policies and practices and induce behaviour and attitudes in their members or supporters which are conducive to cost-effective and technologically dynamic forms of economic behaviour. The first and second of these three agendas will be examined, as appropriate, in different parts of later chapters (pp. 127–35 and 183–8). This chapter will focus solely on the third, exploring the impact of labour movements in a number of leading capitalist economies on the competitiveness of the firms and industries located within each.

The debate on trade union power

As was evident in the material surveyed in part I, there are at least two related but distinguishable views of how trade unions (and left-wing political parties) affect the competitiveness of economies that can be discerned in both academic and popular understandings of the determinants of economic growth in advanced capitalist economies. There is a neo-liberal argument, espoused with enthusiasm by political forces of the Right; and there is a more consensual and corporatist argument, espoused by parties and intellectuals of the Centre Left. In the neo-liberal version, trade unions are the particular *bête noire*. There they stand condemned as institutions which price workers out of employment, block labour market flexibility and (by their political influence) sustain excessive welfare provision. In the centre-left version, trade unions are seen more positively: as institutions whose pursuit of industrial rights and welfare provision can, under certain circumstances, trigger long-term labour market flexibility and overall productive efficiency. As a result, the relevant academic literature and political commentary is criss-crossed by a variety of mutually exclusive views of the relationship of trade union power to the competitive position of individual firms and consequently of whole national/regional economies. At one extreme lies the argument that trade union power *is responsible on its own* for economic underperformance, such that its removal would quickly and effectively restore firms' or national competitiveness. More moderate right-wing arguments (of a broadly neo-liberal kind) treat trade unionism simply as *one important cause* of underperformance, and then vary in the extent to which they give union power primacy in their catalogue of corrosive influences on growth. More centre-left treatments of economic decline tend to focus on factors other than trade unionism, so implying the *absence of any significant relationship* between labour power and economic growth; while away on the more radical edge of the debate, arguments can be found that reverse the neo-liberal orthodoxy altogether, linking trade union *weakness* to industrial decline and trade union *strength* to successful capital accumulation. The main axis of debate, however, is that between mainstream neo-liberal and centre-left theses, where the dominant lines of argument are as follows.

The standard neo-liberal case against trade union power and worker rights is normally built around one or more of the following propositions:

1   Trade unions are said to exploit their monopoly position within the labour market to increase the money wages of their members, but to do so only at the immediate cost of other jobs (as employers substitute capital for labour) and at the longer-term cost of both output and employment (as inflated production costs erode competitiveness). Non-unionized firms and economies are, in this argument, much more likely than unionized ones to maintain long-term employment levels and market share.

2   Such long-term union pressure on wages, it is claimed, then redistributes jobs and earnings between unionized and non-unionized employees, and so increases income inequality. It does so directly (as unions win settlements for their members alone), and it does so indi-

rectly (if by political pressure unions persuade governments to over-spend, when the resulting inflation further erodes the real incomes of workers excluded from union-negotiated wage deals). Heavily unionized labour forces, so the argument runs, are more vulnerable to inflation and wage inequality than labour forces in which union-ism is weak.

3   Trade unions are also said to distort the optimal distribution of pro-ductive resources by establishing blockages on the allocation of labour, on the extraction of high effort levels and (via strike action) on the smooth organization of production. Trade unions, that is, sup-posedly erode productivity and investment, and slow innovation and change, as well as contributing to inflation, unemployment, inequal-ity and excessive welfare spending.

Cumulatively, these three tendencies are said to establish trade unions as the major institutional source of labour market inflexibility, and as such, an important barrier to successful international competitiveness and sustained economic growth. This is definitely the view of trade unions articulated by neo-liberal intellectuals of a conservative or centre-right persuasion; and it is even the view (less stridently asserted, but implicit none the less) which underpins the currently more fashionable 'new growth theory' approach to labour market flexibility. For, as we saw earlier, even in New Labour circles in the UK the view is paramount that flexibility in markets (and especially in labour markets) is the key to competitiveness and growth, and that trade union and worker rights, in the main, undermine that flexibility. In New Labour circles, as in neo-liberal ones, 'flexibility' is understood as requiring 'disposability'; and because it is, the new growth thinking, no less than its purer neo-liberal predecessor, suggests that labour market regulation must appear on the debit side of any growth accounting. The policy consequences of this view are clear: New Labour initiatives in contemporary labour markets are necessarily limited and apologetic. As Tony Blair put it, when introducing the *Fairness at Work* White Paper, which his government reluc-tantly introduced to meet its electoral commitments to its trade union base, 'it cannot be just to deny British citizens basic canons of fairness . . . that are a matter of course elsewhere', but even so, 'after the changes we propose, Britain will' still 'have the most lightly regulated labour market of any leading economy in the world' (Blair, 1998: 1). For many traditional Labour supporters in the UK, that lightness of regulation was a matter of frustra-tion and regret, but it was not seen in that light by the party leaders, equipped as they were (and still are) with what is ultimately a neo-liberal sense that strong trade unionism and competitive economic performance do not sit easily together.

Centre-left counter-arguments to this dominant view tend to focus on the third of the neo-liberal arguments on trade union negativity: on unions as barriers to growth. The corporatist literature provides counter-arguments to the other two standard neo-liberal claims, as we have already seen in chapter 3, suggesting that strong trade unionism can be a route to wage moderation and income equality; but the general centre-left defence of trade unionism and worker rights offers them as triggers for industrial dynamism, as follows.

1   According to the Harvard economists Freeman and Medoff, 'unions have "two faces" ', not one: 'a *monopoly face*, associated with their monopolistic power to raise wages; and a *collective voice / institutional response*, associated with their representation of organized workers within enterprises' (Freeman and Medoff, 1984: 6). Far from necessarily blocking adaptability, trade union strength can facilitate more optimal distributions of resources by transmitting information and commitment between employees and their managerial superiors. Unions can be obstructive; but they can also – depending on the quality and sophistication of the managements they face – be powerful advocates of efficiency and earnings equality.

2   Strong trade unions also contribute to the long-term dynamism of industrial capital by blocking off 'sweat shop' routes to competitiveness, making it more difficult or impossible for firms to compete on the basis of low wages and intensified labour processes, and obliging employers to compete by investing in new equipment and training. In this argument about 'flexible rigidities' (Dore, 1986) – recently illustrated by Wilkinson's longitudinal study of the British iron and steel industry (Wilkinson, 1991) and welcomed by Streeck as 'rational voluntarism being beneficially corrected by social constraint' (Streeck, 1997c: 200) – it is not that strong trade unionism is necessarily a barrier to successful capital accumulation, but that weak trade unionism might be. As Mishel and Voos have it: 'the fundamental point is that high productivity, worker rights, flexibility, unionization and economic competitiveness are not incompatible. In actuality, they may be highly compatible components of a high performance business system' (Mishel and Voos, 1992: 10).

3   Finally, strong trade unionism and entrenched labour codes are said to aid competitiveness by creating the conditions (of security and trust) within which industrial change can be most effectively implemented. Strong trade unions and harmonious industrial relations may not contribute to a neo-liberal notion of allocative efficiency; but it is claimed that they can (and do) contribute to 'a different kind of efficiency, the efficiency which . . . Liebenstein calls X efficiency, the efficiency that comes from careful planning, attentive maintenance of machines, imaginative sales techniques and so on' (Dore, 1985: 201). There is, in other words, a strong body of research literature which argues that 'labour-management co-operation has positive effects on long-term productivity growth' (Buchele and Christiansen, 1992: 77), and which rejects the notion that strong trade unionism is necessarily a barrier to labour market flexibility. It is a litera-

ture which visibly prefers trust-based models of capitalism to liberal capitalist models, and one which sees trade union strength and the active participation of workers as key elements in the economic (and social)
superiority of the former kind of model over the latter.

So far from trade unionism being inextricably associated with poor economic performance, the centre-left counter-argument to the conventional
orthodoxy expects exactly the reverse. It expects unions to be strong – and
the industrial and social rights of workers to be at their greatest – in
economies with high levels of investment in machinery and training, with
rising labour productivity and wages, and with low levels of inflation and
unemployment. And it expects trade unions to be valued as a crucial force
for change: one that helps to trigger the replacement of old-fashioned productive methods by new and innovative ones.

Testing for the union effect

The logical response, when faced with claim and counter-claim of this kind,
is to seek cutting edge data against which to evaluate contradictory propositions; and whole bodies of research findings now exist that have been put
together with precisely that purpose in mind. Indeed individual disciplines
within the social sciences have deployed their own characteristic and
defining methodologies in the pursuit of the union effect, to leave us with
bodies of information which are themselves of qualitatively different kinds.
At one extreme, there is case study material, largely produced by political
scientists and labour historians, to which we shall come later in this section.
At the other extreme, there are whole bodies of national statistics, organized
primarily as correlations between macro-economic variables and different
institutional structures, put together largely by comparative sociologists; on
these again later we shall draw. There are also sets of growth accounts, which
include calculations of labour contributions to growth (although not, as far
as I know, many that attempt to calculate union effects *per se*) which we shall
use in chapter 5; and there are a substantial number of micro-studies, produced largely by labour economists, which seek to isolate the union effect
on some or all of a range of variables (wage levels, wage dispersal, productivity, investment, profitability, labour turnover and so on) at the level of the
individual firm. It is with those that we need to begin.

It is, of course, a characteristic methodological move in mainstream economics to begin at the micro-level; and indeed, since it is at the micro-level
that trade unionism has its membership base, it is a logical starting point
from which to assess the impact of union activity on economic performance.
Unfortunately, however, it is also an extremely difficult level at which to
isolate the union effect. There are deep-rooted problems of research design
and data acquisition to overcome – not least how to abstract union contributions from other operating variables – and there are immense problems

in generalizing from individual firms' experience to the experience of whole economic sectors and whole economies. There are also immense barriers to any easy interpretation of the research data thus generated, the cumulative result of which is to leave us with a body of research material on which it is possible (and indeed common) to find individual reporters offering totally different 'takes'. So, for example, the latest and most carefully constructed of the UK-based general introductory texts on the economics of trade unions (Booth, 1995) suggests that the impact of unions on economic performance is, in so far as it can be isolated, largely deleterious. The latest and most carefully constructed of the US-based studies on the link between trade unions and competitiveness (Mishel and Voos, 1992), however, suggests exactly the reverse. The contrast between the two assessments is striking and important.

Alison Booth, for example, writing with great care to an audience of professional economists, and drawing almost exclusively on material researched and written by other professional economists, summed up the contemporary state of their knowledge as follows:

> First, unionisation in both Britain and the USA appears, on average, to have a negative impact on productivity and productivity growth in the 1980s. Secondly, while there is scanty empirical evidence as to the impact of unions on investment, the US evidence is of a negative effect, while the British evidence is ambiguous. Thirdly, unionisation appears to have a negative impact on profitability. . . . A fourth measure of economic activity on which unions may have an effect is employment. There is some evidence that unions are associated with negative employment growth, in both North America and Britain. However, studies estimating union effects on employment growth have typically not allowed for the fact that unionisation is associated with bargaining over issues that are likely to encourage union firms to vary hours rather than workers, and this cast some doubt on the results. Finally, the few studies looking at union hours gaps reveal significant differences between union and non-union hours. *(Booth, 1995: 223, 262–3)*

Mishel, Voos and their collaborators, on the other hand, addressing their research findings more widely to the US labour movement, matched those claims point for point.

> What have we learned from a decade of quantitative research? First, contrary to the fears of neo-classical economists, unions do not of themselves lower productivity. The majority of studies find that unions are associated with higher productivity. Of those which have not found positive effects, there is typically either no effect or a negative effect associated with a poor labour relations climate. . . . If the key to economic growth is investment, unionism contributes positively by raising the savings of workers. . . . when estimates were made separately for industries with high and low levels of concentration, unionism was found to have no impact on the profitability of competitive firms. What unions do is reduce the exceedingly high levels of profitability in highly concentrated industries towards normal competitive levels . . . On unemployment, neither theory nor evidence tells a decisive

story. . . . conflicting trends suggest that unions do not cause unemployment. . . . Recent research has not found evidence for any of the claimed adverse impacts of unionism on the trade deficit, wage inflation or unemployment. *(Mishel and Voos, 1992: 62, 70, 154–5, 163)*

So how are we to judge? We can do so partly by the weight of the evidence lying behind each competing summary; and there we should be pulled initially in the Booth direction. For it should be said that the bulk of the research findings built on micro-level analysis is closer to the findings of Booth than to those of Mishel, Voos and their colleagues. It is quite conventional in the relevant US-based research literature to find conclusions which 'doubt . . . the generality and robustness of the unions-raise-productivity thesis' (Hirsch and Addison, 1986: 215); and (as we saw in chapter 2) it is equally conventional in the UK-based research on Thatcherism to find the 'Harvard Approach' criticized and trade unionism linked, if cautiously, to low labour productivity (Metcalf, 1990a; 1990b; 1993; 1994; Crafts, 1991; even Kenworthy, 1995: 183). Time and again, when you open research journals directed primarily to the economic community that is the story line reported (see for example Oulton, 1995). But what is important for our purposes here is that those reports invariably come in a highly qualified form, conceding the tentative nature of the findings and the possibilities of alternative explanatory variables lying behind the results on offer. What is also important for us is the fact that it is equally conventional to find the dominant orthodoxy persistently challenged by studies which assert exactly the opposite case: either that 'there is no simple association between unionism and productivity growth' (Nickell et al., 1989) or even that 'there is *no* evidence . . . for the view that unions reduce productivity growth' (Wadhwani, 1990: 382; also Nolan and Marginson, 1990). Metcalf himself is clear on this: that 'the comparative evidence is mixed' and – citing Addison and Hirsch – that 'there is no compelling evidence that, in general, the net effect of unions on productivity is positive or negative' (1990a: 256).

In fact there are some pretty substantial pieces of evidence that underline the complexity of the relationships at work here, and which simply block off any easy adoption of the notion that trade union strength is bad for economic health. One that is worth citing at length is the UK-based Workplace Industrial Relations Survey data from 1987, which was specifically concerned to examine workers' responses to technical change and which drew on over 2,000 workplaces for its results. That survey differentiated between technical and organizational change – that is between changes related to new technologies and changes in work organization and practice with existing technologies. It found – quite contrary to neo-liberal expectations in these matters – no evidence that the rate or form of technical change were 'inhibited by trade union organisation' (Daniel, 1987: 261). Indeed its data suggested 'that the general reaction was support for change, and often enthusiastic support' (ibid.: 264), particularly among shop stewards (the very people demonized by the Conservative Right in the UK in the 1970s). It found pockets of resistance to technical change. It found far more generalized resistance to organizational change than to technical change; and it found that the publicity given to 'the isolated cases where trade unions do resist technical change' obscured from public view the far larger number of cases where 'the existence of trade unions acted as a positive encouragement to the introduction of advanced technology' (ibid.: 273). So with data of that strength and significance to set against the tentative but extensive evidence of a counter-kind, it seems wisest for the moment to go with the *caution* of Alison Booth's conclusion on the economics of trade unionism, rather than with the *certainty* of her summation cited above: for as she said 'what can we conclude about empirical regularities or stylised facts associated with trade unionism? Sadly, rather little' (ibid.: 262).

That caution then leaves a space for the consideration of evidence created by entirely different methodologies; and the major candidate to occupy that space – in the literature on union power and competitiveness – is that around corporatism, which characteristically proceeds by running correlations on macro-economic variables (employment, growth, wage dispersal and the like) against different national institutional settlements (those with extensive corporatist decision-making structures, those without, those with some degree of concertation). It was from that data that – in chapter 3 – we were able to extract material supporting the *superiority* of corporatist over market-based forms of national economic decision-making, and to find data arguing that both fully market-based and fully corporatist models of capitalism worked well throughout the 1970s and 1980s, but that models seeking half-heartedly to occupy some middle ground did not. If we pick selectively from that literature, as we did in chapter 3, it is reasonably straightforward to establish the proposition (so counter-intuitive to the liberal mind) that strong trade unionism acts as an incentive to greater international competitiveness.

The trouble is that to get that result you do have to pick selectively. For no less than the micro-studies of the union effect, the general comparative statistical research data send out a very mixed message, as a fuller reading of the relevant research literature makes clear. For in truth the performance of economies labelled as corporatist on the full range of economic and social performance indicators is too uneven to sustain the claims for general and permanent superiority. Indeed, the performance of individual corporatist economies on any one set of indicators is too uneven to allow easy generalization of any kind; and the individual studies of economies and performance just vary too greatly in the content and reliability of their findings to permit much certainty at all. Rather, the research data indicates a definite *variety* of relationship between corporatism and competitiveness, which in its turn suggests that factors other than trade union strength and centralized collective bargaining are over-determining the results (positive or negative) that the advocates or critics of corporatism mobilize on their own behalf.

The unevenness and indeterminacy of the corporatist–competitiveness relation cannot really be avoided when the full range of available comparative studies is examined in detail. From what is now an enormous literature a few examples will suffice to make the point. Therborn used a 1973–85 OECD data set to examine the impact of two kinds of corporatism – interest intermediation and concerted public policy-making – on cross-national variations in economic performance, and found little evidence that either form played a significant explanatory role (Therborn, 1987). Crepaz examined the impact of corporatism on macro-economic performance in eighteen industrialized countries between 1960 and 1988 and found a strong and positive impact on unemployment and inflation, but not on economic growth (Crepaz, 1992). Henley and Tsakalotos – using OECD data for the same period and criticizing Crepaz for the methodology underpinning his survey – were equally cautious on growth, but were impressed by the positive impact of corporatist institutional arrangements on investment, inequality and unemployment (Henley and Tsakalotos, 1993). Buchele and Christiansen, comparing US economic performance with that of the four largest European economies (E-4) in order to assess the impact of European labour market institutions and regulations on unemployment, found 'that the evidence is mixed, and more importantly, that the same institutions which may contribute to the E-4's unemployment problem (vis a vis the US) also appear to contribute to the relative success of the E-4 in earnings growth and greater earnings equality' (Buchele and Christiansen, 1998: 123). Pekkarinen and his colleagues, judging economic performance since the 1970s in comparative terms, found that the corporatist countries display considerable variety' Sweden doing broadly very well during their period of research, Austria generally less well, with Denmark poor on unemployment but good on wage dispersal, and so on (Pekkarinen et al., 1992: 6). And even Geoffrey Garrett, whose work contains by far the most sophisticated and compelling evidence for the positive impact of social democratic corporatism on rates of economic growth and levels of job provision prior to 1990, had to concede the poorer performance of such corporatist regimes on inflation rates, speculating that 'it is easier for the leaders of encompassing labour movements to generate real – rather than nominal – wage restraint' (Garrett, 1998: 126).

As Bernhard Kittel has aptly put it, in the literature on 'the impact of trade unions on economic performance' we are faced with 'theoretical elegance and empirical ambiguity'. We occupy a world in which 'while the theoretical arguments put forward are widely accepted, empirical evidence seldom proves the assertions convincingly' (Kittel, 1998: 1, 2). Because of this gap between theoretical assertion and supporting evidence, it seems inevitable that tranches of young labour economists will go on replicating and refining earlier micro-studies; when in truth it seems clear that the interplay of unions and competitiveness at the micro-level is so heavily overlaid by more general social processes that it is now impossible to isolate the micro-level adequately for study, or to say with any certainty what the direction of causality of any relationships posited there actually is. And because of the same gap between theoretical assertion and empirical evidence, we can no doubt expect a continuing raft of comparative correlations of a macro kind – but, again, with the same likely degree of indeterminacy. Maybe that is too pessimistic a view; but if there is any truth in it, it suggests that we might learn more by leaving both methodologies behind, to focus instead on particular cases whose strategic significance offers us a more reliable route to a general assessment of the impact of labour power on international competitiveness.

Case studies in labour power

A number of possible case studies immediately present themselves for that purpose. One is the research data on US labour, given the presence of the claim – on the left edge of the US debate on postwar economic performance – that the current weakness of US labour actually helps to undermine the growth rate of the US economy (Lazonick, 1994b: 106–8; Galbraith and Calmon, 1994: 189; Hart, 1994: 235–7; Madrick, 1995: 82–3). Another candidate for detailed scrutiny is the role of labour in the postwar Japanese 'success story'. A third is the role of organized labour in the current Asian crisis: certainly in South Korea, and even in Indonesia – indeed we shall touch on each of those later in the text, dealing with Japanese labour and industrial relations in the next chapter (around the issue of cultural values and Japanese exceptionalism), before returning to issues of class struggle in both the US and East Asia in the conclusion. But for the moment we shall concentrate instead on two European case studies whose development offers particular insight into the relative claims and counter-claims laid out above. One is the case of the UK economy before and after 1979, an economy whose labour relations were reset on neo-liberal lines, and whose experience can therefore provide unrivalled insights into the ability of strong unions to erode competitiveness and of weak unions to permit its restoration. The other is the Swedish economy, whose postwar combination of strong trade unionism and sustained growth constitutes the most rigorous testing ground for the claims for corporatism, and which constitutes in addition ideal territory from which to offer a preliminary assessment of the theory of 'beneficial constraints' developed (for West German labour) by Wolfgang Streeck. We shall use the UK and Sweden in turn, to test first one side of the argument and then the other, before using the experience of both to establish some propositions about capital–labour relations in the context of a globalized world economy.

Neo-liberalism in the UK

As we have already seen, the relationship between trade union power and international competitiveness in the UK has been used on many occasions to sustain the more general neo-liberal case. Indeed it is not too much to say that there now exists a sophisticated neo-liberal reading of postwar UK industrial relations which is rapidly gathering the status of received truth, a reading (or more properly, a misreading) built around the following propositions.

1   UK economic underperformance before 1979 was largely the responsibility of the trade unions. Full employment in the postwar UK shifted industrial power from capital to labour and produced 'the British disease', a mixture of union-inspired restrictive practices, industrial militancy and 'wage drift', which eroded the UK's price competitiveness and discouraged investment. The power of organized work groups in UK industry before 1979 and their systematic opposition to the introduction of new technology and the full utilization of existing productive techniques pushed UK-based manufacturing down the international league tables. And the political power of the trade unions to which those work groups belonged induced successive governments to compound that competitive weakness by providing special legal rights to trade unions, bloated public-sector employment and over-generous welfare provision. The result was supposedly a wealth-destroying combination of high taxation and runaway inflation.

2   Fortunately for the UK the arrival of Margaret Thatcher in power reversed this union-inspired downward economic spiral. Under her leadership, Conservative governments broke the power of UK trade unions, closing down the corporatist decision-making institutions of Labour Britain, expelling union leaders from the corridors of power, incrementally re-codifying UK labour law, leading a series of public-sector confrontations with militant unions and privatizing vast swathes of the former public sector. The result, so neo-liberals tell us, was reduced inflation, increased labour productivity, extensive job creation, renewed foreign direct investment, and a qualitative improvement in the performance of the UK economy. And as we noted earlier, even among academic commentators sympathetic to New Labour the belief has grown that, whatever else the Conservatives after 1979 did or did not achieve, at least they tamed the unions, and in so doing lifted the UK onto a higher-growth path (Metcalf, 1990b: 283–303).

Superficially this neo-liberal reading of the fall and rise of the UK economy is compelling; but here, as elsewhere, first appearances mislead.

The UK before 1979   Many of the general neo-liberal claims about trade union legal privileges and excessive militancy are intrinsically comparative. They compare the UK before 1979 with even earlier UK experience, and they compare the UK over time with other advanced capitalist economies. Yet they do not do so accurately. Trade union legal privileges in the UK (which were never commensurate with the legal protection provided to shareholders through limited liability legislation) peaked in 1975; but that peak (Labour's 1975 Industrial Relations Act) arrived too late to explain patterns of the UK's economic underperformance that stretched back to at least the 1950s, if not the 1890s. Nor did the terms of Labour's legislation in the 1970s do more than leave the UK at a mid-way point on the continuum of legal codes available to leading labour movements: they left it positioned somewhere between economies that were more successful in the postwar period than the UK yet had more generous labour codes (like West Germany and Scandinavia) and economies (like that of the USA) that had been no more successful than the UK but possessed labour codes even less generous to workers and unions than those prevalent in the UK before 1975. So whatever else the pre-1979 UK experience may or may not tell us about the relationship of trade unionism to competitiveness, it does not establish the claim that union-friendly legislative changes directly undermine economic performance. Legal codes clearly *shape* trade union behaviour (as they also do the behaviour of the other players in the industrial relations drama), but they do not *predetermine* that behaviour, or necessarily lock it onto an anti-competitive path.

Nor does the claim of excessive industrial militancy in the UK in the 1970s easily stand international comparison. It is true that the UK experienced an explosion of industrial disputes between 1969 and 1973; but then so did the majority of major European industrial economies. What is actually striking about the first four years of Labour government in the 1970s is not the level of industrial disputes, but rather how effectively and with what speed Labour politicians and trade union leaders contained them, and how the brief (and subsequently much mentioned) strike wave of the 'winter of discontent' which followed reflected a straining of the relationship between government and unions caused by that containment. Critics of trade unionism in the UK in the 1970s can hardly have it both ways: either the trade unions had the Labour government in their grip throughout (and hence had no need of industrial action), or they did not (in which case any return to industrial militancy must be read as an index of their powerlessness, not of their potency).

In fact, there is little doubt that the trade unions in the UK did enjoy (in 1974 and 1975) a very brief period of unprecedented political influence over the incoming Labour government. The Labour Party in opposition had forged a social contract with the unions, trading wage restraint for government policies on industry and welfare. The explicit nature of that agreement was unprecedented in UK terms – although not in Scandinavian terms – and stimulated an angry, even an outraged response from right-wing commentators, who saw in it an unacceptable widening of the real political class. Much of their anger was contrived – a rare example in UK politics of blatant class pique – but the agreement did have one important long-term consequence to which they could legitimately point. Because of it, the subsequent balance between inflation and unemployment in the UK in the 1970s *was* struck somewhat differently from that struck elsewhere in non-

Scandinavian Europe, with inflation higher and unemployment lower than the general European norms. But it is one thing to note trade union influence on the way a Labour government managed the general crisis of Keynesian economics in the 1970s; it is quite another to say or to imply that union influence was the cause of that crisis. It was not. In all the major industrial economies in the 1970s – whether heavily unionized or not – governments had to trade off inflation and unemployment at levels unanticipated in capitalism's postwar 'golden age'. The need for that choice arrived in the UK earlier than elsewhere in northern Europe because of the UK economy's already emerging weakness (on this, Coates, 1980: 180–201), but it came to them all eventually, in a generalized retreat from Keynesian demand management, for which European trade unionism cannot, and should not, be allocated prime responsibility.

So to claim or to imply that the UK trade unions abused their relationship with the Labour Party in the 1970s for narrow sectional ends is to misread both the comparative and the historical record. As we shall argue more fully when discussing Sweden, close relationships between unions and social democratic parties were (and still are) commonplace across northern Europe and have proved quite compatible elsewhere, with high rates of economic growth. In fact, the UK experience in this regard in the 1970s was both typical and moderate. Tax levels in the decade and levels of welfare spending (together much cited in the UK literature as union-imposed barriers to private wealth creation) were much higher in a number of more successful economies elsewhere. In the Scandinavian and Benelux countries, for example, public expenditure throughout the 1970s absorbed a greater share of GDP than in the UK: 54.4% in an average year between 1974 and 1979 in Sweden, 52.8% in Holland, 52.1% in Belgium and 49.1% in Denmark, as against 44.4% in the UK (Coates and Wiggen, 1995: 191). Only in Japan and the US was the tax take lower than in the UK in the mid-1970s; and that put tax levels in the UK well below those commonplace in such successful economies as Denmark, Norway, Sweden, Canada, Austria, France, West Germany and Belgium (Feinstein, 1988: 11).

What actually happened to the relationship between UK trade unions and the Labour Government in the 1970s was that it quickly fell back into a quite standard social democratic form, the unions delivering their side of the social accord while progressively failing to oblige the government to deliver its. Between 1974 and 1979 UK trade unions repeatedly called for investment initiatives, for planning agreements and for public ownership, while superintending four years of falling real wages for their members. But as usual they experienced the standard 'cycle of union influence' (Minkin, 1991: 639), with ministers first responsive and then not, as stronger industrial and financial forces pushed the Labour government towards an early form of monetarism. Far from trade union political power being a potent cause of the UK's economic underperformance in the 1970s, it seems safer to argue that, if there was a causal process at work here, it was one triggered by trade union political *weakness*. The UK trade unions failed to stop the

Labour government's drift into deflation and non-interventionism, and so failed to prevent a Labour government bequeathing to its Conservative successor an economy scarred by high levels of inflation *and* unemployment and by low levels of investment. No other social or industrial force seemed capable of (or interested in) preventing such a retreat from economic management by the UK state. The unions certainly wanted an active and radical industrial policy from Labour; but they lacked the political resources to impose one, when more conservative voices began to prevail.

The vulnerability of the UK economy to stagflation was rooted then (as now) in underinvestment in manufacturing plant and equipment and in human capital. Most of the main commentaries on the present UK economy agree on this much at least (Kitson and Michie, 1996b: 35). What is more contentious among them is the extent to which that underinvestment was a product, in the 1970s, of trade union and work group resistance to the introduction and full utilization of new technology. The most widely cited research literature says (or implies) that union power did erode productivity (Pratten, 1976; Caves, 1980); but unfortunately, on closer inspection that literature proves to be partial in coverage and inadequate in design. The main 1970s studies on industrial relations and productivity were misleadingly selective in their coverage of what to research. They effectively wrote out of the story of underperformance the persistent TUC calls for policies to stimulate industrial investment and for programmes of industrial retraining and power sharing, which alone might have eased the introduction of new technologies for the workers directly involved. They tended to downplay *greater* impact on costs and competitiveness of factors other than industrial relations: 'factors such as differences in the scale of plant and markets, the age and quality of capital stock, general managerial attitudes and skills' (Coates, 1994: 113). And more significant still, the core 1970s research literature on work groups and industrial productivity was flawed by quite staggering inadequacies of design and measurement. These weaknesses have been documented elsewhere (see Nichols, 1986; Coates, 1994: 110–14), but their effect remains. Their existence makes it illegitimate to treat as uncontentious the claim that, in general, trade unions and work groups in the UK in the 1970s acted as the main barrier to any strengthening of the economy's competitive base. Certain trade unions and work groups may have acted in that way; but the research evidence on the relationship between trade unions and productivity in the UK in the 1970s is ultimately too flawed to permit us to make definitive and general statements one way or the other. The intellectual Right has been too quick to rush to judgement on this matter, when they (and we) would do better to say honestly that – for the 1970s at least – the jury has still to be out.

Yet we do need to be as clear as we can on what did, and what did not, happen in UK industry in the 1970s. The more general research evidence for that decade certainly indicates a limited but real shift in power – at shop-floor level – from line managers to shop stewards and work groups in core UK manufacturing industries, and the associated emergence of a particular form of industrial relations practice that included unofficial militancy and a degree of 'wage drift'. The research evidence also shows that labour productivity in UK-based manufacturing firms in the 1970s was lower than that achieved in competing economies such as West Germany and Sweden. The research evidence does not show, however, that the first of these stylized facts *caused* the second. The timing of the two processes is too out of step to allow an easy move from correlation to causation here. Relative levels of labour productivity began to fall in the 1950s. Shop-steward power, always limited and uneven in coverage, did not fully crystallize until the 1960s, when, at most, it could only play a secondary and supporting role to other causal forces (see Tolliday and Zeitlin, 1986: 9; Coates, 1994: 108–9). And even then, its impact on competitiveness, profits, investment and growth was softened by another feature of UK industrial relations in the 1970s, which is not much mentioned by the critics of trade union power: the extent to which, by then, UK labour costs were 25% lower than the European average (Ray, 1987: 2). Cheap labour is hardly a barrier to competitiveness in most neo-liberal theories of growth; yet labour was cheap in the UK, compared with that in the rest of northern Europe, throughout the 1970s. So it seems churlish to point the finger at UK labour when striving to explain the remarkable decline of competitiveness by UK manufacturing industry in that critical decade. A certain kind of trade union defensiveness may have accentuated that decline: but the evidence in general suggests that the roots of UK economic underperformance in that decade lay elsewhere, in the behaviour and proclivities of social institutions and economic groupings with which UK labour had to relate, but which it could neither change nor control.

The UK after 1979 In spite of that, the neo-liberal case against trade unionism in the UK in the 1970s has now entered the mythology of UK politics. It is a much repeated story of 'winters of discontent' made glorious summer by Conservative usurpation of power in 1979, one whose repetition was vital to legitimate the Conservative Party's resetting of UK labour codes in the two decades that followed. Yet in truth the case against trade unionism made by union critics after 1979 was no stronger than the case made against them before 1979. There can be no doubt that the Conservative Government after 1979 did significantly reduce the power of both trade unions and organized work groups, and did reduce both the size of the public sector and the scale of its welfare provision. Nor is there any doubt that the gap in labour productivity between the UK and its main European competitors did narrow at the same time. But what remains in doubt, for the period after 1979 just as for the period before it, is whether these enormous changes were in any way directly and causally related. The critics of trade unionism say that they were. The evidence suggests that they were not.

To take the productivity issue first: both the level and growth rate of labour productivity in the UK did rise after 1979. But they did not do so on the back of either large increases in the output of the manufacturing sector or the level of investment in machinery and skills. Instead, the UK economy after 1979 experienced periods of growth intermingled with first deep (1980–2) and then prolonged (1989–92) recession, which kept levels of manufacturing output and investment *below* 1979 levels until the end of the 1980s. (Indeed, as late as 1992, as we noted in chapter 2, the volume of manufacturing output in the UK had only crept to a level one per cent higher than it had been in 1973, at the height of Edward Heath's three-day week.) The increase in labour productivity achieved in the UK manufacturing sector in the 1980s seems not to have been the result of extensive industrial modernization. Rather it was triggered by an intensification in the rate and length of work in the context of large-scale unemployment and the widespread closure of the least efficient plants. It was the product less of new investment than of 'piecemeal change in work organisation and production techniques' and 'more intensive work regimes' (Nolan, 1994: 67–8), which left more than 3 million UK employees working a 48-hour week or more in 1994 (in a European Union in which only seven million workers in total were putting in such long hours). As Peter Nolan has argued, the 'concerted offensive against labour' waged by Conservative governments in the 1980s, far from triggering a permanent productivity revolution, 'appears to have reinforced the already powerful obstacles to the emergence of a high wage, highly skilled and productive workforce', not least by preventing UK-based trade unions from closing off 'low wage, labour intensive routes to profitability' (Nolan, 1995: 134–5).

Nor are the employment figures particularly supportive of the neo-liberal case against trade unionism. The 1980s witnessed a culling of more than trade union power: it also witnessed a culling of full-time jobs. In the recession of 1980–2 1.7 million such jobs were lost. A further 1.9 million full-time jobs went in the recession of the early 1990s. Thereafter, it is true, unemployment in the UK steadily fell, to settle by the late 1990s below the EU average. But that positive employment gap – much cited in defence of neo-liberalism in the UK – is deceptive in at least two distinct ways. It is deceptive about the scale of the unemployment which remains, because official unemployment figures in the UK throughout the period of Conservative government obscured the disproportionately high numbers of potential and willing workers excluded from the unemployment register. (UK 'activity' rates, particularly for 'prime age' male workers, did *not* fall below EU levels in the 1990s; and even the broad unemployment figure for the UK was higher than that of the reunited Germany for at least the first half of the decade.) The 'employment gap' is deceptive also because it masks the restructuring of employment in the UK away from full-time and secure employment into part-time and insecure work.

The vast majority of the new jobs created in the UK since 1979 were part-time jobs. In 1993 there were just under 6 million part-time workers in a total UK labour force of some 21 million; and of those 6 million part-time workers, at least 70 per cent worked for fewer than 16 hours a week, and did so for very low wages and with very little training. Then, as more new jobs became available between 1993 and 1996, only 38 per cent of them offered full-time and permanent employment. An equal number were full-time and temporary; the rest were part-time of various sorts (*Guardian*, 19 March 1997: 2). And these figures are suggestive of a particular, and distinctly destructive, mode of response by key sections of UK manufacturing industry to the onset of intensified international competition in the 1980s, a response that protected short-term profitability only by sacking large numbers of workers and resetting corporate activity 'at ever lower levels of output and employment in an enterprise or manufacturing sector which is in a vicious circle of contraction' (Williams et al., 1989: 292). UK manufacturing industry – if Williams and his colleagues are right – did not respond to the diminution of trade union power as neo-liberal theory required them to do. Instead of expanding output as labour market 'impediments' eased, they retained a 'narrow obsession with labour, and the negative control of labour costs through sacking', ending up 'cash rich and output lazy' (ibid.: 300, 293); so while from a neo-liberal point of view *strong* trade unionism was supposed to generate wage inequality and prolonged unemployment, in the 1980s, in the UK at least, wage inequality and unemployment intensified dramatically as trade union power *declined*.

Nor did this diminution in trade union power then trigger a renaissance in price stability and investment. It is true that inflation in the UK is now much lower than it was in the 'union-dominated' 1970s; but so it is elsewhere in Western Europe (and the UK's relative inflation performance remains unchanged). It is also true that the UK has attracted large quantities of particularly Japanese foreign direct investment. But foreign direct investment is not the full story of the UK's investment experience since 1979. Overall in the UK, 'manufacturing net investment (as a share of manufacturing output) has been declining since the early 1960s, with negative figures for the early 1980s and 1990s' (Kitson and Michie, 1996b: 35; see also Kitson and Michie, 1996a: 201–2). FDI alone could not, and did not, reverse that trend. In fact the scale of FDI (and its impact on employment) was tiny throughout the Conservative years, when set against the total movement of capital and employment in and out of the UK. Between 1979 and 1992 the total flows of capital out of the UK exceeded those coming in for each year except 1987 (Radice, 1995; Barrell and Pain, 1997: 65); and the employment effects of Japanese implants in particular (with 25,000 new manufacturing jobs created in the 1980s) were drowned by the destruction of 200,000 equivalent jobs by the top 25 British-owned transnationals (Williams et al., 1990). Neo-liberalism extols low wages and limited labour market regulation as the key to the attraction of FDI. Yet the latest empirical research suggests that France, and not the UK, was the major European recipient of FDI (including investment from the UK) in the last years of Conservative rule; and it indicates that low wages are only one factor explaining capital redeployment and a minor one at that when set against skill levels and social infrastructure (Quilley et al., 1996; Barrell and Pain, 1997). Recent research also suggests that many UK firms have chosen to *invest* in Europe rather than 'raise domestic production, exploit economies of scale, and serve the European market through *trade*, in spite of the relative cost competitiveness and the flexible labour markets of the UK economy and the operation of the Social Chapter in other EU economies' (Barrell and Pain, 1997: 70). All of which presumably helps to explain why the *fall* in union power in the 1980s coincided with a *rise* in the UK's underlying trade deficit, quite contrary to the expectations of competitiveness raised by standard neo-liberal accounts of the relationship of trade unionism to economic growth.

Overall indeed, the original neo-liberal case looks less secure than it first appeared, when its claims are exposed systematically to the complexity of the full UK experience. The rise and fall of trade union power in the UK has not correlated closely with the UK record on investment flows, output levels and the balance of payments. In comparative terms, reductions in trade union power have not improved the UK's inflation performance, or the capacity of the UK economy to provide full-time permanent employment; nor, because of the persistent shortfall in investment, are reductions in trade union powers likely to have effected a permanent productivity revolution. Certainly the latest review of the Thatcher revolution supports such a sceptical view (Brown et al., 1997; 80): and even sympathetic commentators like Crafts and Metcalf doubt whether the Tories did enough to ensure that the UK's 'relative decline has permanently ended' (Crafts, 1993b: 344). For the years of Thatcherism actually suggest that the relationship between trade union power and international competitiveness is not one set in stone, as neo-liberalism would have it. Instead, the compatibility or otherwise of worker rights with capital accumulation and international competitiveness is fixed by a prior decision on *the dominant growth strategy* to be pursued in the quest for profitability. If growth and competitiveness are to be won on the basis of low wages and intensified work routines, then trade union power in whatever form *is* a barrier to growth. The Conservative government in the UK after 1979 opted for this low wage strategy, and in so doing increasingly positioned the UK in the emerging international division of labour as a warehouse and assembly economy on the edge of more affluent continental European markets. Trade union power did not initiate or predetermine that positioning, except in so far as union *weakness* allowed its emergence. But to the degree that UK manufacturing capital is now settled into this particular international niche, any revival of trade unionism must threaten its long-term viability, which is presumably one reason why business groups in the UK, having weakened trade unionism so effectively, are now striving with such determination to keep that weakness in place.

Corporatism and the Swedish case

When we consider the literature on corporatism in general, and on Swedish social democracy in particular, the whole tenor of the argument shifts.

Then, and quite contrary to the general focus of the UK debate, the claims *for* trade unionism become the dominant motif, and the enthusiasts for market systems suddenly become the minority voice. There is a neo-liberal voice in this debate, but it is only now becoming more powerful. It is a voice particularly associated with Assar Lindbeck. It was Lindbeck who first diagnosed what he termed 'eurosclerosis' – a diminution in the capacity of Western European economies to generate employment and growth, which he explained as a consequence, in part, of inflexibilities in labour markets caused by welfare provision and strong trade unionism (Lindbeck, 1985: 155): what he earlier had called their 'dead weight costs' (Lindbeck, 1980: 22). And it was Lindbeck who headed the 1993 government-appointed commission on the economic crisis in Sweden – a commission whose report was a clear neo-liberal call for welfare reform (Lindbeck et al., 1994). In both places, Lindbeck offered his version of the general neo-liberal critique of high welfare spending: that the borrowing necessary to finance it squeezes out private investment, the taxation necessary to sustain it deters private effort, and the bureaucracies necessary to implement it corrode total factor productivity. In the UK, arguments of this kind have swept all before them for almost two decades now. In Sweden, however, they still have to contend with the residues of a strongly entrenched social democratic consensus whose characteristic arguments were laid out in the last section of chapter 3.

The postwar economic and social achievement of Swedish social democracy – in combining generous levels of egalitarian welfare provision with high living standards based on sustained economic growth – has been (and remains) a powerful model and inspiration for the European Centre-Left and a serious challenge to many of the conventional understandings of mainstream economics. Welfare provision expanded rapidly in Sweden only from the 1960s, but once under way it left Sweden by 1980 at the 'top of the equality league in terms of employment (per head of population), female as compared to male wages, progressiveness of tax system, generosity of public pensions, public provision of health, education and welfare services, relative absence of poverty and overall income equality' (Glyn, 1995: 50; also Weiss, 1998: 84). Sweden was also by then second only to Switzerland in Europe in its record on employment and to Norway in income per head. Sweden was (and remains) in comparative terms a high wage and high tax economy, with a larger public sector than that of any OECD country and with very high levels of union membership (union density peaked in 1986 at the quite remarkable figure of 86%) For all these reasons, and with the brief exception of the period immediately following the devaluation of 1982, postwar Swedish industry 'constantly operated with higher labour costs than those of its major export competitors' except the USA (Therborn, 1991: 235), and from the 1970s was subject to extensive labour codes (including the 1976 Codetermination Law) which had no UK parallel. Yet at the same time, Sweden possessed into the 1990s a large, internationally competitive and export-oriented industrial sector, one capable of exporting 30% of its GDP when the unweighted average for exports as a share of GDP in the OECD as a whole was a mere 19% (Henrekson et al., 1996: 247). Sweden, that is, quite against the grain of conventional expectations, managed until very recently to combine West German scales of international competitive performance with unparalleled levels of welfare provision, employment security and wage equality.

As is widely acknowledged, the postwar Swedish combination of successful private capital accumulation and generous public welfare provision was based on a quite unique class accommodation: a historic compromise initiated in the 1930s and presided over thereafter by Swedish social democracy in a long period of virtually unbroken political rule (1932–76, 1982–91, 1994–). 'The formal part of the Swedish Historical Compromise was the so-called Main Agreement between the unions and the employers, negotiated between 1936 and 1938' (the Saltsjobaden Agreement). 'The most important part, however, was an informal agreement or understanding between labour and capital to cooperate to generate economic growth' (Korpi, 1992: 104). In Sweden the Left *was* dominant both industrially and politically for a very long period; and because it was, the postwar Swedish labour movement was free to pursue what has become known as the Rehn–Meidner model.

> The basic idea behind the . . . model was that by demanding 'equal wages for equal work' across industries and sectors, it was possible . . . not only to promote the egalitarian ideals of the union movement, but also to ensure a dynamic modernization of the economy by forcing inefficient firms either to rationalize or close down, while simultaneously assisting the expansion of efficient firms. *(Iversen, 1998: 60)*

Indeed it was a 'a central aim of the Rehn–Meidner programme . . . to squeeze low-productivity firms and industries, forcing them to upgrade or exit from the market, while at the same time, through an active labour-market programme, moving those left unemployed to firms and jobs with high productivity' (Weiss, 1998: 95). Equipped with such a programme and model, Swedish labour was then free to pursue both a solidaristic wages policy and the creation of a universalistic and encompassing welfare state. It was also free to break the tendency of full employment to trigger inflation by trading wage restraint (and opposition to spreading wage differentials) for active and selective labour market policies.

An active labour market policy was the crucial element differentiating the Swedish postwar experience of welfare capitalism from experience elsewhere even in the rest of Scandinavia. The uniquely Swedish dimension here was the emphasis on state intervention in all aspects of the labour market *except* that of pay, which, outside moments of deep crisis, Swedish governments prior to 1990 left the peak organizations of labour and capital to settle between themselves. Incomes policies apart, however, Swedish employment policy relied 'more than that of any other small European state on job creation through vocational training or retraining or public works'

(Rothstein, 1985: 154) such that 2–3% of Swedish GDP was regularly so directed. In 1947 the Swedish government augmented the powers of the pre-war National Labour Market Board (AMS), and subsequently the Board pursued the goal of full employment through a quite remarkable set of initiatives, initiatives which were as significant for Swedish labour, and as defining of the Swedish model, as were MITI's 'administrative guidance' for Japanese capital and the Japanese growth model. In the Swedish case, active labour market policy was crucial to the economy's ability to achieve labour market flexibility without recourse to the disciplining effect of large-scale unemployment. It held the key to why, before 1990, 'Sweden had had one of the lowest unemployment levels in the western world since the mid 1950s, while still managing to keep inflation at an average level' (Rothstein, 1985: 155: also Standing, 1988). In fact, from the 1960s the existence in Sweden of such an institution as the AMS and the combination of its policies with the more general solidaristic wage elements and universal welfare provision of the Swedish model set in motion two related logics. One, at corporate level, triggered industrial modernization by prioritizing training, and by putting pressure on low-productivity and labour-intensive sectors to increase efficiency and/or shed labour (Landesmann, 1992: 262–3). The other, at the macro-level, triggered what elsewhere has been termed a uniquely Nordic system of private capital accumulation based on 'forced saving through taxation' (Kosonen, 1992 203).

The Swedish experience is certainly evidence that it was possible – in the years after 1945 – successfully to combine strong trade unionism, generous welfare provision and economic growth. Indeed it is also evidence that, under the right conditions, such a combination could enable particular national economies to out-compete economies equipped with weaker trade unions and more limited welfare provision. Taken alone, therefore, the Swedish experience seems entirely to reverse the conventionally understood relationship of union power to international competitiveness.

However, it is not entirely wise to treat the Swedish experience in isolation, not least because the performance of the Swedish economy in the 1990s proved less robust in the face of international competition than hitherto, and less remarkable in comparative terms. In particular, the 'exceptional' performance of the Swedish economy on unemployment between 1973 and 1990 was not matched by any commensurately outstanding performance on growth, productivity or investment (Weiss, 1998: 88). On the contrary, Swedish growth rates have settled at 'roughly one percentage point *below* the OECD average over the last quarter century' (Henrekson et al., 1996: 280), such that after an outstanding productivity record in the first half of the century, the productivity performance of the Swedish economy as a whole now lags behind all the major OECD economies. 'Hansson and Lundberg . . . estimated total factor productivity growth at only 0.6% per year during 1970 to 1985, while figures in the 1.2%–2.5% interval were typical for most other countries in [their] study' (Lindbeck et al., 1994: 9). Even unemployment soared in the early 1990s: from 1.5 per cent in 1990 to

14.2 per cent in August 1994: as 'Swedish GDP fell by 5.1 per cent between 1990 and 1993 (as compared to a rise of 2.6 per cent in Europe)' (Glyn, 1995: 51), and as Sweden's standing in the international league tables of per capita income slipped from 3rd in 1970 to 14th in 1991 (Lindbeck et al., 1994: 10). By 1993 indeed, and for the first time since the 1950s, less than half those out of work in Sweden found places in active labour market schemes. In the 1950s the standard percentage of the unemployed in such schemes had regularly been 80 per cent (Clement, 1994: 115). Clearly something had gone seriously awry with the workings of the Swedish model in the 1990s, and had begun to do so even before EC entry and Maastricht convergence criteria made their own serious dent in the space for Swedish exceptionalism.

In part the crisis of the Swedish model in the 1990s was the product of emerging *internal* tensions, and of resulting corrosions of essential internal prerequisites for its success. The Rehn–Meidner model was built upon the wage restraint and solidaristic wage policies of unions representing predominantly manual workers in the manufacturing sector. But its solution to the needs for high productivity growth there (namely the toleration of industrial restructuring to move workers from low-productivity industry to high-productivity industry) eventually gave way to a structural shift of employment from manufacturing in general to the public sector, as state employment 'came to take over the labour-absorbing role of the high productivity manufacturing enterprise in the active labour market policy model of the LO economists' (Strath, 1996: 104–5).* This shift then created a major and destabilizing imbalance between the Swedish economy's marketed and protected/public sectors, increasing the tax on the wages of manufacturing workers without resolving the problem of low productivity in labour-intensive public-service provision; and in consequence it eventually eroded the tolerance of high levels of taxation by key groups of Swedish workers and undermined the enthusiasm of unions in the marketed sector (especially the important Metalworkers Union) for solidaristic wage poli-

* Certain commentators have seen the passivity of the Swedish social democratic state in the face of this manufacturing downturn as the model's central weakness. Linda Weiss in particular has insisted that 'it is not corporatism with labour that is the problem, but rather corporatism without industry', arguing that

> if the Swedish state's transformative capacity is weak, this is not because it is *over-embedded in labour*-dominated corporatist institutions. Rather, it is because the state is *under-embedded in industry*. Bureaucratic capability has been built around distributive goals. Accordingly, both industrial intelligence capabilities and policy linkages with industry remain only weakly developed in the Swedish system. . . . it is not that the Swedish state was structurally prevented from assuming a co-ordinating role in the national system of innovation and investment, but rather that, through an historic class compromise, domestically shaped priorities and subsequent SDP hegemony, the state came to prioritize a distributive project without a corresponding transformative orientation. *(Weiss, 1998: 104, 109, 119)*

This 'state-centred' explanation of the fall of the Swedish model will be discussed in chapter 7.

cies. One consequence, that is, of the 'success' of the Swedish model was the eventual fragmentation – now into four federations representing blue- and white-collar workers in the public and private sectors – of a united labour movement whose high degree of centralization had initially made the model possible.

There is an important relationship between productivity growth and the timing of Sweden's 1990s crisis tucked away in this fragmentation of union solidarity. The high productivity of manufacturing industry encouraged by the Rehn–Meidner model enabled Sweden to hold at bay throughout the 1970s the tensions between sections of organized labour that, in weaker economies such as the UK, was already evident before the onset of Thatcherism, and which (in the UK case) paved the way for the Thatcherite capture of the votes of skilled workers in private manufacturing industry. For as Glyn correctly observed, 'the overwhelming proportion of the cost of egalitarian redistribution' in Sweden was a cost which 'was met out of wages – redistribution within the working class, broadly defined'. The crucial point, however, for the viability of the model in the 1950s and 1960s, was that 'the dynamism of the private sector allowed this redistribution to occur within the context of growing consumption per worker' (Glyn, 1995: 45). But after 1973, that dynamism was harder to guarantee. The 1970s was a lean decade for Swedish investment; and although investment levels then recovered, even in the 1980s total gross investment as a percentage of GDP in Sweden settled 5 percentage points lower than the levels achieved in the 1960s. So as productivity eventually dipped in Swedish manufacturing, the standard conflict of interests between workers in different sectors emerged in Sweden too, and pulled away at the unity of purpose and policy which had hitherto sustained so remarkable a period of industrial peace. Swedish labour still remained more willing than other European labour movements to tolerate the redistribution of resources away from productive workers in manufacturing to less productive public-service provision. The social wage was still more tolerated and valued in Sweden than elsewhere by the workers whose taxes financed it (Mishra, 1990: 63–4); but that tolerance lessened in Sweden in the 1990s, as the Swedish economy failed to deliver the rapid economic growth which – in the model's heyday in the 1950s and 1960s – enabled private consumption and public provision to rise together. That just did not happen with the same regularity and ease after 1973 as before: indeed, between 1973 and 1985 'consumption out of the average worker's earnings *fell* by nearly 2% per year or some 20% in total' (Glyn, 1995: 51).

Moreover, as even one of the model's architects, the economist Rudolf Meidner, conceded, one problem with the original model was that 'firms with high profitability [made] "excess profits" since their capacity to pay high wages [was] not fully used' (Meidner, 1992: 167; also Meidner, 1993: 218). This failure had at least two consequences. It reinforced the concentration of capital in Swedish industry in a remarkably limited number of hands – 'fifteen families clustered around two banks' (Gordon et al., 1994: 146) – and so reinforced the strategic significance of the higher industrial bourgeoisie as underwriters of the Swedish historic compromise. It also left incomplete the final stage of Swedish social democracy's original radical project – the socialization of investment flows. By 1976 the Swedish Left was ready to embark on that final stage, through the initiation of collective wage earner funds that would absorb surplus profits and slowly transfer ownership or control from capital to the unions. But this proposal, far more than any other initiated by Swedish social democracy since the 1930s, challenged the fundamental class compromise at the heart of the Swedish model – and in particular antagonized the very group of large-scale export-oriented capitalists with whose predecessors the original compromise had been made (Pontussen, 1987: 22–4). Swedish capital – through its employers' organization, the SAF – then responded with a series of moves against centralized wage bargaining, welfare provision and trade union rights. The SAF began to campaign actively in the 1970s 'against growing public expenditure, against the welfare state, against collectivism in general' (Fulcher, 1987: 245), and to urge on successive Swedish governments a steady stream of conventional neo-liberal policies. Sections of Swedish capital also systematically withdrew from centralized collective bargaining amid a series of industrial disputes and lockouts which they triggered, effectively by 1990 killing off this key element of the Swedish model. And most important of all, in the 1980s major Swedish companies began to export capital on a large scale for the first time. 'Outward foreign direct investment increased from around 3 billion SEK in 1980 to 43 billion SEK in 1988' (Solvell et al., 1992: 230), taking Swedish capital exports from 1 per cent of GDP in 1980 to about 6 per cent in 1990 – from a level in the early 1980s that was normal among capitalist economies to one in the 1990s that was higher than elsewhere (Wilks, 1996: 103: also Albo, 1997: 9).

It is the increasingly global nature of large-scale Swedish capital which now poses the major threat to the viability of Swedish exceptionalism. To work properly, the Rehn–Meidner model required low levels of internationalization among high productivity Swedish companies, since it 'rested on the premise that the 'excess profits' generated by solidaristic wage restraint would translate into increased production and employment by firms or sectors with above-average productivity' (Pontusson, 1992: 322) within Sweden itself. But the model worked less well when (and to the degree that) Swedish firms moved percentages of their production and employment abroad, which they did progressively after 1960 and at a quickening rate after capital controls were eased in 1985. Here then we see the corrosion of one vital element in the postwar Swedish equation. A key precondition of the willingness of the Swedish employing class to hold to its side of the 'historic compromise' with Swedish labour was its degree of involvement in (and dependence on) the Swedish home market for sales and profits, and the associated degree of dependence of Swedish financial institutions on the home-generated profitability of Swedish industrial capital. The export of capital from Sweden in the past decade has lessened that set of dependencies, and with it the willingness of Sweden capital to tolerate the costs and constraints imposed upon it hitherto by the power of Swedish labour.

The fate of the Swedish model tells us much about the determinants of international competitiveness and the role of trade unions in its enhancement. It makes very clear that the unions are not the only – or ultimately even the decisive – determinants of the persistence and effectiveness of 'historic compromises' between major social classes. The Swedish model is now in difficulties not primarily because of divisions on the side of labour, but because dominant groups within the Swedish capitalist class are no longer willing to participate in its central institutions. That unwillingness is in part a product of the intrusion into their interests, resources and freedom of action created by the rules and institutions of Swedish corporatism, and by the revitalized radicalism of the Wage Earner Fund initiative. The unwillingness is also in part the product of a major revival of neo-liberal ideas (and confidence) in Swedish governing circles. But it is also a product of the changing nature of capitalism as a global system: a product of the intensification of international competition – and the changing modes of work organization being developed by successful international competitors – to which Swedish manufacturing industry is now subject, and of the greater facility now available to holders of capital (including Swedish holders of capital) to shift both their portfolios and their productive investments off-shore. With the benefit of hindsight it is becoming clearer that the success of the Swedish historic compromise – as a growth model for Swedish capital and as a source of rising living standards and social justice for Swedish labour – was intimately associated with the productive conditions prevailing in capitalism's postwar 'golden age': an age of Fordist regimes of accumulation and high levels of national economic autonomy (Ryner, 1994; 1995: 8). And by association, the fall or deterioration or challenge to the model (depending on how pessimistic a reading of the future is made) is therefore a product of the extent to which those conditions have been eroded by changes in forms of production and by processes of global economic integration.

Conclusion

This link between 'class compromises' and wider social structures of accumulation in the Swedish story is the point of vulnerability in the whole centre-left argument on labour power and competitiveness; and it is one that neo-liberal critics have been quick to exploit as the Swedish success story has soured (Lindbeck, 1985; 1994). But as the empirical record of the postwar UK indicates, neo-liberal theses on trade unionism and competitiveness have their own deep problems, of which three general ones stand out.

(1)   One is the inability of such arguments (however much their advocates genuflect in this direction) to grasp or allow for the full significance of the

qualitative difference between a labour market and any other form of commodity market in capitalist societies. Labour is not just any old commodity, to be analysed in abstracted models of labour market performance. On the contrary: it is a very special commodity, which, because it is both highly perishable ('it cannot be stored, and if it is not used continuously it is wasted' (Rothstein, 1990: 325)) and highly active (with workers needing to be present at its delivery), requires managing in a very particular kind of way. This is especially the case in a capitalist mode of production, where there is a perpetual wage–effort bargain to be struck between managers and workers within a context of highly differentiated patterns of reward. Labour markets are inherently complex social systems, and have to be understood and studied with a sensitivity to the wider social universes in which they are inserted (Rubery, 1994: 341). At the very least this means that the definitions, goals, motivations and stocks of knowledge that individual labourers bring to the production process inevitably shape productive outcomes (Buttler et al., 1995: 8). It also means that the workings of labour markets are shaped by sets of social forces (institutions, histories, cultures and practices) which lie beyond the immediate control of any one individual labour market actor (labour markets are quintessentially not the appropriate territory for forms of analysis based on the interaction of socially abstracted rational individuals). And most important of all, it means that conventional neo–liberal enthusiasms for factor 'flexibility' cannot be reduced to a simple capacity to hire and fire, since the resulting insecurity of employment is bound to corrode the capacity of labour – as a self-motivating factor of production – to function at full capacity. If neo–liberal intellectuals genuinely want labour to be efficient, they have to treat workers as people, and not simply as commodities; and yet that is something which neither their theoretical systems nor their policy predilections encourage them to do.*

(2)   The second limitation of neo–liberal analyses of trade unionism is this: it is just not the case that labour markets will 'clear' at socially and economically optimal levels but for trade union intervention, or that what we face, without trade unionism, is a level playing field between capital and

---

*   Ronald Dore is very clear on this:

> Of all the buzz words used in the managerial literature to describe the proper pre-occupations of those who seek to improve their industrial performance, the word 'flexibility' must surely be among the most frequent. It has become so – over the last decade – because its antonym, 'rigidity' became in the early 1980s the favourite word of the neo–classical economists in their attacks on the various deviations from free market liberalism . . . which they saw as responsible for economic stagnation in the western economies. . . . And of all the rigidities, it was not so much those in product markets – price cartels, oligopolies, conventional mark-up practices – nor those in capital markets which attracted their attention so much as rigidities in the labour market. (Dore, 1990, 92)

labour which trade unionism then distorts. We do not. Labour markets in a capitalist economy are stacked heavily against labour. There is a basic asymmetry of power between the individual worker and his or her employer that trade unionism attempts to redress. There is a gradient of power running against labour in capitalist societies unless unions act to pull it back (Coates, 1983a: 58–62; 1984: 88–91). That retrenchment or redressing has never been more than partial, although it has been at its greatest, historically, in the corporatist labour codes of the Western European welfare states. In those societies, trade unions have pulled the gradient down a little in favour of workers, giving them rights in the workplace, welfare rights beyond it and higher wages. If neo-liberals now want to reduce those rights and make the gradient steeper once again. they are saying that rapid capital accumulation currently requires an intensification of inequality and a reduction in the degree of redress previously achieved. And in truth, that is the core of the right-wing critique of UK trade unionism in the 1970s – that capital accumulation, UK-style, required a significant imbalance of power and reward between capital and labour, an imbalance which the modest pro-labour reforms of the mid-1970s then threatened and challenged. But put that way, it throws a light on the role of unions and their members in postwar UK economic underperformance entirely different from that characteristically generated by neo-liberal critics: that trade unions and their members were more sinned against than sinning, the victims of deeper processes and stronger social forces, before which the unions' main crime was to be, not too strong, but too weak.

(3)   So to claim, as neo-liberals often do, that trade unions are a (or the) source of income inequality in a capitalist labour market is quite ludicrous, and invariably deliberately disingenuous. Capitalist labour markets work only by entrenching inequalities of power and income between whole social classes. They are machines for the manufacture of social hierarchies, not of individual equality (Botwinick, 1993). To criticize trade unions for allowing wage inequalities within one social class both ignores the important Swedish counter-case (of solidaristic wage policies) and masks the extent to which income inequality as a whole is likely to intensify as trade unionism is weakened. That was certainly the UK experience after 1979. Even in Sweden, for all the wage solidarity achieved within the working class, income inequality between classes was the price even Swedish labour was obliged to pay for the sustenance of its 40-year-long exploration of the limits of class collaboration within corporatist institutions. Inequality, that is, is not a product of trade unions. It is a product of unregulated labour markets and of the untrammelled workings of the privately owned market institutions with whose interests the neo-liberal advocates of trade union restraint invariably identify. Neo-liberalism is quite wrong to market its own policy proposals as the only viable ones available. The issue is not a lack of alternatives now facing privileged and non-privileged classes alike, but an unwillingness of

the privileged to pay the cost of radical policies for employment and growth. Neo-liberalism is in that sense a class project, as well as a theoretical argument, and needs to be recognized as such.

With this in mind, we can go back to the arguments in defence of corporatism laid out at the end of chapter 3, and in particular to the arguments of Garrett and Lange. Their defence of corporatism as a viable growth strategy is also best understood in class terms – as advocating a strategy of collaboration between classes for strategic international advantage, in its Swedish manifestation as an alliance between organized labour and large-scale Swedish industrial capital. Now it is very hard to argue, as much neo-liberal theorizing implicitly does, that in social terms – for the labour forces caught up in it – the experience of life under Swedish corporatism was *inferior* to that under Thatcherite neo-liberalism. On the contrary, and on virtually any morally defensible performance indicator you care to name – industrial and social rights, living standards, gender equality, job security, human dignity – corporatism was (and is) superior. That is why the issue for us, in examining the theory and practice of centre-left arguments on unionism and competitiveness, is not whether the centre-left model is better: it clearly is. The question is rather whether it remains a viable model; and to that question there are a number of troubling things to say (for a general critique, see Albo, 1997).

1   One point of caution concerns the relationship of productivity growth to the maintenance of class alliances. The significant ghost in the machine throughout the Swedish story is the productivity of labour in Sweden's manufacturing sectors. As productivity there rose, and as its rise was encouraged by the Rehn–Meidner model, the collaboration between classes at the heart of the Swedish model held – profits and wages rising together for a prolonged period. But in the end they did not. Overall productivity in the economy slowed, as the weight of public-sector employment failed to be compensated by commensurate increases in labour productivity elsewhere. In the end, that is, the Swedish model hit the same contradiction between sectors as had the UK economy a decade earlier: a contradiction or asymmetry between sectors onto which neo-liberal anti-statism could easily latch. In Sweden, as in the UK, the rise in public sector employment was a *response* to the falling capacity of the manufacturing sector to sustain rising labour productivity and jobs. It was not, as neo-liberalism has it, the *cause* of that fall; but once underway, dwindling manufacturing productivity was then accentuated by levels of public spending whose financing took the sorts of toll that neo-liberalism so often emphasizes – and in the process did, internally as it were, erode the space within which corporatist class compacts could be sustained.

2   Such a rise and fall of industrial productivity – and the associated opening and closing of a space for a certain kind of class politics – brings

the issue of *time* back into our understanding of the relationship of unions
to competitiveness, and raises the possibility that such a relationship may
itself be contingent on the presence and character of a wider set of economic and social institutions and processes. Neo-liberal critics of trade
unionism implicitly discount dimensions of time and contingency: for them,
trade unions are *always* an impediment to output, production and costs. In
their stridency, they have invited and stimulated an equally universal
counter-claim from the Centre Left, one that asserts the compatibility of
trade unionism with high performance on neo-liberalism's chosen economic
indicators, and also with high performance on indicators (such as employment and equality) to which neo-liberalism pays less attention. But when
we look at the evidence deployed in support of that counter-claim, we find
that much of it derives from the functionality of welfare regimes, government spending and high wages to the realization of profits in the accumulation regimes established in Western Europe in capitalism's postwar
'golden age'. Class compacts of a corporatist kind did function satisfacto-
rily for both labour and capital in a number of leading European economies
in the heyday of Fordism; and in doing so, they did provide powerful
counter-factual evidence to neo-liberalism's general anti-union case. But the
question we have to ask is whether the special conditions permitting such
class compacts are not now beginning to erode, whether we are not, in some
fundamental sense, now at or approaching the end of Fordism?

3   Fordism may or may not be going – that is a much discussed issue to
which we shall return in the last chapter – but at the very least it is changing, as a new international division of labour and the emergence of more
globally mobile forms of capital reduce the degree of national autonomy
available to policy-makers keen to reconstitute compacts between locally
based social classes. Labour is still available for those compacts. Capital
increasingly is not. Which brings us back once more to the Garrett and
Lange argument that we currently face *two* viable growth packages: one corporatist, one neo-liberal (Garrett, 1998: 4, 10). For behind such a view lies
an unexplored assumption about the character, not of labour and trade
unionism, but of capital and of capitalism. If strong trade unionism was
compatible with high levels of investment in local manufacturing industry
in Sweden, but was not in the UK, then, since both economies contained
for most of the postwar period highly organized labour movements, it suggests that variables other than labour were at play, and that in particular *the
character of local employing classes*, and their role in the world economy, may
in fact have had a far more potent impact on patterns of economic performance than trade unions *per se*. And if that is so, it is not the symmetries
of institutional arrangements that hold the key to why unionism has different economic effects in different advanced capitalisms, but the nature of
the integration of different national capitalisms into the overall world
system. In the 1960s and 1970s the UK capitalist class was already internationally oriented and globally mobile. The Swedish was not, that was the

key difference. Then the question becomes – which capitalist class is now representative of the situation of capital as a whole? If it is the UK's – if capital in general is becoming internationally mobile and globally oriented (as it surely is) – then it is the Swedish case that has been 'exceptional' and the UK case which is a better guide to the norm. In other words, the argument of Garrett and Lange, when explored more deeply, is as vulnerable as corporatism itself to a critique based on the globalization of capital.

So where do we turn, intellectually? Do we turn back to a neo-liberal enthusiasm for markets, or do we turn towards more radical theories of growth, in our search for an understanding of the political economy of modern capitalism? Certainly the confidence of Scandinavian neo-liberals has recently been strengthened by the difficulties of Swedish social democracy, but the UK experience of the full-blown application of a neo-liberal-inspired political project for nearly two decades now would suggest that much of that confidence is misplaced. The UK evidence seems to suggest that unregulated market forces compound economic inequalities within and between national economies, rather than trigger a move from one growth trajectory to another. It does seem clear, however, that the economic and social space within which the Swedish labour movement managed – for a period – to effect that move in a socially progressive form (to combine the achievement of extensive welfare rights with the sustenance of high rates of private-sector economic growth from an economy which hitherto had enjoyed neither welfare nor growth) was always contingent on a wider set of global patterns of capital accumulation. And it was always dependent on the associated (and very particular) global balance of social forces into which the postwar Swedish economy was inserted. What also seems clear is that the Swedish model is now in difficulties of an apparently terminal kind because, at the level of the world economy as a whole, that balance has shifted again: ostensibly because capital is more globally mobile, actually (as we shall see in chapter 8) because of the steady proletarianization of key parts of the Asian peasantry. In that shift, one particular historical option is visibly being foreclosed – that of nationally based class compacts that allow wages and profits to rise together in core capitalist economies; and one model (of a negotiated or consensual capitalism) is losing its competitive force. There are general lessons for the future organization of capitalism in that foreclosing, and general lessons for the future of the European Left; but they are lessons that will become fully clear only when the other possible interaction between labour power and competitiveness has been explored too: that between the competitiveness of national economies and the deployment of labour as a factor of production.

5

Education, Training
and Culture

The other great claim often made about 'labour' as an element in the growth equation – particularly when the question of the power of labour movements has been set aside – is that it is the *quality of labour as a factor of production* which holds the key to the competitiveness of national economies. 'Quality' here means many things, some of which link back to issues of power, some of which do not. There are those who argue that labour forces can be differentiated, one from another, by the dominant attitudes and values each brings to the exchange of effort for wages, in a continuum that stretches from the 'bloody-mindedness' of shop stewards in UK manufacturing industry in the 1970s to the high levels of cooperation evident in Japanese quality circles in the 1980s (Caves, 1980; Dore, 1973) – a continuum which is then normally explained in broad cultural terms. And there are those who, more prosaically, note the variation in levels of educational attainment characteristic of, and range of industrial training available to, particular national labour forces, and who then seek to relate those variations to differences in patterns of national economic performance. In other words, there is a narrowly focused education and training argument here, and there is a broader and more wide-ranging cultural argument; we need to examine both.

Education and training as the keys to economic performance

The claims

The first thing to note about the current enthusiasm for the use of education as an instrument of economic policy is that it is a very old enthusiasm, certainly a very old enthusiasm in somewhere like the UK, whose political class has been long aware of its economy's diminishing international competitiveness and standing. In fact, in the UK case, these concerns go so far back that they even pre-date the Industrial Revolution and the resulting mid-Victorian period of world industrial supremacy. Educational historians have had no difficulty finding them in the writings of Adam Smith, or even earlier, in the way in which in the 1690s an apparent 'weakness in mechanicks' meant that the UK was 'supplied from foreign parts with divers Commodities which, if the kingdom were replenished with Artizans they would furnish us here at home' (Aldcroft, 1992: 1). But prior to the 1850s official anxiety about the economic consequences of educational provision in the UK was never more than sporadic and muted. From the 1850s to a degree, and from the 1880s in a more consistent manner, it becomes a far more regular feature of the UK educational debate. Indeed for more than a century now, it has been possible to trace in the mainstream debate four persistent themes or claims. One has been that the scale of educational provision in the UK – first at university level, and later at secondary – is inadequate to the needs of a leading industrial nation. The second has been that the education syllabus is inadequately geared to the production of capacities, attitudes and values vital to industrial success. The third has been that vocational and technical education is dangerously underdeveloped in the UK relative to its scale of provision in leading economies elsewhere. And the fourth has been that the diminished standing of the UK economy in league tables of international economic performance is directly linked to these defects in education and training (Reeder, 1980; Mathieson and Bernbaum, 1988; Aldcroft, 1992; Barnett, 1995; Rose, 1997). Indeed it is conventional to cite the Taunton Report on the state of UK schools *in 1868*, to establish how little has subsequently changed both in official thinking and in educational provision. The Report said this:

> our industrial classes have not even that basis of sound general education on which alone technical instruction can rest. It would not be difficult, if our artizans were otherwise well educated, to establish schools for technical instruction of whatever kind might be needed. But even if such schools were generally established among us, there is reason to fear that they would fail to produce any valuable results for want of the essential material, namely disciplined faculties and sound elementary knowledge in the learners. In fact, our deficiency is not merely a deficiency in technical instruction but . . . in general intelligence, and unless we remedy this want we shall gradually but surely find that our undeniable superiority in wealth and perhaps in energy will not save us from decline. *(cited in Aldcroft, 1992: 2)*

Perhaps not surprisingly in the face of so pessimistic a scenario, such arguments have periodically then triggered major bursts of educational debate and reform in the UK. They triggered an expansion of basic university provision at the end of the nineteenth century. They triggered the creation of an extensive system of secondary education after 1944. They inspired a second tranche of university (and polytecnic) provision – and a resetting of the system of industrial training – in the 1960s; and, after the 'Great Education Debate' of the 1970s, they inspired a set of Thatcherite educational reforms through the 1980s (which brought, among other things, a national curriculum in the UK school system for the very first time). But apparently to little avail, if some of the bleaker claims of contemporary commentators on UK economic performance are to be believed. For as late as 1996, the UK government's own international skills audit was showing at best a patchy UK educational performance. The audit found an internationally respectable level of 'graduate production', particularly in science, but a continuing shortfall in the generation of intermediate level skills, and of basic numeracy and literacy – in all of which the UK level of educational performance fell well short of the levels achieved by labour forces in Germany, France, Singapore and the US. The figures on international educational underperformance by UK students are legion. In 1990 only 27 per cent of 16-year-olds reached A–C grades in national examinations in maths, languages and science. The French figure that year was 66 per cent, the German 62 per cent (*Observer*, 5 November 1995: 18). In the global maths league in 1997, 13-year-olds in Singapore averaged a score of 643 (and came top). UK 13-year-olds averaged 506, and came 25th (*Guardian*, 28 April 1997: 23). And so on. And this is presumably why a series of analysts have despaired of the UK's capacity to raise itself onto a new and higher growth path. What he termed poor 'factor creation mechanisms' were certainly a major element in Michael Porter's pessimism about the UK's economic future in his 1990 study *The Competitive Advantage of Nations* (1990: 497–8); and in similar vein, 'weaknesses in the training of British workers' and 'a shortfall in British schooling standards' were singled out by Nick Crafts to justify his view that Thatcherism had not 'succeeded in permanently reversing Britain's relative economic decline' (Crafts, 1992: 33).

For what is so striking about the 1996 UK educational figures cited in the previous paragraph is not simply that they were issued by the UK government. It is also that they were issued in a White Paper on economic competitiveness, and explicitly linked there to the UK's standing in international league tables on GDP per head. For the contemporary concern with the link between education and economic performance which the UK government shares with analysts like Porter and Crafts is not just to be understood as this generation's reproduction of a long-standing and uniquely English 'tradition' of blaming the schools. It is also to be understood as the product of a new set of arguments on the importance of education as an economic input, an importance triggered by the intensification of international competition in the post-1973 period, and one with an international resonance. For, as Ashton and Green have rightly observed, 'across the industrialised world, and in many developing countries too, the thought is paramount that the way to economic growth is via skill formation to raise labour productivity and hence average living standards' (Ashton and Green, 1996: 1). At the heart of that new thought stand three distinct theses.

1   The first is that education is now the nation's key resource – its ultimate guarantor of economic success – because it alone focuses on the one
input into economic activity which is still nationally anchored. As Robert
Reich put it:

> skilled labour has become a key barrier against low wage competitions for the
> simple reason that it is the only dimension of production in which existing
> capitalist powers retain an advantage. Technological innovations may be
> bought or imitated by anyone. High-volume, standardized production facili-
> ties may be established anywhere. But production processes that depend on
> skilled labour must stay where that labour is. *(Reich, 1983: 127)*

In an age of global capital, that is, investment in human capital is all that
remains as an instrument of policy for a government keen to attract global
investment to its territory and economy; and educational performance
becomes the central determinant of where, in the end, high-value-added
production facilities settle and stay.

2   The second central thesis in the new orthodoxy on the importance of
education to economic performance is that the relationship between educational input and economic output is likely to be more direct and unmediated in the future than it has been in the past. Of course, a belief in this
direct and unmediated input–output coupling was always popular – especially among commentators and politicians – with their strongly held (if
largely unsubstantiated) conviction that educational provision (or vocational
training, depending on the argument) was both a necessary and a sufficient
condition for economic growth (for examples, see Bliss and Garbett, 1990:
196). But the credibility of this direct input–output coupling between education and economic growth has now been given renewed potency by those
who believe that employers and policy-makers face a qualitatively new work
paradigm, one in which knowledge has itself become a crucial factor of production. In the old paradigm, as Porter explained to the incoming President
Clinton, the general quality of the labour force was not vital. 'The old
paradigm was one where companies that could enjoy a large home market
gained economies of scale and prospered.' In the new paradigm, by contrast
'success depends on relentless investment by companies . . . not just in
physical assets [but] also in less tangible assets such as research and development, training' (Clinton, 1993: 41). For in what Martin Carnoy has
termed 'the changing world of work in the information age', new information technologies are said to have so transformed work processes and
imperatives that economic success now requires not 'simply higher levels of
education for the workforce, but also education that equips people to think
and work collectively' (Perraton, 1998: 122). On this argument, the successful firm is the flexible firm, and flexibility and learning are inextricably
linked. The firms that reward flexibility prosper; and their organizational
flexibility requires, more than anything else, a labour force sufficiently edu-

cated to be able to move smoothly and rapidly from job to job and task to task. In this vision of the future, successful economies will be staffed by labour forces whose exposure to a particular kind of post-secondary education has equipped them with 'self reliance, rapid adjustment to change, and mobility' (Carnoy, 1998: 127). In this vision too, although the nature and modes of delivery of education have to change, the centrality of education to economic success does not.

3   The third element in the renewed enthusiasm for educational routes to economic competitiveness is the way new growth theory gives investment in human capital a critical role in the workings of the modern economy. As is explained more fully in the Appendix, traditional growth theory (and the associated growth accounting literature) did not do that. It noted the relationship between rates of growth of human capital and rates of growth of GDP, but since it believed that 'the ultimate sources of output and productivity growth [lay] elsewhere', it simply treated 'growth in human capital just like in physical capital as a necessary though not sufficient condition' for economic growth. The new growth theory, however, goes further, arguing that 'a higher *level* of human capital causes a higher *growth rate* of output' (Oulton, 1995: 61) by facilitating either the growth of new knowledge or the capacity of backward economies to catch up by absorbing existing knowledge quickly. New growth theory treats educational investment as both a private and a public good, as investment which, at one and the same time, increases the skills of the individual worker and raises the productivity of the economy as a whole. Some of that investment is understood as straightforwardly a matter of R&D (we shall come to that in chapter 6); but the rest is understood as expenditure on both conventional and life-long forms of general education and industrial training. As Crafts has it, in the new growth theory the 'key idea' is that, for both forms of investment in human capital, 'social returns . . . are much higher than private returns' (Crafts, 1992: 17).

The evidence

There is plenty of evidence that levels of educational performance and degrees of industrial skill vary significantly among advanced capitalist economies, evidence which, more than anything else, points up the inadequate level of formal education and training offered to middle- and lower-skill categories of worker in liberal capitalist models when compared with 'trust-based' ones (Prais, 1987; 1988; 1997). This is particularly marked in the different scale of vocational qualifications found in the UK and the German economies in the 1980s. Research suggests that 60.3 per cent of UK workers lacked even a basic vocational qualification in 1987, as against 28.6 per cent of German workers: a lack of formal skilling which, in the UK case, was particularly marked 'at the level of technician, foreman, office clerk and (to a lesser degree) at the level of manual workers' (Lane, 1989: 82; also Prais, 1995: 15–42). Similar differences in levels of formal education and training appear in studies of managerial cadres (Handy, 1987; Keeble, 1992); and these are underpinned – as we have already observed – by international studies of educational standards which show significant differences in levels of attainment, in participation rates in higher education, and in the distribution of subjects studied by recruits to different categories of industrial employment in different national capitalisms (Carr, 1992: 84). And most telling of all, there are some research data indicative of different specific skill levels in similar groups of workers in different national contexts, quite separate from the degree of formal education or training involved (Prais, 1995: 5–73).

The comparative research data show one other vital piece of information as well: namely that these different patterns of educational performance and levels of skill are neither random nor accidental in origin, but rather emerge from qualitatively different national *systems* of education and training, which themselves vary in scale and quality. There is now a considerable body of evidence on the defining features of the system in each major national capitalism in turn, evidence that lays great stress on the complexity of the German VET (vocational education and training) system, the quality of Japanese internal company training provision and the capacity of the US system to generate technological innovation and breakthrough (Ashton and Green, 1996: 117–76; Green, 1998: 137; Shackleton, 1995: 157–80; Lane, 1989: 62–115; Whitley, 1992b: 16–17; Sako and Dore, 1988; Nishizawa, 1997). Frances Green has written of the existence of:

> three paradigms. . . . First . . . the much lauded German dual system of youth training. In this system a combination of relatively low youth wages, legal and institutional constraints imposed by the social partners, and historically determined social norms lead firms to offer and support apprenticeships. Second, in Japan the predominance of large firms containing internal labour markets means that well managed training (and other learning devices such as job rotation) have a palpable internal pay-off. In the third model, exemplified in the development of the East Asian newly industrialised economies, strong developmental states have to an extent been able to coerce and encourage firms into stepping up their training efforts. *(Green, 1998: 137)*

In the comparative research literature emerging from the UK in particular, heavy emphasis has been placed on the way systemic interactions, dynamics and logics have pulled the German training system (and wider economy) onto a high-skill, high value-added, high-wage trajectory, while the UK's training system settled into what Finegold and Soskice termed a 'low skills equilibrium, in which the majority of enterprises staffed by poorly trained managers and workers produce low-quality goods and services' (Finegold and Soskice, 1988: 22). On this argument and evidence, Germany and Japan – for specific historical reasons – chose or settled on the high-skill path and created institutions, corporate practices and trust relationships to generate and reproduce such a training and growth trajectory (Ashton and Green, 1996: 137–54). However, the UK (and to a lesser degree the US (Wever and Berg, 1993)) did not. In the UK case, so the argument runs, the resulting 'low skills labour force is a consequence of the long-term policy adopted towards training and education in the UK, reinforced by cultural attitudes and practices' (Rubery, 1994: 339). It is also said to be a key element in the UK's subsequent pattern of economic underperformance (Soskice, 1993: 102).*

This last point serves to remind us that *descriptions* or *specifications* of this kind are also necessarily *arguments* or *interpretations* about causes and effects, and as such constitute a kind of tentative evidence that sits half-way between unsubstantiated claim and irrefutable data. As an argument, the description of the German model first surfaced here in chapter 3, as a set of claims that German vocational training systems and substantial rights for workers and unions fuse together to both oblige and enable German employers to compete successfully on the basis of high wages yet low unit costs. The claim is that the German training system generates multi-skilled workers who are able to respond flexibly to new technological opportunities and demand conditions, while the entrenchment of rights to job security and industrial consultation gives those same workers the incentive and security to maximize that flexibility (Soskice, 1991; Lane, 1990: 253; Broadberry and Wagner, 1996: 226, 265). The counter-argument on the UK side is that the logics there work in reverse. The absence of strong worker rights encourages managers to meet competitive pressures by holding down wages, intensifying work processes and adding unskilled labour – while discouraging them from pursuing technological innovation or extensive industrial retraining; and the resulting underskilled, underpaid, undermotivated and insecure labour force is then said to settle into a defensive attitude to new

---

* Broadberry and Wagner have argued in similar vein that systems of

> human capital accumulation can only be understood in relation to the overall production strategy pursued by firms. In America, firms have tended to pursue a policy of standardized mass production, which has required heavy investment in managerial and research capabilities but relatively little investment in shopfloor skills. By contrast, British and German firms have pursued a policy of craft/flexible production, intensive in the use of skilled shopfloor labour. Nevertheless, we also see some differences in the strategies pursued by British and German firms, particularly after 1945. After World War II, whereas German firms maintained their reliance on skilled shopfloor labour, British firms made a relatively unsuccessful move in the direction of standardized mass production and allowed a serious decline in the training of shopfloor workers. This has left British firms in a relatively weak position to take advantage of the information revolution which has been effectively exploited by German firms using skilled workers to produce small batches of high-quality goods. ...Although Britain appears to have moved back towards a more skilled-labour-intensive production strategy during the 1980s, there is still a large skills gap to be made good after the neglect of the previous three decades. *(Broadberry and Wagner, 1996: 265; for a different understanding of the pattern of post-war training in the UK, see Reynolds and Coates, 1996: 252)*

technology and an antagonistic and uncooperative relationship with management. In that way, according to Finegold and Soskice:

> Britain's failure to educate and train its workforce to the same levels as its international competitors [has to be understood as] both a product and a cause of the nation's poor relative economic performance: a product, because the ET system evolved to meet the needs of the world's first industrialized economy, whose large, mass-production manufacturing sector required only a small number of skilled workers and university graduates; and a cause, because the absence of a well educated and trained workforce has made it difficult for industry to respond to new economic conditions. *(Finegold and Soskice, 1988: 21–2)*

But although such arguments constitute evidence of a sort in support of the education–economic performance relationship, they are hardly by themselves strong enough to clarify exactly what that relationship is, or how precisely it works. In fact, hard evidence is very thin on the ground in this area of contemporary research. More readily available are arguments that proceed by assertion and hypothesis. A particularly influential one in the late 1990s pointed to the diminution in the number of unskilled jobs in core capitalist economies, emphasized the intensification of international competition and asserted that in consequence 'a manufacturing policy of concentration on diversified quality products is the only one for advanced societies in order to remain competitive on world markets' (Lane, 1990: 255; also Streeck, 1989: 90). By implication, of course, in that argument the skill level of the labour force – if not important in the past – will be vital to competitiveness in the future. And that argument sat alongside another, which pointed to the way in which – in advanced capitalist economies – the rise in service employment meant that future productivity growth would increasingly depend on service-sector efficiency, and then linked that to the emergence of 'new patterns of work organization and customer interaction in the service sector' and to the resulting need for a service labour force trained in interpersonal skills and computer use (Soskice, 1993: 105). Both arguments seem intuitively reasonable – the latter very reasonable in fact – but in their present condition neither could be thought of as more than tentative, even speculative, in kind.

The search for harder data does throw up some ostensibly stronger research findings, particularly from cross-national analyses undertaken by educational sociologists and aggregate productivity studies by growth accountants. Traditional growth accountancy certainly contains some fairly precise calculations on the impact of educational investment on different growth rates. Denison, for example, in his 1985 study of the UK's economic growth between 1929 and 1982, attributed '27 per cent of the growth of output per person employed to the rise in school levels' in that period (Abramovitz, 1993: 231); and other similarly designed studies have 'shown that the quantity of education provided by an economy to its inhabitants is one of the major influences determining whether per capita income in that society is growing rapidly enough to narrow the gap . . . with the more prosperous economies' (Wolff and Gittelman, 1993: 147). But those studies are bedevilled by the difficulties of adequately measuring even the *quantity* of education inputted, let alone its *quality* (on this, Rubinson and Browne, 1994: 583–4); and at best they can only suggest proximate causal relationships of a preliminary kind (causal relationships which may very well, in the case of education and economic performance, run in more than one direction at once, or run from economic growth to educational inputs, and not the other way round). In fact, broad accounting techniques seem at their strongest when we compare developed and underdeveloped economies over a long period (Maddison, 1995a: 37; Aldcroft, 1992: 9–14). That may be in part because the effect of educational investment on economic growth is at its strongest in just those countries whose 'low incomes and low rates of literacy are likely to be very responsive to additional education and training' (Aldcroft, 1992: 20). But the 'heroic assumptions' underpinning growth accountancy, even at its most sophisticated, leave that mode of analysis just too blunt for the isolation of the impact of educational and training variables on the different growth performances of *advanced* capitalist economies in one short period – and yet it is precisely that impact which policy-makers need to know and which our exercise requires we determine.

There are some research data addressed to precisely that issue, particularly research data designed and implemented by the UK's National Institute of Economic and Social Research in the 1980s. In producing what David Soskice hailed as 'among the most compelling research results of applied economics in the UK since the war' (Soskice, 1993: 102), Prais and his colleagues took a series of matched samples of manufacturing plants in Britain and the Continent (mainly in Germany, but also in the Netherlands and France), covering a range of industries: some 160 establishments in the metalworking, woodworking, clothing manufacture, food manufacture and hotel industries. In each they found a significant productivity difference between the UK and the Continental factories, even though both sets of establishments had 'access to the same machinery' on world markets, and noted, for the German factories unlike the British, that 'it was with the help of a thoroughly qualified workforce that advanced machinery and advanced production methods were introduced, put into operation and fully exploited' (Steedman and Wagner, 1987: 94). Earlier and later NIER studies produced similar results. A 1985 study of 45 matched plants in Britain and West Germany ('mainly manufacturing simple metal products') found skills rather than machinery central to productivity differences, concluding that 'the fault for poor maintenance, poor production and poor diagnosis of faults, has its origins in technical skills at the level of foremen and operators' (Daly et al., 1985: 60–1). A later NIER study of the clothing, garden tools and manufactured food industries argued that 'higher operative skills [in German factories] permitted change-overs in production to be carried out more rapidly and efficiently' and that 'the training of designers and technicians in Germany included greater practical content than in the UK, enabling them to marry theory and practice more effectively than UK workers' (cited in the *Financial Times*, 20 November 1995).

The cumulative impact of these studies was thus very clear: that past UK economic underperformance, relative to Germany at least, owed much to inadequate levels of skill among ordinary UK manufacturing workers, and that future UK economic recovery depended, in part at least, on the expansion of those British workers who possessed craft and vocational qualifications. As Prais reported in 1995 on the generality of their findings, time and again the less than full use of new machinery in the UK factories studies was the product of a 'dearth of diagnostic skills' in the attendant work force, and, because it was, investment in new machinery (although welcome) would not be enough. Action was needed instead across the entire UK training and educational system, in which 'attention must be given to the incentives to acquire technical skills, and to the provision of better basic school-leaving standards – so that the average school-leaver does not regard the acquisition of high technological skills as presenting an insuperable intellectual challenge' (Prais, 1995: 73).

On the surface, the Prais data look convincing, and are now often cited as unambiguously demonstrating 'a positive relationship between levels of skill and qualification in the workforce, and higher productivity and enhanced quality of goods and services' (Keep and Mayhew, 1998: 383). Yet in fact the Prais data are not without their critics, a number of whom have pointed to serious methodological weaknesses that are potentially corrosive of their force. Among their problems 'is the inability to control adequately for differences in the amount, age, composition and layout of capital equipment' in the factories being compared, in a context in which capital is the other recognized source of productivity growth. 'Another is the concentration on formal qualifications as an index of training' in a context in which 'qualifications are only a proxy for economically relevant skills, and sometimes not a very good one'. Yet a third 'is the interpretative burden placed on the observed correlation between high qualification levels and labour productivity' in a context in which 'correlation does not necessarily imply causation' (Shackleton, 1995: 32, 234); and a fourth is the ease with which *general* statements of proof are built on the basis of case work in only a limited range of industries whose representativeness of industry as a whole is seriously open to question. In the NIER studies of 'matched samples' it just was not possible to make a perfect match – differences between the machinery in the chosen factories were evident throughout; the selection of simple production processes to facilitate ease of factor identification pulled the research effort away from cutting edge technologies, where productivity differences are competitively significant; and the complexity of the interplay between machinery and operatives even in these simple production processes made the identification of particular 'skill contributions' highly judgemental and arbitrary. The treatment of the NIER findings *are* informative: but the information they release is as much about those who pursue the causes of productivity differences as about the causes themselves. For, as Paul Chapman has rightly observed, 'the fact that findings from [the NIER] research programme have received such widespread attention despite these methodological weaknesses draws our attention to the wholly inadequate research effort to estimate the real contribution of human capital to productivity' (Chapman, 1993: 114).

In fact, Tony Cutler has been prepared to push the critique of the Prais findings one step further, seeing in these methodological difficulties a troubling continuity between the National Institute specification of the problem of the UK economy in the 1980s as one of underskilling and the early neoliberal argument that the problem in the 1970s was overmanning (for a critique of their methodology, see above, p. 90). In the latter, workers (and their representatives) were portrayed as villains. By Prais and his colleagues, they were at least portrayed as victims. But in both cases the central problem faced by the UK is still said to be a problem of labour (and not of capital or of the state), and it is still one that is supposedly substantiated by hard data. Cutler found that focus on labour distorting, and the data underpinning it methodologically suspect. So while some critics found it 'difficult to avoid the feeling that this [was] a research programme with a predetermined outcome' (Chapman, 1993: 114), for Cutler the problem ran deeper still. He saw Prais's arguments on vocational training and economic performance as merely 'a new instalment of the British Labour Problem', as a moment of retreat by the UK's Centre-Left from any attempt to re-regulate capital; and he argued that, 'just as the British Labour Problem was a bogus characterization of the British economic problem in the 1970s and 1980s, which played a significant role in the economic errors of those decades, so the current nostrums on vocational training promise to play an analogous role in the 1990s' (Cutler, 1992: 165).

The National Institute studies are not, however, the only example of micro-focused research in the training area. There are a number of others (Oulton, 1996), not least one on the biscuit industry in Britain, Germany, France and the Netherlands that adopted a similar 'matched sample' approach. It too found a relationship of skill to product, and denied that differing national levels of productivity could 'be attributed to inter-country variation in the age and sophistication of capital equipment in use' (Mason et al., 1996: 175). Its general view was that 'there is a close correspondence between the structure of workforce skills delivered by Britain's vocational education and training system over recent decades – polarised between a large majority of low-skilled workers and a small minority of highly qualified personnel – and the continued specialisation of large numbers of British manufacturers in highly automated, low value-added production activities' (ibid.: 191). In other words, the Mason study too asserted a strong positive correlation between skill levels and productivity; but it also emphasized – far more than did the Prais studies – the complex interlocking of inputs and outputs in the training–production relationship. What it asserted was a *two-way* relationship between the demand for skills and the supply of them. In the biscuit case study, Mason and his colleagues suggested that there was a correspondence in different countries between the supply of skills (as shaped by national systems of education and training) and the demand for skills by employers (associated with their chosen product mix, capital utilization and work organization. The predominant strategic choices made by employers in any country reflect the extent to which a skilled workforce is available or achievable. But they also affect the supply of skills by signalling to individuals the value of investment in vocational education and training *(Mason et al., 1996: 176)*.

Studies by, among others, Maurice et al. (1986), Wever and Berg (1993), Rubery (1994), Keep and Mayhew (1998), Shackleton (1995), Ashton and Green (1996) and – in relation to university training – Sanderson (1986) all make a similar point: that skill levels sit within wider systems of training that possess their own institutional and social architecture. Some produce a high skills trajectory, some a low skills trajectory (Ashton and Green, 1996: 117–75; Green, 1998: 137); and movement from one to the other requires not simply the re-skilling of the labour force but the resetting of the entire architecture. This task was enough to persuade David Soskice, when considering the UK case, to advocate a 'non-training route out of the low skills equilibrium' (1993: 107), because the institutional structures needed for a company-based training system of the German or Japanese variety were just not there in the UK. Frances Green has been clearer still: if economies are to be moved from one training regime to another, it is vital to 'secure commitment to skill formation policies' from all the principal actors involved: not just organized labour (which is invariably attracted to the idea) but critically from the government (via adequate funding) and from employers. It is Green's judgement that, in the UK case at least, it is with the last two, and *not* with organized labour, that the current problem now lies, in 'a serious question mark about the financial commitment of the state to education' and a 'concern too that the rhetoric of employer commitment is reflected only in pockets of excellence, and not in substantive widespread rises in training activity' (Green, 1998: 138). And this is but the UK version of the general Green (and Ashton) view that, for high levels of skill formation to emerge, 'fractions of the ruling class, especially those in control of the state apparatus, must be committed to . . . high level skill formation', 'groups of leading employers must also be committed', and 'there must be mechanisms for overcoming the externalities associated with investment in training, mechanisms which must induce employers to take account of the social benefits of training . . . and which open up the process of training in ways that allow both employers and employees to assure themselves of the quality of the training provided' (Ashton and Green, 1996: 102).

Training and growth

Yet if Green, Ashton and the others are right – and there seems little reason to doubt the quality of their judgement here – important things follow. The main one is that the focus on labour – its education and training no less than its organization and power – pulls us away from the prime determinants of how (and why) economies perform. At the very least it suggests that those determinants lie in the predominant set of institutional structures and relationships which run through the economy and society as a whole, institutions and relationships in which, at most, labour is simply one player. It also suggests that the driving forces within those institutional complexes are not primarily to be found in the labour camp. They are to be found – depending on the degree of radicalism in the scholarship under review – either back in the mists of time (in the legacy of history and culture), or in the nature of governing institutions within the economy and the state or within the social classes whose character and interests prevail in (and are expressed through) dominant institutional arrangements. If labour then enters (either uncooperative or unskilled) as a contributory element in the workings of those institutions, its presence there (and in that form) is necessarily responsive and subordinate, constituting at most a secondary and reinforcing set of pressures on a system of relationships whose overarching logic and trajectory is fixed elsewhere. And if critics claim otherwise, then the force of their criticisms serves to obscure the more basic processes at work, which is why Tony Cutler was right to treat the current enthusiasm in the UK for vocational training and the 1970s enthusiasm for union-bashing as part and parcel of the same thing: an ideological onslaught on *labour* that served to reduce the potency of calls for the regulation and reform of *capital* as the key to economic recovery.

All this suggests that the three arguments canvassed earlier for the importance of education and training as the key to different growth patterns are all, in their different ways, defective. The writings of new growth theory on the importance of investment in human capital are ultimately too narrow in their specification of variables, abstracting labour from institutional processes and relationships of power which have far greater explanatory impact on how economies perform (as the next chapters will show). The notion that education has now become the critical resource in an information-based production system flies in the face of empirical data (some of which we have hinted at, some of which we shall see later) that stresses the persistence of low-grade production technologies in large parts of the world's manufacturing sectors, and sees labour-intensive, low-skilled service employment as a major employment outlet within advanced capitalist economies into the foreseeable future. And the Reichian argument about re-skilling to attract foreign capital, and its Streeckian embellishment about advanced capitalist economies surviving by concentrating on high-skilled, high value-added production – seem equally overoptimistic. For what is it about newly emerging proletariats in far away places that must oblige them to stay in low-skilled, low value-added production? And if the answer is nothing, where is that safe niche in which already established labour movements can successfully hide? And what is it about the new imperatives faced by local employing classes in liberal capitalist economies in particular that will persuade them to undergo so profound a mental sea-change as to pursue comparative advantage by 'diversified quality production' alone? Supply-side changes in the education and training of workers can do little if the dominant pattern of class relationships within a national economy (and their associated strategies for capital accumulation) do not also change; and such changes are notoriously hard to effect, particularly by the Left. Which is presumably why Keep and Mayhew were right to forecast – for the UK at least – that 'the great danger of current policies is that we will end up with a more highly qualified workforce, many of whom will occupy low-paid, insecure, dead-end jobs, producing low-cost, low-spec goods and services, with no discernible improvement in competitive performance resulting' (Keep and Mayhew, 1988: 392).

In fact, for all these reasons, the data on the relationship between education, training and economic performance are, in general, very tentative, indeterminate and approximate. There is really a 'weak' and a 'strong' version of the relationship on offer here. The weak one is that education and training is a good thing, that 'it seems intuitively likely that on average a more highly educated and trained labour force will be better equipped to meet the rapid changes in technology, tastes and organizations which are characteristic of modern economies' (Shackleton, 1995: 233). That intuition seems entirely unobjectionable. What is less secure is the stronger claim that better education and training is the key to economic competitiveness in the contemporary age or, less secure still, that it is the only key. It is not. As Shackleton has it, 'training can improve a worker's potential productivity. However, his or her actual productivity often depends more proximately on the machines and equipment he or she uses, the way in which work is organized and monitored, and the incentives provided to individuals to work hard and effectively' (ibid.: 234). A steady increase in labour skills may be a vital prerequisite to standing still in the competitive struggles between national capitalisms, and may be highly desirable for a whole set of social values of a progressive kind; but the research material on education and skilling suggests that it is not the safe and easy route to economic renaissance for advanced capitalist economies that particularly moderate governments of the Centre-Left imagine it to be. As Bienefeld so aptly put it, 'training must not be treated as a "cargo cult". One cannot assume that "if we train them, the jobs will come"' (Bienefeld, 1996: 430).

In fact, the adoption of educational solutions to economic problems by such governments in the 1990s tells us less about economic realities than about political ones. For the enthusiasm for training as *the* solution to economic underperformance appears to be part of a general retreat – by European social democratic political parties – from any attempt to control capital, or to offer a qualitatively different analysis of the sources of economic difficulties from that canvassed by neo-liberal intellectuals. In the sphere of vocational training, as Cutler put it, 'it is possible to chatter about "market failure" but, equally, make it clear that one is impeccably respectable and that such "market failure" is only applicable to quite determinate and limited areas' (Cutler, 1992: 180). Centre-Left governments in a globalized capitalism seem to encourage the training of workers, that is, as much to guarantee themselves a successful niche in the political world of electoral markets as to guarantee their firms a successful niche in the economic world of commodity markets.

Cultural factors and economic growth

For many analysts of economic growth, however, the education and training agenda does not exhaust the space occupied by 'ideas' as triggers to economic performance. For them, the knowledge locked away in the minds of workers and managers is but one element in the entire mosaic of economic growth, one that sits inside, and is often subordinate to, wider networks of values and attitudes. The most sophisticated of the 'skills theorists', as we have just seen, insist that training regimes be located in wider 'business' systems, systems that stretch beyond simple modes of knowledge transmission to include institutional arrangements between financial and industrial sectors, and between state agencies and workers' representatives. Invariably one element mentioned in those wider arrangements is the dominant set of understandings and expectations running through them; and indeed occasionally the whole package is referred to as a 'business culture' (Randlesome, 1994). But that labelling can often confuse, by privileging in its categorization one element in a wider configuration (Dobbin, 1994: 14, 18). For our purposes at least, it is more productive to differentiate the complete business system from the cultural elements which it includes, and to treat the impact of each separately. We shall examine the effect of entire business systems on economic performance (business 'cultures' understood as a highly differentiated set of *institutional* arrangements) in chapter 6. What we need to settle our account with here is the effect on economic growth of cultural factors understood in their more precise and narrow sense: as sets of values, understandings and expectations which settle in the minds of managers, workers and politicians, and which then shape their behaviour as economic actors.

The claims

There is nothing new, of course, in the assertion that ideas are important to economic performance. Max Weber's thesis *The Protestant Ethic and the Spirit of Capitalism* established that intellectual territory more than a century ago; and it spawned a tradition of scholarship among both sociologists and economic historians that still shows no signs of abating. The assertion was certainly alive and well in each of the literatures on the postwar performance of particular national economies which we surveyed in chapters 2 and 3. There we saw that US and UK underperformance relative to West Germany and Japan was occasionally explained in cultural terms.

Weiner, for example, explained the UK's economic underperformance from the 1890s by reference to the 'loss of an industrial spirit' (Weiner, 1981); and Robert Reich famously characterized US economic history in the twentieth century as one in which two cultures – one business-driven (and now outdated), one civic (and now essential to future prosperity) – competed for ideological dominance (Reich, 1983: 8). And we saw too that Reich's thesis was in line with, and indeed was partially inspired by, parallel arguments in the German and Japanese literatures – literatures which emphasized the positive impact on growth of the 'trust' relationships cemented in place by (in the German case, Social or Christian Democratic, and in the Japanese case, Confucian) value-systems. Later in this chapter we shall need to look at the adequacy of some of those specific explanatory claims, but before we do we need to recognize as well the more general underlying theses of which they are only a part.

For in addition to specific claims in relation to particular national capitalisms, the cultural literature on different economic performances contains a number of general claims: three are of particular importance.

(1)   The first is that cultural systems can be differentiated by the presence or absence within them of particular sets of ideational attributes. The management studies literature is replete with such schemas, of which those developed by Hampden-Turner and Trompenaars are typical and have recently been the most widely discussed. In his recent writings Fons Trompenaars, the Dutch management consultant, has distinguished cultural systems by the presence or absence within them of five 'value orientations': 'universalism versus particularism (rules versus relationships), collectivism versus individualism (the group versus the individual), neutral versus emotional (the range of feelings expressed), diffuse versus specific (the range of involvement) and achievement versus ascription (how status is accorded)' (Trompenaars, 1993: 29). In collaboration elsewhere with Hampden-Turner, Trompenaars has increased those value orientations in number and re-specified them as 'seven valuing processes crucial to creating wealth': universalism versus particularism; analysing versus integrating; individualism versus communitarianism; inner-directed versus outer-directed orientation; 'time as sequence' versus 'time as synchronization'; achieved status versus ascribed status; equality versus hierarchy (Hampden-Turner and Trompenaars, 1993: 10–11; for another version, see Lodge and Vogel, 1987: 8–23). Such value-lists then provide comparative cultural business analysts with a framework within which to situate particular national business systems, and on the basis of which to explain different economic performances. Trompenaars, for example, has argued that different cultural frameworks encourage the emergence of particular forms of corporate organization (different corporate cultures he labelled, imaginatively, 'family', 'Eiffel tower', 'guided missile' and 'incubator'), in which we find different kinds of relationships between employees, different attitudes to authority, different ways of thinking and learning, different attitudes to people, dif-

ferent ways of changing, different ways of motivating and rewarding and different patterns of criticism and conflict resolution (Trompenaars, 1993: 160). These can then, in his view, be used tentatively to map *national* variations in corporate structure, as shown in figure 5.1.

(2)   The second general claim within the more ambitious or cavalier of the 'culturalist' literature on economic growth is that the distribution of cultural attributes between different national settings makes it legitimate to talk of different 'national cultures' (see for example Dobbin, 1994: 22, 213–17). Hampden-Turner and Trompenaars in particular have recently claimed to have located – on the basis of extensive survey data gathered from managers in the US, UK, Japan, Germany, Sweden, France and the Netherlands – 'the seven cultures of capitalism', each one of which is tied to an individual national economy. They at least are adamant that cultural cohesion, as they term it, gives particular 'cultural fingerprints' to different managerial strata in different national settings – such that 'each of the seven nations . . . believes in a unique combination of the values [enumerated above]' (Hampden-Turner and Trompenaars, 1993: 16). For them, 'the United States is by far the most universalistic culture in our group', 'American managers are by far the strongest individualists in our national samples', 'the Japanese not only have a different approach to quality, they see values and value creation in a different light . . . that follows their cultural orientation', and so on (ibid.: 21, 48, 121). And they are not alone in this view; for their

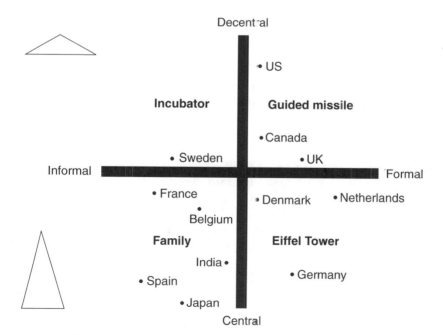

Figure 5.1   National patterns of corporate culture
Source: based on Trompenaars, 1993: 161

findings are entirely congruent with those of other comparative cultural studies – notably the binary comparisons (with Canada and Japan) made by the leading American political sociologist Seymour Martin Lipset in his pursuit of the character of 'American exceptionalism'. Lipset's studies of Japanese and American cultural systems persuaded him that 'the two nations follow different organizing principles' and that 'national traditions continued to inform the cultures, economies and politics of both countries in very dissimilar ways'. The US 'follows the individualistic essence of bourgeois liberalism and evangelical sectarian Christianity', while the dominant culture in Japan 'reflects the group orientated norms of the post-feudal aristocratic Meija era' (Lipset, 1996: 256). And although both national cultures have changed over time, and have done so in similar ways, Lipset has still insisted that the future will not be one of total cultural convergence. On the contrary, value and behavioural differences in the two nations are, and will remain, 'like trains that have moved thousands of miles along parallel railway tracks. They are far from where they started, but they are still separated' (ibid.: 261).

There is in consequence a willingness and a confidence in writings of this kind to list cultural differences country by country – Hampden-Turner and Trompenaars, for example, have an eight-point check list of differences between US and Japanese 'cultural biases' (ibid., 161–2) – and to draw up summary charts of national cultural variations (ibid.: 301; see also Casson, 1993: 430). Of course, academics of the quality of Lipset, Hampden-Turner and Trompenaars are aware of cultural variation *within* national economies, and of the mediation of cultural norms by different personality types. Indeed, Trompenaars likened the distribution of basic attitudes and values to a normal distribution, which could be graphed in the conventional way (Trompenaars, 1993: 25–7). But in his work he insisted on the existence of distinct centres of gravity within each cultural system, gave each a national anchorage and then (with Hampden-Turner) spoke without qualification of American culture, Japanese culture, German culture and so on. North American and Western European business cultures, we were told, are universalistic. South Korean, Russian and many other Asian and South American business cultures are not. And in each culture business leaders will, in consequence, have different attitudes to – among other things – the importance of the detail of the contract, the amount of social time to be spent negotiating a deal, the role of head office in securing and delivering it, and the rights of subordinates to benefit financially from its implementation (Trompenaars, 1993: 43). Applying universalistic practices in particularistic cultures, Trompenaars then told his management readers, was likely to be economically unproductive. To be successful in a universalistic culture, he suggested, it was better to 'seek fairness by treating all like cases in the same way' but in particularistic ones to 'seek fairness by treating all cases on their special merits' (ibid.). Although such advice was underpinned by managerial questionnaire data that purported to establish its validity empirically, it s easy to see how quickly this type of analysis could slide dangerously close to the counselling of practices abroad that would be deemed corrupt at home. It is also easy to see how quickly this kind of analysis could – in less subtle hands than those of Trompenaars and his collaborators – slide at best towards national stereotyping and at worst towards racism.

(3)   The third general claim within the 'culturalist' literature on economic growth – and by far the most vital one of the three for our purposes – is that these ideational differences between national cultures then constitute an important (or even the most important) key to their different postwar performances. It is here that the Weiner arguments on the UK, and the Dore arguments on Japan, are most properly situated: and it is here too that the comparative arguments of such scholars and popularizers as Hampden-Turner and Trompenaars are joined by those of Fukuyama. The thesis of economic development offered by Hampden-Turner and Trompenaars, for example, was that 'each value in [their seven culture pairs] is crucial to success' and that 'the capitalist cultures that succeed in the next century will be those that overcome their cultural predispositions to favour . . . individualism at the expense of community, and bring seemingly opposed values into balance' (Trompenaars, 1993: 10). For they, like Lazonick and Reich before them, saw an increasing gap opening between the requirements of the new conditions of technology, competition and consumer demand on the one side and the strictures of economic liberalism on the other; and, in consequence, they saw growing competitive difficulties for liberal capitalist economies in a future when success would require the establishment of cultures of trust, when managers would be able to develop long-term corporate strategies and mobilize the commitment of entire work-forces. This was also the conclusion of Lodge and Vogel's nine-country study of 'ideology and national competitiveness' in the mid 1980s, a study which ranked economies by their degree of ideological strength (measured by their degree of ideological coherence and adaptability) and then set that ranking against various tests of competitiveness. Individual country rankings on Vogel's scales of ideological coherence (which put Japan, Korea and Taiwan in the first tier, Germany in the second, France and Brazil in the third, the UK, the USA and Mexico bringing up the rear) correlated very closely with their rankings against such measures as GDP growth rates per capita between 1965 and 1984, or the share of investment in GDP over the same period. In the competitiveness rankings as in the ideological rankings, Asian and German economies vied for top placings, while the UK and US competed for the bottom slot.

All of this persuaded Lodge and Vogel, as others have been persuaded before and since, that 'at the present stage in world development . . . countries with a coherent communitarian ideology' are best able to adapt to international competitive pressures, particularly those economies with a 'version of communitarianism that restrains government spending and excessive regulation yet increases the range of co-operation between business management, labor and government' (Vogel, 1987: 321). Such views are now

commonplace in much of the popular literature on the diminishing gap
between US living standards and those elsewhere in the advanced capitalist
world, of the kind alluded to in more detail in chapter 2; and they are
entirely compatible with the way in which, a generation earlier, the economic 'superiority' of the First World over the Third was often explained
by reference to the presence or absence of appropriate 'achievement ethics'
or civic cultures. To underscore the contemporary presence and importance
of such arguments, it is worth citing two further examples, each developed
by intellectuals heavily involved in the development or implementation of
US economic and foreign policy. Lawrence Harrison – a leading USAID
director in Latin America between 1965 and 1981 – has recently argued for
the existence of four 'basic cultural factors' which drive economic progress:
what he termed the 'radius of trust, identification, sense of community';
the 'rigour of the ethical system'; 'the exercising of authority'; and the
dominant 'attitudes about work, innovation, saving and profit' (Harrison,
1992: 226). These, he claimed, hold the key to differences in political, social
and economic development between countries. In his view, for example,
'Britain lost its leadership because it lost its taste for work, saving, creativity, and risk taking' (ibid.: 247). They also hold the key to why the US
economy, in which such values prevailed in exemplary fashion after 1945,
lost its competitive edge in the 1980s. That edge went as those values eroded.
And Francis Fukuyama, from his research base within the RAND Corporation, has recently put the case more strongly still, arguing that economies
flourish to the degree that trust relations prevail within them, and decline
competitively to the degree that their dominant cultural systems succumb
to unbridled individualism. It was Fukuyama's view that 'democracy and
capitalism work best when they are leavened with cultural traditions that
arise from non-liberal sources' (1995: 351) and that in democratic capitalisms economic success depends on the quantity and quality of 'social
capital' present in civil society, social capital which 'rests on cultural roots'.
Economic rationalism is not enough, in this argument, if economic success
is the goal. It has to be underpinned and informed by 'a thriving civil society
. . . habits, customs and ethics – attributes that . . . must . . . be nourished
through an increasing awareness and respect for culture'. Out of such shared
values, according to Fukuyama, 'comes trust, and trust . . . has a large and
measurable economic value'. As he put it, 'one of the most important lessons
we can learn from an examination of economic life is that a nation's well-
being, as well as its ability to compete, is conditioned by a single, pervasive
cultural characteristic: the level of trust inherent in the society' (ibid.: 10,
33, 5, 7; see also Albert and Gonenc, 1996: 188, 190–1).

The evidence

But do cultural factors warrant such 'awareness and respect' as triggers to
economic performance? To decide, there is much to be gained by carefully

examining the two main cases – within the advanced capitalist world – where the argument has been made most strongly that they do: first, contemporary Japan; then, late-nineteenth-century UK.

Japanese 'cultural exceptionalism'   As we saw in chapter 3, cultural factors have also been widely cited as key determinant of postwar Japanese economic success, with the Japanese form of Confucianism regularly mentioned both as a strong influence on the organization of Japanese capital and as an important catalyst to what is often described as the uniquely consensual form of Japanese industrial relations. The relationship of Confucianism to the organizational forms of the typical Japanese firm will be discussed in chapter 6. Here we shall concentrate on culture and industrial relations.

The main claim often made by cultural analysts of Japanese worker–manager relations is not simply that postwar Japanese industrial relations have taken a particularly cooperative and harmonious form, but that they have done so primarily because both parties to the relations – both managers and workers – have carried within their heads particular sets of understandings of how social relations and economic life ought to relate. Japanese workers, we are told, lack the degree of class solidarity characteristic of Western European labour movements; and Japanese managers lack the unbridled individualism of their Anglo-Saxon counterparts. And because they do, because their heads are said to be full instead of a peculiarly Japanese version of Confucianist thought, they have been able to establish among themselves a unique set of industrial relations practices which have harnessed the knowledge and commitment of Japanese workers to technological innovation and productive efficiency on an unprecedented scale – certainly on a scale without precedent in US or UK liberal capitalism, and even on a scale beyond the capacity of the more negotiated capitalisms of the German or Swedish kind.

The principal institutional novelties of the Japanese industrial relations system to which such claims characteristically relate were cited in chapter 3. They include high levels of job security (the 'lifetime employment system'), seniority wage systems, limited wage and status differences between occupational grades, a system of company rather than industrial or national unions and a low incidence of industrial disputes: in total the 'Japanese Employment System'. They also include high levels of labour training, company welfare provision, the extensive use of quality circles and the delegation of 'considerable discretion to monitor and adjust the flow and quality of work on the shop floor' (Lazonick, 1991a: 43) to ordinary Japanese workers. And they are said, by some analysts at least, to extend further still, through a 'shop floor reformation' (Fruin, 1992: 169–70) to the creation of qualitatively different relationships of *trust* between managers and workers, as 'the contractual nature of the employment relationship is obscured or replaced by a sense of common membership in a corporate entity which has objectives which can be shared by all members' (Dore, 1985: 212), with the result that the individual Japanese enterprise is said to

be 'markedly distinguished from both its American and British counterparts by the degree to which company and workers, company and union,
and different levels of management and workers are bound together by the
sense of a common enterprise marked off from its competitors and the surrounding society' (Glazer, 1976: 876). Japanese workers, we are told, have
shown an unusually high propensity to 'work long hours at a steady pace'
and to limit 'their wage demands to levels that reflect the current ability of
their companies to pay without jeopardizing long-term corporate goals', in
the process generating 'widespread agreement that co-operative employment relations have played an important part in the phenomenal success of
the Japanese economy over the past four decades' (Lazonick, 1995: 70; also
Iwaki, 1996: 147).

It should be said (and indeed we shall comment on this again later) that
not everyone describing Japanese industrial relations in this way then turns
to cultural factors by way of explanation: Lazonick certainly does not. Nor
do those offering a cultural explanation always treat culture as the only
factor in play: Dore, to take an important example, admits both to the
difficulties of using the term 'culture' in comparative analysis (Dore, 1993:
76) and to the existence of a wide range of non-cultural sources of postwar
Japanese economic growth, including the character and quality of the
Japanese education system (Dore, 1985: 199–201). But he at least is keen to
add a cultural dimension to that explanatory list and to emphasize the
importance of a Confucianist legacy in Japanese economic life. As he put it
in 1987:

> Start from the assumptions of original sin, as did some of the Confucianists'
> opponents in ancient China, and as did the Christian divines of the eighteenth
> century societies in which our western economic doctrines evolved, and you
> get one set of answers . . . People work for self-interest. If you want a peace-
> ful and prosperous society, just set up institutions in such a way that people's
> self-interest is mobilized and let the invisible hand of the market do the rest.
> Reduce everything to the bottom line. If, by contrast, you start, as at least the
> followers of Mencius among the Confucianists did, from the assumption of
> original virtue, then something else follows. You assume the bonds of friend-
> ship and fellow-feeling are also important, and a sense of loyalty and belong-
> ing – to one's community, one's firm, one's nation – and the sense of
> responsibility which goes with it. And you would be likely to assume that eco-
> nomic institutions which bring out the best in people, rather than the worst,
> make for a more pleasant and peaceful, and probably in the end more pros-
> perous, society. *(Dore, 1987: vii–viii)*

Other analysts have gone further still, asserting the existence of a quite
direct and unmediated relationship between cultural variables and patterns
of worker involvement in the Japanese case. Lipset in particular has linked
Japanese strike patterns, wage restraint and consensual disputes procedures
directly to wider cultural patterns in Japanese society (Lipset, 1996: 225–6);
and Fukuyama has made much of a distinction between 'horizontal' and
'vertical' forms of group solidarity – the first generating class conscious-

ness, the second company loyalty – in order to attribute the superiority of postwar Japanese performance over UK performance partly to the different distribution of the two forms of solidarity between the labour forces of the two economies. The British working class', he has argued:

> has always shown [the] greater degree of solidarity and militancy . . . But that very class solidarity deepens the divisions between management and labor in Britain. Under such conditions, workers scoff at the idea that they and management together constitute one large family or team with common interests. . . . By contrast, horizontal working-class solidarity exists to a lesser degree in Japan than in Britain. . . . Japanese workers tend to identify with their companies rather than with their fellow workers: because they are company unions, Japanese trade unions are despised by their more militant brethren abroad. But the reverse side of the coin is a much higher degree of vertical enterprise solidarity in Japan. . . . This kind of vertical group solidarity would appear to be more conducive to economic growth than its horizontal alternative. *(Fukuyama, 1995: 159)*

And it is not just in the working class that the centre of gravity of thought and action is said to diverge between liberal capitalisms and Asian economies. They are said to do so across the entire managerial class as well. Lipset's arguments here are representative of a wide body of scholarship, which sees US managers and Japanese managers as very different ideational creatures. He reports a tranche of research findings on attitude divergence between the two economies, citing, for example, a study from the 1970s that found fully a half of Japanese managers, but only a fifth of US managers, willing to include the size of a worker's family in the design of appropriate compensation packages, and citing too – from the data gathered by Hampden-Turner and Trompenaars, evidence that US managers are far more focused on profit than their Japanese counterparts (Lipset, 1996: 233, 258). Little wonder, if this is true, that *both* managers and workers are said to set greater store by mutual respect and trust in Japan than they do in societies whose cultural systems are more liberal and Protestant than traditional and Confucian. (For a general assessment of the relationship of Confucianism to capitalist development in East Asia, see Kyong-Dong, 1994.)

Arguments of this kind then invite two kinds of critical response. They invite us to examine whether the Japanese system of industrial relations is accurately captured by the litany of consensual features characteristically deployed to describe it. And to the degree that it is, they also invite us to ask if those features were (and are) primarily put and held in place by cultural forces unique to Japanese industrial society. We need to consider each of those critical questions in turn.

The answer to the first of those two questions is that the Japanese system of industrial relations is *not* fully captured by the litany of attractive institutions and practices with which its advocates are so enamoured, and that on the contrary 'in most western reports, the concentration on the internal labour market in large companies has led to an over-simplified characterization of Japan's industrial relations' (Chalmers, 1989: 33). That system has its downside too, a downside that both underpins its consensual dimensions and helps to give those dimensions a resonance and significance quite different from those conventionally attributed to them. For even at the height of the system's stability (before 1992), the lifetime employment guarantee applied to probably no more than one Japanese worker in four. It was what Chalmers called 'the 25 per cent model' (Chalmers, 1989: 33), applying only 'to a small part of total employment and a minuscule proportion of firms' (Tabb, 1995: 32). Its much cited guarantee of lifetime employment was almost exclusively the preserve of male workers in the large companies, and was enjoyed even by them only to the age of 55, after which even such workers were normally deployed to smaller firms on lower wages. For around those large companies sat (and sit) a myriad of related sub-contracting firms, for whose workers no such guarantees were (or are) available: an entire secondary labour force or 'peripheral' sector, which then acted (and still to a degree acts) as a buffer, softening the impact of market instability on employment security for the more favoured core workers. It was not that large Japanese corporations had somehow managed to transcend the insecurities of capitalist labour markets. It was rather that they had created a system which passed those insecurities down the line to other companies and to other workers.

The result was that even in the most favourable period of postwar Japanese economic growth, the burdens of the employment guarantee enjoyed by core workers fell directly on the shoulders of other Japanese workers, and particularly on the shoulders of Japanese female workers, who were 'predominantly marginalized from core production jobs (not to speak of managerial positions) and relegated to super-exploitation in smaller manufacturing and service enterprises' (Burkett and Hart-Landsberg, 1996: 73) by a culture which was not only consensual but also highly patriarchal and anti-democratic. Women currently make up 40 per cent of the Japanese paid labour force, and their labour (as Price has noted) has 'been mobilized in a profoundly inhuman and discriminatory way from the Meiji period to now by aggressive labour market policies, whether they be to build "a strong army-rich nation" or an "economic superpower"' (Price, 1997: 270). For in truth the Japanese system of industrial relations was (and remains) less consensual than segmented. Japan has a dual labour market. Its whole economy rests on the existence of a vast 'secondary sector . . . of smaller and more labour-intensive enterprises' where 'jobs tend to be low-paying with poorer working conditions' (Chalmers, 1989: 29). Its whole economy contains too 'a strong patriarchal bent. Women and contract workers [have become] the 'other' upon whose shoulders . . . stand the workers in large, private enterprises' (Price, 1997: 272). And in consequence it is an economy whose industrial relations system can be accurately mapped onto a stereotypical view of Japanese cultural traits only by systematically disregarding the work situation and experience of probably 75 per cent of the labour force.

Moreover, even in the Japanese industrial relations system in its prime, core male workers were secure only for so long as they did not find themselves redeployed into that vast and unprotected peripheral sector; and it was the fear of that redeployment – and of the associated 'extraordinary power' of the Japanese personnel department 'in the recruitment and in the promotion of workers' (Lash and Urry, 1994: 68) – which then seems to explain the willingness of even core Japanese workers to work such long hours and to endure such high levels of job-related stress. For working hours and stress levels are extremely high (by comparison with other advanced capitalist economies) even among core Japanese workers. In fact it 'appears that the average Japanese works 500 more hours per year, or an average of ten more hours per week than their counterparts in France and Germany, the equivalent of three extra months per year' (Tabb, 1995: 144; also Sheridan, 1993 219–20), and labours under health-destroying levels of work-intensity, pressure and stress. After all, what other advanced capitalist economy needs (or indeed possesses, as Japan does) a National Defense Council for Victims of *Karoshi* (death through overwork)? (On this see Tabb, 1995: 140–52.) And in what other advanced capitalist economy could a government survey (in 1992) report that one in six male manufacturing employees then worked more than 3,100 hours annually, and add that to work more than 3,000 hours (or 60 hours a week) was potentially lethal (cited in *Time Magazine*, 31 January 1994: 9)?

What Japanese workers face is less a Confucian-inspired set of trust-based consensual work relationships than an extremely burdensome system of employer-dominated labour market regulation. Core Japanese workers are trapped within (and dependent upon) a single corporate employer. Peripheral workers are excluded from a predominantly corporately based system of welfare provision. So even for core workers – and certainly for peripheral workers – the Japanese system of industrial relations was hardly a proletarian paradise even before the recession of 1992; and it certainly has not been one since For as the Japanese industrial crisis deepened in the 1990s, much of the permanence of the industrial relations system began to erode. Large-scale corporate capital in Japan both intensified its pressure on the subcontracting periphery and experimented with compulsory redundancies and redeployments, even among core staff. The result has been a sharp rise in both the number of bankruptcies in the small and medium-size corporate sector and a scale of job loss which by December 1998 had given the Japanese economy the same level of officially recorded unemployment as that of the US (4.4 per cent) for the first time since Japanese postwar unemployment records began, 46 years before.

Seen in that light, more prosaic forces than Confucianism then help to explain the existence and character of the Japanese system of industrial relations; and much of what initially seemed cultural in origin has often been adequately explained in institutional terms (Johnson, 1982: 8; Drucker, 1988: 106; Wilks and Wright, 1991: 22–3; Weiss, 1993: 347; Iwaki, 1996: 162). Core workers in large Japanese companies have very strong material interests in cooperating with their immediate employers in technical change and intensive working practices, and in wage restraint and cost reduction, not least because of their company-specific skills and their dependence on years of service for wage rewards (Glazer, 1976: 877). Employers for their part have equally powerful material interests in sustaining such a set of sharp dependency relationships around the process of production, and in sustaining an image of Japanese culture in the minds of their workers that helps – in Fukuyama's terms – to sustain vertical over horizontal forms of worker allegiance. Indeed postwar Japanese employers have spent a disproportionate amount of corporate energy on creating and maintaining the cultural fiction of unanimity and consensus, and on tying that fiction to a particular definition of Japanese history and national identity; for the hegemony of that thought-system is central to their capacity to control and exploit the labour they employ. As Tabb has noted:

> the multifaceted ways Japanese companies instil and mobilize habits of deference and internalize work discipline are a major factor in higher Japanese productivity. Authoritarian demands and a norm of obedience is less a matter of Japanese character than the brilliantly constructed labor control system. The use of ritual and seemingly consensual processes are designed to force every possible ounce of work effort and rest on a system of rewards and punishment carefully calibrated to play workers off against each other, even as it encourages them to co-operate with each other in the context of individual loyalty to the company. Critics of the system have called it 'management by stress'. *(Tabb, 1995: 163)*

Indeed there is some evidence that the cultural system now paraded as uniquely and permanently Japanese – offered both to us by academic commentators and to Japanese workers by their personnel departments as a pre-industrial set of beliefs and practices which influenced Japanese industrial relations in a unique and consensual way from the outset – was in fact nothing of the kind. It was rather a conscious artefact of state policy in Japan both immediately before and immediately after the war, created under the tutelage of the national state bureaucracy and in the face of opposition from sections of the employing class, to head off and assuage a conventional set of class tensions between capital and labour: tensions which had first manifested themselves around 1905 and again after 1918, and which were at their most potent immediately after military defeat in 1945 (Strath, 1996: 160–93; also Johnson, 1982: 13–14). Linda Weiss, among others, has documented that process of creation in some detail (Weiss, 1993).

So far from believing that Japanese culture took its peculiar Confucianist form because Japan was (and is) uniquely free of class relations of a capitalist kind, it seems more sensible to understand Japanese cultural practices (at least as they manifest themselves in an industrial context) as an important device for labour control within the Japanese class struggle, as a set of institutions and practices created at moments when Japanese labour was weak but militant, and as ones designed to keep Japanese labour weak or contained during the long boom that followed. For it is worth noting that 'the practices of "lifetime" employment, seniority promotion . . . group bonuses, and so forth, did not become common until the 1950s, and represent the triumph of corporate power over what was in the early postwar period a powerful, militant, heavily communist trade union movement organized in US fashion (not enterprise unionism)' (Tabb, 1995: 154). It is also worth noting that it took a series of major *defeats* for the Japanese trade union movement in the late 1940s and early 1950s to clear the way for the creation of a Japanese employment system built on enterprise unions. And in this respect, the fact that only a quarter of Japanese workers subsequently found themselves 'in these lifetime employment pools in large corporations [was] an important aspect of the system' (Tabb, 1995: 158), because it helped to divide the Japanese working class by creating a labour aristocracy, workers in which were prone to identify with their companies rather than with less well-placed workers elsewhere in the network of firms on which the profitability of the large corporations ultimately depended. Which is why it seems wiser to emphasize the industrial and political *weakness* of organized labour – what Okimoto called 'the muted voice of labour' (Okimoto, 1989: 121; also Pempel, 1998: 14, 93–4) – rather than cultural variables *per se*, when explaining any uniquely 'consensual' dimensions of postwar Japanese industrial relations.

And in truth there was nothing particularly unusual about the emergence of a divided and stratified labour force of the Japanese kind, especially after 1945. Post-war labour movements across the advanced capitalist world were all shaped by the manner in which the intense and near universal class struggles of the late 1940s were played out; and the Japanese case was quite orthodox here. In the end, large-scale Japanese capital responded to the postwar militancy of its labour movement – as did employing classes in Western Europe and North America – by establishing a compromise with the better organized sections of the work-forces they faced (Itoh, 1990: 147). In the broadest sense, that compromise in Western Europe took the form of Keynesian welfare capitalism, and in the US of a systematic wage effort bargain with the AFL and CIO unions. In Japan, it took the form of lifetime employment and seniority wages for one Japanese worker in four (Pempel, 1998: 93–4, 109). The balance of cultural forces in those societies in the 1940s may have been one factor shaping the precise form that class compromise took in each national and regional context in turn; but it was class power (and not cultural forces *per se*) which made such a compromise necessary in the first place.

The general problem with cultural explanations of specific institutional phenomena is the asymmetry of the variables in play. Cultures are by their nature both general and persistent phenomena. Institutional practices are inexorably specific and ephemeral. This asymmetry is very evident in the Japanese case. It is difficult to use cultural variables to explain industrial relations practices which encompass only one Japanese worker in four; and it is equally difficult to use cultural variables to explain practices which even the 25 per cent consolidated only in the years after 1945. Demonstrating that the culture itself is only of recent origin helps to square the latter circle, but only at the cost of demonstrating that what has hitherto been referred to as a culture is probably better understood as some kind of dominant ideology or class project. And that is clearer still when we add to the montage data on recent developments within the 'Japanese employment system'. For there is clear evidence that when Japanese managers work abroad (in foreign subsidiaries of Japanese multinationals) they are highly selective in the dimensions of the system they export: long hours, single unions, and quality circles, but not generally lifetime employment guarantees or even seniority wages. And as we have already noted, there is clear evidence too, within Japan itself, of the progressive erosion of central elements of the employment system as the Asian recession of the 1990s deepens, with intensified pressure on subcontracting firms (and their workers) by large-scale Japanese companies, the movement of Japanese capital off-shore and even a degree of compulsory unemployment for core workers. If Japanese industrial relations practices were primarily culturally driven, globalization and recession should not so quickly have produced departures from defining features of the previous employment system; but those changes have occurred, and have done so in rapid order in the 1990s, to leave a clear question mark not only over the future of the Japanese model but also over the appropriateness of cultural forms of social explanation.

All of this suggests that the analytical move favoured by 'culturalists' in the Japanese industrial relations debate is, at best, overdone and, at worst, mistaken. It is simply not necessary to go to cultural factors to locate the role of Japanese labour in postwar economic growth, and it is certainly not necessary to go there first. The proper first move, in the manner of growth accounting, is rather to note that postwar Japanese growth (like that of the other Asian tiger economies) relied heavily on the mobilization of labour: on the increase in the size of the Japanese working class and the persistence of long working hours and intense working practices (Krugman, 1994b; Pilat, 1994: 57–8; Young, 1995; Crafts, 1997b: 78). That persistence was then best explained, quite prosaically, as the product of the weakness of Japanese labour as a social force, such that high rates of economic growth in Japan, as elsewhere in the capitalist world, then became (and remained) partly dependent on the continued ability of the local employing class to increase the size of the pool of available labour and to intensify its work processes. A certain sort of Japanese cultural matrix may then have played a role – in facilitating that intensification – but to the degree that it did it must be understood for what it was: a social construct of limited duration and viability, and a construct moreover which embodied a set of dominant class interests. As Clegg and his colleagues have it, 'much of Japanese "groupism" and "consensus" is not so much an effect of culture as of control from above' (Clegg et al., 1990: 42).

This in its turn suggests a series of linked conclusions about cultural forces and economic growth in the Japanese case. It suggests that the ideational system characteristically referred to as Japanese Confucianism is best understood as a dominant ideology. It also suggests that as a dominant ideology it did indeed work very well as a facilitator of economic growth (as culturalist explanations would expect); but it did so not because of its Confucianism but because of its *dominance*. Indeed it is not surprising that there should be a strong cultural 'voice' in the range of explanations of postwar Japanese economic growth available to us, since cultural variables have in fact been particularly effective as triggers to economic growth in the postwar Japanese case. But it is essential to grasp that this unique degree of effectiveness is *not* the result of any particular affinity between the peculiarly Japanese version of Confucian thought and the requirements of wealth creation; it is rather the result of the degree of dominance established across large swathes of Japanese society (including across sections of its labour force) by a Confucian-inspired ideational system which is so extensively underpinned by a set of material rewards for compliance with corporate requirements (and a set of sanctions for lack of compliance) that it has become a lived ideology within Japan, actively and persistently shaping individual definitions of self and of self-interest. In that compliance it is less the content of the ideational system than the severity and extensiveness of its orchestration which holds the key to its economic significance. Of course, the actual content of the Confucian system then has real effects on the ways individuals and institutions interact; but it does so only because of the distribution of social power that lies behind (and indeed explains) the pervasiveness of the ideology's presence in contemporary Japanese society. So to culturalists, at this stage of the argument, it is right to concede that ideas do influence economic growth; but it is also right to emphasize that such ideas do not influence growth in a vacuum of social power, and that their economic significance cannot be fully grasped without situating those ideas firmly in the power structures from which they emerge, and to whose continuance their persistent dissemination is vital.

The UK's 'loss of the industrial spirit'   Japan's economic performance has not been the only one to attract culturalist forms of explanation. The diminished fortunes of UK-based manufacturing industry in the twentieth century have also lent themselves to arguments of that kind; and the UK case is a valuable additional piece of evidence for us, because of the way the thrust of the culturalist explanation there supplements the Japanese one. For if we have *ended* our Japanese case by concluding that what is often described as a universally shared Japanese culture is probably best seen as some kind of dominant ideology, initially orchestrated by various sections of the Japanese ruling class in order to control and intensify the labour process, the UK case is interesting because it *starts* with an analysis of dominant ideas in the UK in the twentieth century, and makes no claim for their universality throughout society as a whole. As we have just seen, the thrust of the Japanese material (both that created by cultural historians and that created by their critics) is that the dominant ideas orchestrated by ruling groups after 1945, when combined with a set of other institutional and social processes, were extremely important in facilitating rapid rates of economic growth. The thrust of the UK material, as we shall now see, runs exactly counter to that, arguing that the ideas which came to dominate in governing circles in the UK after 1900 acted as barriers to rapid economic growth, and did so precisely through the institutional and social forces they helped to consolidate and sustain. The Japanese case, that is, encourages us to redefine our original question – of 'what is the impact of cultural variables on economic performance'? – to one concerned with the economic impact of dominant ideas, directly on institutional and social relationships and indirectly on growth. The UK case then helps us to see more precisely how such dominant ideas ought to be understood and analysed, and to judge the weight that should be allotted to them in explanations of different economic performances.

The literature on the dwindling competitiveness of UK-based manufacturing industry in the twentieth century is vast. In that literature, cultural arguments are only one strand; but they are an important and widely cited one none the less, not least because the sense they convey – that the UK now lacks entrepreneurial dynamism – is a very general one. It is one that runs through much of the popular commentary on why UK living standards are still low by northern European standards, and it is one that contributes to many serious comparative academic studies (not least those by Porter and by Fukuyama). For, as Aldcroft has rightly observed, 'general impressions, though inevitably imprecise, do suggest that British people do not rate the pursuit of economic progress as highly as the Americans, Germans or Japanese, and that enterprise and profits are not held in such high esteem as in some other countries' (Aldcroft, 1982: 58). It is almost as though – in the popular understanding of why the UK economy continues to underperform – there is a general sense that the contemporary UK lacks an appropriate 'growth culture', and that, as the Hudson Report on UK economic underperformance put it a quarter century ago, 'Britain's present economic difficulties . . . derive ultimately from a kind of archaism of the social and national psychology', from 'a habit of conciliation in social and personal relations for its own sake, a lack of aggression, a deference to what exists, a repeated and characteristic flight into pre-industrial, indeed pre-capitalist fantasies, a suspicion of "efficiency" as somehow common, a dislike for labour itself' (Hudson Report, 1974: 113). In fact recent commentators have often found a strange cultural paradox in the UK case: the combination of entrepreneurial inertia (and associated economic decline) with a breath-taking arrogance about the superiority of all things British. The British, it would appear, now combine economic underperformance with a culture of complacency and self-deception in a way which has no easy parallel elsewhere in the advanced capitalist world (for this, see Hampden-Turner and Trompenaars, 1993: 297–336).

In the light of that, it is not surprising that we find a clear space in the UK debate on relative economic performance for a coherent and full-developed culturalist voice; and it is a space that has been filled most effectively of late by Martin Weiner's highly praised study *English Culture and the Decline of the Industrial Spirit 1850–1980* (1981). The Weiner thesis – which Fukuyama among others adopted unreservedly and apparently without question (Fukuyama, 1995: 249–51) – is that UK economic underperformance in the twentieth century is best explained as the long-term consequence of a more general 'loss of the industrial spirit' since 1850, a loss whose roots lie in the emergence, in the last half of the nineteenth century, of a 'cultural *cordon sanitaire* encircling the forces of economic development: technology, industry, commerce'. The result was a 'mental quarantine' of a highly conservative kind, full of 'suspicion of material and technological development' and 'uncomfortable with progress' (Weiner, 1981: 5). According to Weiner, nineteenth-century industrial development in the UK was, at best, marked by a 'certain incompleteness' from which 'stemmed long-lasting cultural consequences' (ibid.: 7). The degree of social transformation it effected was more limited than at first appeared. What the UK experienced in the nineteenth century was not a complete capitalist revolution. Instead it saw 'the containment of capitalism within a patrician hegemony which never, either then or since, actively favoured the aggressive development of industrialism or the general conversion of the society to the latter's values and interests' (ibid.: 10). The social and political accommodation that Victorian industrialists made with the ruling aristocratic class, that is, left undisturbed 'a pervasive culture that was both non-industrial and anti-industrial' (Warwick, 1985: 103). As Weiner has it:

> Over the past century, then, high among the internal checks upon British economic growth has been a pattern of industrial behaviour suspicious of change, reluctant to innovate, energetic only in maintaining the status quo. The pattern of behaviour traces back in large measure to the culture absorption of the middle classes into a quasi-aristocratic elite, which nurtured both the rustic and nostalgic myth of an 'English way of life' and the transfer of interest and energy away from the creation of wealth. *(Weiner, 1981: 154)*

This notion that UK capitalism lost its ideological edge around 1900, through the social accommodation made by a rising bourgeoisie with a threatened aristocracy, has been reinforced in three ways by other writers sympathetic to a culturalist explanation of twentieth-century UK economic decline. Some have emphasized how that cultural accommodation was built around, not simply the glorification of a pre-industrial past, but the privileging of the UK's imperial present. The resulting cultural mix in the UK was thus not simply archaic, it was also preoccupied with the maintenance of Empire and the UK state's world role, with its associated downplaying of the importance and needs of locally based capital accumulation (Warwick, 1985: 103). Others have stressed too the important role of the UK's public schools in both cementing that social accommodation (by taking the sons of northern manufacturers and turning them into southern 'gentlemen') and in generalizing an anti-scientific educational culture and ethos throughout UK society, through their control of the educational syllabuses of the state system of mass education which emerged incrementally in the UK after 1918 (Mathieson and Bernbaum, 1988). And still others have insisted that a bourgeois-based 'growth culture' has been squeezed out of the UK's economic and political life not just by the dominance of aristocratic antipathies to industrialism *per se*, but also by the presence in UK ruling thought of a strong social democratic and welfarist antipathy to the inequalities associated with unregulated capitalist development (Barnett, 1986). The result, so the argument runs, is that UK industrial capitalists failed after 1900 to establish their own cultural hegemony. They allowed themselves to be boxed in between two broad anti-capitalist classes – one aristocratic, one proletarian – and to be drowned in a cultural nexus that was half-feudal, half-socialist, one which left the British 'never fully reconciled . . . to the virtue of the profit motive, profits being regarded as somewhat sinful' (Aldcroft, 1982: 52); and because they did, the UK allowed its leading role as a world manufacturer to slip inexorably away.

Needless to say, these claims have been fiercely contested by others in the UK 'declinist' debate. Partly that refutation has turned on the specification of factors other than cultural ones that are said to have triggered manufacturing underperformance; and partly it has turned on the historical accuracy and conceptual adequacy of the claims about the impact of cultural variables that are being made. It certainly looks as though the Weiner thesis systematically overstates the degree to which late-nineteenth-century northern industrialists did consciously and on a large scale buy in to a set of aristocratically dominated institutions and value systems. There is plenty of evidence of sons continuing to run family businesses after attending public school (and continuing to run them well) and, indeed, of strong elements of a scientific and technologically informed syllabus being delivered by those public schools from the 1890s (Rubinstein, 1993: 102–40; Edgerton, 1991a: 159–60). It also looks as though the Weiner thesis overstated the degree of anti-capitalist feeling evident in the nineteenth-century UK aristocracy, underestimated the strong bourgeois elements in *fin-de-siècle* UK ruling thought, and understated the degree to which aristocratic cultures in more successful capitalist economies – most notably those in Germany and Japan – contained even more stridently anti-capitalist and pro-imperialist strands than the aristocratic culture in the UK. After all, the UK aristocracy by 1900 had a century-long record of involvement in capitalist agriculture, industry and commerce; UK culture was as much shaped by Adam Smith, Charles Darwin and Samuel Smiles as by Coleridge and Carlyle; and UK culture had no depth of anti-capitalism to match the strictures of a Nietzsche or a Marx (Rubinstein, 1993: 52–8, 69). And if the rhetoric of UK social democracy was one that privileged the distribution of wealth over the creation of wealth – was full of the anti-capitalist 'New Jerusalem' romanticism that Barnett attributes to it – the practice of Labour governments in relation to wealth creation was very different. Both the 1945–51 and the 1964–70 Labour governments clearly prioritized industrial investment over welfare provision; yet they could not by themselves prevent the steady erosion of the world standing of the UK's manufacturing base.

All this has been enough to persuade at least some prestigious commentators on the UK's economic performance to discount cultural explanations altogether – to see them as a distraction from the more serious business of addressing the institutional arrangements (and underpinning patterns of class power) which explain why UK manufacturing industry has suffered such low levels of investment in new plant and equipment for more than a century now. They at least have been prepared to extract from the inadequacies of the Weiner thesis a general assertion that an economic or material explanation is always to be preferred to a cultural or sociological one (on this, Hobsbawm, 1968: 187), and by implication at least have downplayed the importance of ideas as shapers of economic performance both in the UK and beyond. And yet – given the pervasiveness, in the more reflective sections of UK society, of this sense that something ideational is going on (and is going wrong) in the contemporary UK – such a total rejection of the importance of cultural factors seems misplaced. For in the UK after 1890, just as in Japan after 1945, it would appear that the ideas that sat in people's heads (both the things they valued and privileged and the total stock of categories and stories with which they defined themselves, their situation and their past) did at the very least act as a filter through which more material forces influenced their behaviour, and did have a part to play in producing slightly different responses from them to what were broadly a similar set of material experiences. So rather than discount totally the impact of ideas on growth performance, perhaps the more productive way forward (at least for those of us who share Hobsbawm's broad theoretical approach) is to recognize that the centre of gravity of dominant patterns of thought does vary between national economies (and does vary over time within each national economy in turn), and then to establish a materialist explanation of the ways in which such dominant ideological packages influence economic performance. The trick, that is, for us at least, is not to throw the 'ideological' baby out with the 'cultural' bath water, by discounting the role of ideas altogether. It is rather to create a non-culturally based explanation of how sets of ideas come to be in people's heads in the first place, and of why the stock of ideas, concepts and values available to workers or managers in one place at one time is different from the stock available to other workers and managers at other places and at other times – and then to find a way to relate both those explanations to the analysis of economic performance.

The question, of course, is how to do that: and here the UK experience offers valuable guidelines. It suggests that the best way to relate cultures to economic performance is to link ideas to classes, and to see cultures as layered sets of class ideologies sedimented over time. For as Rubinstein has correctly argued, what Weiner saw as an all-pervasive aristocratic embrace

drowning late-nineteenth-century UK entrepreneurship is better understood as the ideational consequence of a changing set of relationships
between a number of entrepreneurial social classes: in the specifics of the
UK case a changing set of relationships between 'three rival elite groups
whose interaction with each other, and with the majority of the population,
constituted the substance of modern British history – the landed elite, the
commercial-based London elite . . . and the northern manufacturing elite'
(Rubinstein, 1993: 140). The key to understanding the weakness of the
UK's manufacturing industry in the twentieth century, for Rubinstein, is to
grasp how limited was the economic and social power of that northern elite,
even at the height of the economy's mid-century period of world domination, and certainly thereafter (Rubinstein, 1993: 24–5). The key for *us*, in
going that one stage further in our understanding of the impact of ideational
variables on economic performance, is to supplement Rubinstein's class
analysis with an ideological mapping of the manner in which those changing social relationships triggered, among other things, the layering and re-
layering of popular culture and elite understandings.

For at the end of the nineteenth century each of those social groupings,
and indeed the other classes on their edge as well (both aristocratic and proletarian), demonstrated, as social classes invariably do, a certain 'idea prone-
ness', a certain propensity to identify with, and to articulate, particular sets
of values, categories and explanatory systems. Once articulated, of course,
those idea systems then came to possess an autonomy and trajectory of their
own, which allowed them to disseminate into the thinking of other social
classes and to persist in popular consciousness long after their originating
classes had vanished or moved on. But the emergence and original impact
of such ideas was none the less closely associated with the social power of
their originating or 'sponsoring' class. So in the ideological market-place of
UK society by 1900 there is clear evidence of a distinctly aristocratic culture
which combined paternalism towards the lower orders and disdain for trade
and industry with an enthusiasm for the traditional institutions of Church
and state. That aristocratic culture mingled with a more conventionally
bourgeois culture of a liberal kind, one built around an enthusiasm for the
rights of private property, market exchange and the pursuit of profit; and
both battled for ideological space and supremacy with an as yet underdeveloped set of broadly proletarian ideologies which sought to regulate (or
even, in extreme versions, to replace) the property base of aristocratic and
bourgeois power within the economy through some form of state control or
ownership. The relative strength of those ideas – both at elite level and in
the general populace – shifted over time, rising and falling then (as now) in
line with the social and economic strength of the classes most closely iden-
tifying with each. Which is why what began as a 'loss of the industrial spirit'
(if that is what actually happened) has more properly to be understood (as
in truth Weiner himself attempted to say) as the ideational consequence of
inadequate bourgeois power, as a twentieth-century 'failure of the UK's
industrial bourgeoisie'.

Yet there has been no twentieth-century bourgeois failure in that sense. For where Weiner's analysis misleads – and where his critics are stronger – is less in his underlying propensity to relate ideas to classes, or to explain ideological dominance in terms of class power (all of which is fine), and more in the detail of the dominant ideology specified, and in the associated understandings of class relationships implied. In the Weiner analysis, the UK declined because an anti-capitalist culture drowned out an emergent pro-capitalist one. One culture, that is, entirely replaced another. Yet in truth – in the UK as elsewhere – dominant patterns of thought were actually layered mixtures of competing ideologies; and in that layering bourgeois rather than aristocratic thought remained dominant throughout. There were (and indeed there remain to this day) vestiges of both a pre-capitalist aristocratic and a post-capitalist social democratic/labourist ideology in both popular consciousness and elite opinion in the UK; and those vestiges presumably do help to make UK society slightly less growth-oriented, and slightly more socially compassionate, than those of any competing economies which lack either an aristocratic past or a strong social democratic labour movement. But from as early as 1900 the aristocratic elements in UK ruling and popular culture (and since 1979 even social democratic ways of thinking) have been (and are now) only minor strands in both popular and ruling thought. The UK is not a society whose culture is predominantly aristocratic, or even (as in postwar Scandinavia) social democratic, since the centre of gravity of dominant ideas in the UK this century has been, and remains, not so much pre-capitalist as *early* capitalist. Weiner notwithstanding, throughout the twentieth century the UK has been predominantly a *liberal* society with a liberal culture; and indeed it has been liberal ever since – as Keynes put it – 'Ricardo's doctrine conquered England as completely as the Holy Inquisition conquered Spain' (Keynes, 1936: 32) in the 1830s and 1840s. Liberal categories, liberal assumptions and liberal policy prescriptions run through its entire common sense; and liberal ideas about how economy, state and society should interact have particularly shaped the self-definitions and understandings of the world held by the leaders of UK industry as a whole for more than a century now.

Weiner was therefore quite wrong in the substance of his claims. It is not that the UK manufacturing sector declined in the twentieth century through some aristocratically induced 'loss of the industrial spirit'. It is rather that it did so as its dominant classes failed to break with their nineteenth-century identification with *laissez faire*. As David Marquand put it: 'having made one cultural revolution in the seventeenth and eighteenth century . . . Britain has been unable to make another in the twentieth century. In the age of the industrial laboratory, the chemical plant, and later of the computer, she stuck to the mental furniture of the age of steam' (Marquand, 1988: 8). It is not that UK manufacturing declined because UK ruling thought retreated. UK manufacturing declined because UK ruling thought became stuck.

Culture, class and power

What the UK experience suggests, therefore, is that the culture surrounding capital accumulation in any one capitalist economy has to be understood as the result of long periods of ideological sedimentation; that is, it has to be understood as the product of a long and complex history in which particular ideas were laid down one upon another, like rocks settling into a landscape over vast millennia. Some of those ideas (particularly the pre-capitalist ones) are likely to have been nationally or regionally specific; but the ideas triggered around industrialization itself (from nationalism and liberalism to social democracy and Marxism) definitely were not. How those ideas all settle down together, into particular national mixes, is then largely to be understood as the product of the struggles between social groups (for economic control, political power and cultural dominance) in each national capitalism in turn. The result will be slightly different in each case – national cultures will have different ideological centres of gravity – because the class patterns and ideational legacies operating in each do differ a little; but the result will only be slightly different, because capitalist industrialization imposes a common agenda everywhere, and invites (and triggers) a broadly similar range of responses. Capitalism comes in certain 'models', that is; but all the models are recognizably capitalist.

There is a real sense in which the choice between models of capitalism with which we are concerned in this book is to a degree a choice between dominant cultures. It is certainly the case that the various models can be differentiated (both between examples of particular models, and between broad model camps) in part on a cultural dimension. UK capitalism in the 1980s may have been 'liberal-market-based' rather than 'trust-based', but its characteristic institutional structures showed far greater residues of both a social democratic concern with welfare and an aristocratic paternalism towards the poor than did those in the other great liberal capitalist economy, the US, which possessed neither an eighteenth-century aristocratic past nor a strong twentieth-century social democratic presence. And both societies were more liberal than either Germany or Japan, where, as economies which developed later, liberal ideas (and the associated middle class) were correspondingly weaker and a military-nationalist aristocracy stronger. Germany, not Japan, consolidated a strong labour movement too: so social (and Christian) democratic welfarism left a strong institutional and cultural legacy there which had (and has) no Japanese equivalent. Cultures, that is, do figure in the determinants of economic performance; but they do so only in a fusion with the social classes who originally articulated them and with the institutional structures which their presence and strength are able to establish and defend.

Three conclusions on the place of cultural factors in economic explanation seem to rise from the two case studies now completed.

1   The first is that the relation between culture and economic performance is an extremely difficult one to pin down; and in its difficulty it can
often degenerate into crude caricature and circular argumentation. If used
loosely, the term 'culture' implies a set of values and practices which are of
long standing, which persist without change, and which apply universally
throughout a society. Yet if that is what a culture is, then it simply cannot
explain patterns of economic activity which differ from one period to
another, or which apply to some sectors of an economy but not to the rest.
As Ozaki correctly has it, there is something profoundly wrong with a form
of explanation which attributes a general work ethic to Japanese society in
order to explain the postwar success of the Japanese car industry, yet has
nothing to say about why 'the same Japanese apparently lose' that work ethic
'once they step into the petro-chemical industry' (Ozaki, 1991: 83). There
is also something wrong with the argument that culture holds the key to
performance, when the culture remains constant but the performance dips.
It may suit a certain kind of literary historian to go to a series of cultural
products – normally drawn, it should be said, from 'high' culture rather
than 'low' – to create an image of a national culture; but the very methodology leaves unexamined how representative that culture is of wider popular
thought (or of the thought patterns of key economic groups), and does not
of itself show the precise link which transform general ideas into specific
triggers to economic action. It just leaves a great gap between culture and
performance, with the causal link implied or asserted but not demonstrated;
and so ultimately it can neither demonstrate the direction of causality nor
indeed prove the existence of a causal relationship at all.

2   The second general concluding point is this: that although the resulting temptation for many economic analysts is to discount cultural variables
altogether, that inclination needs to be resisted. For intuitively we all know
that national cultural differences do exist – that Japanese social practices are
not the same as British social practices, that American ways of treating the
poor are not those of Scandinavia, and so on. What we need instead – as a
replacement for a total cynicism about cultural variation – is a methodology
which enables us to move closer to any link that might exist between general
social ideas and individual economic action. That methodology, as both case
studies suggest, is one that must begin by disaggregating cultures into their
component ideological formations, must then situate those ideological formations in the complex historical stories which underpin their development,
and must end by grounding those disaggregated formations into the institutional structures they inform and into the social classes with which they
are most closely associated. That class–ideology link is itself a complex one
to unpack – full of difficulties and controversies – but it at least offers a
mechanism for linking ideas to economic performance through the social
actors whose economic interaction is the ultimate source of economic
growth.

3   The third concluding point is this. Both the Japanese and UK case studies suggest that the potency of ideas as economic forces turns not simply on the nature of the social classes with whom those ideas are associated. It turns also on the power of the classes themselves. And because it does, it demonstrates yet again that the ultimate responsibility for different patterns of economic performance does not lie primarily with labour. Labour forces, labour institutions, even entire labour movements, have never thus far enjoyed such a degree of economic, social and political power that they have been in a position to exercise cultural power as well. Economic performance does seem to be affected – to a degree which is hard to measure but also hard to deny – by the ideas which dominate in particular capitalist economies. But those ideas have so far rarely been ideas primarily developed and articulated by labour movements. Sweden in the heyday of the Swedish model is perhaps the exception. Elsewhere the ideas that have dominated capitalist economic performance have been the ideas of the dominant classes; and the institutional arrangements surrounding the processes of production have been largely defined and designed by them. In the end, therefore, neither the level of skills prevalent in a labour force nor the ideas which prevail within it are largely of its own creation and control. The principal classes shaping institutions and ideas have been employing classes. The principal social force has been capital, not labour. It is to capital, therefore – to its industrial organization and its political practice – that in our pursuit of the sources of economic performance we must now turn.

6

The Organization of Capital in the Pursuit of Growth

As we saw in more detail in chapters 2 and 3, there is more in dispute between the various models of capitalism than simply the power of their labour forces, or the nature of their ruling ideas. In fact neither the role of labour nor the impact of cultural forces are the prime definers of particular systems of capitalist organization and governance. Rather, the major capitalist models can be distinguished, one from another, primarily by the manner in which, within them, capital is organized and the state is deployed. The role of the state as an economic agent within particular national capitalisms will be discussed in chapter 7. The focus of this chapter is on company organization and management and on the different ways in which companies relate to each other, to their sources of finance and to those they employ.

The Centre-Left critique of liberal capitalism

It has been a consistent theme of recent centre-left critiques of the liberal capitalist model of capitalism that its forms of corporate governance are one of its two main sources of competitive weakness (state policy, as we shall see in chapter 7, being the other). The critique has characteristically taken one of two routes, each leading from a sense that liberal capitalist ways of running the economy rely too heavily on *market* institutions to link companies together and make far too little use of *networks* for that purpose.

The first form of the critique concentrates on the relationship between industry and finance: a relationship which is specified as defective in one of at least three ways:

1   Liberal capitalist economies are understood as linking sources of investment to their major companies primarily through the use of stock markets rather than banks. In such economies, so the argument goes, large companies seeking new funds raise equity capital rather than bank loans. They leave bank-lending to the small-firm sector; and in the process they create a logic of short-term profit-taking at the heart of the model. For equity holders require strong and immediate dividend payments if they are not to sell stock; and corporate managers must generate these dividends to avoid falls in share prices and resulting takeovers. Systems of investment funds based on stock markets, that is, have a propensity to generate 'exit' rather than 'voice' relationships between financial and manufacturing institutions (Zysman, 1983; Pollin, 1996; Watson and Hay, 1998: 411; Blackburn, 1999: 8–10). That in its turn gives liberal capitalist economies a tendency to short-termism in investment decision-making; and short-termism is said to be a major barrier to the kinds of investment necessary to the protection of long-term competitive strength. This argument, as we saw in chapter 2, lay at the core of Hutton's explanation of twentieth-century UK economic decline (see above, pp. 50–1). It also constitutes a key element in Porter's more multi-faceted explanation of US economic underperformance in the 1980s: that postwar US (and, by extension, UK) industry suffered from 'fluid capital', while Japanese and German industry enjoyed 'dedicated capital', and that these differences in the 'external' systems of capital allocation in the various countries then had (and continue to have) important 'internal' effects on managerial practices and corporate performance indicators (for similar arguments, see Ellsworthy, 1985; Pollin, 1996: 270–76; Hollingsworth, 1997b: 292–30).

2   The insertion or existence of money markets between locally based manufacturing firms and locally based banking systems is then said both to reflect and to exacerbate a competitively damaging gap between industry and finance, which quickly becomes self-sustaining. Locally based banks do not invest heavily in leading local companies. They invest instead in smaller businesses (from whom they extract burdensome rates of return) and they invest abroad, locking their own profitability into a systematic dependence on the competitive success of foreign firms and overseas labour forces. The supply of bank-based finance to such overseas competitors then hits locally based manufacturing industry in two ways. It denies local industry a bank-driven incentive to modernize; and it opens a gap between levels of productivity and performance at home and levels of productivity and performance in the better-financed economies abroad. The result is that locally based banks have progressively less and less incentive to invest at home, since to do so is to put bank assets into industries whose lack of competitiveness bank absenteeism has already helped to create (on this, see Coates, 1994: 51–4; Hutton, 1994: 110–31).

3   The cumulative effect of bank-based capital export and stock-market-induced short-termism is then said to be the creation of an inter-

locked system of path-dependent growth. Liberal capitalist economies gather to themselves manufacturing sectors suffering long-term investment shortfalls, and settle onto growth paths in which competitiveness progressively depends on low wages and long hours, while economies based on close industry–bank links settle onto pathways in which investment in manufacturing plant and equipment, in R&D and in training, is high, so enabling their competitiveness to be based on the development and exploitation of cutting-edge technologies. And that, we are told, is a large part of the reason why – in the postwar period – the US economy saw the gap between itself and its major competitors shrink, why the UK economy went into rapid competitive free-fall, and why economies of the German and Japanese kind so flourished. UK banks and UK industry in particular stayed apart for far too long, and UK fund managers came to demand far too high a rate of short-term dividend payment; and because they did, the UK's manufacturing sector in the postwar period experienced a level of underinvestment from which its German competitor was systematically free – with obvious and predictable consequences for relative rates of growth. For German banks, so the argument runs, provide for the industries they support investments that are 'neither short-term nor arms-length'. In Germany, 'as in the case of the Japanese *zaibatsu*, bank representatives bec[o]me involved in the affairs of their client companies over prolonged periods of time' and because they do, they '(like their Japanese counterparts) provide a degree of stability in financing that permits German companies to take a longer-term perspective in their investments than American market equity-financed companies' (Fukuyama, 1995: 214). That at least is the claim.

This particular form of the argument, pointing the finger of responsibility at financial institutions, has been *the* major strand in recent centre-left arguments on twentieth-century UK economic performance. Similar arguments can be found in the US debate, but the issue of 'industry and finance' has mainly been mobilized to explain differences in postwar economic growth rates *within Europe*, between two of its leading economies. In the US literature on the deficiencies of liberal capitalism, by contrast, the main point of comparative reference (as we saw earlier) has been Japan rather than Germany; so the central focus of the critique of corporate capital developed by the US Centre-Left has been slightly different. US corporate capital has been criticized not just (or even primarily) for its inadequate articulation of industry and finance. Rather it has been criticized for the general inferiority of its forms of corporate organization and practice when compared with the more successful wing of large-scale Japanese business; and here again the lines of argument have run in three linked but distinguishable ways.

1   For some commentators what has distinguished (and strengthened) Japanese corporate capital has been its collaborative nature – its status as 'alliance capitalism' (Gerlach, 1992). The basic claim here, as we saw in detail earlier (pp. 59–62), is that 'the core idea underlying Japanese-style

capitalism is *networking*, while the essence of . . . US-style capitalism is found in the concept of *market* as defined by Adam Smith' (Nakatani, 1995: 43: also Gerlach, 1992: 3). US corporations relate to each other – as to their sources of finance – as independent companies answerable to distinct bodies of share-holders. Japanese companies do not. In Japan, large companies are (to an unparalleled degree) linked through interlocking share-holdings into distinct groupings, each of which possesses its own main bank. These corporate holdings and internal banking supports then prevent external share-holders from exercizing any significant influence on corporate policy, with the result that the cost of capital to large Japanese companies has been low throughout the postwar period (when compared with the cost of capital faced by foreign companies), that Japanese companies have been freer than their US counterparts to take a longer-term view of how and when to cover their capital costs, and that the rate of return required of them (even in the long term) has been commensurately lower. Indeed there is clear evidence that Japanese rates of return on industrial capital have been *poor* by leading international standards throughout the postwar period – averaging 8.6 per cent in 1991, compared with a world average of 15.1 per cent and figures for the US and UK of 19.1 and 20.2 per cent respectively; yet, of course, it was Japanese industrial capital (and not its US or UK industrial rivals) that achieved rapid rates of economic growth in the three decades before 1991. Japan's corporate networking systems have been offered by many scholars as the key factor to explain that vital paradox.

2   For other scholars of Japanese corporate capital, however, the competitive strength of postwar Japanese industry has lain less in the *external* relationship of company to company than in the *internal* structure and workings of the typical Japanese firm. Analysts have characteristically contrasted American, European and Japanese corporate structures – variously labelling them the 'M' form, the 'H' and the 'J' (Fruin, 1992: 302) – and have seen in the less hierarchical structures of what Fruin called the 'Japanese enterprise system' an enhanced capacity to borrow, adapt and develop technologies initiated elsewhere. Japanese firms – so the argument runs – characteristically avoid a sharp division 'between information-processing and decision-making on the one hand, and operational implementation on the other', and so possess an enhanced capacity to mobilize shop-floor skills and commitment, 'providing incentives for wide-ranging learning among a relatively large body of employees' (Aoki, 1994: 13, 23). The information systems and incentive structures within large Japanese companies are said to leave those companies particularly flexible in response to market volatilities, and particularly equipped to generate innovative forms of work organization and resource deployment (of which Toyota's *kanban* or 'just-in-time' production system of the 1970s is often presented as both archetypal and emblematic). And the subcontracting networks underpinning the larger Japanese firm are said to have combined with the horizontal information flows and job flexibility characteristic of Japan's system of 'human

capitalism' (Ozaki, 1991) to facilitate what became the typical Japanese marketing and production strategy in its period of postwar growth: of first 'conquering the low end of the market with volume and price competition, and then moving up through "diversified quality competition" ' (Lash and Urry, 1994: 72) – Japanese car sales to the US after 1970 being a classic case in point.

3   The experience of the US car industry was in fact more than just a case in point. As we saw in chapter 2, the speed and severity of the Japanese onslaught on the US car market after 1973 triggered a more general analysis of US industrial deficiencies – a third theme for us here – one that argued for the need for a paradigm shift from *mass* to *lean* production if US corporate capital was to withstand the Japanese challenge to its dominant position in world commodity markets. For the third strand in the eulogy on Japanese capitalism which emerged in the US management literature in the 1980s was that set by Womack et al.'s study *The Machine that Changed the World*: that Western capitalism, which had once moved from craft production to mass production (and in the process from UK to US world economic leadership), now stood on the brink of a third phase, one which would be characterized by Japanese economic leadership unless US corporate capital shifted its production methods (Womack), reset its attitudes to the training and skilling of labour (Reich) and abandoned its passion for untrammelled managerial control (Lazonick). We met this argument in detail in chapter 2. Japanese corporate capital, not US corporate capital, had – we were told – found the forms of corporate governance, the structures of corporate control and the forms of labour management vital to competitive success in a new economic environment; and because it had, future competitive success depended, more than anything else, on replacing liberal capitalist forms of corporate structure and behaviour with more cooperative forms of a broadly Japanese type. Lean production, we were told, will in the end 'supplant both mass production and the remaining outposts of craft production in all areas of industrial endeavour to become the standard global production system of the twenty-first century'; and when it does 'that world will be a very different, and a much better, place' (Womack et al., 1990: 287).

Controlling for catch-up and convergence

The largest single weakness in much of this literature is that (notwithstanding the value of many of its individual insights, on which we shall comment favourably later) in general terms it claims more than its data base will legitimately allow. For the general thrust of many centre-left reflections on the different postwar performances of capitalist models (as we have just seen) is that those differences are to be explained primarily by reference to institutional variations between the models; the definite implication is that, once locked on to those divergent growth paths by such institutional differences, these economic records will continue to diverge until and unless major institutional change is effected in the liberal capitalist case. These are very big claims indeed; and in making them it is significant that critics of market-based ways of orchestrating capital accumulation characteristically focus their fire only on the inferior *rate* of productivity growth in the US after 1945. They tend to discount the full significance of the superior *level* of US productivity performance, which continues to be demonstrated in the comparative growth figures on which they draw; it is a tendency to emphasize rates rather than levels of productivity, which, it should be noted, was common among growth economists and economic historians right through to the 1970s (Broadberry and Crafts, 1990: 386). It is also significant that, when inviting US policy-makers to learn from (and copy) German or Japanese corporate practices, centre-left critics of current US deficiencies tend to make insufficient allowance for the degree to which postwar German and Japanese economic success might derive from earlier and equivalent processes of learning and copying.

In their enthusiasm for bank-led capital accumulation and alliance capitalism, many Centre-Left analysts do not give sufficient weight to (or adequately control for) the possibility that what lies behind different postwar economic performances is not the superiority of one economy's institutional arrangements to those of another, but rather the *different* position that each economy occupied after 1945 on a broadly common growth trajectory. They do not give sufficient weight, that is, to the possibility that growth differences between advanced capitalist economies in the postwar period might themselves be explained by the positioning of those economies at different points on their own long-term growth trajectory – to what Hall and Jones, following Barro and Sali-I-Martin, term their 'transition dynamics' (Hall and Jones, 1997: 173) – and that the speed of any one trajectory might be (and almost certainly was) influenced by its interaction with others. The nature of that interaction is a highly contentious (and ultimately deeply theoretical) issue. It might, as neo–classical growth theory would suggest, be a broadly positive one, bringing higher growth rates to underdeveloped economies as factors redeploy. It might alternatively, as post-Keynesian and Marxist theories would suggest, be broadly negative, amplifying existing growth differences through processes of cumulative causation and the 'development of underdevelopment'. But no matter how in the end the relationship between economies is theorized, that relationship exists; and because it does, any attempt to isolate organizational sources of permanent competitive advantage must first control for it. It must control for that dimension of existing (and recent) growth differences caused by interaction between economies at different points in their own long-term growth trajectories; and it must at least allow for the possibility that differences in growth performance might diminish over time (that there might be a *convergence* of growth rates), as temporarily rapidly growing models catch up with (and then come to resemble) their more staid (but historically more successful) competitors.

It is this sensibility to the impact of convergence and catch-up that the more enthusiastic advocates of trust-based forms of capitalism characteristically fail to demonstrate. In mobilizing evidence from the postwar growth record of advanced capitalist economies to support their push for bank reform, corporate networking and active industrial policies, they claim too much when (and to the degree that) they imply that *all* the growth differences thrown up by the comparative statistical data can be attributed to such institutional arrangements. They certainly never systematically address the contrary possibility – that in reality there is nothing significant to explain in the figures on postwar growth differences between national economies – that the rapid growth achieved by certain economies and models after 1945 was simply a temporary phenomenon associated with their relative backwardness in technology and use of labour (Feinstein, 1990: 291–2), a growth that would necessarily give way to a common (and lower) rate of growth across the entire capitalist bloc as soon as full convergence of production modes occurred – as soon, that is, as catch-up was complete. Nor do the more enthusiastic centre-left critics of liberal capitalism normally concede that, even if the situation is more as they describe it, even if convergence and catch-up are at best only part of the postwar story, it still remains the case that their presence requires a resetting of the central claim, to make allowance for the degree of convergence and catch-up running through the different growth performances of different capitalist models which is being used as evidence in support of institutional change. For in truth there is a postwar catch-up and convergence story, and in assessing the past strengths and weaknesses of particular capitalist models we need to allow for the following dimensions of it.

1   We need to be able to account first for the existence of *initial postwar US productivity leadership*, for the manner in which, from a position of nineteenth-century industrial leadership – when its labour productivity was higher than elsewhere in the emerging capitalist world economy – the UK economy between 1870 and 1913 experienced convergence with a number of Western European economies and complete catch-up (and bypassing) by the US economy: the US economy established a very large (28 per cent) lead over the UK in levels of aggregate labour productivity by 1913, pulling away in the process from the average (and much lower) figure on labour productivity achieved by the other fifteen leading capitalist economies. We need to note, and be able to explain, the manner in which that US lead in labour productivity was then further extended by inter-war dislocation, and the differential impact of the Second World War, such that by 1950, 'after recovery from the most severe after-effects of the wartime destruction and dislocation, the average relative productivity levels of the other [leading capitalist] economies had sunk from 54 to 43 per cent of the American level' (Abramovitz and David, 1996: 28).

2   We need to be able to account too for the *unprecedented degree of both catch-up and convergence in levels of aggregate labour productivity (and asso-*

ciated income per head) that was such a feature of the capitalist section of the world economy between 1950 and 1973. Capitalism's postwar 'golden age' actually witnessed an unprecedented degree of catch-up with the world leader, in that during those years levels of labour productivity in the leading fifteen economies closed on the US level at a rate of 1.8 per cent per annum, even though the US was experiencing its most rapid period of productivity growth. Indeed, in this regard at least, the contrast with the pre-war period could hardly have been starker here, in that 'from 1870 to 1950 13 of the advanced capitalist economies . . . were falling behind US productivity levels, whereas 15 of them were catching up on the USA after 1950' (Maddison, 1995b: 45). The capitalist sections of the world economy also experienced unprecedented *convergence* during its 'golden age', both in that 'the variance of their productivity levels declined more rapidly and with greater consistency across [those fifteen] countries than ever before' (Abramovitz, 1994a: 86), and 'because the process of catch-up now involved somewhere between 20 and 40 countries, depending on the criteria used' (Baumol, 1994: 64). Indeed by extending the period, key new players in Asia can also be made to join that list: not just Japan, but by 1992 South Korea, Taiwan and Thailand, which were by then (as we noted in chapter 1) the fastest growing of the Asian economies, taking 1950 as the base year (Maddison, 1995b: 22).

3   We also need to be able to account for the pattern of *much more ambiguous convergence and catch-up after 1973*, when the capitalist sections of the world economy witnessed both a significant slowing of the rate of convergence and catch-up of levels of labour productivity among leading capitalist economies after 1973 and the already mentioned arrival of a second wave of new industrializing economies based predominantly in South-east Asia. World capitalism after 1980 witnessed the persistence of an absolute US lead in aggregate labour productivity, in the 1990s a narrowing of the UK's productivity gap with Germany, and a more general European convergence, such that by the early 1990s the continent possessed 'a "core" group of nine countries with a very similar per capita income all within +/−8.0 per cent of the median, whereas in 1950 only two were' (Crafts and Toniolo, 1996: 5), whose existence we need also to be able to explain.

4   And finally, we need to be able to account for the existence of both *national and sectoral variations in postwar economic performance*. We need to recognize and explain the way in which, even in the 'golden age' of rapid convergence and catch-up, not all national economies were involved. For the vast majority of such economies, differences in performance persisted over time − rich economies stayed rich, poor economies stayed poor; only some economies were able so to alter their productivity performance as to join what has been termed the postwar 'convergence club' (Baumol, 1994: 64). And even among the economies which did effect significant degrees of

catch-up and convergence, not all their sectors demonstrated similar capacities to narrow the leader–follower performance gap. Nor was convergence consistent across all the measures of productivity performance.* These national and sectoral variations also need to be explained.

One way to effect that explanation – and at the same time to dismiss the importance of differences in capitalist models – is to follow the route adopted by Feinstein and by Krugman (the Krugman argument that surfaced briefly in chapter 3): denying the existence of a 1950s European 'economic miracle' or a 1980s Asian one by reducing the entire postwar growth story to one of nothing but catch-up and convergence, and the economic growth miracles to simply an issue of 'the temporary advantages of backwardness'. That is certainly how Feinstein handled German *and* Japanese postwar growth, by insisting that 'a very large part of the discrepancy in economic performance of the postwar years can be explained in terms of the lower level from which the fast-growing followers started their advance' and by claiming that 'the rapid rates achieved in Germany [and] Japan . . . owed far more to their low starting point than to any special merits of their economic and social arrangements' (Feinstein, 1990: 291). Likewise Krugman has more recently argued – in a highly controversial and widely disputed piece (Krugman, 1994b) – that there was nothing particularly special about forms of capital organization in South Korea, Taiwan, Singapore and Hong Kong that could account for their recent spectacular economic growth. Basing his case on the careful growth accounting of Young and others, he has insisted that the remarkable rates of economic growth achieved by the Asian tiger economies prior to 1997 simply reflected their effective mobilization of hitherto unused economic resources in a one-off growth spurt that would inevitably slow down as the mobilization was exhausted. 'Asian growth,' Krugman wrote, 'like that of the Soviet Union in its high-growth era, seems to be driven by extraordinary growth in inputs like labor and capital rather than by gains in efficiency', such that 'once one accounts for the role of rapidly growing inputs into these countries' growth, one finds little left to explain' (Krugman, 1996b: 175).

* Stephen Broadberry has demonstrated clearly that European convergence on the US was *not* a product of superior productivity performance by European-based industry, that, on the contrary, from as long ago as 1870 'labour productivity in US manufacturing has fluctuated around a level of about twice the British level, while German manufacturing labour productivity has fluctuated around a level broadly equal to the British level' (Broadberry, 1997: 337). The Japanese catch-up, by contrast, did involve improvements in manufacturing productivity which were in excess of improvements in the Japanese economy as a whole: improvements which have now put Japan ahead of Europe (and close to the US) in output per worker, although only level with Germany in output per hour worked. (Japanese workers, as we saw in chapter 5, work many more hours.) In fact, as these data on manufacturing productivity suggest, the Japanese and European experiences of post-war catch-up and convergence were very differently grounded. European catch-up largely rested on rapid total factor productivity (TFP) growth, whereas a significant part 'of the Japanese growth came from the accumulation of human and physical capital' (van Ark and Crafts, 1996: 4).

Yet in truth there was still much to explain, as Krugman's many critics have been quick to point out. Certainly there was for Japan, where, as Krugman himself conceded, the postwar growth performance seems to have involved both 'high rates of input growth and . . . high rates of efficiency growth', and where, in consequence, even though 'the era of miraculous Japanese growth now lies well in the past, most years Japan still manages to grow faster than other advanced nations' (ibid.: 178). And there was too for the Asian tiger economies, because they at least managed suddenly to mobilize large quantities of hitherto unused economic resources, when they had not managed to do so before, and when the bulk of the underdeveloped world was unable to follow suit. Similar questions remained to be probed for Europe in the 1950s, where West Germany grew rapidly and in sufficiently sustained a manner to significantly narrow the productivity gap with the US economy, but where the growth performance of other European economies (from Italy to Spain, from Greece to Ireland) did no such thing. So both *membership* of the 'convergence club' and *different economic performance* within it remain to be explained, even when the pattern of convergence has been written into the record; and that explanation does require more than the statistical apparatus of conventional growth accounting, important as that apparatus is for an initial specification of what precisely is at stake.

Rather than follow Krugman (and Feinstein) it seems wiser to leave open the possibility that different forms of capitalist organization do hold the key to the different capacities of particular national economies to grow rapidly at different periods since 1945 – that capitalist models historically have mattered – by understanding the determinants of catch-up and convergence in the manner of Moses Abramovitz, the leading figure in what is now an extensive research literature on these questions. For Abramovitz has argued persuasively that membership of the postwar 'convergence club' was not automatic, and that catch-up was not simply a problem-free process of mobilizing hitherto under-utilized economic resources. Rather it depended on a particular interplay of *technological congruence* and *social capability*. Abramovitz has argued that 'changes in the character of technical advance . . . make it more congruent with the resources and institutional outfits of some countries but less congruent with those of others' (Abramovitz, 1986: 406), and that, although productivity differences between economies definitely create a strong potential for subsequent convergence (as follower economies copy the technologies of more advanced ones), those followers are able to catch up only if they have a particular 'social capability', only if they possess a 'capability to exploit emerging technological opportunity', which 'depends upon a social history that is peculiar to itself and that may not be closely bound to its existing level of productivity' (ibid.: 406). Like Krugman and Feinstein, Abramovitz has argued that convergence is to be expected. He has been as aware as they that 'economic backwardness' gives advantage in the pursuit of economic growth, that late-comers can (more easily than established industrial economies) achieve rapid rates of productivity growth (and hence a degree of catch-up) by moving workers from low productivity sectors to high ones (invariably agriculture to industry), by adding capital stock to workers who hitherto had very little capital at their disposal, by adopting state-of-the-art technology copied from more advanced economies and by enjoying the dramatic increase in market size and economies of scale which are likely to result from these other changes (Abramovitz and David, 1996: 22). He has been clear, that is, that there is a '*potential* for relatively fast growth that countries with comparatively low productivity enjoy' (Abramovitz, 1994a: 87). But unlike Krugman, he has also insisted that convergence and catch-up will occur only to the degree that, and only in economies where, such potential is able to be *realized*: and realization requires a certain endowment of natural resources, a certain technical congruence, and a certain 'social capability'.*

Conceptually equipped in this way, Abramovitz has been able to give a particular (and highly credible) reading to the postwar pattern of convergence and catch-up. He has explained initial US productivity leadership in the twentieth century as the product of 'a fortunate concordance between America's own exceptional economic and social characteristics and the nature of the dominant path of technological progress and labour productivity advances': a path which was broadly 'not only resource-intensive but also tangible capital-using and scale-dependent' (Abramovitz, 1993: 230; Abramovitz and David, 1996: 25, 41). The early-twentieth-century US economy, that is, combined rich natural resource endowment and large-scale domestic markets with technologies it had initially largely borrowed from abroad (von Tunzelmann, 1995: 191) and with more indigenously generated forms of business organization ('the American system of manufactures'), to create what Chandler and Lazonick called managerial capitalism, and regulation theory known as 'domestic Fordism'. The timing of the subsequent catch-up – and the story of rapid postwar convergence – is then understood (and explained) as a product of the erosion of some of these concordances (particularly the eventual erosion of the US's natural resource advantage, and the gradual shift of technological progress from a reliance on tangible-capital to intangible-capital) and the removal of blockages to the ability of mainly European (but also Japanese) economies to exploit their undoubted 'social capabilities'. Once the weight of agriculture in the European and

---

* Abramovitz has defined 'social capability' on a number of occasions, broadly as follows:

> This is a vague complex of matters, few of which can be clearly defined and subjected to measurement. It includes personal attributes, notably levels of education, an attribute that is subject to measurement, however imperfectly. But it also refers to such things as competitiveness, the ability to co-operate in joint ventures, honesty, and the extent to which people feel able to trust the honesty of others. And it also pertains to a variety of political and economic institutions. It includes the stability of governments and their effectiveness in defining and enforcing the rules of economic life and in supporting growth. It covers the experience of a country's business people in the organisation and administration of large-scale enterprises and the degree of development of national and international capital markets. (*Abramovitz, 1994a: 88*)

Japanese social formations began to decline, once the blockages on world trade occasioned by the Great Depression and the Second World War were out of the way, and once the spread of higher education and greater experience with large-scale production had enlarged social capability, a quite predictable process of catch-up and convergence ensued.

The only economies able to grow in this way, according to Abramovitz, were those able to realize the general potential for catch-up created by US technological leadership. At play here, helping some and hindering others, were: facilities for the diffusion of knowledge (including channels of international technical communication such as multinational corporations); conditions facilitating or hindering structural change in the physical location, occupational composition and output patterns of particular economies; and 'macro-economic and monetary conditions encouraging and sustaining capital investment and growth of effective demand' (Abramovitz, 1986: 390). Some economies experienced or created those conditions. Most did not; and only the former experienced rapid postwar economic growth in consequence. And since for Abramovitz 'the pace at which potential for catch-up is actually realized in a particular period depends on factors limiting the diffusion of knowledge, the rate of structural change, the accumulation of capital, and the expansion of demand' (ibid.), he was also to explain the post-1973 slackening in the rate of catch-up and convergence among core club members. It was all a matter of the erosion of the conditions underpinning capitalism's postwar 'golden age', and the emergence of internally generated barriers to generalized economic acceleration thereafter. As he put it, 'in realization, as well as in potential, the convergence boom itself produced conditions unfavourable to continued productivity convergence at the boom's rapid pace or with the same degree of systematic association between initial levels and subsequent growth rates. The convergence boom was an inherently transitory experience' (Abramovitz, 1994a: 119).

Telling the postwar story in this way helps to explain why certain economies, and only certain economies, grew and converged. It helps to explain membership of the convergence club; and it also tells us something of their *common* convergence experience. What it does not do is help us much with an analysis of why, within a common pattern of convergence, some advanced capitalist economies grew more quickly than others. Nor does it help us to explain the arrival into the convergence club of a number of late-comers who joined long after the 1973 slowdown. The idea of 'social capability' suggests a way of constructing that explanation: by carefully analysing institutional differences between advanced capitalist economies (in the way, indeed, many of the studies cited in section 1 of this chapter did) in order to locate the degree to which the different growth performances of advanced capitalist economies throughout the postwar period can legitimately 'be attributed to differences in the elements of social capability, and, if so, to which of them' (Abramovitz, 1994a: 97). Abramovitz himself has explicitly declined to make that explanation, 'pleading incompetence' (ibid.), and restricting himself to a series of hints about individual country performances within a broad listing of 'realization factors which have mainly to do with international conditions' and which 'are in fact the external environment for individual latecomers' (Shin, 1996: 25). But we clearly need to do more. We need to interrogate the notion of 'social capability' further. For it does hold the key to the different capacities of individual national economies in the postwar period to mobilize unused or underused economic resources and to increase the efficiency of their use, once mobilized; and, because it does, it also reopens the explanatory space for centre-left institutional analysis of the kind closed out by more conventional growth accounting, by re-establishing the importance of non-economic prerequisites of successful convergence strategies.

The need to mobilize capital

Ultimately economic growth is the product of the coming together of two distinguishable processes. The first is an increase in the volume of labour and capital mobilized for productive purposes. The second is an increase in the efficiency with which, once mobilized, those resources are used, either an increase in the efficiency with which individual factors of production are deployed (increases in the productivity of labour or capital) or increases in the efficiency of their interaction (increases in total factor productivity: TFP). In the growth literature surveyed in the Appendix to this book, there is much controversy about the relative contribution of each of those distinguishable processes to the growth performance of particular economies in particular periods. It is generally recognized, of course, that labour supply is broadly fixed by rates of population growth, and that 'the rate of growth of the labor force is seldom higher than two per cent per annum, even with international migration' (Boskin and Lau, 1992: 17); but on the supply and significance of capital there is no equivalent unanimity. Rather, depending on the definitions used and the measurements taken, increases in the volume or quantity of capital are said to play a larger or a smaller part in the stimulation of labour productivity; and certainly in the first wave of growth accounting (associated in particular with the work of Edward Denison in the 1960s), factor inputs of this kind were thought to have played only a modest role in the growth of labour productivity in the twentieth century US, with the remaining (residual) growth said largely to reflect the impact of technical progress (that is, improvements in the *quality* of capital). Developments since then have refined our understanding and measurement of the role of capital, allowing it a greater role in the generation of productivity growth (Kendrick, 1993: 141); and the residual forces generating increases in total factor productivity are now understood to involve more than technical change, stretching out to include the restructuring of employment distribution between economic sectors, improvements in the education and skill levels of both workers and managers and economies of scale associated with market size and large production runs (Abramovitz, 1994a: 93).

Later studies have still made clear that the relative contribution of capital intensity and TFP to postwar growth patterns has varied between economies and altered over time (Dowrick and Nguyen, 1989: 1025). In particular it has effectively been established that the volume and modernity of capital was particularly important in the postwar growth performance of certain northern European economies, those which lacked the ability to rapidly improve labour productivity by shifting employment out of agriculture, in the manner of a number of their Asian and southern European competitors. The available econometric evidence certainly suggests that capitalism's postwar 'golden age [was] a time of exceptionally high investment' (Crafts and Toniolo, 1996: 578), and that the 1960s in particular 'saw a great investment boom in Europe and Japan in which growth rates of capital stock per worker rose above the high rates of the 1950s and in which the composition of capital shifted towards higher-yielding assets' (Abramovitz, 1989: 195). It should perhaps be said in passing (as we briefly noted earlier in this chapter) that no such unanimity surrounds the more recent growth of the Asian tiger economies, where fierce disagreements persist on the relative contribution of factor inputs and improvements in factor efficiency (Krugman, 1996b; Drysdale and Huang, 1997). But perhaps the fierceness and content of that debate is not so critical, given that later studies have also made clear the interconnected nature of the various growth sources in contention and the capital-augmenting nature of much technical change, with capital investment now understood as both triggering *and* responding to technical innovation and diffusion, with 'the effect of technical progress on real output [depending] on the size of the capital stock' (Boskin and Lau, 1992: 51) and with 'the pace at which countries . . . exploit their potential for productivity advance . . . itself governed by investment and growth of capital' (Abramovitz, 1989: 195). Indeed it is now possible to discern a general recognition, across the full swathe of the relevant research literatures, of the central importance for rapid economic growth of improvements in both the *quantity of investment funds available* and the *quality of the technologies* into which that investment is then put. It is now widely recognized, that is, that although capitalist economies in the postwar period survived by the mobilization of wage labour, they flourished by deepening and widening the productive capital with which that labour was linked. It is also widely recognized, as table 6.1 shows, that their capacity to flourish in this way definitely differed during the period as a whole, in line with their differing propensities to direct resources into gross fixed capital formation.

The importance for postwar economic growth of capital investment of this scale and kind, as a set of mainly Schumpeterian-inspired economists and economic historians have now demonstrated, has primarily to be filtered through the question of technology. There are now clear research data to show the importance of technology to growth, establishing 'a clear long-run

Table 6.1 Gross fixed capital formation as a percentage of GDP

Country	1960–7	1968–73	Average 1974–9	1980–9	1960–89
US	13.1	18.4	18.8	17.7	18.2
Japan	31.0	34.6	31.8	29.5	31.4
Germany	25.2	24.4	20.8	20.5	22.6
UK	17.7	19.1	19.4	17.4	18.2
Total EEC	22.7	23.4	22.2	20.1	21.9
Total OECD	21.4	22.7	22.2	20.8	21.6

Source: Young, 1992: 2

relationship between the development of technology indicators such as R&D and patents, and economic growth in the form of labour productivity trends' (Verspagen, 1996: 239; Pianta 1995: 176). There is also clear research evidence linking investment to growth in total factor productivity (Dollar and Wolff, 1993: 14; Broadberry, 1997: 334) and technical change to capital accumulation, establishing what Wolff has termed 'complementarities between capital accumulation and technological advance', and particularly – if De Long and Summers are correct – between investment in machinery and equipment and GDP growth (Wolff, 1994: 53, 55). Indeed there is research evidence for the existence of a 'virtuous circle' of cumulative causation linking R&D expenditure, capital accumulation, economic growth and further R&D expenditure (Pianta, 1995: 177). There is also clear evidence that only economies with a certain level of capital investment, and a certain level of independent research capacity and activity, are able to benefit from the technological innovation of others, that 'technical progress does a country with a high level of capital stock much more good than a country with a low level' (Boskin and Lau, 1992: 51; also Fagerberg, 1988: 451). And there is overwhelming evidence that the process of catch-up by the northern European and Japanese economies during capitalism's postwar 'golden age' involved primarily a reduction in (although not a complete elimination of) the technology gap established between US industry and its leading international competitors prior to 1950 (van Ark and Crafts, 1996: 20; Dollar and Wolff, 1993: 13–14; Wolff, 1994: 72). All this strongly suggests that the growth rates of leading capitalist economies in the postwar period did not diverge primarily because of the strength of their labour movements or because of the nature of their dominant cultures. They diverged primarily because of their differing capacities to mobilize capital for technological innovation and imitation

This is very clear in the literature on the 'erosion of US technological leadership as a factor in postwar economic convergence' (Nelson and

Wright, 1994). In that literature it is widely agreed that the initial postwar US lead in labour productivity rested on US technological superiority, which was itself the product of the capacity of US-based firms for technological and organizational innovation. That initial lead, according to Nelson and Wright, had two components. 'One was American leadership in mass production industries', in which the US had excelled since at least 1900. The other was American leadership in high-tech industries, in which US superiority was of briefer standing, 'the consequence of massive and unprecedented American investments in research and development after the war' (ibid.: 129). The subsequent process of catch-up and convergence by a club of leading capitalist economies in Western Europe and Japan was initially a consequence of technology diffusion, a reflection of their 'social capability' to imitate and disseminate technologies and forms of corporate organization of a US kind, in a situation in which, given the scale of the US lead, 'the opportunities for catch-up . . . were very large indeed' (Maddison, 1996: 53). Implicit in that argument is the view that the rate of convergence between the US and other leading capitalist economies slowed after 1973 primarily because that copying and dissemination process was coming to completion, so leaving future rates of growth of labour productivity dependent on more generalized capacities for innovation across the capitalist bloc as a whole. As Abramovitz and David put it: 'the post-World War II conjuncture of forces supporting catch-up' had 'largely done its work', bringing 'the labor productivity levels of the advanced capitalist countries within sight of substantial equality' and so creating a situation in which 'the significant lags that remain among the advanced economies . . . are no longer to be found in a marked persistence of backward technology embodied in obsolescent equipment and organizations' (Abramovitz and David, 1996: 60). Economies that had initially prospered by benefiting from rapid immediate postwar reconstruction, and then from aping US forms of corporate behaviour, had then to maintain their productivity growth paths by more internally generated forms of technical and managerial change, without any guarantee that capacities for imitation could be easily reset into capacities for innovation *per se*. The slowdown in productivity growth in Europe and Japan after 1973 suggests that this resetting was difficult to make.

In fact Pianta has recently argued that postwar economic growth in advanced capitalist economies 'has mainly relied upon one of the two "engines of growth" offered by technology: either the generation of knowledge and innovation of a disembodied nature . . . *or* the use of technology embodied in investment' (1995: 181–2). Measuring the first by expenditure on R&D per head and the second by capital formation per employee, he observed distinct differences in the postwar performances of leading economies, with Japan between 1970 and 1990 out-performing the OECD average on both measures of technologically induced growth, with Germany (and to a lesser degree the UK) meeting the OECD average on the first measure but not the second, and with the US under-shooting the OECD average score for both innovation and capital investment and so enjoying 'a much weaker virtuous circle between technology and growth' (ibid.: 183). Pianta's research data also show a convergence in patterns of behaviour across OECD economies over time and the need for a more balanced reliance on both modes of inducing growth, as the technology gap between the US and other leading capitalist economies diminished. As he put it, 'at first the scope for catching up was so large that countries could "specialise" either in the production of innovations, reaching high R&D intensities, or in the diffusion and use of technology through higher investment per employee'. But later, 'as the room for catching up becomes smaller, less diversity in the combinations of R&D and investment intensities emerges, and growth needs to be sustained by a more balanced use of the two "engines of growth"' (ibid.: 185). That need was reinforced by the clear evidence – after 1973 – of the way productivity growth in both Europe and Japan slowed down in spite of the rapid rise in particularly Japanese expenditure on research and development. That slowdown in the context of rising R&D spending per head is one of the great puzzles of contemporary economic history. It has a name – the Solow paradox – but it does not yet have a definitive explanation (for a recent attempt, see Gittleman and Wolff, 1998).

Such a critical lacuna leaves an important research space – now being filled by a new generation of micro-based research on technology innovation and diffusion – and a policy gap which, as we saw in chapter 2, theoreticians of many varieties in the 1980s were keen to fill. US governments in that decade were not short of advice on how to re-trigger rapid productivity growth, much of it entirely in line with a set of general findings on growth performance which existing research data do now appear to have confirmed. For in general it seems safe to argue that the capacity of particular national economies to mobilize capital for technological innovation and imitation does depend, as Abramovitz has argued, on a particular fusion of 'technological congruence' and 'social capability'. Technological congruence does seem to be vital to successful economic growth. Certainly the technical requirements of the First Industrial Revolution sat particularly easily with the natural resource base and emerging market conditions of industrialists in the UK, just as the technical requirements of the Second Industrial Revolution mapped most empathetically onto those of the US. In the most general terms, the technology of early industrialism required small units of investment, skilled and artisanal labour and craft-based flexible production methods. The UK has those in abundance. By contrast, the mass-production technology of the Second Industrial Revolution required 'certain special features, such as very large markets and cheap resources' (Nelson and Wright, 1994: 131), which the early-twentieth-century US economy provided more adequately than did the initially more developed UK one. And in that very important sense, there may be some explanatory mileage in the idea that the capacity to mobilize capital is dependent on the nature of what Freeman and others have called the dominant 'techno-economic paradigm' (Freeman and Perez, 1988; Freeman and Soete, 1997). Not everyone is comfortable with the drawing of sharp breaks in the sequence of technical change; yet the idea that technologies cohere in dominant clusters, and are linked to sets of supporting institutions, is a fertile one. For, if true, it gives one reading of the postwar growth story, and one reading of why – after 1973 – productivity rates slowed in advanced capitalist economies. It suggests that when one paradigm is in place, leading economies tend to experience very little catch-up by less developed economies; because 'technologies are clustered within the paradigm . . . institutions have evolved to support the paradigm' (Shin, 1996: 18), and existing investments in core economies attract increasing returns. But it also suggests that when one techno-economic paradigm is in the process of being replaced by another, economies can and do converge or even pass, because then of course 'previous technological or institutional development no longer acts as an advantage . . . rather it becomes a costly burden to the structural adjustment of forerunners' (ibid.). In periods of paradigm shift, so the argument runs, it is late-comers that are 'lighter and faster' in the new technology system (ibid.), and that grow more rapidly than established economies in consequence (see also Brezis et al., 1993). And in those periods too, overall rates of productivity growth can be expected to dip, because new technologies require a long learning period before generating significant efficiencies, and old technologies (and the knowledge and experience base associated with them) experience diminishing returns.

As we saw in chapter 2, the whole force of the centre-left criticism of US industrial performance in the 1980s turned on thinking of broadly this kind, insisting that a new technological paradigm was emerging to which Japanese forms of industrial organization were better suited. That claim may or may not be valid. It is certainly disputed, and is actually not essential to any explanation of the diminishing technology gap between the US and its main competitors. The emerging technological congruence between them and the existing paradigm is enough for that explanatory task (on this, see Nelson and Wright, 1994: 155–6). But even scholars not fully wedded to notions of 'paradigm shift' have noted the capacity of technologies, once adopted, to become locked in, path-dependent and self-sustaining – to experience the so-called QWERTY phenomenon (David, 1985: 292) – with resulting entry-costs for new industrializers and tendencies to industrial inertia for well-established ones. And some of them have noted too that, even if advanced capitalist economies at the end of the twentieth century are not moving from one techno-economic paradigm to another, they are experiencing recognizable processes of qualitative technological change which have distinct consequences for comparative rates of economic growth. The argument here is that as (and to the degree that) dominant technologies are becoming more science-based over time – as investment is moving, in Abramovitz's terms, from tangible capital to intangible capital (Abramovitz, 1993: 230) – so the tightness of the fit between the natural resource base of an economy and the capacity of industrial capitalists to exploit those dominant technologies itself declines. As Nelson and Wright put it, 'the advent of science-based technologies has significantly increased the extent to which generic technological understanding is possessed by trained scientists and engineers, *wherever they live*' such that now there is 'little that [is] intrinsically American about the technology' (Nelson and Wright, 1994: 159, 131) informing high-quality production in advanced capitalist economies. Those economies may or may not face a new technological paradigm; but they certainly rely for the competitive edge of the firms within them on a technological base which itself requires high-quality scientists, engineers and operatives. And because they do, the ability of those economies to exploit the full productive capacities of contemporary technologies now depends on more than their resource base and domestic market size. It also depends, as the new growth theorists persistently tell us, on their investment in research and development, and in human capital.

So what is clearly salvageable from the 1980s enthusiasm of certain intellectuals for all things Japanese is the recognition that technological congruence is no longer fixed primarily by the distribution of *natural* resources. Japan, after all, was (and is) deficient in a number of basic industrial inputs. What gave Japanese industrial capital its edge over US capital before 1992 was its unprecedented capacity both to mobilize hitherto underused economic resources and to intensify the effectiveness of their use, once mobilized. And by the same token, what gave US industry its earlier competitive edge over UK industry was not simply the larger scale of the US domestic market or the plentiful supply to US manufacturers of cheap natural resources. It was not even simply the enhanced quality of US industrial technology, which developed to meet the demand for the large-scale extraction of those natural resources. It was also, as Alfred Chandler has documented, the capacity of US-based firms to create the professional managerial cadre and the internal organizational structures vital to the full exploitation of the new technical and market opportunities, to develop what Chandler called 'the three-pronged investment in production, distribution and management that brought the modern industrial enterprise into being' (Chandler, 1990: 8). For what seems ultimately to establish the impact of technological congruence on competitive performance is not natural resources or market size. It seems rather to be the presence or absence of economic institutions and social relations which possess the capacity to enable the owners of industrial capital rapidly to adopt existing technologies, quickly to extend the scale and intensity of their use, and ultimately to initiate technical innovation and change. What seems to fix the impact of technological congruence on the pattern of growth, that is, is the nature of an economy's 'social capability'.

The capacity to mobilize capital

Once the importance of 'social capabilities' is recognized, the space emerges again for an examination – in different national capitalisms – of the char-

acter of discrete institutions and of the relationships between them. Indeed
the space is open for an examination of entire business systems: both the
systems of technological innovation and diffusion in each leading economy
and the more general systems linking company to company, industry to
finance and capital to labour. This is quintessentially the territory of the
'new institutionalists', a sweep of intellectuals, based in a range of social
science disciplines, prepared to make two general arguments. They are prepared to argue that the way particular economic institutions operate differs
between national capitalisms, and that those differences have direct and
powerful consequences for patterns of growth and competitiveness. They
are also prepared to argue that such institutional differences are systematic
rather than random. They are structural rather than accidental, and they
reflect the impact on economic activity of wider 'societal effects' (Maurice
et al., 1986) which are themselves predominantly nationally rooted. The line
of argument here differs in detail, depending on which piece of research is
being deployed: but the general thesis – of the 'social embeddedness' of economic action (Granovetter, 1985) – does not. Economic performance is
affected by institutional practices. Institutional practices vary between
economies. Those variations are systematic and mutually reinforcing. They
are also socially rooted and nationally constrained. Collectively they constitute a social system of production. And that social system holds the key to
why growth rates differ.

   The notions of 'societal effects' and 'social systems of production' were
initially developed by a series of scholars concerned with the way systems
of education and training, industrial relations and patterns of work organization varied between different European economies (Maurice et al., 1986;
Sorge and Warner, 1986; Sorge, 1991). Their research suggested that 'firms
did not respond with infinite elasticity to perceivable market and technological environments', but rather responded in ways 'conditioned by past
investment into capital and manpower, and by the nature of their specific
social, political and institutional environments' (Sorge, 1993: 273–4). Their
research also suggested that the way firms organize themselves internally
was closely linked to surrounding systems of education and training, social
stratification and industrial relations, and that firms could strengthen their
competitiveness by enhancing this alignment of their internal practices with
those prevailing in the society around them (Sorge, 1991; 163, 186). The
social parameters of economic action were therefore a crucial determinant
of economic behaviour, for these scholars, and a critical factor in their explanation of different growth performance: and such social parameters were
understood as being neither random in effect nor idiosyncratic in origin.
Rather they were presented as socially created, institutionally coherent, persistent over time and reciprocally related (Sorge, 1991: 163). Hollingsworth
and Boyer have expressed the important general idea at play here as follows:

   By a social system of production, we mean the way that the . . . institutions
   or structures of a country or a region are integrated into a social configura-

tion . . . these institutions, organizations and social values tend to cohere with each other, although they vary in the degree to which they are tightly coupled to each other into a fully-fledged system. While each of these components has some autonomy and may have some goals that are contradictory to the goals of other institutions with which it is integrated, an institutional logic in each society leads institutions to coalesce into a complex social configuration. This occurs because the institutions are embedded in a culture in which their logics are symbolically grounded, organizationally structured, technically and materially constrained, and politically defended. *(Hollingsworth and Boyer, 1997: 2)*

The impact of such social systems on differential growth performance have been recognized by economists from a variety of theoretical traditions – neo-classical and Marxist as well as Schumpeterian – and has been used for a range of analytical tasks which cumulatively have deepened the notion of capitalist models with which this text is centrally concerned. There is, for example, an entire scholarship preoccupied with the exploration of national systems of industrial relations, in which – as we have already seen – both social democratic and Japanese systems' figure large (Tolliday and Zeitlin, 1986; Howell, 1992; Kogut, 1993; Edwards, 1994; Cooke and Noble, 1998). There is an extensive body of literature on national systems of innovation (Lundvall, 1988; Nelson, 1993) concerned to show that 'historically there have been major differences between countries in the way they have organised and sustained the development, introduction, improvement and diffusion of new products and processes within the national economy' (Freeman, 1995: 19). Comparative literatures also exist on different systems of corporate governance (Hollingsworth and Boyer, 1997), state practices (Crouch and Streeck, 1997), political economy (Pempel, 1998) and accounting and finance (Zysmann, 1983; Williams et al., 1990); and covering them all, we now see emerging a burgeoning literature on national business systems (Whitley, 1992a; 1992b).

Throughout these literatures, leading practitioners are aware of some of the dangers of this form of conceptualization of the world of capital: dangers of emphasising homogeneity over heterogeneity in any national economy; dangers of missing critical sub-national and supra-institutional patternings; dangers of over-systematization and of functionalism; and the problems of locating sources of institutional change (see Rubery, 1994: 337–8). But for them, the pay-off is worth the pain, since the notion of distinct business systems provides them with a vital comparative device within which to integrate and systematize various key features of the different ways in which particular national economies organize themselves internally for the purposes of competitiveness and growth. Playing with a set of distinctions between different forms of economic coordination – particularly different degrees of dependence on markets, hierarchies, networks and the state – analysts of business systems have argued that competitiveness is affected by the dominant combination of at least the following sixteen business characteristics.

1　The nature of the firm
- The degree to which private managerial hierarchies co-ordinate economic activities
- The degree of managerial discretion from owners
- Specialisation of managerial capabilities and activities within authority hierarchies
- The degree to which growth is discontinuous and involves radical changes in skills and activities
- The extent to which risks are managed through mutual dependence with business partners and employees

2　Market organisation
- The extent of long-term co-operative relations between firms within and between sectors
- The significance of intermediaries in the co-ordination of market transactions
- Stability, integration and scope of business groups
- Dependence of co-operative relations on personal ties and trust

3　Authoritative co-ordination and control systems
- Integration and interdependence of economic activities
- Impersonality of authority and subordination relations
- Task, skill and role specialisation and individualisation
- Differentiation of authority roles and expertise
- Decentralisation of operational control and level of work group autonomy
- Distance and superiority of managers
- Extent of employer–employee commitment and organisation-based employment system. *(Whitley, 1992b: 9)*

The use to which distinctions of this kind are then put varies between scholars. For some (J. Rogers Hollingsworth being an important recent example) they are the core of the already-told story in which liberal capitalist economic domination gave way to that of trust-based capitalism as technologies and markets changed. For him, the 'hierarchy-market' mixture of US-type mass production was effective (and remains so) 'when markets are stable, consumer tastes are homogeneous, and technology is not highly complex and slow to change'. But the 'less hierarchical and more network-like' modes of coordination characteristic of late-industrializing economies of the Japanese and German variety 'proved more effective once markets became unstable and consumers demanded products based on complex and changing technologies' (Hollingsworth, 1997a: 140). The US business system is still seen have considerable strengths, 'its institutional arrangements facilitating creativity, individualism, "short termism" and flexible labour and capital markets' being particularly good at the stimulation of new industries. But it is also seen to have particular weaknesses: particularly a suitability for continued dominance in 'stable homogeneous markets . . . for . . . products of low technological complexity', markets and products no longer at capitalism's cutting edge (ibid.: 142, 145). Hollingsworth, that is, echoes many of the concerns of those centre-left critics of US capitalism in the 1980s whose work was discussed in chapter 2, although his work adds a deep pessimism about the ease of change which was characteristically missing in the pre-Clinton US policy debate. For the defining feature of these business systems for scholars like Hollingsworth is their embeddedness, their path dependency and the associated difficulties of implanting institutional practices on an incremental basis from more successful business systems elsewhere, and (in the absence of major crisis) of breaking from one path to another. It is his view that 'short termism and institutional inertia' will make for a very 'difficult American transition', and that 'its prevailing practices of industrial relations, its education system, and its financial markets – in short, the constraints of its past social system of production' might even block that change altogether (Hollingsworth, 1997b: 293).

On the other hand, Richard Whitley, who drew up the sixteen points, writes in ways that are more agnostic about the superiority of particular business systems, if equally sensitive to matters of path dependency and social specificity. His list was created as part of an argument that 'no single pattern [was] clearly superior to all the others', and to deny the value of 'the search for some set of universal correlations between abstract contingencies and effective organisation structures across all market economies'. For Whitley, universals are not available in a world in which 'business organization is institutionally relative' (Whitley, 1992b: 5); and analysis instead is best directed to the origins of institutional diversity. To that end, Whitley suggests we relate the sixteen characteristics listed here to what he terms 'six broad background institutions', with which affect they interact: six institutions concerned with 'the availability of, and conditions governing access to, financial resources and different kinds of labour power' and with 'the overall political and legal system which institutionalises property rights, provides security and stability and varies in its type and degree of support for private business activities' (Whitley, 1992b: 25). The 'Whitley 6' begin with state variables (business dependence on the state, and state commitment to industrial development and risk sharing), at which we shall look in chapter 7. They end with labour variables (including training systems and skilled unionism), with which we have already dealt. But they also include the capital-focused variable 'capital market or credit-based financial system', which Hutton and others singled out as particularly generative of UK economic underperformance: it is at that variable that we need now to look in some detail.

The gap between finance and industry in the UK and West Germany

The claim that the institutional distance between financial and industrial companies is a principal determinant of economic performance has been used, as we have seen, to indict UK financial institutions in the postwar period and to praise German ones. The available research evidence suggests however that this awarding of points needs considerable refinement if it is to survive intact, given that in its basic form it is stronger on the UK than on Germany, and is seriously underdeveloped on both.

There is certainly evidence to indicate the existence of a larger gap between industry and finance in the UK than in Germany for most of the postwar period, and to support the argument that this larger gap had a number of deleterious consequences for the bulk of the UK manufacturing sector. That evidence includes the following.

1   Forms of corporate governance among large corporations do differ significantly between the UK and Germany (and indeed Japan). Banks do not play the role in corporate governance in the UK that they play in either Germany or Japan, where 'equity stakes, a proportion of the lending, and seats on the board give . . . the banks a different association with companies than is typical in the UK' (Prevezer and Ricketts, 1994: 247). External share-holders are the main reference point in UK corporate decision-making (Prevezer, 1994: 196). The company's share price is the key performance indicator guiding senior managers; and the threat of hostile take-over is a major preoccupation for UK boards of directors in ways that have no easy German (or Japanese) equivalence (Prevezer and Ricketts, 1994: 245).

2   Large UK companies do raise a larger percentage of their investment funds as equity than German and Japanese firms; and dividend payments are high by German standards. Investment levels are not, however (Buxton, 1998: 169–76). Nor are levels of expenditure on research and development. In Japan, it should be noted, 'real expenditure on R&D increased more than fourfold between 1972 and 1994, and in West Germany and Italy by two-and-a-half times' (Buxton, 1998: 170). In the UK in the same period R&D expenditure rose only by 20 per cent. Yet at the same time UK (and US) companies had a significantly higher equity proportion among their liabilities than companies in Japan and Germany. Japan's debt:equity ratio among non-financial institutions in 1988 was 4.19. Germany's debt:equity ratio that year was 4.25. The equivalent US figure was 0.76. The UK's was 1.03 (Prevezer and Ricketts, 1994: 254). Between 1973 and 1988 the proportion of gross operating surpluses paid out as dividends by UK-based manufacturing firms was 'typically 3–4 times as high as in German manufacturing' (Williams et al., 1990: 475). And in 1988 the ratio of dividends to gross income for non-financial institutions in the UK was 42 per cent. In Japan that year it was 10 per cent (Prevezer, 1994: 202).

3   The cost of borrowing investment funds from UK financial institutions is significantly higher than the costs faced by their German and Japanese equivalents; and the typical period for the realization of loans is significantly shorter. The House of Commons Select Committee on Trade and Industry recently calculated the median required internal rate of return

in UK manufacturing at a staggering 21–25 per cent for low-risk operational investments, and at 16–20 per cent for strategic ones, with a median completion period of only 19–24 months; understandably in consequence it issued a series of strictures against City-induced short-termism, inadequate bank–industry links in the small- and medium-firm sector, and restricted levels of investment across UK manufacturing industry as a whole (Lee, 1997b: 238–9).

4   Financial institutions in the UK are now major international players, and have increased their weight in the UK economy as the contribution of UK-based manufacturing industry to employment, GNP and the trade balance has declined (Lee, 1997b: 250). City earnings have grown as a contributory element on the plus side of the UK's balance of payments; and the City has acted as a major conduit for the export of capital (on which those earnings rest). And, as we saw in chapter 4, the UK remained both a major and a consistent net exporter of capital throughout the 1980s and into the 1990s, creating a situation in which, as Lee has it,

> whilst the City's costs to the performance of manufacturing industry are widely acknowledged, the gains in output, productivity and profitability that might accrue to manufacturers from the provision of lower cost capital for long-term investment remain notional, whereas the City's benefits to the balance of payments, whilst they might be smaller than those which would accrue from an industrial revival, actually exist and are tangible to those who receive them. *(Ibid.: 249)*

All this may indeed now be deleterious to UK competitiveness and growth; but it remains fully intelligible in historical terms, since the gap between UK industry and UK financial institutions is both of long standing and entirely structural in origin. The gap was initially the product of a divergence of interests first established during UK manufacturing's brief nineteenth-century period of world monopoly. In that period, UK-based industrial concerns did not require bank capital to anything like the degree demonstrated by the fledgeling industries of Germany and Japan. The UK's world monopoly gave its industrialists surpluses on which internally financed long-term investment could proceed apace. It also gave sterling a particular role in the nineteenth-century world economy broadly similar to that of the dollar between 1944 and 1971, and attracted to London foreign borrowers keen to draw on those surpluses for their own industrial take-off. From the 1870s the English banking system simply found it more profitable to finance foreign trade and to handle portfolio investment abroad than to seek out domestic industrial demand for long-term finance – found it advantageous indeed to fuse with a set of London-based commercial interests long involved in that trade, a fusion (which we noted in chapter 5) that then established both a distance between industrial and financial interests and an international focus for UK banking practices with no close parallel elsewhere. It was not that UK-based banks ceased to lend to UK manufacturing firms after 1900. It was rather that they proved increasingly reluctant to grant long-term credit to such firms, or to use their position as creditors to encourage industrial rationalization. Certainly before 1945 the UK banking sector does not appear to have consolidated extensive habits either of long-term industrial involvement or of industrial coordination; and since it was precisely in that period that German and Japanese banks were doing both those things, the reluctance of UK banking to become extensively involved with local manufacturing did set their relationship with industry on a trajectory different from that emerging elsewhere in Europe and Asia.

As is more fully documented elsewhere (Coates, 1994: 155–6), the twentieth-century consequences of this unique trajectory have been many and various. UK-based banks have not been totally dependent for their survival on the 'health' of the local manufacturing economy. They have not therefore been under any systematic pressure either to make long-term credit available (to protect the profitability of lending in the past) or to act as coordinators of industrial modernization (to guarantee the profitability of lending in the future). Instead, when UK banks have lent to UK industry, the bulk of that lending has been short-term. Indeed Williams and his colleagues have insisted that 'unlike the banks in all the other advanced countries, through the long boom of the 1950s and 1960s British banks did not lend money over periods longer than two years for the purchase of capital equipment like machine tools' (Williams et al., 1983: 69). 'And although long-term loans for such purposes were available after 1973', Williams later suggested, 'the banks did not change their criteria for lending. They remained pre-occupied with the taking of security over fixed assets.' They remained committed to what the American Banking Association, in its evidence to the Wilson Committee, called 'the liquidation approach' (Williams, Williams and Haslam, 1989: 78).

Such a set of banking orientations, and the persistently low percentage of bank assets tied up in local industry, reflect the uniquely wide options faced by UK banks because of London's strength as an international financial centre. UK-based banks have long faced the option of financing local industry or of making money from financing the UK state, lending abroad, and servicing the circulation of money by others. All this appears to have given UK-based financial institutions in the twentieth century a particularly acute version of the bankers' general predilection for 'maximum flexibility and liquidity' (Fine and Harris, 1985: 42). It has left them willing to lend to industry only on terms by which loans could be quickly retrieved, and only in forms which avoided a heavy dependence on any one firm, industry, or even one economy. In fact, as Zysman has argued, this is the characteristic form of relationship between banks and industry whenever strong capital markets (of the London type) exist alongside them. Put simply: 'where capital markets emerged to finance industrial development, bank lending has been traditionally limited to short-term purposes. Where the capital markets were neither adequate nor reliable sources of development funds, banks or specialised institutions filled the gap with loans'

(Zysman, 1983: 61). They did that in Germany and in Japan, but not – given the existing strength of the London capital markets *before* full industrialization – in the UK.

It should be noted, however, that of late, under the impact of the liberalization of world financial markets, much of this gap between UK companies and financial institutions has diminished. There is evidence of enhanced lending by commercial banks to small and medium-size UK companies (Prevezer, 1994: 201) and of the growing willingness of those banks to lend long-term (Laverack, 1996: 56). There is evidence of the emergence of UK bank-led blocks of companies of a kind historically associated with Japanese rather than UK capital (Scott, 1997: 121). There is evidence too of greater dependence by large-scale UK companies on a range of financial institutions and instruments outside the UK itself (Prevezer, 1994: 200). But there is *not* evidence of any resulting change in the tendency to export capital. Rather, and in the 1980s in particular, UK manufacturing industry experienced a generalized 'hollowing out' of both output and employment (Williams et al., 1990: 480) as large-scale UK industrial capital and UK financial capital went abroad together, moving productive activity and employment out of the UK, in parallel to the export of portfolio funds. In the Williams sample of 25 giant British manufacturing firms, their UK-based employment fell by 330,000 between 1979 and 1989, while their overseas employment rose by 200,000. Large-scale UK industrial capital is no longer as distant from UK financial capital as it once was – so radical institutional reform is not the panacea it might once have been – but both are as distant as ever from the bulk of the UK manufacturing base, which remains in consequence short of low-cost investment funds and less and less capable of contributing either to GNP or to employment growth. To this degree at least, the institutional matrix surrounding the flow of funds to UK-based companies does appear to have locked the UK economy onto a particularly low growth trajectory; therefore there is some legitimacy in pointing to these features of the UK's overall social structure of production as major barriers to economic growth, as Hutton and others have done.

It should also be noted that the data on the hidden comparator in this argument – namely Germany – are much less straightforwardly supportive of the finance/industry 'gap' theory than they are in the UK case. There is, however, supporting evidence of a kind.

1   It is clear that the institutional links between German banks and German companies are significantly different from those prevalent in the UK. The German banking system is built around a number of large universal banks, created in the 1870s and combining the services of a merchant bank with those of a deposit bank. Either directly or indirectly these universal banks do have a close and long-term relationship with a set of German companies, to whom they act as a house-bank. The relationship is direct, in that German universal banks own industrial shares and sit on

supervisory boards of German companies. It is also indirect in that, in their capacity as board members, German bankers control proxy votes for shares deposited with them by their customers and proxy votes lent to them by other banks. As late as 1975 West German banks and investment companies reportedly owned 9.1 per cent of the shares of West Germany's seventy-four largest enterprises, and controlled as trustees an additional 53.6 per cent (Scott, 1997: 147); and the 'Big Three' universal banks in particular 'held more than 25 per cent in shares (in effect, a power of veto) in 28 of the top 100 companies' (Dyson, 1986: 129). In that year, West German banks held 15 per cent of all the seats on the supervisory boards of those 100 companies, and in thirty-one of them provided the chairman.

2   It is also clear that German firms typically do enjoy the capacity to raise long-term loans from their banking system, and to do so at lower rates than those operative in the UK. Small and medium-size firms in Germany are particularly advantaged here relative to their UK equivalents (Anglo-German Foundation, 1994: 11; Midland Bank, 1994), since they can draw on the expertise and support of a differentiated set of regional, municipal and cooperative banks, and of a set of financial institutions geared to long-term fixed-rate industrial investment (particularly the KfW) which have no direct UK equivalent. These savings and cooperative banks, which collectively control half the assets of the entire German banking system, 'usually accept lower dividend payments than shareholders . . . do not seek rapid capital gains . . . and assure SMEs of a comparatively predictable and reasonably priced supply of capital' (Lane, 1995: 48, 53). If Schneider-Lenne's calculations are correct, by 1990 almost two-thirds of all bank loans advanced to companies in Germany were long-term and fixed rate, whereas 'by contrast, the maturity structure of bank loans in the UK appear[ed] to be exactly the opposite': two-thirds of UK bank loans to companies were short-term, and 'in the case of long term loans, it [was] the exception rather than the rule for a fixed interest rate to be agreed for the entire maturity' (Schneider-Lenne, 1994: 293).

3   It is also clear that German manufacturing industry is significantly more competitive in overall terms than its UK equivalent. For even though the productivity gap between UK and German industry narrowed after 1979, German manufacturing industry still possesses a general capital-based productivity edge over UK manufacturing industry. The research data available to us confirm 'the view that investment by firms in Germany has generally been higher than in the UK throughout the period 1950–1989' (Edwards and Fischer, 1994a: 17); the gap was particularly marked in the 1950s and particularly narrow in the 1970s. Certainly, as late as 1989 'German manufacturing had at its disposal about 30% more physical capital (equipment and structures) per worker-hour than British manufacturing' (O'Mahoney, 1994/5: 12); and in 1992 the capital stock per worker in Germany was US$50,116 whereas in the UK it was only US$22,509

(Hutton, 1997: 28). In consequence, German-based companies have a presence in European and world markets which is far in excess of any achieved by the majority of their UK equivalents. In 1985, for example, 'West Germany had a 38% share of EC 12 manufacturing output compared with ... just 12.8% for the UK' (Williams et al., 1990: 483), and the West German economy ran a trade surplus bigger in 1989 than Japan's, even though its population was only half Japan's. In fact, while West Germany outstripped Japan in world markets, the UK economy in the 1980s (although by then growing in real per capita terms faster than the German) still ran a trade deficit with the rest of the European Union, two-thirds of which was caused by trade with West Germany, caused, that is, by the Germans 'sending us their finished exports to fill out the hollowed space' (Williams et al., 1990: 485) created by the export of capital by UK-based transnational corporations.

It is of course tempting to run those separate propositions together in a causal chain, arguing that German manufacturing superiority is a product of the role played in German industry by German banking institutions. But that would be an illegitimate move. All that can be legitimately said – and all that is claimed by serious scholars – is that the institutional relationships between German banks and German manufacturing firms give the former the *potential* to exercise significant degrees of industrial leadership, and to create different (more long-term) sets of expectations and imperatives around German management. As Zysman has it: 'in drawing conclusions about the German case, we cannot go much beyond the contention that long-term banking finance encourages industrialists to take a longer view both by providing long-term capital resources and by substituting a longer-term view of industry needs for a concern with the short-run fluctuations of the stock market' (Zysman, 1983: 265). And we cannot go much further because in practice the exercise of that potential for control by German financial institutions is a highly nuanced one, so nuanced in fact as to allow space for a new revisionist literature to deny that UK and German industry–bank relations really differ at all (Edwards and Fischer, 1994a; Schneider-Lenne, 1994).

At the heart of that revisionism is the argument that the apparent gap in practices between the two economies is in large part a statistical mirage, a product of different forms of company accounting, such that when the figures are standardized it becomes clear that both the UK and German industrial sectors rely predominantly on internally generated funds, and that German banks relied *less* on bank loans as a source of finance than UK banks between 1970 and 1989 (Edwards and Fischer, 1994b: 259, 265). It is also argued that the supervisory boards on which German bankers sit do not exercise effective industrial leadership. The effective power in German industrial companies is said to lie one layer lower down, in the executive boards from which all the social partners are effectively excluded (Esser, 1990: 27; Lane, 1995: 54; Schneider-Lenne, 1994: 291). Add to that the recognition that large German companies, like large companies elsewhere, have effectively freed themselves of dependence on particular house-banks (Esser, 1990: 29), and that indeed the Big 3 universal banks in Germany have now reduced the proportion of lending going to large German companies (Schneider-Lenne, 1994: 288), and a more accurate picture emerges of where bank–industry links in Germany are at their most distinctive. 'Among large firms house bank relationships definitely do not exist' (Edwards and Fischer, 1994b: 267). It is among the small and medium-size German companies – the *Mittelstand* – that banks and industry most effectively articulate in the German case; and it is there that the competitive advantages of long-term low-interest lending seem to be most potent. In the large-company sector, bank control is neither sought nor exercised.

> To sum up, the banks in Germany have quite considerable potential influence on the business world as a result of their participations, supervisory board functions and proxy voting rights. However, companies are not dominated by the banks, nor is it in the banks' interests to assume responsibility for other firms' business: they would not be able to do this satisfactorily owing to a lack of the necessary expertise in this area. Moreover, the banks – alongside companies, trade and other associations, and unions – are only one factor in an intricate system of checks and balances governing the wide range of business interests. Nor, finally, are the banks themselves a homogeneous block, but compete intensely with each other. *(Schneider-Lenne, 1994: 292)*

The revisionist material on German banking is very powerful. The work of Edwards and Fischer in particular has shown 'that the argument that German banks perform a corporate control function lacks both solid theoretical and adequate empirical support' (Dyson, 1986: 129), so destroying the credibility of the earlier thesis that the structure of corporate finance in the two economies was qualitatively different and poles apart. But such a claim was only ever one-third of the argument about UK–German institutional differences. The other two elements in the case for the reform of UK financial institutions were concerned with the adverse effect of capital markets on UK investment patterns and managerial criteria for action, and with the creation of long-term growth trajectories rooted in nineteenth-century banking practices. They were theses about 'short-termism' and about systematic industrial underinvestment; and there the evidence is less damning, and the jury is still out. For, bank lending apart, there is certainly much validity in the claim that the other important distinguishing feature of the German financial system, when compared with that of the UK, is the weakness of its capital markets. Latest figures may suggest that – in the large-firm sector – bank loans are the main form of external financing in both the UK and Germany; but among medium-size firms that is not the case. Medium-size UK firms are more likely than German ones to go to the stock market for their external finance (Schneider-Lenne, 1994: 293); and the whole weight of German economic history suggests that for the bulk of the twentieth century German industrial firms of whatever size were more institutionally protected from over-exposure to short-term pressures for immediate profits and high-dividend returns than their UK equivalents. Globalization may now be ending that, and producing convergence: UK banks are now becoming universal banks, and large German companies are seeking equity capital on world stock markets. But equity capital of this kind was historically of little importance in the German case, and is still only of minor significance; all of which suggests that any discussion of the sources of past German industrial strength must allow some weight to the closeness of financial to non-financial economic institutions, even if current trends suggest that future German development is likely to be able to draw on only vestigial elements of any German exceptionalism of this kind.

In fact what is clearly salvageable from the arguments on bank–industry relations in the German case is the place that bank representation on the supervisory boards of large companies plays in a wider system of close coordination within the ranks of large-scale German industrial capital. Even Edwards and Fischer recognize this, the possibility that bank representation on supervisory boards is simply 'the most pronounced aspect of a different institutional feature, whereby large firms are represented on each other's supervisory boards' (Edwards and Fischer, 1994a: 238). German capital is highly organized internally, not least through a developed set of interlocking directorships. John Scott found that 'multiple directors made up 10.7 per cent of the directorate of the top 250 German enterprises of 1976, and they tied over three-quarters of the enterprises into an extensive network of connections'. He also found that 'bank directors were especially important in this network', and that 'the density of this network . . . was higher than that found in any of the Anglo-American economies', and close to Japanese levels (Scott, 1997: 149, 193). German industrial capital is also – by UK standards – characterized by high degrees of both vertical integration and horizontal combination, with horizontal links between both competitors and suppliers particularly marked among small and medium-size enterprises. German business organizations, that is, 'are connected by a multiplicity of ties both to a very dense socio-institutional framework and to each other', while 'their British counterparts tend to be more institutionally isolated' (Lane, 1992: 76). The full economic significance of this is yet to be established empirically (so the claims made for it have to be tentative); and the latest research evidence suggests a degree of convergence between models in the past two decades. But it is at least safe to say that, historically, corporate coordination through networking relationships was a significant and distinguishing feature of German (and as we shall see next, Japanese) capitalism, and that 'the tight intertwining of universal bank and industry facilitate[d] – more than anything else – a highly organised system of capitalist production and reproduction' built around a series of 'financial groups' (Esser, 1990: 29, 30). And to that degree at least it seems legitimate to argue (as many have done) that the distinctive business system established in Germany from the 1870s holds one important key to its sustained economic growth thereafter.

It is possible to go at least that far with the institutionalist claim for German superiority, because ultimately the problem with the argument lies less in its substance than in its parameters. Institutionalist explanations of different economic performances are limited ultimately not by what they say but by what they do not. It is the emphases they contain and the level of analysis at which they settle that is ultimately their undoing. As we have seen, when institutionalist accounts of UK and German postwar economic performance focus on the role of different business systems, they place the weight of their analyses on the *systemic* nature of the institutional differences they privilege. One consequence of this is that the logic of the argument pushes towards policy proposals of a cherry-picking kind – towards the suggestion that slowly growing economies should seek out and adopt the institutional practices of more rapidly growing ones – so obliging the more sophisticated of the institutionalists then to emphasize the notion of 'embeddedness' and the associated difficulties of extracting one element from what is seen as an integrated system of institutions and practices. But by putting the emphasis in their analysis of business systems on the notion of system, institutionalists understate the importance of the fact that the systems being analysed are *business* systems. For the historical record suggests that it is the character of the business classes within those systems that holds the key to the manner of their operation, not the fact that business classes relate to each other in a systematic way, and that in consequence it is the classes themselves, and not merely their institutions, which would need to be borrowed if catch-up was to be effected in this cherry-picking way.

By recognizing the class basis of different national business systems in this way, their defining institutional differences can then be anchored in a different, and more incisive, form of explanation. In the specifics of the UK–German comparison, that explanation makes clear that behind the institutional differences of the two systems lie different relationships between the financial and industrial fractions of each national capitalist class, differences that principally derive from the distinct positions occupied by UK and German capitalisms in the global economy after 1870. For, as we saw in chapter 5, financial capitalists in the UK played a critical world role long before UK industrialization, and indeed had that world role strengthened and underpinned by the temporary world monopoly enjoyed by UK industrial capitalists in the mid-nineteenth century. In consequence, the accumulation of industrial capital in the UK in the twentieth century operated against the background of extensive capital export and within internal parameters set by the imperial ambitions of the UK state elite (as well as within those set by the defensive and moderate labourism of a well-organized but conservative working class). The class parameters driving and containing German industrialization were from the outset simply different. The financial strata within the German capitalist class did not develop an international role and orientation. The German state (as we shall see in chapter 7) played an entirely different role in relation to local capital accumulation. The German labour movement (as was the way with working classes created later and more abruptly than that of the UK) was politically more militant than the UK labour movement both before 1933 and after 1945; and those differences were all ultimately the product of the *later* arrival of German capitalism into the emerging world capitalist economy, and of the resulting different location initially occupied globally by German capital.

The gap between finance and industry in the UK was not simply a gap between institutions. It was a gap between fractions of a common class, whose location in the emerging world capitalist system after 1870 gave its financial strata both a set of international orientations and the market power to superimpose them on local industrial capital. That was not true in the German case: and the trajectory of German industrial development differed from that of the UK accordingly. Convergence now – under the impact of the intensification of global competition – may well be pulling large-scale UK industrial capital out of the UK, and giving large-scale German industrial capital access to international funds and production sites it hitherto eschewed. But that convergence is occurring at the end of a century of different *internal* capital accumulations: and that different legacy is ultimately to be explained by reference to the balance and character of class forces in each economy, and not simply by reference to the institutional structures and organizational practices into which those class relationships have cohered. What we are dealing with in the German case is not simply a superior set of institutional practices: we are dealing with a stronger industrial bourgeoisie.

Coordinated capitalism: the Japanese case

The research question which that then leaves is whether industrial bourgeoisies that relate to each other through network forms of coordination are necessarily and permanently stronger competitively than industrial bourgeoisies that handle their intra-class relations predominantly through market-based forms of coordination. As we saw at the start of this chapter, and more extensively in chapter 3, that is certainly what is claimed for postwar Japanese industrial capitalism in particular: that the networked structure of large-scale Japanese capital facilitated capital accumulation, technology transfer and innovation after 1945, that the internal structuring of large-scale Japanese companies left them particularly well placed to exploit the underlying technical and market imperatives of capitalism's 'Third Industrial Revolution', and that the subcontracting underbelly of this dual economy gave it a flexibility and a dynamism that others lacked. So, on one of the widely cited arguments, the success of the postwar Japanese economy rested centrally on its possession of large-scale (positively Schumpeterian) enterprise firms capable of generating the 'collective reflexivity' vital for success in the competitive universe of the new information-based technological paradigm (Best, 1990: 137–66; Lash and Urry, 1994: 65–80). Or, as one of the more widely cited counter-arguments has it, Japanese postwar success was embedded in the specificity of its articulation of large and small firms, and in the associated dynamism (flexibility and specialized skills) of its small-firm sector, embedded, that is, not in its large-firm sector so much as in the ability of its networks of small firms to establish a competitive advantage in the new era of flexible specialization (Friedman, 1988). Or postwar Japanese success was embedded in the fierce competition between large Japanese companies (Patrick and Rosovsky, 1976: 43), or it was embedded in the balance between competition and cooperation that they somehow miraculously struck (Hutton, 1994: 269), or it was embedded in the way Japan mixed institutional features which appeared in isolated form in other economies – in what Okimoto termed 'the dynamic interactive chemistry of the whole' (Okimoto, 1989: 175). In the pre-1992 literature on why postwar growth rates differ among advanced capitalist economies, the organization of Japanese capital was everyone's favourite answer (see Kenney and Florida, 1993: 24–7); and that was true whether you were a post-Fordist, a neo-Schumpeterian, a post-Keynesian or even a neo-classical economist. Japanese capital provided many faces to the world, and was acclaimed simultaneously for the dynamism of its small-firm sector, the networking of its industrial groupings and the competitiveness of its firms both large and small.

Reaching the facts through this cacophony of claims is extraordinarily difficult, but a number of crucial things do seem to distinguish the general organization of Japanese capital from that of American capital in the postwar period.

1   One distinguishing feature of postwar Japanese capitalism appears to be the complex networks linking many of its main industrial companies (Gerlach, 1989; 1992; Lincoln et al., 1992). Large sections of Japanese industrial capital before 1945 were organized by (and within) ten large *zaibatsu*, integrated networks of companies organized around a family-dominated holding company. Although formally dissolved by the occupation forces after 1945, the *zaibatsu* companies reconstituted themselves to a significant degree as soon as economic and political circumstances allowed; and new coalitions of firms emerged, organized around particular banks or large manufacturing companies. In consequence, large sections of Japanese industrial capital after 1945 came to be organized in something akin to what for Germany Esser called 'finance groups'. The Japanese research literature invariably labels these as 'industrial/enterprise groups', and the Japanese themselves apparently refer to them as either *kigyo shudan* or *keiretsu*, depending on their antecedents and width (Esser, 1990: 30; Scott, 1997: 194–5). As a result, large companies in the Japanese economy were (and indeed still are) linked together through interlocking reciprocal share-ownership: in a real sense they partly own each other. 'A typical listed firm in Japan has extensive interlocking shareholdings with transaction partners

(banks, insurance companies, suppliers, customers, trading companies) and affiliated firms' (Sheard, 1994: 310). The largest corporate groupings characteristically extend across a range of industrial sectors, each grouping trying to have at least one major company in each major business sector – the so called 'one set' principle (Gerlach, 1989: 147–8). Groupings originating after the war are invariably organized around a Japanese equivalent of a German house bank, and tied in to one or more of the leading securities houses. And even those major Japanese companies that are not part of the 'horizontal' *kigyo shudan* networks (and that includes *keiretsu* like Nissan, Toyota and Toshiba) are 'vertically' interlocked with their main banks, and with their chain of supplying subcontractors, so that overall and on average, 'a typical Japanese firm has about 70% of its shares held by other corporations' (Sheard, 1994: 312).

2   Within each 'enterprise group' companies do not face each other as isolated market entities, but as component elements of a coherent network of capitalist enterprises: networks which then compete fiercely with each other. 'Members of the corporate sets are linked together', Scott tells us, 'through reciprocal capital, commercial and personal relations; they engage in preferential trading, joint ventures, and technical integration; and their aligned participations are reinforced by preferential loans supplied by the group bank and by funds from the trust and insurance companies within the group' (Scott, 1997: 193). Stockholding, interlocking directorships and group controlled finance are the lynch-pins to group coherence, and cumulatively establish a degree of linkage between financial and non-financial institutions in Japan – between industrial and financial capital – which certainly has no US or UK equivalent, and exceeds even the degree of bank–industry interaction in the German economy. These industrial networks provide 'an effective mechanism for ciffusing and diminishing risk in Japan's industrial system' acting as 'a kind of keiretsu-based insurance system' for private sector 'risk diffusion and crisis management' (Okimoto, 1989: 139), which again has no liberal capitalist equivalent; and in the process they help to shut out foreign ownership and make it difficult for foreign-based firms to penetrate the Japanese home market (Gerlach, 1992: 262–5). What is unique about the Japanese pattern is not simply that banks own large numbers of shares in the companies they lend to, although it should be noted that across the large corporate sector as a whole 'the most prominent interlock, in terms of both shares and value, is with the bank that would be recognised as the firm's "main bank"' (Sheard, 1994: 314). What is also unique is the degree to which the shares of the banks are themselves owned by the industrial corporations that are the bank's main customers. While 70 per cent of most companies' shares are held by other companies, as we have just noted, according to Paul Sheard the twenty-one major financial institutions in Japan find 92 per cent of their shares held in this way. Sheard looked in particular at the Daicho Kangyo Bank. He found the top twenty share-holders in that bank were corporations, in all of which

DKB was a prominent shareholder, and to almost all of which DKB was the largest bank creditor. 'In other words, the bank is owned in large part by firms to which it acts as a main bank' (Sheard, 1994: 334–5): and this for a bank which sits at the heart of one of Japan's six largest postwar industrial networks.

3   A third distinguishing feature setting the general organization of Japanese industrial capital apart from the organization of US capital in the postwar period has been its penchant for subcontracting. Japan is not an economy of large employment units. On the contrary, 88 per cent of Japan's non-agricultural labour force work in the small- or medium-enterprise sector: over 50 per cent work in establishments employing fewer than 30 regular staff, and 42 per cent work in firms with fewer than 10 (Chalmers, 1989: 47). Even large-scale Japanese companies are not large employers, at least by North American or Western European standards: Toyota, for example, employed 65,000 people against General Motors' 750,000, when producing 4.5 million vehicles a year against General Motors' 7.9 million (Fruin, 1992: 256). Instead, the process of industrial production – in a number of key industrial sectors, including automobiles – is extensively subcontracted. It has been estimated, for example, that 'unlike the US [auto] firms in the 1980s that produced 60–70 per cent of their own parts, the major Japanese producers made only 30 per cent and contracted out the rest through their system of affiliates' (Tabb, 1995: 122). Certainly the major Japanese car companies came by the 1970s to preside over a virtual mountain of smaller firms: MITI estimated for 1978 that 'the average Japanese auto maker had 171 first-layer, 4,700 second-layer and 31,600 third-layer part makers' (Lash and Urry, 1994: 73); and Toyota in particular had by then developed its renowned 'just-in-time' production system, gaining competitive advantage by the central orchestration of component flows from an integrated set of formally independent subcontracting firms. And this was not just a feature of the Japanese car industry. In practice, each of the broad industry groups in the contemporary Japanese economy is hierarchically organized with, at every level within the group, a high degree of company specialization. Japanese companies, that is, show a marked tendency to focus on one particular field of business (Okimoto, 1989: 125; Gerlach, 1992: 27), and to compete in that field with specialized firms from other industry groups, while being themselves locked into complex hierarchical relationships between major and minor companies within their particular industrial grouping.

4   This process of networking and subcontracting coexists alongside a particular set of internal managerial practices (and forms of internal corporate organization) which are again said by many management specialists to set Japanese companies apart from their main American rivals. It would appear that in general Japanese firms did not copy the M (multi-divisional) organizational form that was adopted by large US corporations with such

success in the first half of the twentieth century, or the European H-form
(holding company), so that even today major Japanese companies are reportedly not only 'smaller in number of employees' but also 'less integrated vertically, [and] less diversified in product line . . . than comparable American
and leading European firms' (Fruin, 1992: 26; for the link to the system of
lifetime employment, see Okimoto, 1989: 125). They are also said by Fruin
to have been pushed by the logic of their late development and resource
scarcity into organizational practices geared to the full utilization of borrowed technologies – from early on to have emphasized the importance of
organizational learning and cooperative structures linking factory, firm and
network (ibid.: 13) – establishing in the process team-based models of work
organization which gather productive efficiency by the sharing of information and the systematic development and utilization of employee skills. The
postwar Japanese industrial firm, that is, is said to have prospered by becoming 'a learning organisation that is continuously creating new productive
services by teamwork and experience' (Best, 1990: 166), and by combining
a focus on high-volume output with production facilities that minimize
complexity. It is also said to have prospered by linking the advantages of
cooperation between firms with high degrees of cooperation between capital
and labour; and certainly Toyota's 'just-in-time' relationship with its subcontractors is normally presented as one part of a wider system of 'lean production' in which job flexibility is extensive, employee-involvement is
encouraged and quality control is high. And if imitation is the sincerest
form of flattery, and diffusion the best guide to potency, it is significant that
the 'Japanese Enterprise System' has now 'acquired mainstream legitimacy
in the theories of scholars and the practices of managers' (Lincoln, 1993:
55) throughout the advanced capitalist world, with the work of Aoki and
Fruin in particular much discussed and cited in the relevant research
literatures.

There can be no doubt that, before 1992 at least, these interlocking features of Japanese corporate organization did facilitate the full exploitation
and development of mass production technologies initially developed in the
US. The story of postwar Japanese economic catch-up is not complete
without a discussion of the role of the Japanese state (to which we shall
come in chapter 7); but nor can it be adequately explained without reference to the high level of informal orchestration of long-term investment
strategies and production systems within the networks of Japanese companies. As Calder has it, 'research presents the long term credit banks and the
keiretsu industrial structure as key elements in the "corporate-led strategic
capitalism" that has been central to the prosperity of Japan's most successful industrial sectors' (Calder, 1993: 21). And those sectors, as US industrial planners became only too aware by the 1980s, included not simply
ships, steel and automobiles, but also by then consumer electronics, robotics, super computers and telecommunications (Kenney and Florida, 1993:
51).

The role of bank finance, for example, was (and remains) central to the facility with which postwar Japanese companies acquired and mobilized new resources: both capital and labour. There is plenty of research evidence to show that Japanese industrial firms were more dependent on bank finance than even German firms after 1945 (Corbett, 1994: 306, 311; Edwards and Fischer, 1994a: 68), and that Japanese banks historically were far less internationally focused than their UK contemporaries (Calder, 1993: 11). There is clear research evidence too that the cost of loans made by Japanese banks to companies within their industrial groupings was low by international standards, at least until the 1990s (Tabb, 1995: 103; Nakatani, 1995: 51). There is clear evidence that the system of interlocking and stable shareholding to which the banks were central freed Japanese industrial managers from any pressure for high-dividend distribution (Okimoto, 1989: 121; Masuyama, 1994: 333; Corbett, 1994: 307; Lash and Urry, 1994: 77), and enabled them to privilege the building up of market share over short-term profit-taking (Drucker, 1988: 106; Lash and Urry, 1994: 77; Johnson, 1995: 61). There is also clear research evidence to show that the system of interlocking shareholdings freed Japanese companies from hostile takeovers (Hiroshi, 1988: 81–2), that it was created to close out the danger of foreign ownership associated with moves to liberalize capital controls in the 1960s (Hiroshi, 1988: 82; Masuyama, 1994: 328), and that it did facilitate the orderly restructuring of companies and sectors in competitive difficulties both before the 1973 oil crisis and after it (Pascale and Rohlen, 1988: 149–70; Calder, 1993: 166–73). Japanese industrial capital, that is, throughout its long years of rapid postwar growth, was institutionally positioned to subordinate financial logics to manufacturing ones (Clegg et al., 1990: 56) in ways that UK-based industrial capital, for example, was not. The competitive struggle between banks, and the high involvement of banks in long-term industrial lending, guaranteed that (Hidaka, 1997: 166); and they gave Japanese industrial capital, in consequence, access to investment funds at prices and on terms which (to a degree greater than that experienced by either US or UK industrial capital) facilitated rapid capital accumulation and persistent industrial modernization.

There can also be no doubt that this flow of capital was used, in the first instance, to bring Japanese heavy industry and mass production consumer good production up to US standards; but it would be quite wrong to treat Japanese growth after 1945 as simply a question of catch-up from a late start. For it is clear too that sections of Japanese industrial capital developed by the 1980s capacities for the development and application of new technologies, capacities developed by information-sharing within Japan's corporate networks, and capacities which by then had extended to the new high-tech industries. There is also clear research evidence that this capacity for technological innovation was itself linked to Japan's earlier economic backwardness, as a long-term spin-off from the way in which Japanese industrial companies after 1945 had prospered initially by 'reverse engineering', by acquiring finished products from abroad, de-constructing them, and creating the industrial capacity to reproduce and then refine them (Freeman, 1988: 335). The result, it would appear, was the emergence of a particular system for industrial research and development (Westney, 1993: 37): one characterized by a heavy propensity for 'process innovation rather than product innovation . . . focused on incremental innovation rather than radical innovation' (Imai, 1992: 225), one in which firms established a closer working relationship between R&D departments and production engineers and process controllers than was normal in the US and Europe, one biased towards the generation of high-quality consumer products – 'according to recent estimates, nearly nine-tenths of Japan's total R&D effort is devoted to product development' (Kenney and Florida, 1993: 58). The sensitivity of Japanese R&D departments to the competitive advantages of process innovation predisposed them to recognize early the industrial potential of computer technologies initiated in the US, and encouraged them to apply those technologies to existing mass production systems, transforming them as they did so. Indeed 'by 1989, Japanese corporations had deployed 219,667 industrial robots in manufacturing compared to 36,977 for the United States and 22,395 for Germany' at a time when 'no other country had deployed more than 10,000 industrial robots' (ibid.: 71). Free from any distorting impact on the distribution of R&D capacities created by military-industrial production – Japan was by 1990 spending a full 1 per cent more of its GNP on commercial R&D even than the US – Japanese companies concentrated their growing R&D expenditures after 1973 on product development in the 'fastest growing civilian industries, such as electronics' where 'patent statistics showed that' by the 1980s 'the leading Japanese electronics firms outstripped American and European firms in these industries, not just in domestic patenting but in patents taken out in the United States' (Freeman and Soete, 1997: 302). The result, by 1990, was a significant repositioning of US and Japanese firms, not just in mass production assembly industries of the Fordist variety, but in 'the new high-technology sectors of semiconductors, computers, telecommunications, software and biotechnology' (Kenney and Florida, 1993: 50) as well.

It is also clear that the system of subcontracting and the associated internal managerial initiatives on production flows and labour incorporation were well geared to achieving the full utilization of capital and labour, once mobilized. Together these left Japanese firms well placed to 'combine product and process specialization at the manufacturing level, co-ordination in strategic planning and marketing at the corporate level, [and] product and market-breadth at the inter-firm level' (Fruin, 1992: 10). Subcontracting is a case in point. The deployment of senior managers and core workers to subcontracting firms, and the extension of credit facilities from the top to the base of the industrial grouping, did lock small and large firms together. The competitive struggle of those small firms for large-firm business did encourage dynamism and innovation among them; and the existence of a differentiated and entrepreneurial small-firm sector did provide a cushion for the large firms, protecting their ability to guarantee job security to (and underwriting the value of their investment in the training of) core workers and central managerial staff. To this degree at least, it is possible to go with the 'flex spec' thesis of Japanese growth, in recognizing the competitive and technological dynamism of Japan's small-firm sector in the years of high growth each side of 1973. But the general assertion that Japanese growth was primarily driven by its small-firm sector is not persuasive (see Fruin, 1992: 300; also Williams et al., 1987). For the postwar Japanese economy (including its small-firm sector) was dominated by the large firms within each industrial grouping. It was they that drew greatest competitive advantage from the subcontracting system; and in automobiles and consumer electronics at least, it was the reorganization of mass production systems under their leadership that produced truly remarkable results (in both productivity growth and capture of global market share) particularly from the 1970s. As the MITI white paper of 1980 estimated, while it was 'capital increases in the 1960s [which] contributed most heavily to increases in production' in Japan, 'in the 1970s . . . the importance of technology and other factors rose' in industries as diverse as chemicals, textiles, metal products and electronics (Hajime, 1988: 147). In the crucial automobile industry, among 'those other factors' must be included the whole paraphernalia of 'lean production', which left Toyota's inventory costs by the 1980s averaging a mere US$40 a car, when the US Big Three had inventory costs averaging between US$600–700 a car! (Tabb, 1995: 123; see also Fruin, 1992: 251–95; Cusomano, 1989).

It would appear that 'lean production' was initially purely a Toyota phenomenon, but that after the first oil crisis in 1973 large sections of Japanese manufacturing industry adopted some or all of its precepts: 'employment rationalisation, the introduction of new technology (including computer-aided machinery), developing energy-saving capacities, reducing inventories and reorganising stock control systems, work reorganisation and reskilling' (Peck and Miyamachi, 1994: 657). Technically, 'lean production is distinguished by the absence of indirect workers, buffer stocks and the rework characteristic of mass production, and by the presence of re-skilled, multi-tasked workers using flexible equipment for small lot, just-in-time production with rapid changeover' (Williams et al., 1992: 324). The claims made for this form of organization of the labour process by its most enthusiastic advocates have been enormous: that 'it uses less of everything compared with mass production – half the human effort in the factory, half the manufacturing space, half the investment in tools, half the engineering hours to develop a new product in half the time' (Womack et al., 1990: 13). And since it was only after 1973 that the Japanese export sector really asserted itself in world markets, it is perhaps not entirely surprising that the enormous productivity gains apparently associated with lean production should have come to be so enthusiastically canvassed, particularly by those outside Japan who were seeking to enhance the competitiveness of their own industrial base. For what could anyone possibly find objectionable in forms of labour organization described as follows, especially if they were being canvassed as *the* key to competitiveness, growth, employment and rising living standards:

> The distinctive features of Japanese organization include long-term employment, seniority promotion, flexible and overlapping role assignments, extensive cross-training, team production, cohesive work groups, strong vertical relationships, finely graded hierarchies combined with low inequality, broadly participatory yet formally centralized decision-making, enterprise-based unions, a rich bundle of employee welfare services, and ceaseless efforts to build morale and commitment through appeals to core company values, rigorous screening and socialization of recruits, and an abundance of ritual and ceremony. *(Lincoln, 1993: 71)*

The answer (as we began to see when discussing Japanese industrial relations in chapter 5) is that there is much that is objectionable and distorted here, both in the claims made for lean production, and in lean production itself: objections and distortions which limit it both as a route to permanently successful capital accumulation and as a model for any form of progressive settlement between capital and labour. For what is missing from the description (and advocacy) of lean production by scholars deploying the ostensibly neutral analytical categories of organizational science is a clear sense of the power relationships that run through it, and of the consequently intense forms of labour exploitation which are, in truth, the key to its impact on productivity and growth.

Certainly the Womack, Jones and Roos study is deeply flawed as a piece of reliable scholarship, as has been indicated by, among others, Karel Williams and his colleagues (Williams et al., 1992). As they demonstrate convincingly, the study's research data (published separately in background papers from MITI) did not sustain its claims for the scale of the productivity gains made by lean production, or for the centrality of lean production systems of labour organization for the productivity gains recorded. The conclusions of *The Machine that Changed the World* ignored the critical role of automation levels, design factors and capacity utilization, which its own research indicated played so critical a role in the market impact achieved by Japanese car producers after 1973. Nor did the study allow adequately for the catch-up dimension of an initially backward Japanese car industry in the narrowing of productivity differentials; as Williams and his colleagues put it, 'the basic story of labour hours per vehicle is . . . that the Japanese have been on a long trajectory of improvement but started so far behind the stationary Americans that the current performance gap between the American and Japanese industries is relatively small' (Williams et al., 1992: 333). Moreover, Womack and his team seem entirely to have missed the significance of the fact that Japanese car productivity, once having caught up, then stabilized: that lean production did not and could not generate permanent productivity growth. And most of all, in selecting just some of the productivity determinants located in its research data for special emphasis in its report, the MITI study closed in on what Williams and his colleagues rightly called 'the soft organizational features' (team work and the like) and studiously ignored the critical role of long hours, intensified work routines and low wages in the competitive success of the Japanese auto industry in the postwar period.

Lean production, as applied in the postwar Japanese car industry, was (and remains) in reality a superb system for extracting surplus from labour, by 'combining intense effort with long hours' (ibid.: 342). There is a healthy debate – particularly in the labour process and post-Fordist literatures – on whether lean production is just a version of Taylorism and Fordism, or something new; and that literature includes fierce disagreements about whether the trade-off between the job security and intensified work processes that Toyota and other Japanese companies offer their core workers is or is not preferable to the wage–effort bargain struck by labour movements elsewhere (on this, see Peck and Miyamachi, 1994: 651–2; Kenney and Florida, 1993: 24–5). But these disagreements notwithstanding, those research literatures demonstrate quite clearly the *downside* of lean production, which its advocates studiously ignore, that lean production depends for its effectiveness upon:

- a highly coercive and exploitative relationship between the main company and its system of subcontractors, and through them between the main firm and the labour employed in the subcontracting network (Kenney and Florida, 1993: 47);
- a seriously weakened labour movement, unable and unwilling to assert any degree of control over the design, distribution and pace of work (Dohse et al., 1985);
- excessive hours of work by its core workers: Tabb reports Japanese auto workers clocking up 2,210 hours in 1989, including 291 in overtime, more than the average for all Japanese industries, an average which was itself – as we saw in chapter 1 – higher than elsewhere in the advanced capitalist world (Tabb, 1995: 120);
- intensified work routines both in the main factories and in the subcontracting system (Cusomano, 1989; Dohse et al., 1985: 129–34);
- a gradation of wages: high for core workers, but lower and lower as we go down the supply chain (Arrighi, 1994: 343–4; Kyotani, 1996).

'Every year workers in the Japanese automotive industry man their production lines and machines for 250 to 800 hours per person more than their German counterparts: each year Toyota utilises its production capacity (plant operating hours) for about 900 hours more than Volkswagen' (Bosch and Lehndorff, 1995: 1–2). And it is not without significance that it was from the Toyota labour force that Kamata Satoshi could publish his diary of working the just-in-time system under the title 'The Automobile Factory of Despair' (Cusomano, 1989: 305). In Japan at least, it would appear that the underside of lean production is worker stress, factory accidents and high rates of suicide.

Lean production, when exported back into the US, has played its own role in reversing the originally inexorable rise of Japanese car exports, but only (as we shall discuss more fully in the last chapter) at the price of lowering wages and intensifying the wage–effort bargain. For in a real sense, lean production is not a qualitatively new kind of labour management, but one of a very old kind. It offers individual firms a rapid growth in market share for so long as they, and they alone, can intensify the process of surplus extraction from their workers. But it also invites (indeed compels) duplication and diffusion to competitor firms elsewhere, and eventually leaves the competitive gap as it originally was, but at a higher level of work intensity and with lower returns to labour. Lean production is, in this sense, not a new and permanent solution to capitalism's growth problem, but a key mechanism for temporarily resolving that problem by ratcheting down workers' rights and workers' rewards.

In any event, it would be unwise to swallow the fiction that the Japanese economy after 1973 became entirely reset on such lines, or that its industrial capitalist class had found the key to productivity growth across the economy as a whole. Neither fiction would be true. Lean production did not become hegemonic, even in the Japanese car industry, and certainly not beyond it. Nissan struggled to adopt the *kanban* system from the 1970s (Fruin and Nishigushi, 1993). Neither Honda nor Mazda went fully over to the Toyota system, and each underperformed compared with improving US car producers throughout the 1980s (Williams et al., 1992: 326). And more generally, Japanese productivity proved 'extremely variable across industries' (Oulton, 1994: 53): high in cars, electronics and steel, but low in food, drink, agriculture, textiles and retail services. Wolff found productivity in Japanese agriculture in 1988 to be just 18 per cent of US levels, in food, beverage and tobacco 35 per cent and in textiles 57 per cent (Abramovitz and David, 1996: 33). Little wonder then that Porter thought Japan 'a study in contrasts', one divided between world-beating companies in some sectors and other sectors in which companies 'not only fail to measure up to the standards of the best world-wide competitors but fall far behind them' (Porter, 1990: 394). That division did not affect overall Japanese international performance and standing, of course, as long as export industries were not among that second list; but it began to matter enormously when, after 1992, the wheels began to come off Japan's hitherto spectacular trade performance. After 1992, as we have already observed, the advocates of the Japanese model have fallen understandably silent.

A note on trust-based capitalisms in the 1990s

The 1990s have not been a good decade for the economic performance of trust-based capitalisms. The German economy, newly united east and west, spent the decade (as we shall discuss in more detail in chapter 8) struggling with unprecedented levels of unemployment and low profitability in its manufacturing sector (while still maintaining a GDP growth rate of 2 per cent per annum in the second half of the 1990s). The Japanese economy, once its manufacturing sector felt the full internal consequences of the collapse of share prices on the Toyko stock market in 1990, did less well even than that. It spent the decade in economic stagnation and ended it in recession. Except in 1996, Japanese GDP grew at less than 1.5 per cent per annum from 1992, well below the average growth rate of either the US or UK economies in that period. Each major capitalist economy then ran into the turbulence created by the general East Asian financial crisis (on which again we shall comment in chapter 8); but Japan alone had its own minicrisis from 1992, one whose origins threw sharp light back on the strengths and weaknesses of its growth model, one whose resolution indicated clearly the unsuitability of the 'Japanese Enterprise System' as a model for the European and North American Centre-Left.

The Japanese downturn of the 1990s threw into relief the weaknesses of what hitherto had looked an impregnable set of corporate relationships between industrial and financial institutions. The internationally closed, highly networked and state-directed nature of the postwar Japanese banking system had produced, as we have seen, a steady flow of cheap capital for the Japanese manufacturing sector, and had transformed large Japanese companies into major exporters after 1973. But that very growth loosened the dependence of large companies on bank credit, and brought the Japanese state under heavy international pressure to liberalize its financial markets and to revalue the yen. Internal and external developments, that is, ate away at the institutional underpinnings of Japan's postwar growth performance.

Externally, pressure from the US administration produced the 1985 Plaza Accord, committing the Japanese state to the toleration of a stronger yen (which then nearly doubled its value against the dollar in just eighteen months). Squeezed in export markets, large Japanese corporations moved capital abroad, both into the US and Europe (their main markets) and into the Asian tiger economies (their main source of cheap labour), as the Japanese policy regime moved from what Pempel called its 'embedded mercantilist' phase to its 'international investor' phase (Pempel, 1998: 16). In fact, 'after 1985 there was . . . a massive outsurge of outward FDI from Japan'. In the three years to 1988 Japanese capital exports 'exceeded the cumulative value of FDI during the previous three and a half decades . . . from 1951' (Hobday, 1995: 20), and between 1987 and 1990 ran at almost double the level of US FDI (Brenner, 1998: 217). Then, from 1991 to 1995 'annual foreign direct investment in manufacturing by Japan grew' again 'by almost 50 per cent. . . . with almost all of the increase absorbed by Asia' (Brenner, 1998: 223–4), in the process locking the Japanese and Asian tiger production, finance and export systems together to such a degree that the East Asian financial crisis of 1997 then threatened the survival of major Japanese financial institutions.

Internally, the Japanese government sought to head off the pressure on corporate profits triggered by the yen revaluation by deliberately running a cheap money policy, and the resulting over-supply of available funds induced progressively more speculative investment by Japanese financial and manufacturing institutions, particularly investment in marginally viable industrial projects and in non-productive outlets such as land and financial assets. Inflated land and asset prices then gave a false sense of the value of corporate collateral, and induced lending to ever more marginal and risky corporate ventures, while the strong networking links between banks, industrial firms and the bureaucracy encouraged over-lending and the paper-inflation of corporate worth, while being themselves lubricated by cronyism and corruption. Between 1985 and 1990 investment in industrial plant and equipment increased at more than 10% per annum, and the economy in total averaged growth rates of nearly 5% (Brenner, 1998: 216). But at the same time 'the value of property in Japan increased by over 200 per cent . . . rapidly appreciating values in an already expensive property market' (Leyshon, 1994: 142) as large Japanese corporations spent in total Y40 million between 1985 and 1990 speculating in what Noguchi has termed a 'land fever' (Noguchi, 1994: 295) When the resulting 'bubble economy' burst in September 1990, the result was a string of scandals, corporate collapses and diminished investor confidence – a crisis of confidence (and bad debts) which then locked the entire Japanese economy onto a low-growth trajectory until the second half of 1995, and again from 1997.

In the process, the Japanese-based car and consumer electronics industries lost their world market share, as US manufacturing capital 'bounced back' (Lester, 1998) in the 1990s and as Japanese export dependence shifted into high-technology-intensive products (Yoshitomi, 1996: 69). By 1998, in consequence, Japan looked far more a typical advanced capitalist economy than it had a decade before. Technology transfer and diffusion had by then run in both directions (in and out of Japan), to leave Japanese corporate networking no longer so visibly *the* model that aspiring national capitalisms elsewhere ought properly to follow.

The response of large-scale Japanese industrial capital to the more difficult trading conditions of the 1990s also demonstrated that the Japanese model under whatever name – Fruin's 'Japanese Enterprise System', Hutton's 'peoplism', or Ozaki's 'human capitalism' – was (and always had been) an inappropriate model for Western progressive forces of a centre–left variety. Even in the heyday of Japanese economic growth, centre–left enthusiasts had always rather cherry-picked from the Japanese model, focusing on the conditions surrounding the favoured 25 per cent of core workers while underplaying the fate of the rest; but even they could not but notice the general intensification of work routines, and the greater job insecurity, triggered by stagnation and recession in the 1990s. Large-scale Japanese manufacturing firms responded to diminished profitability in exactly the same manner as capitalists elsewhere. They progressively shifted their centre of gravity from manufacturing to financial services (Leyshon, 1994). They intensified their pressure on their subcontractors, and they ate away at the rights of their core employees. They also responded by moving productive capacity abroad, to cheaper and less organized labour elsewhere in East Asia, as indeed they had already done at least twice before, moving light manufacturing industries abroad in the 1950s and basic material industries abroad after the oil crisis of 1973. The share of Japan's imports from Asian affiliates of Japanese companies rose sharply in the early 1990s, to account 'for 15 per cent of total manufactured imports in 1994, as compared with less than 5 per cent in 1985', with significantly 'most of the exports of Asian affiliates being . . . home electronics, electrical appliances, and standardized components for the transportation and electrical industries' (Yoshitomi, 1996: 69), which were then in increasing competitive difficulties. In other words, large-scale Japanese industrial capital in the 1990s reacted to its own immediate profit problems by intensifying the extraction of surplus from the workers it employed (both directly in Japan and abroad and indirectly in subcontracting systems). In this way, lean production in that decade became very lean indeed for the workers exposed to it, which made a mockery of, among other things, the eulogies for all things Japanese developed by Lazonick and others in the 1980s, and the claim by Womack, Jones and Roos that a world dominated by lean production would be a better place. For Japanese and other East Asian workers in particular, the 1990s made clear that it was not.

7

The State as an Element in the Growth Equation

At the heart of the debate about capitalist models, as we have now seen, are disagreements about the rights of labour and the powers of capital, disagreements which invariably come together in a fiercely contested set of views about the appropriate role of the state as an agent in the process of economic growth. Indeed, since the shaping of public policy is a central concern of much of the academic scholarship (and all of the popular advocacy) on particular ways of organizing capitalist economies for growth, the question of the state is invariably the central issue in dispute between them. In the broadest sense, attitudes to the state as an economic agent map quite directly onto the intellectual traditions laid out in the Appendix. As has been argued more fully elsewhere (Coates, 1996: 4–16) researchers, commentators and policy-makers of a broadly neo-liberal persuasion invariably present the growth equation as a matter of 'states versus markets', and restrict state activity to policies designed to *strengthen markets* and to correct unavoidable market failures. Policy communities of a more Keynesian hue tend to argue for a degree of *economic management* by the state, particularly through the orchestration of levels of aggregate demand. Those influenced by more Schumpeterian understandings tend to argue for state action on the economy's supply side, *creating market advantage* by policies designed to enhance the quality of local factors of production, both capital and labour. And radical scholarship invariably presses for a high degree of *state regulation and control* of economic processes, which it otherwise sees as driven by the private interests of privileged classes. In the sphere of the state, more obviously than elsewhere in the debates on capitalist models, technical arguments about the determinants of growth and value positions on the appropriateness of private ownership sit inextricably together.

The interface of the political and the economic has long been a major research area in the social science disciplines camped on either side of the divide; and it is now the central concern of the burgeoning sub-disciplines of international and comparative political economy. There has long been in existence a rich research literature on the impact of economics on politics, particularly one concerned with the economic (and social) prerequisites for the emergence of stable democratic political systems (Lipset, 1959; Moore, 1966; Therborn, 1977; Rueschemeyer et al., 1994). There is also a comparative literature on the general impact of 'state–societal' relations on technological innovative capacity and diffusion, and thereby on competitiveness (Hart, 1992a; 1992b) and on the relationship between 'regime type' and economic growth (Sirowy and Inkeles, 1990; Haggard, 1990; Helliwell, 1994; Siermann, 1998). There are also sets of research materials linking the performance of particular national economies in the postwar period to particular kinds of government policy. We met some of that material briefly in chapters 2 and 3; and from it we now need to extract its three central threads. We need to examine the adequacy of the argument that both the US and UK economies in the postwar period underperformed in part because of their exposure to inappropriate forms of state intervention and management. We need to examine the adequacy of the argument that state policy was central to the postwar convergence on US productivity levels and market performance achieved by Germany and Japan; and we need to examine the argument that the space for state intervention of a growth-inducing kind is now seriously restricted by the phenomenon of globalization. We need, that is, to examine both the degree to which *past* differences in the competitive performance of leading capitalist models can be explained in state terms, and the extent to which *future* differences in their competitive performance might be similarly triggered.

Liberal capitalism and the state

It is a defining feature of the liberal model of capitalism that the state plays a very limited role in determining how capital and labour interact in the pursuit of growth. There is no enthusiasm among advocates of such a model for the state to play either a planning or a regulating role. The task of the state, for them, is simply to underwrite and facilitate the full functioning of market processes, by creating sound money, preventing monopoly distortion of factor and product markets, and ensuring open and free trade. Beyond that, the state's economic activity should be restricted, in this model, to the provision of public goods – to the delivery of goods (such as defence and basic social infrastructure) which are both 'non-appropriable and non-depletable' (Sharp and Pavitt, 1993: 5); if it is not so restricted, economic underperformance is likely to ensue. Indeed, as we saw in chapter 4, it was central to the explanation of postwar UK economic decline developed by neo-liberal economists in the 1970s that this self-limiting role had been breached by postwar UK governments, and that it had to be reconstituted if the UK's economic record was ever to be improved. But, as we also saw earlier, such a neo-liberal explanation of what was wrong with UK state–economy relations in the postwar period was not the only one widely canvassed. Left-wing commentators of various intellectual persuasions told a different story, one that attributed the weakening of the competitive position of the UK (and also the US) economy, not to over-government, but to under-government and to mis-government: to the lack (in volume and in kind) of appropriate industrial policies, and to the distorting impact on the international competitiveness of consumer-goods industries of heavy government involvement in the orchestration of military-industrial production. Neo-liberal critiques of state performance were predominantly focused on the UK, so that particularly in the 1970s the UK state found itself criticized from both the Right and the Left, whereas the US state a decade later found itself critiqued predominantly from the Centre-Left. Given their importance, impact and widespread currency, both sets of criticisms deserve careful empirical scrutiny.

The case against the UK state

At the height of the political battle for control of the UK in the late 1970s, a revitalized Conservative Party under Margaret Thatcher made generally available to the British electorate a strongly articulated neo-liberal critique of the economic activity of the postwar UK state. The UK economy in the 1970s, so the argument ran, was over-governed, over-regulated and over-taxed. Its processes of wealth creation had been weakened by three decades of Keynesian demand management, with its associated 'neglect of supply and structural policies to the detriment of the long-term potential of the economy' (Aldcroft, 1982: 42). Its investment performance had been eroded by the effect on labour costs of over-full employment, and by the impact of high rates of government borrowing on the cost of raising capital. Its entrepreneurial capacities had been undermined by the high marginal rates of tax made necessary by excessive government spending and by the state's propensity for egalitarian social engineering; and the work ethic of its labour force had been corroded by the dependency mentality or culture created by extensive welfare provision. The growth of state bureaucracies triggered by Keynesianism, so the Thatcherites claimed, had tipped the balance of advantage in the labour market away from capital, and had exposed particularly small- and medium-size businesses to stifling levels of regulation and form-filling. And the persistent willingness of politicians to take the credit for postwar economic growth had fuelled the illusion that economic growth was something you could *talk* into existence, rather than something you actually had to *create* by investment, competition, hard work and the taking of risks (Coates, 1994: 57–8). The Thatcherite Conservatives thus came to power committed to 'rolling back the state', committed to a set of internal policies that would strengthen the UK's international position (both economic and political) by releasing market forces from the grip of an interventionist politics.

To the Conservatives' critics both before and after 1979, however, such a rolling back of the state in the pursuit of a stronger international role was precisely what the UK economy did *not* require for the rapid reconstitution of its competitive position. The argument from the Centre-Left was rather that among the most important reasons for postwar economic underperformance (the UK's slippage from the second most powerful capitalist economy in 1951 to the middle of the pack three decades later) was the propensity of the UK state in the postwar years to subordinate the needs of the local manufacturing base to a higher set of priorities: to the defence of sterling as a reserve currency, to the protection of London as an international financial centre and to the maintenance of the 'Great Power' status of the UK political elite. Centre-left critics of that subordination pointed to the willingness of successive UK governments to trigger internal recessions by increasing interest rates, undermining local investment in manufacturing plant and equipment (the so called 'stop–go' policy cycle of the 1950s and 1960s), in order to maintain overseas confidence in sterling, and to attract into London short-term speculative capital flows which could then finance balance of payments shortfalls triggered by excessive military expenditure overseas and dwindling industrial competitiveness at home. They pointed to the absence of high levels of government expenditure on the modernization of the civilian industrial sector, to the government's privileging of the agricultural sector for grants and protection and to the heavy concentration of government spending (and government research and development capacities) in the military sector. Far from believing that the postwar UK state had drifted from a proper 'liberal' recognition of the role of market forces as catalysts for growth, the critics of the Thatcherite programme thought the UK state *too liberal*, too locked into a nineteenth-century mind-set that was no longer appropriate to the competitive requirements of the postwar world order. Lacking both a strong conservative *dirigiste* tradition of a French or Japanese variety and a labour movement willing to establish and participate in active partnerships with local industrial capital in the Swedish or German manner, left-wing advocates of competitive modernization were prone to look to state leadership as the key to success, to bewail its absence (and the associated lack of industrial expertise within the state bureaucracy itself) and to treat the post-1979 Thatcherite reduction in state economic activity as part of (and indeed as a fatal accentuation of) the UK's long-term economic problem (on this, Coates, 1994: 60–70).

Given the depth of disagreement between these two views of the state's contribution to postwar UK economic underperformance, they cannot both be right – although of course they can both be wrong. The available evidence seems to suggest that the balance of credibility lies more with the centre-left than with the neo-liberal argument, but that neither is blemish-free.

To take the Thatcherite arguments first: we have already seen the limitations of the trade union dimension of the Thatcherite case (earlier, pp. 91–4), and it is now worth noting in addition the vulnerability of the neo-liberal case to much of the available comparative evidence on the functions of the state. It is simply not the case that, for the critical periods when different growth patterns were established, UK tax levels and scales of welfare provision were higher than those in economically more successful Western European economies (most notably the Swedish and German economies). As we saw in more detail in chapter 4, they were not. Nor, if the comparative framework is shifted from the dimension of place to that of time, does the causal sequence implied by the Thatcherite argument fit the facts. On a neo-liberal argument, high levels of government expenditure should precede and trigger loss of competitiveness; whereas in the UK case the explosion of government spending actually followed the loss of competitiveness and was a response to it. The share of GNP passing through state hands fell in the 1950s, and the degree of state direction of private-sector economic activity diminished, as the UK was caught and passed by its main European rivals. Government spending (and the proportion of it used for purposes of industrial modernization) then rose in the late 1960s and early 1970s, as the UK state belatedly attempted to trigger its own European catch-up. In fact, the 1970s were years of heavy government involvement in industrial (and more broadly economic) management of a largely unsuccessful kind: on that the Thatcherite case is strong. But the rot started much earlier, and started in the unregulated private sector, to which neo-liberalism looked for its solution, which suggests that the questions to be asked about the UK state are not 'why did it intervene so heavily?' and 'why did it do such damage?', but 'why did it intervene so belatedly, and to such little effect?' There are answers to those questions, as we shall see; but they are not neo-liberal answers.

For what the neo-liberal critique of UK state economic activity failed to recognize, particularly in its critique of the adoption of Keynesian methods of demand management in the 1950s, was the *functionality* of high levels of state spending to capital accumulation (and rapid productivity growth) during capitalism's 'golden age'. Successful capital accumulation in the 1950s and 1960s required secure and growing markets, to absorb the output of the newly established semi-automated production systems of the consumer goods sector. It also required new outlets for employment, to absorb workers displaced by the rising productivity of the new capital-intensive mass-production industries. Government spending, and its extension of welfare provision, met both those requirements. The growth of state expenditure became *dysfunctional* only when the productivity growth of the private sector slowed: for then public-sector wages did eventually become a pressure on private-sector wage costs and profit levels, and public-sector wage funds did progressively suck in more competitively priced commodities from abroad. We saw that, for the 1980s, in our discussion of the Swedish model in chapter 4; and the dating is important here. The UK economy ran into 'the productivity problem' even earlier than the Swedish economy. It met it acutely in the 1970s – to give neo-liberal ideas a renewed popular appeal, but it did so for reasons that the Thatcherite project declined to address. It did so because investment levels in the mass-production sectors of the UK economy throughout the postwar period fell below those common in leading capitalist economies abroad, and it did so, as we have said, *before* state expenditure as a percentage of GNP began to rise (on this, see Coates, 1994: 178–9).

This is where centre-left arguments then gain their purchase. Under-investment was definitely accentuated by repeated 'stop–go' government policies. There is plenty of research evidence to sustain that (Pollard, 1992: 368–9). Those policies were triggered by balance of payments crises, which reflected not simply previous UK underinvestment, but also heavy military expenditure abroad. That too is clear from the empirical evidence. And that expenditure was part of a wider government propensity to privilege indus-tries producing military-related products. For the UK retained throughout the postwar period (and still does) a leading presence in world markets for military equipment (including military aircraft) and a leading presence in the related production of civilian aircraft; and it does so because the UK state did play a persistent, effective and *dirigiste* role in the reorganization and modernization of the appropriate industries (Edgerton, 1991b). Overall, throughout the postwar period, as David Edgerton's work demon-strates, 'Britain remained the second largest spender in absolute terms on defence R&D in the capitalist world', which meant that 'in relative terms the [UK] commitment to defence R&D was staggering'. Certainly through-out the 1970s, of all the major capitalist powers 'Britain spent the highest proportion of total national R&D spending (approximately 28 per cent) and between 1976 and 1981 the highest proportion of government R&D spend-ing (over 50 per cent) on defence' (Edgerton, 1991a: 164). Japan may have had its MITI, but the UK had (under various titles) its Ministry of Defence; and the MoD and its predecessor ministries definitely acted as a very effec-tive industry ministry for the postwar UK state. Indeed, when neo-liberals point to the UK in the 1980s (and to the Thatcher governments) as clear evidence of economic growth linked to a rolling back of the state, they would do well to remember the very active role played by those Thatcher governments in the marketing of UK-made armaments, the seriousness with which leading Conservative ministers took the government's respon-sibility for the reconstruction and modernization of the companies making those weapons (to the point of Cabinet division in the Westland Affair in 1986), and the intensification throughout the 1980s of the UK manufac-turing sector's dependence on arms production for its profit and employ-ment levels. The result, as Edgerton noted, was that the UK 'entered the 1990s with the largest and strongest military-industrial-scientific complex in Western Europe – a complex that retained its strength while other parts of the British economy . . . fell apart' (Edgerton, 1991a: 164), and ended the decade with its arms sales at record levels, and its position as the world's second largest weapons exporter firm and secure (Norton-Taylor, 1998: 16).

By contrast, it would appear that the volume of funding for civilian industry in the UK was negligible until the 1960s, and that the criteria guiding its allocation during that period were disproportionately preoccupied with regional development, the funding of military R&D, and the rescuing of bankrupt firms and industries. It would also appear that the implementation of what funding was provided was distinctly passive and non-directional, such that a real opportunity to strengthen the competitive position of the UK's industrial base in the 1950s (of the kind begun by the Attlee governments between 1945 and 1951) was effectively squandered. As late as 1961, 'the British State spent over £270 million on aid to agriculture, and less than £50 million on industry and employment' (Hall, 1986: 273). By the 1970s, it must be conceded, the UK state 'supported civil technological development on a scale more lavish than any other European nation' (Edgerton, 1991b: 83), and by then almost 50 per cent of all UK industrial aid went to fund research and development; but 70 per cent of that still went to the defence, aerospace and nuclear industries. Such priorities stood in sharp contrast to those evident in Germany, France and Japan, whose states spent 'equivalent sums on a broader spectrum of promising industries: including chemicals, electrical goods, transportation and machine tools' (Hall, 1986: 274). Moreover, as late as 1979 'the proportion of public expenditure devoted to regional aid was twice as great as in most other European nations', in a non-directional climate of industrial policy that was quasi-corporatist at best. As Hall noted: 'with the exception of the occasional nationalisation, compulsory schemes have been avoided . . . since 1918 industries in Britain have been asked to rationalise themselves' (ibid.: 275) ; all this while industrial policy elsewhere – in much of Western Europe and Japan – was more generous, more focused on industries producing goods for civilian consumption, more preoccupied with profitable industries, in places more *dirigiste*, and overwhelmingly more successful (Coates, 1994: 186–7).

However things definitely altered after 1964, in a more *dirigiste* direction. Between 1964 and 1979 (with a brief interlude in the first half of the Heath government's tenure of office in the early 1970s) both Labour and Conservative governments did turn their minds (and their policies) to industrial modernization. In the 1960s in particular 'a very serious attempt was made to redirect state support for R&D away from the defence sector to the civil sector, and away from long-range to short-term projects' (Edgerton, 1991b: 105). For a very brief moment the UK possessed, in the Ministry of Technology created by the first Wilson government, 'an Industry Ministry of much greater scope than any other in the capitalist world; Japan's much-vaunted MITI was a minnow by comparison' (Edgerton, 1991b: 105; also Tomlinson, 1997). Edward Heath's Conservative government broke that ministry up; but then it too, after its famous policy U-turn, produced an Industry Act under which it (and the Labour government that followed) poured resources into industrial reconstruction, and both the Labour governments of the 1964–79 period armed themselves with interventionist agencies (the IRC in the 1960s, the NEB in the 1970s) with which to take public control of large ailing private manufacturing companies. Aerospace, cars, and civilian engineering were all beneficiaries of this state largesse, largesse that in the end did not effect the competitive renaissance it was specifically created to produce.

That statist failure did more than trigger a Thatcherite revival and a reduction in the proportion of the UK's R&D expenditure that was government financed: down to 39 per cent of the total by 1986 (Walker, 1993: 173). It also told us much about the weaknesses of the UK state as an instrument of industrial modernization, and about the character of the industrial sector it so singularly failed to modernize. At one level the failure was one of policy and institutions, as the Thatcherites claimed, although it was hardly a failure of policy and institutions of the kind they described. At the level of policy, state-induced industrial modernization failed in the UK because so much of the resources deployed by the state were directed to the bailing out of firms and industries (specifically the car industry) which by then were already so weakened in competitive terms by years of underinvestment and inadequate restructuring that any amount of state finance could never be more than too little and too late. And at a deeper level, the failure was one of institutional interaction within the state machine itself. The UK state in the 1970s, like that of the US, was in essence a triangulated one, whose centre of gravity oscillated between its finance ministry, its defence ministry and its ministry for civilian industry production: a triangulated state in which civilian industry ministries always played the Cinderella role (Coates, 1994: 205). In the UK state of the 1970s, even before the Thatcherite Conservatives returned to power to accentuate these institutional power imbalances, the Treasury and the Ministry of Defence simply packed too great a political punch to allow a perpetually redefined and re-titled industry ministry to win the resource and policy battles over interest rates, spending priorities and trade policy which were vital for civilian industrial reconstruction. And at a deeper level still, the DTI lost those battles because the social forces with which it – as a civilian industry ministry – articulated were weaker than those surrounding both the Treasury and the MoD.

It is worth dwelling on that deeper weakness in more detail, because it points up a general dimension of the argument being developed here on the role of the state. In each of the national capitalisms with which we are concerned, the capacity of the state to act as an element in the growth equation depends in large measure on the character of the social classes which surround it, and through which it is obliged to govern. For, notwithstanding the trappings of power with which democratic politicians like to surround themselves, both they and their state bureaucracies ultimately depend for economic performance on the behaviour of others: workers, employers and bankers at the very least. State policy can shape the behaviour of those groups in important ways – the state is to a degree an independent agent –

but it is their behaviour that in the end determines the degree of economic success. The state in this sense can exercise only relative autonomy. In the case of the UK state in the 1970s, that autonomy was already heavily constrained by the set of class relationships that had been built around it over time (on this, see Mann, 1988: 217–18). By the 1970s financial institutions in the City of London had enjoyed a close working relationship with the Treasury for more than two centuries. That section of UK industrial capital concerned with the production of military and military-related goods had enjoyed a close working relationship with the Ministry of Defence for almost half as long. UK-based producers of consumer goods, by contrast, had no such tradition of close state involvement. Indeed, they themselves had subscribed since at least the 1870s to a liberal ideology which required the absence of such a close working relationship (Wilks. 1990: 145; Boswell and Peters, 1997). They had spent the bulk of the twentieth century treating the possibility of state regulation as inherently socialist, and had been prepared to turn for assistance to the state only as a matter of last resort, when they were already too weak competitively to be rescued easily. Not for them a right-wing statist tradition of close working relationships with a pro-active business-friendly industry ministry. For unlike dominant class blocs in non-Anglo-Saxon capitalisms, the entire bloc of privileged social classes which had surrounded the UK state since 1900 had consistently combined a commitment to Empire (and to Britain's great power role in the world) with an antipathy to any systemic state involvement in the orchestration of private capital accumulation. The state they had created and sustained was embedded both in liberalism and in militarism (see Mann, 1988: 228; Edgerton, 1991b; Reynolds and Coates, 1996: 241–6; Lee, 1997a: 134–59); and because it was, attempts to transform it into an instrument for the modernization of the consumer-goods sector of the UK industrial base after 1964 were doomed to be as half-hearted, ineffective, and ultimately transitory as they eventually turned out to be.

That would have mattered less if heavy state involvement in the orchestration of a strong military-industrial base after 1945 could have acted as an effective *alternative* modernizing strategy for UK industrial production as a whole. The postwar UK state could still have acted as a general agent of economic modernization if the spin-off from military-focused R&D, for example, could have triggered competitive developments in those sectors of the UK's industrial base that were directed towards the production of mass-consumption goods. There is much debate within the literature on UK military expenditure – and even more within the literature on US military expenditure – about this capacity of the military-industrial complex to trigger general economic competitiveness; but for the UK at least it does appear that the price paid by the postwar UK civilian industrial sector for the commitment of successive UK governments to the maintenance of a strong world role (and of an independent capacity to generate cutting-edge weaponry) was extraordinarily high (Coates, 1994: 193–201). The proportion of the UK's scientific resources geared to military-focused R&D in the critical opening decades of the postwar period was staggering. We should never forget what David Edgerton called 'the deeply warlike orientation of English science and technology' (Edgerton, 1991b: 85). The impact on the UK's balance of payments of arms exports on the one side and of overseas military expenditure on the other was broadly adverse. And there is no avoiding the sharpness of the contrast between the postwar economic performance of those advanced capitalist economies that won the Second World War (and thereby retained their military capability) and that of those which lost it (and were thereby prohibited from building up either military forces or the engineering complexes to arm them) (Kaldor et al., 1986: 36). In a very real sense, the UK won the war and lost the peace; and that loss was in large measure triggered by a state 'mind-set' which persuaded successive governments to strut their stuff on the world stage and to privilege (in their industrial policy) those sectors geared to the production of the armaments that strutting required.

The residual imperialism of the British state committed it to overseas economic and military policies after 1945 that, directly through their impact on the UK's balance of payments and indirectly through the industrial policy priorities they triggered, fuelled the underinvestment in civilian industrial modernization in the first two postwar decades which sent the UK's industrial base into competitive free-fall in the next two decades (Blank, 1977). The associated liberalism of the UK's employing class and the associated absence of state traditions (and state expertise) of industrial modernization then undermined subsequent attempts to correct that free-fall by state spending, planning and public ownership in the 1970s. The fusion of this militarism on the one side and deeply engrained liberalism on the other then produced a Thatcherite neo-liberal response after 1979, at precisely that moment when, as first Western European corporatism and eventually even Japanese capitalism faltered, the UK state faced its last opportunity to reposition the UK economy internationally before the full force of globalization shut the door on such state-initiated change. The Thatcherites recognized the strategic importance of their moment, but chose to seek economic success by accentuating the domestic impact of global competition on an already uncompetitive industrial base, removing capital controls and state subsidies, and removing trade union and worker rights. And the result, as we can now see all too clearly, was disastrous for the future long-term competitive strength of UK-based industrial capital. For what emerged from nearly two decades of Thatcherism was a further intensification of the structural imbalance between financial and industrial capital in the UK which had already weakened UK-based industrial capital for more than a century: a strong City, an internationally competitive military-industrial sector, a shrunken civilian industrial base and a labour force working long hours, on low wages, with inadequate structures of training. This was hardly the repositioning of the UK economy internationally which Labour politicians had envisaged as they created and expanded the role of MinTech in the late 1960s; but it was (and it remains) thé repositioning left to a later Labour government by the intervening decades of neo-liberalism.

Industrial policy and the US state

Of course the UK state has no monopoly on 'liberal militarism', or on the residual imperialism with which it is associated. The burden of running global capitalism switched long ago from the UK to the US, and the relationship between the postwar American state and its underlying economy does in consequence demonstrate many of the liberal and militarist features we have just documented. Just as in the UK, so in the US (particularly at federal level) state policies towards industries manufacturing consumer goods have long been (and remain) *liberal* in inspiration (and so are broadly voluntarist in character, reactive and passive in form, limited in scope and predominantly market-forming in focus) and *militarist* (anchored in the Pentagon, with procurement policy as the chief instrument, state-funded R&D heavily focused on arms production, and a definite and limited range of client industries serviced, including aerospace) (on this, for the UK see Reynolds and Coates, 1996: 243–4; for the US see Weiss and Hobson, 1995: 235–7). Those features of state policy have not, however, impacted on US economic performance in quite the same way as they did in the UK, since in the end 'though politically and culturally from the same historical mould, America is not a re-run of British political economy' (Weiss and Hobson, 1995: 219). For, as we shall explore in more detail next, the adverse consequences of the way in which, as Michael Porter correctly observed, postwar 'US governmental policy . . . largely ignored industry' in favour of 'the social agenda and . . . national security' (Porter, 1990: 531) were minimized in the US by the self-generated productivity superiority of industrial capital, and by the size and (until the 1970s) by the largely import-free nature of the internal market for consumer goods. Moreover the sheer scale (and centrality) of the US military-industrial complex gave it a presence in US manufacturing as a whole which initially triggered advantageous spin-offs into the civilian industrial sector of a kind that had no UK equivalent (Porter, 1990: 305). But in the end, the postwar US economy did pay the same kind of price – in terms of competitiveness – for the world role played by its state elite that the UK economy had paid before it. Like the UK state after 1870, the US state after 1945 did eventually experience the contradictory consequences of imperial dominance, as its exercise of an international political and military hegemony which was predicated on industrial superiority ultimately corroded the industrial superiority on which that hegemony was based.

There is no doubt that, in a very special sense, the relationship between the US state and the consumer-goods sections of its industrial base is informed by a deeply embedded set of *liberal* ideas, and that those ideas have both a distinct content and a powerful impact on policy, including as they do:

assumptions in the United States about state structure, the positive-sum nature of open markets, and the key role of multinational firms in generating and distributing global wealth. Liberal ideology intellectually justifies the free movement of capital and is buttressed by the claim that the postwar global economy has developed into an interdependent system from which it is both practically unfeasible and normatively undesirable to try to extricate a national economy. *(Reich, 1995: 60)*

Those ideas have not precluded the development of federal policy in relation to civilian industrial production (Diebold, 1982: Mowery and Rosenberg, 1993), but they have affected its form. They have consistently built into US political debate an antipathy to state involvement in the design of long-term industrial strategy; and they have weakened the role of federal departments as orchestrators of industrial renewal. The US state, at federal level and in its dealings with civilian-focused industrial producers, has never come within a whisker of producing an equivalent of even the UK's relatively ineffectual Department of Trade and Industry, let alone a Japanese MITI. The very structure of the federal state, as well as the political traditions embedded within it, simply block its capacity to act as a 'developmental state' in the East Asian manner.

It is true that 'some parts of the federal state are endowed with impressive administrative and bureaucratic capacities and are able to operate within a system of state–society linkages that belie notions of a weak state' (Lindberg and Campbell, 1991: 391); but, as Weiss and Hobson have noted (1995: 225), those parts are almost exclusively concerned with defence and agriculture. In those sectors at least 'the United States does have a relatively extensive set of policies towards industry: it does, in fact, target "winners" and encourage the movement of capital and labour away from losers' (Vogel, 1987: 92). David Vogel may well be correct to stress that 'the Department of Defense, NASA, the National Institutes of Health and the Department of Agriculture have proven no less – or more – capable of picking winners than has MITI' (ibid.: 95); and Chalmers Johnson was equally right to stress that 'the real equivalent of the Japanese Ministry of International Trade and Industry in the United States is not the Department of Commerce but the Department of Defense which in its very nature and functions shares MITI's strategic, goal-oriented outlook' (Johnson, 1982: 21). But in relation to the civilian manufacturing sector, and in direct contrast to defence and farming, the extent of the postwar US state's 'direct intervention in industry' has been 'among the lowest in the world'; and although its indirect activity (via the provision of social and physical infrastructure) undoubtedly 'yielded benefits that flowed to industry, these were rarely the prime motivating force'. Rather 'American economic strength was used' by the postwar US state 'to advance other goals' (Porter, 1990: 305) primarily of a foreign policy variety.

The strength of liberalism in the US political culture did not prevent the emergence of what Simon Reich termed 'an active, routine set of state responses towards indigenous industry in recurring contexts. . . . which aggregate into a routinized process of decision-making that amounts to a de facto industrial policy' (Reich, 1995: 58). Nor did it prevent either massive New Deal initiatives in times of crisis or, as we shall see, the pursuit of an active and interventionist *foreign* economic policy. And in the 1970s it was even compatible with a limited number of high-profile government 'bail outs' of firms in difficulties: Lockheed in 1971, Chrysler in 1979. But more normally it restricted the willingness and capacity of the US state to develop more than 'a few, relatively blunt interventionist instruments' (ibid.: 61) in relation to civilian manufacturing industry. In particular, it pushed indus-trial policy towards a regulatory stance – restricting it to the strengthening of competitive processes within particular sectors – and it blocked the emer-gence of policies of industrial support which were capable of discriminat-ing between home and foreign producers, smoothing or reversing sectoral industrial decline or consciously designing long-term competitive (and ulti-mately comparative) advantage. In fact, the US state was urged by many on the Centre-Left to adopt just such a set of discriminatory and targeted policies to counter intense Japanese competition in the first half of the 1980s; but ultimately it declined to do so (Johnson, 1984; Thompson, 1989; Graham, 1992). In the event, the limited amount of discriminatory indus-trial policy which did occur in that decade emerged primarily at state level, where it was predominantly restricted to moving industrial capital around *inside* the US, where it could not, by virtue of its sub-national scale of operation, substitute for federal policy directed at US industrial capital as a whole (Eisinger, 1990; Borgos, 1991). It was this non-discriminatory stance of the *federal* government towards consumer goods industries – this com-mitment to a 'level playing field' of competition within the US for home-based and foreign-based companies alike – that was then castigated by many on the Centre-Left as an *additional source* of competitive weakness for locally based producers, and criticized for denying them state orchestration of industrial activity of the kind provided by overseas governments to their firms before entering the US market (Reich, 1995: 56). The Centre-Left wanted coherent industrial policy and managed trade; and it got neither.

Yet by contrast to this state parsimony in relation to producers of con-sumer goods, the size of the US military budget has remained enormous throughout the postwar period, peaking first around the Korean War, then around the Vietnam War, and again in the 1980s. This pattern of postwar largesse stands in contrast to the scale of US peacetime military spending prior to 1946, which was typically around 1 per cent of gross national product (Edelstein, 1990: 421). For after the war, 'the US government devel-oped a vast science/technology infrastructure which linked government agencies; industrial, university and government laboratories; and business enterprises' behind 'the publicly stated purpose [of] national security' (Best and Forrant, 1996: 225). In consequence the percentage of US GNP going into military spending settled at around 7 per cent in the quiet years of the Cold War, and 8.5 per cent during the Korean and Vietnam conflicts. And in the process, sections of US industrial capital became the largest single national supplier of arms to governments outside the Soviet sphere of influence, and the proportion of the US state's expenditure on R&D that was militarily related rose significantly. In the US, approximately half of all R&D is now funded by the federal government, and two-thirds goes on defence. Best and Forrant report a total US defence R&D budget for 1988 of US$40.1 billion. The equivalent figure for Germany that year was US$1.1 billion (ibid.: 225).

This expansion of military production was presided over by the Pentagon, which, as a relatively autonomous department within the US federal government, implemented throughout the postwar period a *de facto* industrial policy of a potent and extensive kind. Best and Forrant called it 'an invisible industrial policy' (ibid.: 226) and Markusen and Yudken a 'closet' one (1992: 51); while Adams referred to the closed nature of the policy-making process linking the Pentagon to Congress and the defence industries as 'the iron triangle' (Adams, 1982: 24). For if industrial planning is understood 'as the state's effort to shape production and distribution in specific industrial sectors, including interventions and negotiations with individual firms' (Hook, 1990: 359) then the postwar US state has been as active an industrial planner as any Asian tiger state. It has simply done the bulk of that planning through the Pentagon's (and NASA's) R&D and procurement initiatives.

As a percentage of GNP, US government procurement throughout the postwar period has been at least twice as large as that of the Japanese government, apparently accounting for 'more than a half of all aircraft, radio and TC communications equipment: a fourth of all engineering and scientific instruments; and a third of all electron tubes and non-ferrous forgings manufactured in the United States' (Reich, cited in Weiss and Hobson, 1995: 228). Indeed Graham notes of DARPA (the Pentagon's R&D funding agency) that 'by the close of the Reagan presidency' it 'had moved, partly by choice and in part propelled by congressional frustration with administration inactivity, into the role of venture capitalist for America's high technology industries', spurring initiatives in areas such as 'high-definition television, superconductors, and other advanced electronic technologies' and being hailed in the process as 'America's answer to Japan's MITI' (Graham, 1992: 228). Pentagon direction certainly played an important role in the postwar reconstruction and modernization of the US aircraft industry, and more recently in the development of the emerging electronics industry (Hook, 1990), in two, that is, of the key industries in which the US enjoyed prolonged postwar world competitive advantage. Indeed many commentators have insisted on a close and direct link between Pentagon sponsorship and competitiveness, noting – with David Vogel – 'that virtually all the sectors in which American industry continues to enjoy a competitive advantage – from aircraft to pharmaceuticals to biotechnology – have been the beneficiaries of direct and substantial governmental assistance' (cited in Weiss and Hobson, 1995: 228). As Best and Forrant put it, after noting that in 1987 the Department of Defense purchased 17% of the 'shipments of the fifty largest defence-related sectors':

> The reality behind the appearance of public and private separation was one of pervasive government involvement in industry both as a major funder of corporate R&D and as a major purchaser of high technology products. . . . the federal government funded 85 per cent of the R&D for the emerging electronics industry in the 1960s. . . . [and] as late as the mid-1980s purchased over two-thirds of the output of the aircraft industry. In the critical early phases of the semi-conductor industry, the government purchased an even greater proportion. In fact, the major export industries of the USA in the postwar period all received both substantial government R&D and purchasing support in their formative, low productivity years. This includes aircraft, computers, electronics, telecommunications and instruments. *(Best and Forrant, 1996: 226)*

It is therefore perhaps not entirely surprising that some scholars have noted close similarities between the nature of the relationships established between sections of US industrial capital and the Pentagon and those characteristically attributed to state–industry interactions in Japan (Johnson, 1982: 21, 311; Weiss and Hobson, 1995; Best and Forrant, 1996). What is surprising, however, is how bad a press the Pentagon generally receives for the industrial policy it pursues, even from those who would have the US adopt Japanese-style institutions and practices. For since MITI's practice of 'administrative guidance' is invariably accorded by them a central explanatory role in Japan's postwar economic growth, and we now see that the Pentagon too exercised (and indeed still exercises) similar forms of guidance, it is not unreasonable to expect similar plaudits for Pentagon-based industrial policy. Yet they are relatively rare. It is possible to locate bodies of scholarship prepared to assert the positive impact of Pentagon policies on the general competitiveness of postwar US industrial capital; but that scholarship exists amid a welter of research-based material arguing the counter-case. In fact, claim and counter-claim are very finely balanced, as we shall now see.

On the plus side of the account stand four broad arguments. The first is that the wartime mobilization of large-scale military production runs did lay the foundations for the postwar Fordist productivity boom. The second is that for a large part of the postwar period, the R&D expenditure directed by the Pentagon into militarily focused production did have important spin-offs for the productivity and competitiveness of US-based civilian industrial production. The third, linked to that, is that for that period at least the cluster of industries loosely labelled 'the military-industrial complex' did play the kind of general catalytic role played by cotton in the UK Industrial Revolution and by railway construction in US (and German) nineteenth-century industrial development. The fourth is that the scale of postwar US military expenditure sustained employment and demand across US industry as a whole, while its character (dependent as it was on highly skilled labour and intensive R&D) created a highly paid and well-organized labour force of the kind increasingly required in a knowledge-based industrial environment. In other words, there is research material arguing that the size of the US military budget was not as negative for indigenous competitiveness as earlier the UK's had been. In the UK, liberal militarism (as we saw) reinforced the dominance of financial over industrial interests. In the US, by contrast, so the argument runs, it was of a size and character that gave it a developmental potential for US industry as a whole (on this, Weiss and Hobson, 1995: 223–30).

Against that interpretation of the economic consequences of US military expenditure stand a range of arguments that do not so easily enable US and UK experience to be differentiated. There is some very carefully constructed research evidence to suggest that the size of this budget did squeeze out other forms of expenditure, although considerable disagreement remains about whether the major casualty was investment in civilian industry (Smith, 1977), private consumption (Edelstein, 1990) or various forms of social spending (Mintz, 1992). There is research evidence too sustaining, for the US no less than for the UK, the adverse impact of overseas military spending on the balance of payments (Dumas, 1982) and – via the associated neglect of civilian industry and the slowing of productivity rates there – on inflation and unemployment (Markusen and Yudken, 1992; Dumas, 1982). Certainly the general claims for job creation associated with US military expenditure look less progressive and all-encompassing when set against the research evidence showing that the defence sector's labour aristocracy is predominantly white, and that a disaggregated look at the general employment impact of defence expenditure in the US in the 1980s reveals 'harmful effects for blacks and helpful effects for whites' (Abel, 1990: 418). And the general case looks less impressive too when the Pentagon's undoubted role in encouraging the development of a US-based microelectronics industry is set against the subsequent competitive history of the industry the Pentagon encouraged. Defence support did not enable that industry successfully to resist serious competition from initially Japanese-based industrial companies in the 1980s, leaving space again for the argument that the 'cost-plus' nature of much defence procurement feather-beds the firms supplying commodities to the US military, with long-term adverse effects on their competitiveness in wider, civilian-driven markets (Dumas, 1982: 7; Adams, 1982: 22). 'Destruction by neglect' is how Markusen and Yudken characterized the fate of the US consumer electronics industry in the 1980s (1992: 63), one of a list of industrial areas (beginning with steel and ending with semi-conductors) in which a Pentagon-led industrial strategy fell victim to Japanese-based competition (on this, Best and Forrant, 1996: 227).

In such a climate of controversy, partial truths invariably lie on both sides of the debate: and the balance of argument in any particular case has to be probed for from a mass of contingent variables, not read off a set of fundamental axioms. Defence sectors of the US size are not destructive of competitiveness by definition. They always carry the potential of job creation, demand maintenance and technological spin-off; but equally they always carry the danger of crowding out, R&D distortion and balance of payments shortfalls. To find the right balance of such effects in any particular case is difficult, in part because it is very hard to devise adequate measures of key variables and to design research strategies which can accurately isolate the military effect. The balance of effects is also difficult to find because much of the empirical research concerned with the economic consequences of military expenditure is itself embedded in competing theoretical systems (neo-liberal, post-Keynesian and Marxist in the main) which predispose analysts to move in conflicting directions (on this see Dunne, 1990). But at least for the case of postwar US military spending it seems possible to extract three reasonably secure general findings.

1   The first is that most of the research data suggest at best a broadly neutral impact of US military expenditure on more general US competitiveness, and at worst a slightly negative one, at least by the 1980s. Certain localized industrial regions within the US – the so-called US 'gun belt' (Markusen and Yudken, 1992: 38) – have clearly benefited greatly from Pentagon largesse, since in the US, as elsewhere, 'military expenditure has strong regional and industrial constituencies in the few areas where the bulk of the work is done and the bases are located' (DeGrasse, 1983: 153). Clearly too certain occupational categories depend heavily on such expenditure for their employment (not just service personnel, but also certain categories of professional and technical workers). But the general industrial and employment consequences of high military spending have not been so beneficent; and while it would be quite illegitimate to attribute declining US competitiveness exclusively to military expenditure, it would appear that, for the US economy in the 1980s at least, 'higher arms spending magnifie[d] the difficulties' (ibid.: 156) of the civilian goods sector, such that overall 'the net impact of defence on growth [was] negative' (Sandler and Hartley, 1995: 220).

2   The second reasonably secure conclusion that we can draw in this area is that the functionality of US defence expenditure to US-based capital accumulation in general varied over time. It was clearly highly functional at the start of the postwar Fordist boom, lubricating the spread of Fordist production methods across US industry and, via its negative impact on the US balance of payments, enhancing the global money supply (and hence global levels of demand) at a time when American goods were in short supply in world markets. But as the Fordist settlement unwound, US defence expenditure became less and less functional to continued US industrial supremacy, triggering the collapse of the dollar as the cost of the Vietnam War flooded world money markets with unwanted dollars in the late 1960s, and, through the industrial and state policy priorities it engendered, leaving US export (and later home) markets vulnerable after the Vietnam War to competitive capture by the retooled consumer-goods industries of the US's satellite economies in Germany and Japan.

3   The third conclusion we might draw is this: that, although the Pentagon's procurement policies were not as detrimental to the competitiveness of the US industrial base as were MoD policies to that of the UK, it remains the case that a defence-led industrial policy was not as effective a modernizing device as a civilian-led policy, even during the easier competitor conditions of capitalism's postwar 'golden age'. Even in its prime, defence expenditure was an expensive way of creating jobs; and that prime has now passed. The capacity of defence expenditure to generate commercially significant spin-offs has progressively declined (there is now more 'spin-in' than 'spin-out' of the military-industrial complex); and the general indifference to (and lack of policy instruments for assisting) civilian industry immobilized the state when changing global conditions lessened the central role of defence budgets in general economic performance. And because that was (and is) so, it is hard to disagree with the general judgement made by Sandler and Hartley at the conclusion of their extraordinarily thorough study of the relationship between defence inputs and the industrial base: that 'defence reallocations are not the desired pathway to growth' (ibid.: 220).

There is one other important point to be made about the general economic consequence of postwar US defence spending. It is this: spending on military equipment and the maintenance of large military staffs have been but one part of a US foreign policy which, since 1945, has had an active economic dimension. That economic dimension has been overwhelmingly *neo-liberal* in inspiration. US policy-makers have been determined to open and deepen overseas markets for US manufactured goods, and to orchestrate significant rates of growth in the capitalist world economy as a whole through the active encouragement of American capital export and technology diffusion. The Bretton Woods system of fixed exchange rates against the dollar was designed for precisely those purposes (as was the distribution of Marshall Aid); and in the wake of the dollar's fall in 1971, the US state regularly pressed for reductions in trade barriers in leading markets. Two such markets in particular have consistently preoccupied US trade negotiators – the European Union and Japan – where, in each case, open entry to US internal markets has been traded for greater access to closed markets abroad. The US state has also, of course, created its own free trade area in North and Central America (through NAFTA). So it is not, in that sense, averse to protectionism if open markets fail; and indeed protectionism (normally in the form of voluntary export agreements) was a strong element in the US state's initial response to the rise of Japanese competition *within* US domestic markets in the 1980s. But 'given the general commitment to free trade' which has underpinned US foreign economic policy since the war, such protectionist initiatives for particular industrial sectors have normally been 'established on narrow grounds and for purposes as limited as political pressure would permit' (Tyson and Zysman, 1983: 56). They have also largely been ineffectual, and even counter-productive, consolidating the outmoded forms of production that created market weakness in the first place without successfully excluding the more enterprising and competitive of the foreign-based producers.

It is clear that the postwar policy of the US state towards industry – both industries at home and industries abroad – moved from initially triggering and reinforcing the competitiveness of US-based industrial producers to eventually helping to erode that competitive edge. Military expenditure between 1941 and 1945 triggered US military Fordism. Overseas military expenditure after 1945 (and the wider international financial architecture which the US state designed in negotiation with the British) fuelled the export of US goods. And the general standing of the dollar enabled the postwar US economy to run a balance of payments deficit without having to deflate internally. But in the space created by this US economic and political empire strong competing economies re-emerged. The geo-politics of the Cold War put the two defeated Axis powers at the front line of the new world divide, and made their reconstruction as powerful and stable capitalist democracies a crucial element of US state policy. Denied the right to arm themselves, both benefited from the military spending of others, the Japanese economy in particular soaring to rapid growth in the 1950s on the back of US military expenditure in Korea,* and between 1965 and 1975 on the back of even greater volumes of US military expenditure in Vietnam. Preoccupied with its world role, and with the protection of its military-industrial base, the US state left its consumer-goods sector to modernize itself, and was helpless to prevent the heavy loss of market share experienced by the US car and consumer electronics industries in the 1980s. So, like the UK state before it, the US state in its imperial guise failed to protect and develop the internal economic strength on which ultimately its world role rested; but unlike the UK state before it, the US state went one stage further. Locked in battle for world supremacy with a qualitatively different economic and social system after 1945 – in a Cold War struggle that had no nineteenth-century equivalent – the US state did more than ignore key sectors of its own industrial base. It also *actively reconstructed competitor*

---

* This was such an important moment in the postwar Japanese success story that it is worth recounting in detail. This is how William Tabb described it, drawing on the research of Robert Angel.

> Through the global postwar recession of 1949–50, the United States insisted that Japan follow the orthodox deflationary programme of the Dodge Line . . . Japan pleaded for relief from this killing austerity. Then . . . salvation came from an unexpected source. Just two months after . . . the Korean tinderbox burst into flames . . . as the only nearby industrialized nation with adequate manufacturing capacity, Japan's under-employed factories and workshops benefited enormously from Korea's misfortunes between 1950 and 1955, first as suppliers of war materials and services for United Nations forces and, after the July 1953 armistice, as suppliers of materials needed for the reconstruction of South Korea. . . . special procurement, broadly defined, pumped between $2.4 and $3.6 billion into the capital-starved Japanese economy and accounted for an amazing 60 to 70 per cent of all Japan's exports. Also significant for Japan's postwar economic development, this unanticipated expansion of demand was strongest in industries such as textiles, steel products and automotive equipment, the very sectors that would lead Japan's export drive during the 1950s and 1960s. *(Tabb, 1995: 91–2)*

economies on the front line of the Cold War, and then stood by as the industrial competitiveness of those economies created rust belts in the heartland of the US's indigenous manufacturing core. US state policy may not have helped the US car industry in the 1980s: but it was certainly of immense assistance at critical postwar moments to the car industry of Japan.

The state and late development

So it is both a paradoxical and an important consequence of US foreign economic policy in the postwar period that the US state figures more unambiguously on the credit side of the Japanese growth equation than it does in the economic growth accounts of the US itself. And the US state was not entirely alone in playing that bizarre and unexpected role: there has to be a similar entry in the West German growth accounts for the UK state's immediate postwar role, in reconstructing key elements of the German car industry (Reich, 1990: 170–86).* In both cases, and at brief but strategic moments in the postwar economic story – for a mixture of geo-political, and in the UK case, short-term resource and humanitarian reasons – US and UK administrations treated foreign (car) manufacturers more favourably than they did their own – so helping directly to reconstruct an indigenous manufacturing industry in the manner of a truly 'developmental state'. They just happened to play that role when temporarily acting as the 'state' in a conquered territory; and they just happened to do it when explicitly not acting in a similarly 'developmental' way at home. By so doing, they inadvertently added a state dimension to the growth story of the two economies whose economic success would later surpass their own, and lead us to an examination of the other state dimension to those success stories. They lead us, that is, to an examination of the role, if any, played by the German and Japanese states in the orchestration of postwar economic growth once the brief period of Allied occupation was over.

The economic role of the postwar West German state

Here, of course, we are firmly in the territory of the much cited and widely discussed Gerschenkron thesis – that economies industrializing late (in his

---

* On the UK state, Reich reported the Ministry of Supply's opposition to the reconstruction of Volkswagen being over-ridden by the Treasury, which was concerned with the short-term problems of financing German food supplies. In its view,

> relief could most easily be secured by reinvigorating the German economy. Volkswagen was considered a cornerstone of the German economy, and so the Treasury in cooperation with the CCG (the British military administration in Germany) made strenuous efforts to find it resources and profitable markets . . . Treasury officials suggested that every effort should be made to maximise the foreign currency that could be generated by the production and export of Volkswagens, to the advantage of the British exchequer . . . in simple terms, the Treasury placed a higher priority on the short-term problem of supporting the German population than on the long-term problem of British competitiveness. *(Reich, 1990: 309, 175)*

case, those industrializing later than the UK and the US in the nineteenth century) do so by the development of 'different institutional instruments of industrialization' (Gerschenkron, 1966: 16), not least universal banks and the state. In the original thesis, Germany figured as a 'bank-led' example of the advantages of backwardness, and the economy cited as the prime example of state-led industrialization was Russia before and after 1917. But subsequently it has become conventional, in following a broadly Gerschenkron line, to use the state as a key variable in all the major examples of successful catch-up by leading capitalist economies; and as we saw in chapter 3, (above, pp. 68–9), there now exists a body of scholarship prepared to attribute a significant, if largely covert, role to the postwar West German state as an economic modernizer, and to link the priorities embodied in the economic policy of the postwar West German state (its preference for investment over consumption, its welfarism, and its proximity to a well-organized private sector) directly to Germany's 'late'-nineteenth-century start (Weiss, 1998: 123–5). Linda Weiss's work, cited in chapter 3, is not the only example of the genre. Indeed the most impressive recent piece of similar scholarship in the English literature is that of Simon Reich, which has argued that the pre-war (fascist) German state played such a modernizing role (at least for the German car industry), establishing in the process a state tradition (of deliberately fostering a number of core German-owned car producers, by discriminating against US inplants) which carried on in unbroken fashion into the 1960s, if not beyond (Reich, 1990: 65, 67, 145). The 'fruits of fascism', as Reich terms the resulting economic advantage to core car producers, was evident in the Japanese case too, and in his view left such car producers competitively positioned to take market share from the car companies of the more 'liberal' economies (of the UK and the US) in which state orchestration of private capital accumulation was deemed less legitimate.

The Reich and Weiss theses sit ill with the formal position of the postwar German government, that it was committed to a *social market economy* based on 'the belief that industrial modernization and structural change should best be left to the market' (Abromeit, 1990: 61). Nor are their theses easily compatible with a state structure as extensively decentralized as that of the German state both before and after unification; yet their arguments are none the less persuasive, for at least the following reasons.

1   One is the important role played by the German state in underwriting the labour codes of the German corporatist 'model'. In line with a state welfare tradition that stretches back to Bismarck, one that reflects the strength of the German working class, which (outside the fascist period) has had to be accommodated as the price of social peace, postwar Federal German governments consolidated a very distinctive capital–labour accord (of a kind discussed already in chapters 3 and 4). West German workers came in the postwar period to enjoy levels of job security, training and

workplace participation which had no US (or even UK) equivalents; and West German governments (in the manner of Swedish and other Scandinavian governments) pursued active labour-market and welfare policies which contrasted sharply with the broadly inactive labour-market policies and limited state-welfarism of successive US administrations (on this, contrast Knoke, 1996: 36–48). To the degree that postwar West German competitiveness rested on a high level of labour cooperation with industrial management (and that, as we saw earlier, has been widely said to be the case, although never incontrovertibly established), then to that degree too the West German state's covert and indirect role as the guarantor of that cooperation has also to be conceded.

2   Moreover, for all their formal commitment to a neo-liberal relationship between state and industry, successive West German governments directly affected local rates of industrial accumulation in a number of critical ways. Throughout the 1950s and 1960s they deliberately maintained a low dollar exchange rate for the Deutschmark, to facilitate the build-up of German manufactured exports; and they gave active support to the banking system's provision of long-term industrial finance, particularly to small and medium-size enterprises. From the 1970s they showed what Porter called a 'stubbornly persistent tendency to subsidise ailing sectors' (Porter, 1990: 378): not least shipbuilding, railways, coal, steel and agriculture. Regional support for industrialization was, and remains, extensive in postwar Germany; and public funding in Germany for civilian-focused R&D remains high. The Anglo-German Foundation reported (1994: 11), for example, that the public provision of loans, grants and guarantees for SMEs in West Germany amounted in 1988–9 to £1,093.4 million, when in the UK the figure was only £3.8 million; and Sig Vitois reported total R&D expenditure in Germany as a percentage of GNP at 2.9 per cent – that is at a level 'comparable to Japan's and roughly a percentage point higher than non-defence R&D in the US and UK'. He also reported West Germany as second only to France by then as 'one of the big promoters of basic research', noting in both cases the crucial role played by the state in this provision, 'both in its support of an external, public and quasi-public . . . infrastructure and in its programs for boosting the internal innovative capacity of firms' (Vitois, 1997: 10–11). And Henry Ergas persuasively argued that technology policy in West Germany (and Sweden) has been primarily *diffusion oriented* rather than (as in the US and the UK) *mission oriented*, that postwar governments in Germany and Sweden have been more concerned than their Anglo-American equivalents to encourage the diffusion of 'technological capabilities throughout the industrial structure, thus facilitating . . . ongoing and mainly incremental adaption to change' (Ergas, 1987: 52). His evidence suggests that, if the test of R&D policy is that it encourages 'widespread access to technical expertise' and reduces 'the costs which small and medium-sized firms face in adjusting to change', then 'policies have been very successful', not least by their prioritizing of investment

in human capital, their systematization of industrial standards, and the encouragement of cooperative forms of research, both between companies and between industry and academia (ibid.: 67–75).

It must be conceded, of course, that the scale of involvement in the guidance of the postwar economy played by public bodies in West Germany was nowhere near as extensive as that in Japan, and that the official adoption of even Keynesian demand management techniques in West Germany after 1967 was neither as early nor as prolonged as in the UK (on this, Allen, 1989; Thompson, 1991). For the orchestration of capital accumulation in West Germany by state bodies has been normally *indirect*, operating through (and in close liaison with) the German banking system, and being most obvious and direct only in the areas of labour training and welfare provision. It has not been the German way normally to bail out individual industrial firms (although, as in the US, there are examples of this – AEG Telefunken in 1982 being the most prestigious). Rather, 'in sector-wide intervention, the government's role' normally 'has been to support measures of industry-led adjustment. . . . always in concert with the banks, business and labour' (Chandler, 1986: 180). So, for example, when Volkswagen met competitive difficulties in the mid 1970s, it received no direct federal government funding to parallel that poured so unsuccessfully into British Leyland by the UK government in the same period. Instead measures were agreed 'by the combination of federal and state governments, the shareholders and the trade union . . . for rationalization and modernization, with a social program to ease the costs of adjustment for each worker'; and 'the only significant cash subsidy' provided from public funds was reportedly 'for new investments in the region affected by the layoffs' (ibid.: 161). But even so, there can be no doubting the importance to the German pattern of postwar economic growth of this mixture of direct and indirect state inputs. The centre of gravity of the German model of 'organized capitalism' does appear to lie in the private rather than the public sector – in its industry–bank linkages rather than in any industry ministry; but none the less the public underpinning of those linkages, and the state integration of labour into the German system of private governance as a subordinate partner, also appear critical to the postwar German economic success story. As Linda Weiss has it: the German system of private-sector governance 'does not preclude state involvement; it presupposes it' and 'in this sense, the capacity of the German state is deeply embedded in the . . . system' (Weiss, 1998: 136).

The Japanese 'developmental state'?

If Germany is one example of what Dore referred to as 'an early case of late development' (Mutel, 1988: 146), Japan is clearly the other; and even more than Germany's, Japan's state has attracted attention from a range of scholars convinced, in the words of Chalmers Johnson, that 'in states that were late to industrialize, the state itself led the industrialization drive, that is, it took on developmental functions' (Johnson, 1982: 19). As we saw in chapter 3 (pp. 62–4), Johnson in particular is associated with the argument that postwar Japanese economic growth owes much to the developmental role played by state planning and guidance, primarily through the agency of Japan's MITI. As we also saw there, this 'developmental state' thesis on the 'Japanese miracle' has never been without challenge. It has been challenged on the one side by neo-classical economists, for whom 'the main impetus to growth has been private – business investment demand, private saving, and industrious and skilled labour operating in a market-oriented environment' (Patrick and Rosovsky, cited in Anchordoguy, 1988: 509). And it has been challenged on the other side by a range of 'new institutionalists' for whom 'the bureaucratic dominance thesis can no longer be accepted' (Wilks and Wright, 1991: 39), since it underplays the primacy of politics and private capital in the postwar Japanese growth story. But in spite of the controversy surrounding it, the case for the Japanese bureaucratic elite as the principal economic modernizer in postwar Japan has not gone away. Indeed Johnson has defended it persistently, emphasizing as he has done continuities between the pre- and postwar Japanese bureaucracy (between the authoritarian Japanese state of the Meiji restoration and the liberal democratic state imposed by the Americans) and parallels between modern Japan and medieval Venice, both of whose economic superiorities he has linked to their capacity 'to fuse in an ad hoc manner the effectiveness of the absolutist state with the efficiency of the bourgeois market' (Johnson, 1995: 29).

The 'developmental state' thesis on Japan runs broadly as follows: that Japan after 1945 is best described as a 'state-guided high-growth system' (Johnson, 1982: 309) built around a close and detailed working relationship between state bureaucrats and privately owned firms and industries. Such a growth system was made possible in Japan by the coincidence of certain vital prerequisites for a successful capitalist developmental state: 'the existence of a small, inexpensive but elite bureaucracy staffed by the best managerial talent available in the system' (ibid.: 315), a political system able to allow that bureaucracy considerable autonomy, a commitment to market-conforming methods of state intervention and the existence of a pilot organization such as MITI (ibid.: 314–19). The emergence in postwar Japan of such a model Schumpeterian state – combining as it did the Schumpeterian prerequisites for successful democratic government with an understanding of his sense of the dynamics of competitive advantage – was made possible, in this view, by the legacies of state economic management laid down in the post-Meiji restoration process of forced industrialization; and it was made necessary by the parlous economic condition into which Japan had been forced by wartime defeat. Indeed the First World War (and particularly the state's reorganization of Japanese capital and labour relations during it) figure strongly as a supporting explanatory variable in the development thesis case, the war being the moment when (and state policy the route whereby) much of what was unique about the postwar Japanese system came into existence: the shift to heavy industry, agrarian reform, bank rationalization, the subcontracting system, lifetime employment, seniority pay and even enterprise unions (Johnson, 1995: 29–34: also Weiss, 1993: 199). Both Johnson and Weiss were aware how that postwar settlement had to be *re*-established in Japan, initially in a context of American hostility to Japanese reconstruction and amid fierce class struggles within Japan itself. But that re-establishment, in their hands, was also state-induced and state-guaranteed. It was induced by the US state (in the guise of its occupying military administration) in response to the rise of the Cold War and in order to defuse labour unrest; and it was then guaranteed by the reconstituted Japanese state, as part of its general developmental thrust (Johnson, 1995: 29).

It should be said that there is considerable supporting evidence for this thesis. There is certainly considerable evidence that the postwar Japanese state (primarily through MITI) initially set out quite deliberately to restructure the entire economy in a series of what its critics later termed 'scrap and build cycles' (Burkett and Hart-Landsberg, 1996: 70), moving its centre of gravity first out of agriculture and textiles into steel, chemicals, machinery and other heavy industries, then (after the 1973 oil crisis) out of those into transport and electrical goods (cars, motor bikes, televisions, videos, calculators and the like) and, later still, into a range of high-technology products. On a negative reading of that process, Japanese capital simply redeployed declining industries off-shore towards the end of each cycle, intensifying the processes of labour exploitation as it did so, with the last cycle (in the 1990s) failing for the first time to re-establish a high growth trajectory (hence the underlying nature of Japan's contemporary crisis). On a more positive reading, Japanese capital regularly repositioned itself at the front edge of each technological revolution, on each occasion first copying and then developing the production potential of the latest forms of R&D, corporate management and marketing strategies, in the process transforming Japan into the world's second most prosperous economy. But on either reading Japanese capital did not pursue such growth strategies on its own. It did so in a close and ultimately guided relationship with agencies of the postwar Japanese state.

The general industrial strategy pursued by the postwar Japanese state is normally periodized. In the first key 'period of *reconstruction* and *high growth* . . . from the end of the Second World War until the middle to late 1960s . . . the government–industry relation upon which industrial policy was predicated could be characterised as the "governmental industrial guidance model" ' (Boyd, 1987: 78). Of course, until US foreign policy changed in 1947, the original intention of the occupying authorities had been to use state policy to *de-industrialize* Japan, removing heavy machinery as part of reparations and repositioning Japan as an underdeveloped economy dominated by agriculture and small business. But once US state officials had decided that Japan must be rebuilt as a bulwark against communism – once

Japan had become (to follow Arrighi) 'a US invited guest in the exclusive club of the rich and powerful nations of the West. . . . in a perfect example of what Immanuel Wallerstein has called *development by invitation*' (Arrighi, 1994: 340) – American loans and credits poured in. In its first phase of postwar reconstruction (up to 1955) the new Japanese state then sought first to re-establish Japan's basic economic infrastructure within that American framework. Before 1955 (under both US military control and the fledgeling democracy), Japanese state planners initially targeted resources at the coal and steel industries, and later at textiles, shipbuilding and chemicals, while also mobilizing available capital reserves through a series of new banks (including a development bank and an export-import bank). These were the years in which, in the judgement of many analysts of recent Japanese economic history, 'the extensive involvement of government in industrial development was decisive in saving the country from a crippling economic and political dependence upon the industrial West and in creating the conditions for a phenomenal economic success' (Boyd, 1987: 85). Even Michael Porter, whose 1990 report was broadly critical of the propensity of the Japanese state for protectionism and subsidies, was obliged to concede that 'in the early Japanese successes, such as steel, shipbuilding and sewing machines, this sort of government role was constructive' (Porter, 1990: 414).

By 1955 the confidence of Japanese state planners was sufficiently developed for that year's white paper to discard any fatalistic view of Japan 'as an overpopulated poor country without resources or accumulated capital' (Sheridan, 1993: 136) and to seek ways of breaking free from excessive dependence on US aid and procurement spending. In a policy decision which is now famous, they plumped for the achievement of high-speed economic growth by *targeting*: deliberately creating comparative advantage in international trade in capital and technology-intensive industries such as 'autos, large machine tools, industrial machines, large computers, speciality steel [and] petrochemicals' (MITI, cited in Johnson et al., 1989: 66) in which in 1955 Japan had no obvious international market advantage. To create that comparative advantage, MITI encouraged the systematic import of foreign technology (to upgrade the quality of the Japanese industrial base) while maintaining high tariff protection around infant industries, in a deliberate piece of state-induced industrial restructuring. As Sheridan has it, 'from 1955 until as late as the mid-1960s, there was virtually no restriction on MITI officials improvising and enforcing any policy measures they thought would help to protect and nurture their selected industries' (ibid.: 151). Okimoto described Japanese industrial policy in that period as follows:

> During the 1950s and 1960s industrial policy played a central role in meeting the historic challenge of industrial catch-up (a role that has shrunk with the passage of time, as Japan has closed the gap). Showing little faith in the magic of Adam Smith's invisible hand, the Japanese government intervened in order to (1) establish sectoral priorities; (2) mobilize resources to hasten their devel-

opment; (3) protect infant industries; (4) issue guidance on investment levels; (5) organize rationalization and anti-recession cartels; (6) allocate foreign exchange credits; (7) regulate technological flows in and out of Japan; (8) control foreign direct investment; (9) issue 'administrative guidance' enjoying quasi-legal status; and (10) publish white papers on mid- and long-term visions of Japan's future industrial structure. *(Okimoto, 1989: 23)*

But from the mid 1960s, as the success of that policy turned Japan into the capitalist world's second largest economy, policy again changed. 'While continuing to pursue the goal of industrial catch-up, the Japanese government turned its attention to the task of dealing with the potentially far-reaching effects of trade liberalization' (Okimoto, 1989: 25). State priority shifted to the creation of strong export industries – first in medium-technology-dependent consumer durables, such as cars and consumer electronics, and later in more technologically sophisticated consumer products. 'To compete against giant foreign producers, MITI took the lead in pushing for "structural rationalization" in a number of key industries, like steel and automobiles' (ibid.: 25), encouraging firms to merge in the pursuit of size. In the process, the degree of direct intervention by MITI diminished; and MITI was reorganized internally, away from a vertical structure linking it to specific industries, and into a set of horizontal bureaux concerned with inter-industry and cross-industry issues. Its use of resource rationing and 'administrative guidance' eased in the 1960s, was progressively restricted to Japan's small and medium-size industrial sectors, and for the economy as a whole was replaced by the production of longer-term 'vision' statements. 'In those "Visions" the focus of industry policy shifted from heavy and chemical industries to a group of knowledge-intensive industries, such as machine tools of various kinds (electrical, transport and precision machinery), high-tech industries (integrated circuit computing, robotics, fine ceramics and new metals), vertically integrated assembling industries, fashion industries and information-related industries' (Sheridan, 1993: 164–5).

Central to MITI's strategy in the 1980s was the nurturing of indigenous R&D capabilities, linked to the development of high-growth technology industries: a policy shift, of course, from MITI's earlier enthusiasm for imported technology. It was, 'in essence, the transition from latecomer to pioneer' (Okimoto, 1989: 28), one implemented primarily through tax concessions and MITI-orchestrated private-sector collaboration. And in 1978 and 1983 legislation was introduced to facilitate MITI's rationalization of declining industries (Young, 1991). According to MITI there were then eleven such 'structurally depressed' industries: textiles, sugar refining, corrugated cardboard, chemical fertilizers, vinyl chloride, open-hearth steel, electric furnace steel, aluminium refining, shipbuilding, plywood and shipping. The Japanese state, that is, acted for a second time in the 1980s to trigger what Burkett and Hart-Landsberg termed its 'scrap and build' growth strategy, in the process establishing a distinctive *time pattern* of state intervention. The postwar Japanese state intervened heavily at the start (the

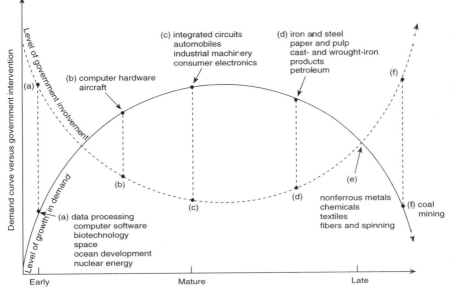

Figure 7.1   Industrial life cycles and government intervention
Source: Okimoto, 1989: 51

'build' stage) and at the end (the 'scrap' stage) of an industry's life cycle, while withdrawing from detailed intervention in the middle of the cycle. Okimoto's diagram captures that sequence well.

There is considerable evidence too (particular for the years before 1975) of the widespread use by different ministries of the Japanese state, and particularly by MITI, of a series of policy instruments directed to the achievement of this developing economic strategy. These policy instruments were larger in number than and different in kind and mixture from those characteristically deployed by liberal-capitalist governments for their own civilian industrial bases in the same period. These included – as is often recorded – 'bank finance and directed credit, import controls and protection, restrictions on entry and exit of firms in the domestic market, control over foreign exchange, and not least, controlled importation of foreign technology' (Singh, 1993: 281). The postwar Japanese state did not have at its disposal two of the major policy instruments favoured by capitalist states in Europe and the US. It made little use of public ownership; and it enjoyed no large military procurement budget by which to shape industrial behaviour. MITI in particular 'possesse[d] practically no budget for public procurement' (Okimoto, 1989: 98). Instead, in the heyday of MITI's power in the 1950s and 1960s state planners used preferential financing, tax-breaks and import controls to protect and develop targeted industries, and orchestrated cartels and bank-based industrial groupings to trigger competitiveness, in what MITI itself in 1974 retrospectively termed a 'plan-oriented market economy system' (Johnson, 1982: 10). If Johnson is correct:

> Before the capital liberalization of the late 1960s and 1970s, no technology entered the country without MITI's approval: no joint venture was ever agreed without MITI's scrutiny and frequent alteration of terms; no patent rights were ever bought without MITI's pressing the seller to lower the royalties and make other changes advantageous to Japanese industry as a whole; and no programme for the importation of foreign technology was ever approved until MITI and its various advisory committees had agreed that the time was right and the industry involved was selected for nurturing. *(Johnson, 1982: 17)*

In the 1960s, however, 'Japan was forced to liberalize to accord with international agreements: as a result MITI lost many of its cruder and more direct tools'; but that simply forced it back on 'more indirect, subtle, sometimes informal methods' (Krauss, 1992: 313): in other words, onto more informal mechanisms of maintaining 'a moving band of protectionism' (Tyson and Zysman, 1989: 130) and onto the increased use of administrative guidance. For MITI, like other Japanese ministries and government agencies, was able to exploit its legally established powers to issue directives, requests, warnings, suggestions and encouragements, and in the process to gather to itself 'a quite remarkable degree of discretionary and unsupervised authority' (Johnson, cited in Coates, 1994: 226–7). It was (and indeed it remains) a degree of unsupervised authority without parallel in the civilian industry ministries of any other major capitalist economy.

Okimoto has reported, however, that 'like other tools of industrial policy, such as anti-recession cartels, administrative guidance has come to be used less and less as Japan's economy has matured' (Okimoto, 1989: 94). Yet even in the 1980s, according to Johnson, MITI still retained the capacity to do broadly four things. It made medium-term economic forecasts (its vision statements). It arranged for the preferential allocation of capital to selected strategic industries. It targeted industries it believed vital to future economic success, and designed policy-packages to develop them; and (after 1978) it actively formulated policy for 'structurally depressed industries'. Some of the policy instruments it used did change over time. It used 'foreign exchange controls (until 1964), protective customs duties (until the late 1970s), control of foreign capital investment (until about 1976) and control of imports of foreign technology (until 1980)' (Johnson, 1986: 202), and certainly maintained effective tariffs, quotas and hidden trade barriers longer than other leading industrialized economies. None of these policy instruments are now either available or as potent. Yet, as Johnson said, although 'the particular mix of tools change[d] from one era to the next because of changes in what the economy needs and because of shifts in MITI's power position in the government' the underlying purpose remained firmly intact: it was to find 'market-conforming methods of intervention' (Johnson, 1982: 29) that could engineer comparative advantage in international trade for Japan's chosen industries. The Japanese state was uniquely preoccupied with such a purpose for five critical decades after 1945; and until 1992 it at least experienced unprecedented degrees of success in its pursuit.

It is thus possible to go a considerable distance with the thesis that the Japanese state played *a* key developmental role in postwar Japanese economic growth, and that its role was particularly pivotal to the great catch-up spurt prior to 1973. But it would not be right to go the extra inch and attribute to the Japanese state either the sole or a totally independent catalytic role here, or to leave the impression of bureaucratic infallibility. For on the contrary, the research evidence now available to us – much of it stimulated by Johnson's 1982 study – also makes clear the limits of the Japanese state as a developmental agent (for a general report and survey, see Abe, 1997).

It certainly makes clear the *mixed* record of agencies like MITI as strategists for growth. MITI has its failures as well as its successes: and those failures include both industries it tried and failed to restructure – shipbuilding, machine tools, the car industry in the 1960s, petrochemicals (Friedman, 1988; Krauss, 1992: 316; Okimoto, 1989: 5–6) – and those (such as coal and textiles) it subsidized because of heavy political pressures of a kind familiar to governments across Western Europe. There is clear research evidence that some industrial sectors in Japan did not flourish in spite of close relationships with a sponsoring ministry: Japanese pharmaceuticals and the Ministry of Health and Welfare being examples (Howells and Neary, 1991). There is also clear research evidence of the success of firms – not least in automobiles and consumer electronics (Japan's two great success stories of the 1970s) – that occurred without MITI's close involvement or guidance. In the 1950s MITI was slow, for example, to grant permission for the transfer of transistor technology to what later became the SONY corporation, and indeed only did so when presented with a *fait accompli* by the company's management at the time; and this episode serves to highlight 'the fact that some of Japan's most successful export industries – consumer electronics, cameras, watches, and other precision equipment – managed to grow up strong and healthy outside MITI's incubator for targeted infant industries' (Okimoto, 1989: 65). It also appears to be the case that in the 1980s – after a particularly successful start in the preceding two decades (Anchordoguy, 1988) – MITI proved increasingly inept at picking winners in the new and rapidly changing high-tech industries on which the planners hoped to build Japanese competitive dominance in the 1980s and beyond. In these industries, for which the issue was no longer importing technology but developing it, 'recent Japanese efforts' have been likened to 'the industrial policy equivalent of flogging a dead horse' (Callon, 1995: 2). Although by the late 1980s Japanese high-tech companies had joined battle for market share with their US rivals, the research data suggest that MITI played only a modest role in that catch-up (Okimoto, 1989: 7), and that 'it is companies, not government bureaucrats, that have been at the heart of Japan's stunning postwar ascent to international competitiveness' (Callon, 1995: 3) in this crucial new field.

We know too that MITI was never a totally autonomous and all-powerful state agency. There is plenty of research evidence to show persistent differences of policy and approach, and regular 'turf wars' between MITI and other parts of the Japanese state machine (Callon, 1995: 31–54). There is evidence to show effective resistance from key industrial sectors to MITI's administrative guidance (Wakiyama, 1987: 225), and also of 'how constrained the bureaucracy was and is in achieving its policy objectives by the organisational strengths of the firms and their associations, and by the resources which they employ in their transactional relationships' (Wilks and Wright, 1991: 44). In fact Richard Samuels has even asserted, in relation to the energy sector at least, that 'in *no* case did the state prevail against private interests' (Samuels, 1987: 289), and Callon has argued that increasingly – in high-tech industries at least – 'large Japanese firms [have] cast off their dependence on MITI and refused to contribute funds to MITI consortia' (Callon, 1995: 183).

There is also plenty of evidence of political influence and control over MITI even in its heyday (Calder, 1988; 1993): evidence that, as Samuels put it, 'the Japanese state can create and manipulate interests, but it can also be colonized by them' (Samuels, 1987: 287). And there are also a lot of data showing that, at its most effective, MITI did not issue orders to Japanese industry, but rather worked in a close collaborative relationship with key firms and industries. There is clear evidence, that is, that the Japanese growth strategy which so impressed Western centre-left commentators from the mid 1960s was one predicated on a close and mutually beneficial state–capital relationship, not on a state-led one. This has been very thoroughly documented for the energy sector by Samuels, who has insisted that the relationship between MITI and Japanese private industry was sufficiently that of 'reciprocal consent' and a search for mutual accommodation as to make the inference of state leadership problematic (Samuels, 1987: 1–22, 261). The absence of public ownership in Japan and the general emergence there of 'powerful and stable private actors [in] enduring alliances with politicians and bureaucrats [to] vigilantly check market-displacing intervention' (Samuels, 1990: 37) does seem to suggest that the experience of the energy sector in this regard can safely be taken as representative of Japanese industry in general (see also Abe, 1997).

There is clear research evidence of MITI's diminishing powers over time. There is even some dispute in the relevant literatures about how potent MITI actually was (how much the direction of private sector economic activity actually changed) during the dash for growth between 1951 and 1973 (Johnson, 1982: 31; Saxonhouse, 1983: 269–71; Calder, 1993: 249), although it should be said that the balance of informed opinion is as Callon reports it: 'that despite certain negative costs, MITI's policies from the 1950s through the 1970s in the main played a positive, if limited, role in promoting Japanese economic development and growth' (Callon, 1995: 4;

also Boltho, 1985). But there is little disagreement that MITI's role in the last two decades has been more limited and less central to private capital accumulation in Japan than it was before, in part because of the very success of the state–capital relationship triggered by MITI after 1945. In the critical area of state control and direction of investment funds in particular, the evidence is overwhelming that 'these powers have waned progressively as Japan's capital markets have developed and its financial system has become internationalized', and that this diminution in state authority is 'symptomatic of a much broader shift in the balance of power between the state and private enterprise, one in which the relative autonomy of the private sector has increased with the growth of the economy' (Okimoto, 1989: 143, 144). Indeed the most potent criticism of the unbridled developmental state thesis currently on offer from 'new institutionalist' scholars is that the Johnson thesis 'is now seriously out of date' (Callon, 1995: 2), that times and conditions have changed, and with them the importance and role of MITI itself.

Be that as it may, one other thing is also very clear. No matter how good or bad MITI was in triggering growth between 1945 and 1973, it certainly was not able to prevent either the slow down in Japanese growth rates after 1973 or the stagnation into which the Japanese economy settled after 1992. That is an ominous set of failures for those who would explain MITI's diminishing powers by reference to Japanese economic success and maturity. Japan came out of recession from the late 1940s behind a MITI-led industrial revival. It is now failing to come out of its 1990s recession in any similar kind of way; and it is failing because a growth strategy geared to achieving technological catch-up in a context of limited capital export and expanding global demand is clearly not reproducible in a world of technological convergence, extensive capital flows and low levels of consumer confidence. MITI may have been able to save Japanese industrial capital once; but it is clearly failing to do so again.

It is in that sense that the end of the Japanese economic miracle provides a much clearer vantage point from which to clarify the true nature of the economic role of the postwar Japanese state than was available to commentators before 1992. The state fulfilled a number of strategic planning roles for Japanese industrial capital in the initial dash for technological and economic convergence. That much is clear. In the 1950s Japanese planners took full advantage of the opportunity provided by the existence of spaces in the emerging postwar world economy to reposition Japanese industrial capital in the international division of labour. The Japanese state also twice played a role in facilitating the orderly export of industrial capital – once after 1955, and again after 1978 – in response to the emergence of cheap proletarian labour elsewhere on the Pacific rim; and throughout the postwar period, the Japanese state played a crucial role in both the management of money and the reproduction of the Japanese labour force. In all those senses, it acted as what in a Marxist intellectual tradition would be recognized as an 'ideal collective capitalist': first nurturing its initially vulnerable industrial bourgeoisie and then facilitating the restructuring of their basis of accumulation in a way which other, more liberal, capitalist states did not.*

But the postwar Japanese state could not, by the simple fact of working closely with sections of industrial capital, thereby free either itself or its class-base from the generalized logics of accumulation which characterized world capitalism as a whole. It found neither a way to quicken rates of productivity growth after 1973 when those were slowing across the advanced capitalist economies as a whole, nor a means of escaping the generalized tendencies to financial instability and overproduction which beset the *entire* Pacific rim in the 1990s. So, while the initial economic 'success' of the Japanese state demonstrated to the full the potential for state-orchestrated private capital accumulation that the uneven development of the capitalist world system made available to late-comers in the immediate postwar period, its diminishing capacity to trigger a successful third cycle of 'scrap and build' for Japanese industrial capital after 1973 also demonstrated the manner in which that potential for state action was then eroded by successful catch-up on the one side and by increased globalization on the other.

State action in a changing global order

When Andrea Boltho set out to answer the question 'was Japan's industrial policy successful?' he ran into the dilemma that all of us face when dealing with the state as an element in the growth equation. He believed he had an answer to that question, but he knew he could not prove it. He knew that 'a counter-factual experiment [was] impossible', that one could not, as he put it, 'rewrite history and see how Japan would have developed in the absence of an industrial policy' (Boltho, 1985: 188). Indeed, many of the critics of the development state thesis have ultimately rested their case on this point: that the research methodologies sustaining the thesis focus too heavily on policy inputs and too little on economic outcomes, and that when outcomes are examined, no control is introduced for the impact of other variables. Boltho still went on to say that on balance he 'came down in favour of attributing to Japan's policy a very important role in shaping the country's postwar economic development' (ibid.). But from the same data base, Gary Saxonhouse concluded with equal certainty that 'when the Japanese experience is properly normalised for capital stock, labour force, geographical position and natural-resource endowment, there is little left to be explained by an industrial policy' (Saxonhouse, 1983: 271). The temptation is therefore enormous to shrug and walk away, and to remain at the end

---

* So too it would appear, from the weight of the available research evidence, did the South Korean and Taiwanese states. See Henderson (1993a; 1993b), Henderson and Appelbaum (1992) and, among others, Deyo (1987), Amsden (1989; 1990), Wade (1988; 1990; 1992), Chowdhury and Islam (1993), Pilat (1994), Fitzgerald (1995); but also Haggard (1990) and Hamilton (1997).

of the research review as agnostic and uncertain about the true role of the state as an economic agent as at its outset.

However that temptation must be resisted. What the overlap of potential causal variables makes difficult (to the point of impossibility) is any fully adequate growth accounting assessment of the part played by discrete factors (including political ones) in any particular growth trajectory. Institutional and historical material of the kind we have examined here does not lend itself to mathematical forms of rigour, however carefully constructed the indices of performance turn out to be. But what it does lend itself to are tentative judgements of the Boltho (and indeed of the Saxonhouse) variety. It lends itself to judgements rooted (as we have seen progressively throughout this middle part of the book) in the careful gathering of empirical data, the setting of that data in an appropriate comparative framework, and its insertion in an implied trajectory of the 'what would have happened but for . . . ?' variety. This last move – the attribution of causality to a particular factor which rests ultimately on the positing of a *growth path which did not occur* because of the factor's presence – cannot, by the nature of the beast, be established empirically; but that does not mean it is either valueless or arbitrary, or that such an attribution is to be avoided. It is not, so long as the trajectory foregone is one projected on the basis of an underlying theoretical framework of an appropriate kind. For the construction of causal analysis in the area of economic growth always has its own unavoidable moment of theorizing, one which, in the context of this study, necessarily takes us back to the material discussed in the Appendix. In the end, judgements on the role of the state as an agent in the growth equation depend on our theoretical understanding of how capitalist economies work; and that includes our theoretical understanding of the various roles played within them by the institutions of the state.

Such a theoretical move is not, however, empirically unconstrained. Facts do matter. They help to indicate what is not credible, even if they cannot unambiguously indicate what is. It is extraordinarily difficult, for example, to sustain a purely neo-liberal understanding of the role of the state in the postwar growth story once the facts are known about the German state's underwriting of welfare provision and the Japanese state's involvement in industrial targeting. Even Saxonhouse had to concede a role for the Japanese state in the triggering of savings and the managing of trade; and even the World Bank has now come round – in a limited and somewhat grudging way – to conceding a role for state policy in world development, 'protecting and correcting markets' (Panitch, 1998: 15–20). New growth theorists can certainly find much support for their emphasis on the importance of human capital in the West German (and Swedish) postwar combination of generous welfare provision, active labour market policies and export strength; and economists of a Schumpeterian persuasion have no difficulty in explaining both the effectiveness and the desirability of MITI-type strategies that combined the encouragement of cartelization with an insistence on intense internal competition (Dosi et al., 1989). My own view, however, is that none of these perspectives can do more than cherry-pick from the full range of state practices covered in this chapter. None of the theoretical approaches mentioned thus far in this paragraph can adequately explain the liberal militarism of postwar US and UK state policies, the changing effectiveness of interventions by the Japanese state, and the global parameters within which our chosen economies and states interacted over the fifty-year period. As far as I can tell, if we wish to attain that level of explanatory adequacy we need to make use of analytical frameworks that are ultimately rooted in some form of Marxist understanding of capitalism as a world system.

With that in mind, three broad conclusions on the role of the state in the postwar growth equation seem legitimate here.

(1)   First, politicians and administrators do not directly produce economic growth. Nor do they, by their own immediate actions, produce commodities which domestic and foreign consumers choose to buy; and to this degree at least, neo-liberal preoccupations with private economic processes are entirely valid. Where neo-liberalism falls short is in its insistence on treating markets as spheres of exchange between isolated individuals, abstracted from the class positions and unequal relationships into which they are inserted in a capitalist mode of production, and in its associated failure to recognize the crucial functions played by the state in the orchestration of private capital accumulation. Under capitalism, markets do not work unaided. Nor are they level playing fields. Rather, capitalist markets are terrains of struggle between and within capitalist classes; and because they are, the state has three possible points of entry into the private sphere of unequal market exchange. It can act to orchestrate the relationship between different sections of the capitalist class. It can act to orchestrate relationships between capital and labour. And it can act to orchestrate the reproduction of labour power itself.

Indeed the creation of the conditions under which labour power is sold has historically been one of the basic and unchanging functions of the capitalist state (the regulation of property relationships and of money as the medium of exchange having been the others) (Brunhoff, 1978). Whether then states expand their role – to orchestrate capital–labour relations, or to tilt the balance of power between sections of the dominant capitalist class – varies over time and between national capitalisms: but it does not vary randomly. Rather, the degree and scale of state action vary with the balance and character of class forces surrounding it, and then in a dialectical fashion play a critical role in reproducing and shaping that balance over time. US military spending after 1945 played a critical role in shaping the weights of different sections of capital within the US social formation. German state power underwrote a certain role for German labour; and so on. What we have examined over the course of this chapter are a series of capitalist states exercising an important degree of autonomy in relation to the national class forces surrounding them, while being ultimately constrained by the nature of those class forces and by the rhythms and logics of the capital accumulation on which they all depend. Therefore, the first general conclusion to be drawn from the material examined here are that over the postwar period state apparatuses visibly enjoyed a degree of *autonomy* in relation to patterns of accumulation within the territorial space they controlled, that the exercise of that autonomy clearly affected those patterns of accumulation in decisive if indeterminate ways, and that the degree of autonomy available was limited in important and predictable ways by the class forces and economic processes surrounding each state in turn.

(2)   Secondly, if Marxist theory is correct to argue that all capitalist states enjoy a degree of relative autonomy, that theoretical insight does not of itself then explain why particular states chose to use their autonomy in different ways. Yet this is the crucial question for us: why did particular states play different roles in orchestrating local capital accumulation in the postwar period? The scholarship of the 'new institutionalism' offers one answer to that question, emphasizing state 'autonomy'. Marxist scholarship, broadly defined, offers another, emphasizing state constraints. As we have now seen repeatedly throughout the last four chapters, the 'new institutionalist' writings invariably draw attention to the differential distribution of institutional practices, state traditions, cultures and political programmes, and then offer typologies and explanations of particular state practices within the framework of the general assertion that the world is irreducibly pluralistic and complex (Hollingsworth and Streeck, 1994: 270–300; Hollingsworth and Boyer, 1997). Marxism goes the extra explanatory inch, arguing that all this complexity and surface plurality has an underlying structuring logic of its own, tied to the uneven development over time of capitalism as a world system. Of course, certain major non-Marxist comparative historians and sociologists (from Gerschenkron to Barrington Moore and beyond) have gone most of that inch as well, noting the existence of different routes to modernity (Barrington Moore) and the effect of late industrialization (Gerschenkron) and even tying those routes and that lateness to the character of pre-capitalist social classes and political formations. But what Marxism then adds is the notion that the routes interact, and that late and early industrialization can (and must) be explained in a consistent – and class-based – way: and in a way that is geared to the strength and character of capitalism's formative classes, and not just to the strength and character of its pre-capitalist ones.

There is certainly explanatory mileage in re-specifying early and late industrializers as what elsewhere we have termed 'stage 1 and stage 2 capitalisms' (Looker and Coates, 1986: 98–101), and in then treating the UK and the US as core examples of 'stage 1 capitalisms' and Germany and Japan as 'stage 2 capitalisms'.

- For in stage 1 capitalisms industrialization followed a lengthy period of *internal* social differentiation, which had already established capitalist social relationships before the arrival of factory production. Stage 1 capitalisms, that is, already possessed a strong bourgeoisie engaged in the process of suppressing, containing or accommodating pre-capitalist social classes. They already possessed a relatively powerful and centralized nation state and a well-developed civil society capable of blocking state involvement in the emerging private economy. It is stage 1 capitalisms that were (and are) infused with a developed liberal and secular culture, and in which indigenous middle classes set the pace of economic change, presiding over an industrialization process whose tempo was, in retrospect, relatively slow, but whose reach and penetration into the economy as a whole was relatively thorough and dense from very early on, and whose position in the emerging global order was periodically hegemonic.

• Second-wave capitalisms were (and remain) rather different. There the impulse towards capitalist industrialization arose less from the internal evolution of their societies than from external pressures working on their ruling groups from an emerging industrial capitalist world beyond their borders. Capitalism and industrialization arrived together in these societies. The move from feudalism to capitalism, and from agriculture to industry, was historically fused rather than, as in first wave capitalisms, historically distinct (or in the US case with feudalism, non-existent). As both cause and effect of this process, the industrial bourgeoisies of second-wave capitalisms were weaker, modernizing aristocracies were stronger, liberal and secular ideas were less central and dominant, and proletariats were initially more radical, than in the first-wave cases. The state in consequence retained stronger rural roots while paradoxically being more intimately involved in capital accumulation than was the case with first wave capitalist industrializers; and the penetration of capitalist modes of life and thought was less deep and thorough.

Such a schematization then helps us to tie together many of the features of state practice and political philosophy dividing the various postwar capitalist models. It suggests, for example, that the liberalism that is so visibly entrenched in both US and UK capitalisms can (and should) be traced back to the class and ideological formations surrounding their economies' early start, and that the subsequent militarism of the UK and US states can equally be derived from the periods of world economic dominance that the manufacturing sectors of each stage 1 capitalism briefly enjoyed. And by the same token, it suggests that the pattern of different performances between national capitalist economies with which we are concerned here is best respecified as a set of shifting national trajectories on a map of combined but uneven economic development, where the spaces for catch-up and convergence were predetermined by the prior character of class relations distributed across that map by almost five centuries of class struggle, capital accumulation, production and trade. And such a schematization helps to remind us that the state apparatus in each major capitalist economy did not start from the same point in 1945, and should not be thought of as of equal potency and potential. Rather each state should be thought of as the legatee in 1945 of the manner in which its own national class history interacted with wider global processes of uneven development. Such states should be thought of as institutional centres of power facing different classes, inheriting different histories and occupying different locations in the global economic order – and accordingly as being structurally predisposed to act in dissimilar ways. The second general conclusion that we should therefore draw from the research data on postwar state economic activity is that such state action differed between national capitalisms after 1945 in relation to the positions each occupied on a shared map of social classes and global patterns of production and trade, and is best explained by reference to the prior establishment of that map and those patterns.

(3)   Then, as a third and final concluding observation on the role of the state in the postwar growth equation, there are things to say about the relationship of state action to such global positions and processes. For in the postwar period state action has differed not only in kind and effectiveness *between* capitalist economies. It has also differed in any one economy *over time*: and indeed the centre of gravity around which those policy differences have been organized seems itself now to be differently located than it was in the 1950s and 1960s. Then, in what in the older capitalisms at least is often termed 'the golden age', the state was a very active and involved economic player. State policy varied between national capitalisms, as we know, but it did so around a recognizably common agenda of extensive state involvement in economic life. Now it seems to vary around a much more restricted agenda, from which such things as public ownership, the picking of national champions and the expansion of state welfare expenditure seem to have been removed. Patterns of global interaction between national economies which in the 1950s and 1960s allowed a considerable variation in local state practices (which allowed, that is, for the existence of a *range* of capitalist models) seem now to be in the process of forcing convergence onto a *single* model, of a liberal capitalist kind.

Whether that is so, and what follows for progressive politics in the next century, is *the* big issue which awaits us in the next and final chapter. But in drawing the material on the economic role of the state together in preparation for that discussion, it is worth noting the manner in which the accumulation process in the first half of the postwar period did allow an extensive economic role for the state, of at least two kinds. In those capitalist economies where levels of labour productivity were already high, it allowed (indeed it seemed almost to require) state action to orchestrate the relationships between capital and labour on which the full potential of Fordist production methods could be realized. In those economies, state action on what Keynesian economists would characterize as the *demand* side of the equation was essential if local rates of capital accumulation were to be maintained or enhanced: either direct action (via demand management and/or military expenditure) or indirect action (via the consolidation of trade union and worker rights, which then triggered a private-sector wage–profit dynamic). In less productive economies, by contrast, state action was both possible and necessary on the *supply* side of the equation: orchestrating private savings, the transfer and diffusion of imported technologies, the protection of infant industries and the subordination of local labour movements; and economies flourished (or failed to flourish) in the hitherto underdeveloped areas of the global economy to the degree that their local states (and supporting employing classes) had the capacity to meet those possibilities and needs (to the degree that they had, as Abramovitz put it, the appropriate 'social capability'). In the first half of the postwar period, that is, states facing a particular level of already established capitalist development could (and did) establish for themselves different degrees and forms of orchestration of the three basic relationships at play within a capitalist economy – between sections of capital, between capital and labour, and between labour and the domestic economy. Here then is the third general conclusion which we can safely draw from the research data on the state as an element in the growth equation: that in the first half of the postwar period the nature of the global order allowed a significant space for both consensual and developmental alternatives to a purely liberal market order. The question before us now is whether, in the changing conditions of the second half of the postwar period, the space for those alternative models is diminishing or has already gone.

Part III

Conclusion

8

Capitalist Models and the Politics of the Left

The rise and fall of particular capitalist models has both an immediate and a long-term lesson for all of us. The immediate one is the more obvious: that some of the enthusiasms (especially centre-left enthusiasms in the 1980s for the wonders of Japanese capitalism) now look particularly misplaced. The longer-term one, more obscure perhaps, is that the volatility of capitalist systems inevitably makes the decision to pursue any model an inherently precarious and unreliable process. For it is not just on the British Left, as Martin Wolf would have it, that whenever we 'embrace a particular exemplar, it turns out to be on the verge of collapse' (Wolf, 1996: 18). Centre-right enthusiasts for liberal capitalist models are equally prone to find their chosen cases in terminal decay: either one step away from that significant take-off which perennially eludes it (as the UK economy seems permanently to be) or successful only at the cost of unacceptably high levels of inequality and insecurity (as was the case with US capitalism in the 1990s).

For in the end the problem seems to lie not with modelling but with capitalism. It is not that particular models of capitalism fail to function in a satisfactory manner unless reset in some particular fashion, as both neo-liberal and centre-left theorists would have it. It seems rather that capitalism itself, in whatever form, is capable of functioning only with sporadic effectiveness and always at considerable social cost. And for that reason it seems unwise to treat the present difficulties of model after model as merely temporary aberrations on growth trajectories that are basically sound and reliable, since in truth it is their brief periods of sustained and rapid growth which constitute the deviation from the norm. It was, after all, Western capitalism's postwar 'golden age' between 1948 and 1973 which proved to be the great exception, a period (of rapid growth in profits and wages across the advanced capitalist world as a whole within which a variety of capitalist models could and did flourish) that was as brief as it was unusual, when set in the long history of capitalism as a world system. Even then it was a 'golden age' that depended for its viability on unstable and undesirable conditions: on unequal exchange between the First World and the Third (the success of some models, that is, requiring the failure of others), and on an underlying military Fordism which periodically threatened human survival itself. But it was none the less a 'golden age' – at least when compared to the more difficult conditions for growth that followed for the remainder of the Cold War period, and when set against the intense economic instability into which the new post-Cold War era settled at century's end. Because it was, the expectations of economic performance which it created continue to colour popular expectations of what is attainable by capitalist economic systems. Yet, as we shall now see, each of the major exemplars of that system's postwar success face deeply rooted and structurally induced limits to their contemporary and future capacity to meet those expectations, in even the most modest form; and because they do, the one thing of which we can be certain is that the politics of the Left in the first years of the new millennium will need to be significantly more determined, and more radical, than they have been in the closing years of the old one, if we are truly to prevent the legacy of the past sitting like a nightmare on the brain of the living.

Models in disarray

State-led capitalisms: Japan and the Asian tigers

When the first ripples of the financial crisis of East Asian capitalism rolled out from Thailand through Malaysia and Indonesia into South Korea and then Japan itself in the autumn of 1997, the financial journalist Samual Brittan found some 'modest consolation' in the fact that in consequence 'we should now hear rather less about the much canvassed virtues of Asian capitalism' (Brittan, 1997b: 24). Papers like his, which even in the mid-1990s had run editorials in praise of Korean and Japanese forms of economic organization, quickly reverted to type, extolling the virtues for economic growth of political restraint, financial deregulation, and the free play of market forces. And in truth, they had much to gloat about in the figures on recent Japanese economic performance. For by 1998 the Japanese economy was officially in recession, trapped inside its longest and most severe economic slowdown since 1945, experiencing its first negative GDP growth for 23 years and its greatest year-on-year drop in GDP since the Second World War. The 1998 recession in Japan persisted in spite of record low interest rates, a heavily devalued yen (then at an eight-year low against the dollar, with a resulting boost to the Japanese trade surplus) and a series of fiscal packages aimed at stimulating domestic demand. But domestic demand in Japan in 1998 remained stubbornly flat as, 'fearful of falling wages, rising unemployment, failing banks and a rising budget deficit, Japanese workers . . . squeezed spending and increased their savings' (Persand, 1998: 20). And with recession came a trawl of economic phenomena from which the postwar Japanese economy had until then been remarkably free: low rates of industrial investment (investment fell by 5.6 per cent in 1997 alone), a serious profit squeeze on major industrial conglomerates, a rise in personal and corporate bankruptcies, the spectacular collapse of a number of large brokers, assurance companies and banks (including the country's tenth-largest commercial bank) and the extensive deregulation of Japan's financial sector. Recession also brought the indignity of 'advice' from US Treasury officials on how to reflate the Japanese economy: apparently a 'stimulus of up to 2 per cent of GNP would be very constructive and would provide reassurance to financial markets', the US deputy Treasury secretary told the Japanese Ministry of Finance (cited in the *Financial Times*, 20 March 1998). All to no avail.

Yet this sharp reversal of fortunes between the US and Japan should not lead us to forget how remarkably successful the Japanese economy had been in the five postwar decades taken as a whole, and how large a world role in consequence it now plays. Indeed one reason for the speed and nature of the US Treasury's intervention was doubtless that importance: Washington was presumably worried about the impact on the world economy of a pro-longed and deep recession in what had become by then the world's second-largest economy (with a GDP only slightly lower than the GDPs of Germany, France and the UK combined) and the major source of both demand and investment funds for the entire Asian region. So in dismissing so quickly and with such enthusiasm the institutional forms which had triggered the remarkable growth achievements of the Asian tiger economies, and of Japan itself, neo-liberal commentators on the character of Japan's contemporary ills inevitably failed to do justice to the balance of strengths and weaknesses of the Japanese growth model. A more appropriate balance would have to recognize at least the following.

It would have to concede the effectiveness of such a model for the achievement of rapid catch-up and convergence in the conditions created by the Allied defeat of the Axis powers in 1945. In institutional terms, the arrangements consolidated in Japan between the state bureaucracy and the owners of private capital left the latter particularly well placed to mobilize large volumes of capital for the development of manufacturing industries with a high tradable output. In social terms, those arrangements facilitated the consolidation of a strong national industrial bourgeoisie, who then accu-mulated fixed capital per person employed at the quite remarkable annual average rate of 7.43 per cent for nearly forty years, including a rate of well over 6 per cent per annum from 1973 to 1990, when Japan's 'high growth' period was already over (Pilat, 1994: 46). To a degree far beyond the reach of their liberal capitalist competitors, they also enjoyed the active support of the state in that process. At the institutional level, postwar Japanese industrialists were free of the drawbacks associated with stock-market-based forms of capital generation which so slowed manufacturing investment in the US and the UK; or (to put the same point in social terms) they were free of the pernicious influence on national accumulation rhythms wielded in the US and the UK by a strong and internationally oriented class of rentiers and financiers. Until the 1980s at least Japanese savings fuelled industrial investment at home, not abroad, in ways which US and UK savings did not. And at the same time, the state bureaucrats with whom those industrialists did business were also, for more contingent historical reasons, freer of the international political obligations and preoccupations that pulled state energy (and priorities) away from national economic growth in both the US and the UK. In Japan, the state and capital combined to *manage* Japan's relationship with the rest of the world economy, choosing neither simply to 'open' that economy to international market forces nor to subordinate themselves to a Dutch auction with foreign capital, and in the process orchestrated an unprecedentedly successful process of catch-up and convergence.

The Japanese model seemed (and seems) less strong, however, as a device for moving beyond catch-up and convergence into industrial leadership. Japanese forms of corporate organization were clearly capable of shifting from technology diffusion to technological innovation, but the organizational practices devised to catch the US needed themselves to be reset once Japanese technological leadership held the key to further export growth; and this was neither an easy nor an automatic process, since systems of R&D built up from a background of reverse engineering possessed no particular feature that gave them any automatic superiority over the national innovation systems of liberal capitalism. In that sense at least, the superiority of the Japanese model is likely to be a one-off temporary affair, as Krugman implied. The East Asian tiger economies mobilized resources (labour as well as capital) as Krugman pointed out, to trigger catch-up, and gained productivity advantage by restructuring economic activity out of agriculture into manufacturing, and by exploiting economies of scale, and, in the Japanese case at least, also developed modes of social organization (within the manufacturing sector) which triggered productivity growth. But they were not by that process able to sustain indefinitely the dramatic growth and productivity superiority of their individual 'high-growth' phases. In the end, they all slowed down to more normal growth levels, and all fell victim to more generalized global processes of demand stagnation, diminishing returns on capital investment, financial speculation, currency volatility and debt default. They each had their brief moment as exemplars of strong capitalist models; but they all ultimately succumbed to the general weaknesses of the capitalism they would exemplify.

Moreover, even in their heyday, the successful Asian growth economies depended on the largesse of other 'models' for their own success (this indeed is a feature of models – their mutual interaction – which applies with equal force to the dependence of US and UK capitalism on respectively Japanese and German growth, as we shall see later). In the East Asian case, postwar reconstruction was a deliberate act of US foreign policy; and the subsequent export-led growth trajectory depended critically on rising demand (and therefore rising productivity) particularly in the US home market. As Henderson and Appelbaum have it, 'the economies of Japan, Taiwan, and South Korea – and the militaries of the latter two countries – were deliberately built with US aid and technology transfers as bulwarks against communism' and 'additionally Japanese industry benefited from the increased demands . . . that emerged during the Korean War' (1992: 9). Even the Japanese model in its prime required successful models elsewhere for its markets, particularly a successful liberal capitalism in the US; and it also required the toleration (for political reasons by the US government) of its own propensity to defend its internal market by unofficial forms of protectionism. Whatever else the Japanese model was, it was not a model that could (or ever did) stand and prosper alone.

And of course, we must not forget what Jeff Henderson quite properly called 'the dark side of the miracle', particularly 'labour repression and the exploitation of women workers' (Henderson, 1993b: 213). For behind the ostensibly neutral terminology of Krugman's 'factor mobilisation' and the euphoric descriptions of the special 'trust' relationships linking Japanese companies and Japanese workers lies the appalling social reality of long working hours, intensive work routines, constant managerial pressure to meet corporate goals and the orchestration of a national culture of social unity by and in which labour resistance was (and is) minimized. The actual repression of labour rights has been at its most visible in South Korea (where wages remain low, and hours of work long, even by Japanese standards); but the general subordination of labour is absolutely central to the Japanese growth story too. Labour subordination was true even for the 'salary men' during Japan's period of rapid growth. It was even truer for workers in Japan's subcontracting sectors. It was particularly acute for women and for migrant workers; and all sectors of the Japanese labour force were squeezed when the bubble broke after 1992. Then the trade-off that core male manual and white-collar workers in Japan's largest corporations had settled into from the mid-1950s – long hours, intense working routines and (for office workers) long commuting times in return for regular wage rises, generous overtime pay and total job security – began to corrode (for hours worked, see table 8.1). Little wonder that the 1995 ISR survey of degrees of worker satisfaction found Japanese workers the most discontented of any in its 60-country sample (Taylor, 1995: 8). As Henderson put it, in criticism of those left-wing intellectuals keen to present the Japanese model as a socially progressive one, we must not, as they did, show 'scant regard for the fact that economic development in the East Asian NICs – and in Japan – was (and is being) built at substantial human and environmental cost' (Henderson, 1993a).

Table 8.1 Hours worked per worker
1950–1992

Country	1950	1973	1992
Sweden	1,951	1,571	1,485
Germany	2,472	1,865	1,605
UK	2,224	1,929	1,720
USA	2,121	1,896	1,914
Japan	2,166	2,201	1,965
Taiwan	2,753	2,690	2,386
South Korea	2,200	2,428	2,454

Source: Crafts, 1997b: 79

The other dark side of the miracle was the unregulated nature of capital itself. The close state–industry links made cronyism and corruption an unavoidable element in this model (Pempel, 1998: 202) – indeed the circulation of senior state administrators into lucrative private-sector posts was widely hailed in Japan as *amakudari* (the descent from heaven) – and the politics of Japan in the 1990s was overwhelmed with scandal upon scandal. Corruption apart, the lack of external financial regulation and fierce competition between financial institutions made over-lending a structural tendency, held at bay only so long as export growth could stave off excess production and discourage the movement of funds into property and other forms of speculation (Brenner, 1998: 90). Perhaps not surprisingly therefore, it was the failure of major financial institutions, and the nationalization of major banks to cover their bad debts, rather than the stability of trust-based industry–finance links, that came to be a defining feature of the Japanese model in the wake of the 1997 East Asian financial crisis. Moreover, the commitment of large-scale industrial capital to the protection of its core workers predisposed both state and industry in Japan to a scrap-and-build accumulation strategy, protecting core workers by relocating subcontracting and declining industries, first into the regions of Japan and then into the rest of East Asia. The resulting internationalization of Japanese capital ultimately corroded the institutional arrangements between capital, labour and the state, which had hitherto guaranteed the growth of Japan's indigenous industrial base, by transforming key sections of Japan's industrial bourgeoisie into international players dependent on accumulation rhythms elsewhere (Pempel, 1998: 139, 147); and in the process it weakened the fusion of interests between state officials and the owners of industrial capital on which Japan's uniquely successful postwar economic growth had been based. The 'hollowing out' of Japanese industry by the export of capital is not yet anywhere near as advanced as in, say, the UK; but such a 'hollowing out' is as endemic to the Japanese model of

capitalism in times of crisis as it is to its liberal capitalist competitors, and
the share of employment provided by manufacturing industry in Japan –
like that in the UK – is now well below its peak levels of the early 1970s
(Jackson, 1998: 15).

In this sense, the 'golden geese' image of East Asian economic growth
tigers is both true and misleading (Child-Hill and Fujita, 1996). It is true,
in the sense that much of the industrial development of industry in South
Korea and Taiwan (and more recently in Malaysia, Indonesia and Thailand)
has been the product of the export of Japanese capital. But it is also misleading, because the image it presents is of a benign and mutually beneficial
process, when in reality the process is neither of those things. The export
of Japanese capital into East Asia has been driven by the perennial pursuit
of low wages and intensified work routines, in an attempt to resolve the
internal contradictions of Japanese-based capital accumulation by moving
them out from core to periphery. That movement has done more than create
an increasing interdependence between regional economies. It has also
brought intensified labour processes to wider and wider sections of East
Asian labour, corporate instability as debts have accumulated and curren-
cies collapsed, and yet further job insecurity and poverty for large sections
of the East Asian (and now Japanese) working class (Chote, 1998: 4). And
because it has – because the Japanese economic miracle has these dark sides
– there is no way in which 'the Japanese model' can or should be hawked
around the European and North American Left as a progressive alternative
to liberal capitalism. It was not in the past. It is not now. And it will not be
in the future.

Negotiated/consensual capitalisms:
West Germany and Sweden

The Centre–Left is on much firmer ground when presenting European corporatism as that model. As we have seen in both the Swedish and the West
German cases, postwar Western European corporatism put at its core a set
of workers' rights; and until the 1990s at least both Sweden and West
Germany, as leading examples of the corporatist form of capitalism, did
manage to combine the protection (and indeed the periodic extension) of
those rights with sustained economic growth and rising general living standards. Like the Japanese economy, however, economic performance by both
the Swedish and the by then united German economies proved in the 1990s
to be less impressive than it had been hitherto. In particular, and for the first
time in the postwar period, unemployment in both economies settled in that
decade at levels which were higher, and GDP growth rates at levels which
were lower, than those in the US and the UK; as German and
Swedish labour productivity levels, which were always lower than those in
the US, dropped back towards (in the German case) and below (in the
Swedish case) even UK levels (Albert and Gonenc, 1996: 189). Official

unemployment rates in Germany reached 9.1% in January 1999, and in Sweden 7.6%, when the UK figure was only 6.2% and the US figure was 4.4%. But neither economy in 1998 was (as Japan was) actually in recession. The projected growth rate for Swedish GDP in 1998 was 2.9 per cent (*Financial Times*, 14 August 1998) and for Germany's 2.7 per cent (Pain, 1998: 29); and German manufacturing still remained at century's end what Carling and Soskice legitimately termed 'the exporting powerhouse of Western Europe' (1997: 73). Indeed, as late as 1993 the united German economy was responsible for over 10 per cent of total world visible exports, when the comparable figure for the much larger US economy was only 12 per cent, the Japanese 9.6 per cent and the UK's 4.8 per cent (Streeck, 1997b: 34).

So taking the 50-year postwar period as a whole, any stock-taking of the two economies would have to concede at least the following strengths of the corporatist model of capitalism.

It would have to concede the quality of the labour and welfare legislation put in place in each economy and the associated high performance (in terms of *social* indicators) which then resulted. If we take any of the socially germane economic indicators (hours worked, job security and rights of retraining, welfare provision, income equality or even working-class purchasing power) it is clear that postwar Swedish and German levels of attainment are striking (even remarkable) in comparative terms. Take hours worked, for example: table 8.1 shows clearly how working hours have come down steadily since the war in all our chosen economies (with the exception, significantly, of the post-1973 US). It also shows clearly the significantly fewer hours spent at work in Sweden and Germany than in the successful East Asian capitalist economies. And all sorts of other indicators reinforce the same general point. So at the start of the 1990s the median length of time individuals had occupied their present jobs in Germany was 7.5 years, compared with 4.4 years in the UK and 3.0 years in the US (Japan was highest, at 8.2 years); on average workers in small enterprises in Germany earned 90 per cent of the earnings of workers in large enterprises, whereas the figure in the US was only 57 per cent (Streeck, 1997b: 36, 38); and by the mid 1990s, 'average hourly wages for German production workers stood at $31.87, compared to $17.74 for their counterparts in the US' (Brenner, 1998: 234); and so on. There can therefore be little doubt that manual or routine white-collar workers were (and remain) far better off and protected in social terms in Sweden and Germany than they were (and are) in the UK or the US, let alone in Japan or in any of the Asian tiger economies.

Any stock-taking exercise would also have to recognize the ability of each of these major corporatist economies, prior to the recent intensification in the internationalization of capital, successfully to combine the consolidation of those worker rights with the maintenance of sustained economic growth, capital accumulation and the consolidation of internationally competitive firms.

- *In the Swedish case*, the ability to do this through to the 1980s appears to have turned on the initial success of the Rehn–Meidner model in redeploying Swedish labour into high-productivity sectors of Swedish manufacturing, with the associated consolidation of a high-value-added, high-wage, high-productivity growth trajectory for Swedish manufacturing industry as a whole. The reinvestment of any resulting super-profits back into Swedish industry was of course vital to that growth trajectory; but so long as that reinvestment occurred, the model was perfectly capable of sustaining not simply a self-confident labour movement but also a strong (if tiny) national industrial bourgeoisie.

- *In the West German case*, the combination of welfare and economic growth seems to have rested less on the central orchestration of labour redeployment than on the growing ability of German industry to capture larger and larger shares of world trade in manufactured goods. Initially, in the 1950s and 1960s, when West German growth rates were at their highest, that capture of market share came from the fusion of pre-existing labour skills and capital with (in the 1950s) *low wages* and in the 1960s voluntary *wage moderation* by German trade unions (Brenner, 1998: 65, 77); but from the 1970s the German export drive had to be combined with steadily increasing German labour costs. Then the trick – what Wolfgang Streeck later characterized as 'a socio-economic tightrope walk' (Streeck, 1997b: 42) – seems to have required a redeployment of German export activity into ever higher-quality, higher-value-added commodity production, a redeployment (of both capital and labour) which was facilitated by the existence of uniquely close institutional links between financial and industrial institutions in Germany, the strength of trade union involvement in the diffusion of technology and new forms of work organization (Wever and Allen, 1991), the development of extensive programmes of labour retraining and also (it should be said) the importation of large quantities of cheap (largely Turkish) migrant labour to provide an unskilled and low-paid subterranean cushion. And while the trick was performed, it left West Germany not simply with a self-confident labour movement, but (like Sweden) with a capitalist class in which national and industrial fractions' interests prevailed over international and financial ones.

But the stock-taking would have to recognize also two serious and developing weaknesses in this hitherto successful corporatist model.

One is the weakening of the competitive position of nationally based manufacturing industry, triggered initially by slowdowns in the rate of local capital accumulation after 1970. In West Germany, for example, 'between 1973 and 1979 the manufacturing gross capital stock grew less than one-third as fast as it had during the 1960s and early 1970s' (Brenner, 1998: 174) in direct response to a squeeze on profitability occasioned by tightening export markets and rising labour costs. The growth in the West German stock of manufacturing capital then slowed further between 1979 and 1990, dropping from its annual rate of 2 per cent between 1973 and 1979 to just 1.4 per cent in the 1980s (ibid.: 128), in the process steadily reducing the rate of growth of labour productivity and eroding the capacity of German manufacturing to sustain its share of employment and output in overall German GDP. As we saw in chapter 4, the Swedish experience was similar. Commentators have observed too the propensity of productivity rates to slow in Germany as the technology gap with the US narrowed, suggesting that the institutional structures binding German finance and industry left German industrial capital better at technology adaption and diffusion than at innovation and the opening of new industries (Ergas, 1987: 74; Porter, 1990: 377, 380; Carling and Soskice, 1997: 64–8; Streeck, 1997b: 41, 46), and better at medium-level technologies than at high-tech production. It is clear too that German manufacturing capital is now experiencing increasing difficulties in protecting its share of its export markets by persistently moving up-market while carrying labour costs that are heavy in international terms. Price competition is intensifying across the full range of German export markets, as the technological sophistication of Asian competition increases.

This triple mixture (of low investment, weak innovation and intensified price competition) now places a serious question mark over the ability of the German model to maintain its high-wire balancing act into the first years of the new century. Unemployment (at 12 per cent overall in 1997, and 20 per cent in the East German *Länder*) is already much higher in the united Germany than it was in the old West German economy. Real wages have been virtually stagnant for a decade and a half now (Mahnkopf, 1999: 159). Sections of German manufacturing capital are already pulling out of the centralized collective-bargaining systems (Carling and Soskice, 1997: 57; Mahnkopf, 1999: 161–5); and calls are intensifying from a revitalized German neo-liberal right for major welfare reform. Germany at century's end looks poised to move in the Swedish direction, deconstructing parts of its hitherto entrenched corporatist model as external competitive pressures pull sections of German capital out of the class compact they had hitherto reluctantly accepted. That deconstruction might be slowed by the arrival of the German Centre-Left in power in 1998; but (as we shall see in the last part of this chapter) European social democracy is also in retreat from old-style class compacts, so even that slowdown in the internal unravelling of the German model is likely to be at best only a brief reprieve.

That is particularly so because of the manner in which the emerging internal tensions of the German model are being matched (again Swedish style) by the export of capital. Class compacts of the corporatist kind work, as we saw in chapter 4, only so long as they are accompanied by persistent *internal* capital accumulation, a pattern of local investment in manufacturing industry which (as we have seen) was a defining feature of the German model through to the 1980s (particularly when compared with the way the export of capital was by then already hollowing out significant sections of UK-based manufacturing industry). As Streeck put it, 'the postwar German compromise between capital and labour . . . was conditional on limited mobility of production factors across national boundaries' (Streeck, 1997b: 49). But the export of capital by German companies – east into the former Soviet Union, south into the emerging markets of Spanish America, and even west into existing US and UK corporate capital – is now a significant (and growing) feature of corporate Germany's response to the difficulties of maintaining market share from within the high-wage, high-social-taxation compact of German corporatism. As Brenner has recently noted, before 1985 German FDI was stable (at around DM 10 billion a year); but between 1985 and 1990 'German foreign direct investment more than tripled to 30 billion marks, while investment from abroad stagnated' (Brenner, 1998: 229). More recently still, capital export from Germany has run at unprecedented levels: DM 57.5 billion in 1997, DM 30 billion in the first half of 1998 alone. But some inward investment has also returned – DM 14 billion in the first half of 1998 (Norman, 1998: 20), with US investors apparently attracted by the very features of German labour markets (high skills, high wages, established collective bargaining rights) that neo-liberal economics normally treats as a barrier to capital accumulation (Cooke and Noble, 1998: 600): so the jury is still out on the scale and persistence of this capital leakage. But the signs are not good for German inward investment over the long term. Barrell and Pain's figures suggest a significant *widening* of the gap between capital outflows and inflows for the German economy from 1976 to 1995: from a gap of just US$2.5 million on average each year between 1976 and 1980 to an annual average in the first half of the 1990s of US$23.9 million (Barrell and Pain, 1997: 65). Indeed, part of the pressure exerted by the new German government for tax harmonization (at least on business taxes) within the European Union in 1998 seemed to stem from a recognition of this problem: that unless (and to the degree that) the social costs imposed on German capital could be generalized across the Union, the pressure would be on German industry to relocate an increasing proportion of its productive activity elsewhere within the EU (where labour is cheaper, union rights less entrenched and taxes lower) and out beyond EU boundaries (where taxes, labour rights and wages are lower still).

There is no doubt that Western European corporatism – as a model of progressive capitalism – is now under increasing threat. As a model, it contains considerable inner strengths, and seems perpetually capable of generating fresh examples of 'economies doing well'. The fashion in 1997–8 was definitely for the Dutch and Danish versions of the genre (Brittan, 1997a: 24; Gray, 1998: 17). More generally, European corporatism's cumulative build-up over a 40-year period of capital stock and labour skills (and associated social infrastructure, political stability and market size and sophistication) still seems capable of acting as a powerful magnet for new capital seeking high rates of return in an increasingly unstable global order. The German manufacturing sector still employs over a third of all German labour (a significantly higher percentage than for manufacturing in either the US or the UK), and German inflation and interest rates remain low by international standards (for an enthusiastic endorsement of the model's future, see Henzler, 1992). But the pressure on profits triggered by increasing competition, the capacity of capital to relocate in increasingly developed productive systems abroad, and the speed and extent of technology diffusion into even new labour forces and corporate structures, are all now combining to pull capital in the opposite direction: out of Western Europe into more supine or repressed proletariats abroad. The full ramifications of this balance of pull and push factors in the new global order will be discussed in the next section; for now it is enough to note their more local and immediate impact within Western Europe itself. It is enough to note, that is, that German- and Swedish-style welfare capitalism did represent, at its peak, the most socially advanced form taken by postwar capitalism as a whole, that this peak seems now to have been passed, and that socially advanced forms of capitalism are now in danger of internal deconstruction under the linked impact of increased international competition and the enhanced export of capital.

Market-led capitalisms: the UK and the US

Much has been made in the UK recently of the 'end of relative decline' by focusing public discussion on the shrinking performance gap between the UK economy and the economies of Germany and Japan (Wolf, 1996c: II); and there is no doubt that the statistical indicators of general economic performance do sustain that view to a degree. The performance of the UK economy in the 1990s *relative to its own immediate past* was better on a range of indicators: better on inflation, on unemployment, and on rates of economic growth. Unemployment in the UK in the 1990s fell to 6.4 per cent on the ILO definition. In the mid-1980s it had peaked at 11.9 per cent. Inflation in the UK in the 1990s ran consistently at well under 4 per cent; in the period 1974 to 1983 it had regularly run at well over 10 per cent. The UK economy grew steadily (and without recession) from 1992 to 1998. It had reached a similar growth plateau between 1982 and 1988, but that earlier plateau had been squashed between two very severe recessions: the first, from 1980 to 1982, the deepest and sharpest the UK economy had experienced since before the 1930s; the second, from 1989 to 1992, the longest unbroken period of falling GDP the UK had known since 1945. Set against that economic history, therefore, defenders of the Major government in particular could lay claim to considerable economic improvement, could legitimately bewail their own ejection from office in 1997 as somehow economically unjust, and could claim to have bequeathed to their New

Labour successors the strongest and most vibrant economic legacy inherited by a new government in the UK since the Second World War. And they did.

Similar optimistic readings of recent UK economic performance were again common – particularly on the Centre-Right of British politics – when the argument shifted into a *comparative* mode. Here the claims were basically two. One was that the productivity gap dividing the UK from its more corporatist European neighbours was narrowing to the point of oblivion, and was doing so because of the greater labour market flexibility possible under the more lightly regulated labour market conditions of the UK's post-1979 liberal capitalist policy regime. We met the detail of that argument in chapter 4. The second and parallel claim was that the UK economy in the 1990s was a job-creating economy: that (with the US economy) its modes of labour market organization attracted foreign direct investment, enabled private companies to hire staff with greater impunity and set employment trends on an upward trajectory at a time when the more regulated labour markets of corporatist Europe were experiencing growing unemployment. Statistical indicators on the UK economy in the 1990s, so the argument ran, demonstrated both the long-term competitive viability of UK-based industry *and* the competitive superiority of liberal capitalist modes of economic organization over corporatist ones.

A more balanced stock-taking however must deflate the more fanciful elements of those claims, and do so in at least two ways.

It must do so first by noting – as we first did in chapter 2 – that the narrowing of the gap in performance on a range of economic indicators between the UK and Germany in the 1990s appeared to be far more the product of increasing German difficulties than the product of the transcendence of persistent UK defects, and that in any case the gap (in labour productivity, investment levels, inflation and interest rates) still persisted. Quite what the scale of the productivity gap was by 1998 remained contentious (on this, see McKinsey, 1998: Elliott, 1998); but the existence of a gap, however small, did not. (For various calculations of the size of the gap at the start of the 1990s, see Lansbury and Mayes, 1996: 30; Broadberry, 1997: 36, 41; and at the end of the 1990s, see Department of Trade and Industry, 1998.) As the new millennium approached, the UK economy continued to demonstrate what in comparative terms were below-average levels of industrial investment and serious competitive weaknesses among even its leading manufacturing companies (DTI figures, cited in Brown, 1998). It continued to possess too small a manufacturing base for the scale of its internal requirements for manufactured commodities (with manufacturing GDP contribution and employment provision down from the 30 per cent and 8.5 million workers of the late 1960s to just 22 per cent and fewer than 4 million workers by the late 1990s). In fact the UK manufacturing sector entered 1999 officially in recession – trapped in its most adverse run of monthly output figures since the Thatcher recession of 1981; yet that same manufacturing base still reported serious (and competi-

tively damaging) skill shortages on a regular basis. The UK record on investment in R&D (and on innovation generally) remained poor by
international standards – Michael Porter placed the UK 13th out of the
seventeen industrialized counties whose innovation structures he studied
in 1988 (*Financial Times*, 11 December 1988: 9) – too skewed towards
defence industries, too sectorally concentrated (even in the civilian sector)
in a narrow range of industries (primarily pharmaceuticals and aerospace)
and in volume terms still inadequate to the scale of competitive edge
required by the UK economy to balance its demand for imported manufactured goods. (For balance it should be noted that, the very same week,
the OECD scored the UK higher, because of its enhanced capacity for technology diffusion (*Financial Times*, 15 December 1998: 8).) The UK
economy continued in consequence to run a large and persistent deficit on
its overseas trade, and (1997 apart) an associated shortfall on its overall
foreign payments, which touched 4 per cent of GDP in 1989, one that it
could finance only by the maintenance in London of interest rates that (as
late as November 1998) were still twice the level adopted by the bulk of the
European Union in the run-up to the introduction of EMU. And those high
interest rates then acted, as in the past, as a powerful disincentive to further
investment in manufacturing plant and equipment. The UK had spent the
first four decades of the postwar period locked in a process of cumulative
economic decline caused by inadequate levels of investment in manufacturing plant and equipment, and that growth trajectory remained firmly in
place at century's end.

The immediate effects on living standards associated with the productivity shortfall triggered by low investment could be (and were) cushioned
by high interest rates; but the long-term consequences of that shortfall
could be ameliorated only by a second feature of the UK's current growth
regime little mentioned by those keen to 'talk up' recent UK performance:
namely the manner in which low investment and innovation have been (and
remain) offset in the UK by the persistence of low wages and long hours.
Workers in the UK earn less, and labour costs are inflated by fewer social
overheads, than in any other major European economy. On these indicators,
the UK keeps company with economies like Ireland and Spain. The hours
worked within the UK are among northern Europe's longest. Indeed a suc-
cession of UK governments (both Conservative and now New Labour) have
sought to protect the capacity of the UK economy to create employment of
that kind by negotiating opt-outs from EU-wide agreements on the length
and terms of employment. For the job-creation claims of the UK's advocates obscure the true nature of the employment trends now operating. The
UK economy has created jobs, but most of those jobs have been part-time,
low-skilled and low-paid. The UK economy has experienced a steady (and
during its recessions a rapid) destruction of full-time employment, a
destruction of high-wage jobs, a destruction of jobs in manufacturing
industry and a destruction of jobs requiring extensive training and high
levels of skill. As we saw in more detail in chapter 2, the balance of employ-

ment within the UK has shifted downwards on all those key indicators for two decades, as upwards of 3 million full-time jobs in civilian employment were lost between 1979 and 1993, to leave the UK positioned as predominantly an off-shore warehouse economy, where a low-paid, underskilled and now poorly unionized work-force depended for the attraction of foreign direct investment on the economy's role as an assembly pad within the tariff boundaries of the EU for the export of medium-tech mass-consumer goods into the more prosperous heartlands of corporatist Europe.

The UK economy remains disproportionately a service-based economy, internationally competitive in financial services, but otherwise centred around low-paid service provision to a slowly growing domestic market. It remains one from which, in consequence (and as we documented in chapter 4), the export of capital regularly exceeds its import, and where the capital imported into manufacturing industry by foreign-based transnational corporations rarely brings with it the high-value-added R&D-based elements of the global production process. As Barrell and Pain found, 'whilst the UK has clearly been able to attract relatively labour-intensive investment, it has fared relatively poorly in attracting more capital-intensive investment'; and of course, 'UK firms have more assets located overseas than foreign firms have in the UK' (1997: 69, 70). The UK economy remains in consequence one trapped in what is ultimately a parasitical and subordinate relationship with the rest of mainland Europe, able to survive in the short term by the persistent opting out from European-wide initiatives that would standardize labour codes and labour costs, but in the process unable to break through into a more socially desirable high-wage, high-productivity, high-investment growth trajectory. Government ministers of whatever political persuasion persistently claim to be on the verge of making that readjustment, in order to bring UK productivity and consumption standards up to the Western European average. They persistently offer the UK's electorate different 'models' for achieving that – first ways, second ways, now third ways – which is one reason why the UK debate on capitalist models has been so extensive and so prolonged. But in practice those politicians invariable argue for policies in Europe which would achieve that catch-up by bringing the rest of Western Europe back towards existing UK practices and performance levels; and they certainly lack the political will and courage (and the associated social forces and international legislative freedom) to instigate the radical institutional changes (to the rights of private financial and industrial capital) which such a re-alignment of the UK growth trajectory now requires. Yet (as we shall argue in more detail in the last pages of this book) without major institutional change – without some 'fourth way' – the UK economy will continue to bob along the bottom of the European performance tables; and the more it bobs along there, the weaker grow the economic and social forces within the UK which centre-left politicians would need to mobilize if they truly wanted to effect the leap up those league tables that they and their electorate in the UK have now sought for so long.

So there is nothing particularly desirable about the UK's version of liberal capitalism to place it over Western European corporatism on any scale of capitalist models predicated on progressive social values; nor, in truth, is there anything particularly desirable about the US model either. Rather less in fact, even though the recovery of US capitalism to its previous position of world leadership has been much hailed by neo-liberal commentators throughout the 1990s. They have had a particularly good time pointing up the more fanciful aspects of the US 'declinist' literature of the decade before and celebrating the persistence of US global economic leadership (Spulber, 1995: 114–45). And, as with the UK, the purely economic indicators of overall industrial performance do provide much ammunition for neo-liberal triumphalism. The US economy did enjoy eight unbroken years of economic growth from 1992. Key sectors of US industry, which had previously felt the full onslaught of particularly Japanese competition, did 'bounce back' with a vengeance: most notably the US auto industry. And the US economy did continue both to retain its broad productivity advantage (even over the Japanese economy) and its competitive strength in a series of important new high-tech industrial sectors. Stock-holders in the US particularly prospered throughout the 1990s, and ended the decade reinforced again as speculative capital returned in volume to New York, to avoid the turbulence of Asian financial markets. The real returns on US equities between 1982 and 1997 averaged a remarkable 12.8% (Wolf, 1998: 21). And unlike the European corporatist economies, the US economy in the 1990s even managed (as did that of the UK) to pull unemployment down to rates well below general European ones, to rates equivalent to Japanese ones, and to rates (at 4.4% by late 1998) which the US itself had not seen for three decades.

So what possibly could be wrong with that? Actually two very important things: one economic, one social.

Economically, the US continued to run a massive trade deficit throughout the 1990s, as it had from 1982. Just as the UK's 'prosperity' after 1979, and its ability to attract FDI, turned ultimately on the superior economic performance (and hence market demand) of corporatist Europe, so the US's ability to maintain internal living standards relied on the productive growth of particularly the Japanese economy, and the increasing willingness of Japanese investors to move their capital out of Japan, into US real estate, government bonds and industrial corporations. It relied too on the ten-year decline in the value of the dollar against both the mark and the yen initiated by the Plaza Accord of 1985 – a fall of 60 per cent against the yen and 50 per cent against the mark, a fall whose precariousness was underlined by the yen's own precipitous collapse in 1998. The rate of growth of labour productivity across the US economy as a whole remained low throughout the 1990s both by comparative standards and in relation to previous peaks of labour productivity growth in the first half of the postwar period; and it did so both because of the increasing concentration of US employment in low-productivity service sectors, and because of a restricted flow of capital funds into industrial retooling (Spulber, 1995: 186). US manufacturing industry shed almost 2 million jobs from 1979 to 1996, while employment in the low-productivity service sector grew by nearly 30 million. US industry spent a significant part of the 1990s achieving productivity gains by 'downsizing, out-sourcing, reorganisation of the labour process, and speed up – and only in small part through investment growth' (Brenner, 1998: 187), and by those mechanisms did pull labour productivity growth rates *in the manufacturing sector* back up to 'golden age' levels (Lester, 1998: 43). But in the US, as in the UK, the 'productivity miracle' of the 1980s and 1990s relied far more on the closing of old plant and the intensification of work routines than on investment in what Brenner termed 'state of the art plant and equipment' (Brenner, 1998: 199); and because it did, long-standing sources of US productivity weakness (particularly inadequacies in US systems of industrial training and mass education, and the extensive export of US capital) remained largely unchallenged.

The persistence of those weaknesses points to a further source of US economic recovery, which, while immediately positive for overall US growth, signalled persistent and long-term structural (and social) weaknesses in the emerging *social* structure of accumulation surrounding industry. The industrial recovery of the 1990s was based on more than the intensification of work routines and the devaluation of the dollar. US industrial recovery in the 1990s was also based on a steady and persistent diminution in the real wages of US industrial workers (between 1979 and 1990 real wages in the US *fell* at an annual average rate of 1 per cent). It was based on the accentuation of already (in comparative terms) unprecedented levels of social inequality, and it was based on an increase in the number of hours required of (in addition to an intensification of the work performed by) US workers. In fact US labour has been throughout this story the absent guest at the capitalist feast. The particular strength of unions representing predominantly white male manual workers played an important if subordinate role in sustaining the Fordist dynamic of postwar capitalism's 'golden age' prior to 1973 (Davis, 1986: 190–1; Kotz et al., 1994; Coates, 1994: 219–221); but subsequently even that section of the US labour movement has endured what has been effectively a 40-year 'employers' offensive' against it (Moody, 1997; Brenner, 1998: 60, 191–2, 196). This weakening of the industrial power of US labour has left even male white workers in the US vulnerable to downsizing, wage cuts and increased job intensity and stress; and since white male workers remain by far the most privileged section of the US labour force, it is clear that the pressures on black and Hispanic Americans and on women workers of all ethnic backgrounds have systematically increased.

So the intensification of the labour process and stagnant real wages for the vast majority of US workers underpinned the growth of the US economy in the 1990s, and guaranteed that any resulting prosperity would not be generalized across US society as a whole. The US economy and society enter the next century with the starkest juxtaposition of poverty and wealth of any of the capitalist models we have examined (Mishel et al., 1997: 393–406). Even America's much cited job-creation machine looks less impressive in comparative terms when an ethnic and age element is included. For in the contemporary US, a quite staggering proportion of young black males are incarcerated and the total prison pupulation exceeds 1.8 million; and when we control for that incarceration, we find that US employment rates among 'prime age males' (aged 25–54) are not superior to those achieved in corporatist Europe. In fact, for 1992–3, they were actually worse (Buchele and Christiansen, 1998: 121). To a quite remarkable degree, unemployment is low by international standards in the US only because it incarcerates four times as many of its potential workers as does the UK, six times as many as does the rest of Western Europe, and fourteen times as many as does Japan (Gray, 1998: 22). To a quite remarkable degree too, unemployment is low in the US because of the proliferation there of 'non-standard' forms of employment: part-time jobs, temping, self-employment and multiple job holding, all of which 'typically offer lower wages, fewer benefits, and far less security than regular full-time work' (Mishel et al., 1999: 253). As many as 4 million workers in the US in 1997 reported that they wanted full-time employment but could find only part-time work, in an economy in which by then 30 per cent of all available employment was of this non-standard variety.

Yet for all the starkness of these differences in their employment performance, what is actually more striking about all three models is the commonality of the difficulties into which they are now running. On the side of 'capital' the story seems everywhere to be the same. 'Golden age' rates of productivity growth have gone, price competition has intensified, and profit margins on productive investment are pressed. And from the centre of each model the response of corporate capital seems invariably to be the same: intensify local wage–effort bargains if you can, and if you cannot, leave in search of cheaper labour and higher rates of surplus extraction elsewhere. On the side of 'labour' in consequence, there are equivalent similarities. The settlements arrived at in the core capitalisms during the 'golden age' – the US capital–labour accord, the Japanese employment system, Western European welfare capitalism – are everywhere under challenge. Established (that is male white) workers in each of the core capitalisms have now experienced between 15 and 25 years (depending on where they are) of frozen (or falling) real wages, increased job insecurity and intensified work processes. They have seen welfare rights come under pressure, and, where they have been organizationally and politically weak, they have seen them significantly reduced; and new workers (either new strata within established capitalisms, or whole proletariats in new capitalisms) have largely been denied those wages and welfare rights altogether. In other words, the models have stopped working. They have stopped working as engines of growth and capital accumulation; and they have stopped working as providers of secure employment and rising private and social wages for the bulk of their populations; and we need to know why.

The globalization of capital
and the exploitation of labour

The conventional answer these days, at least for capitalist models favoured by the Centre-Left, is globalization. The enhanced global mobility of capital is invariably cited – by politicians, commentators and neo-liberal academics – as the reason why a new form of convergence is now essential: not between the technologies underpinning industrial production, but between the social structures of accumulation surrounding that production. The dominant thesis in Western policy-making circles these days appears to be that the future lies only with capitalist models in which labour-market flexibility is guaranteed, that such models can be arrived at only by a deregulation of markets of all kinds, and that such deregulation involves a 'rolling back of the state': back from any attempt to impose national controls on the deployment of capital, and back from any attempt by the state to enshrine rights and rewards for labour. What globalization has done, according to those keen to advocate its imperatives, is impose a standard framework of requirements on all national capitalisms, so squeezing (to the point of oblivion) the space for a variety of capitalist models, and requiring that the remaining space be occupied by deregulated (that is, by liberal market) capitalisms.

On this argument, the arrival of globalization has awesome consequences for trust-based capitalist models. It has simply destroyed the space previously enjoyed by growth strategies based on state direction or extensive welfare provision, by restricting successful growth strategies to those which are purely market-driven and entirely under the control of private capital. The new global mobility of capital is having this effect by so penetrating the boundaries of existing national economies with cross-border movements of goods, technologies and investment funds as to create a truly 'borderless world' (Ohmae, 1995) beyond the control of national political institutions. In this borderless environment, only two strategies are open to the growth-seeking national state. One is to cut back on all forms of market 'interference' (on the centre-right, neo-liberal-inspired, understanding of the role of the contemporary state) by cutting taxes, labour rights and capital controls. The other is to refocus its energies on improving the quality of the one resource that is not geographically mobile, namely labour (on the current moderate centre-left, new-growth-theory-inspired understanding of the role of the contemporary state, as advocated particularly by Robert Reich). Whatever happened in the past – so the argument runs – however many models of capitalism were then viable, in the new age of instant communication and inflated financial circuits no state can do more than run either an old or a new version of liberal capitalism and hope by that mechanism to eke out a continually precarious competitive advantage from which a limited degree of welfare provision can, down the line, be adequately funded.

Needless to say, so bleak a policy scenario has been (and remains) much challenged by more radical voices on the European and North American Centre-Left. Such voices have been keen to reassert the space for a more ambitious capitalist modelling, by denying both the novelty and the force of globalization, and by challenging the assumption that, as markets become more global, they automatically become more 'perfect' (in the sense of experiencing effortless factor mobility within them). In consequence, a strong counter-literature now exists, one which asserts the existence of global linkages and flows of contemporary scale in the years before 1914, denies the degree (or weight) of capital export in the social chemistry of many strong national capitalisms (from the US to the German), and reasserts the capacity of the modern state to exercise controls over both capital and labour, given appropriate quantities of political will (for surveys, see Perraton et al., 1997; Radice, 1999). Far from globalization collapsing all models back into a liberal mode, the claim is rather that 'reports of the death of the national economy are greatly exaggerated' (Wade, 1996: 60), that 'national models of growth in the advanced countries are . . . rather undergoing a common transition along distinct trajectories' and that 'government is not so much being squeezed out of the economy, rather the points of leverage are shifting' (Zysman, 1996: 159). In a globalized economy, so the counter-argument runs, state power requires what Linda Weiss has termed 'domestic and international linkages', linkages in which 'the most important power actors' are 'those who participate in them from a position of domestic strength' and linkages which in national governments have an important *catalytic* role to play in orchestrating the participation of nationally based firms in international trade and competition: encouraging foreign direct investment, brokering technology alliances between local and foreign firms, and facilitating the regional relocation of productive networks (Weiss, 1997: 24–5; Weiss, 1998: 167–212). As Wade has it:

> The world economy is more inter-national than global. In the bigger national economies, more than 80 per cent of production is for domestic consumption and more than 80 per cent of investment by domestic investors. Companies are rooted in national home bases with national regulatory regimes. Populations are much less mobile across borders than are goods, finance, or ideas. Those points suggest more scope for government action to boost the productivity of firms operating within their territory than is commonly thought. *(Wade, 1996: 61)*

Both sides of the debate tend to concede that there has been a sea-change in the scale of economic activity at the global level in the past three decades: significant increases in economic flows across national boundaries in the spheres of trade, finance, investment and corporate ownership, and significant increases in the internationalization of certain production processes, supply networks and production chains. They also recognize the particular emergence (and potency) of global financial markets (see Cerny, 1996: 84–6; Zysman, 1996: 170–4). What they disagree about is the extent to which 'on virtually all the important criteria – share of assets, ownership, management, employment, the location of R&D – the importance of the home base remains the rule, not the exception' (Weiss, 1997: 10). In general, those who see globalization as novel and all-embracing go one way on those criteria, emphasizing capital mobility, national state weakness and the erosion of space for variety and social generosity in the governance of successful capitalisms. Those who see globalization as neither novel nor all-embracing go the other, seeing costs to capital exit, the persistence of alternative pathways and the space for a reformist route to international competitiveness. In choosing between them, and finding a way through and beyond what is increasingly a sterile defence of polar positions, we should note the two main ways in which their debate impinges on the question of labour power, and its relationship to the international competitiveness of particular capitalist models.

It is worth noting first that much of the talk of labour-market flexibility is disingenuous, as we saw in chapter 4. There is no avoiding the fact that if markets are only lightly regulated, private capital remains unconstrained and labour remains unprotected. Such a scenario may sound credible to those immersed in a liberal culture, but it is actually a dialogue concerned to shift social power away from labour movements and democratic institutions back into the private boardrooms of companies and back into the hands of one particular (and already highly privileged) social group. Moreover, as a class project, it is not only anti-democratic: it is also economically bankrupt. For 'the logic of the market, left to itself, necessarily tends to be *cumulative* rather than *corrective*' (Anderson, 1987: 72; see also the Appendix, pp. 271–3). A process of uneven economic development created by the unregulated interplay of market forces at the level of the world economy cannot be unwound by those same market forces (on this, see Albo, 1997: 4–8), which is why the centre-left counter-arguments on the limitations of labour-market flexibility are so important. If neo-liberals genuinely believe that factor flexibility is the key to growth (rather than subscribing, behind that claim, to a powerful ideological commitment to unregulated capital markets) then they have to concede the force of the argument (and the evidence) that certain forms of labour flexibility can actually be enhanced by the regulation of the way capital employs labour, by the force of the argument, that is, about the 'beneficial constraints' for capital of corporatist forms of entrenched labour rights. Cutting wages and reducing trade union rights is ultimately self-defeating, as Greg Albo has rightly observed:

> the spread across the capitalist bloc of neo-liberal policies keeping wage increases below productivity growth and pushing down domestic costs has led to an unstable vicious circle of *competitive austerity*: each country reduces domestic demand and adopts an export-oriented strategy of dumping its surplus production, for which there are fewer customers in its national economy given the decrease in workers' living standards and productivity

gains all going to the capitalists, in the world market. This has created a global demand crisis and the growth of surplus capacity across the business cycle. *(Albo, 1994: 147)*

But, as Albo (1997: 8–22) (and Panitch) have also documented, that does not mean that the centre-left strategy of 'progressive competitiveness' is ultimately any freer of self-defeating contradictions. It is not. A strategy aimed at the consolidation of high-tech, high-value-added, high-wage production on the basis of 'the widespread training of a highly skilled, highly flexible and highly motivated labour force' and the encouragement of investment in new technology still presumes, as Leo Panitch has it

> that mass unemployment is primarily a problem of skills adjustment to technological change rather than one aspect of a crisis of overproduction; it fosters an illusion of a rate of employment growth in high tech sectors sufficient to offset the rate of unemployment growth in other sectors; it either even more unrealistically assumes a rate of growth in world markets massive enough to accommodate all those adopting this strategy, or it blithely ignores the issues associated with exporting unemployment to those who don't succeed at this strategy in conditions of limited demand (and with the attendant consequences this would have for sustaining demand); it ignores the reality that capital can also adapt leading technologies in low wage economies, and the competitive pressures on capital in this context to push down wages even in high tech sectors and limit the costs to it of the social wage and adjustment policies so central to the whole strategy's progressive logic in the first place. *(Panitch, 1994: 83)*

For centre-left theorists have also to recognize the poverty of the vision of the world created by the reduction of the state's role to that of investment in human capital. What 're-skilling labour' as a growth strategy does is leave investment as a Dutch auction in which local labour forces (and local states) bid – like whores – for the favours of mobile capital. Such a strategy is equally predicated on leaving capital unregulated as is its neo-liberal alternative, and in both cases lacks the capacity to lift any particular economy to a high growth path without at the same time pushing an alternative economy onto a lower one. That may be electorally popular within the successful economy, but it is neither socially progressive at the level of the world economy as a whole nor free of its own internal propensity to be undermined by similar initiatives elsewhere, whose cumulative effect is to leave individual economies persistently prone to the crises of competitiveness, unemployment and social retrenchment that re-skilling was meant to avoid (on this, Bienefeld, 1994: 112–16; 1996: 429–31). You cannot get off the treadmill simply by running faster. All you can do by that mechanism is temporarily pass others, until they respond by running faster too, with the long-term consequence of having the whole field increase their speed just to stand still. The victor in such a race is not the runner, but the treadmill.

The second thing to note, to which again the image of the treadmill is germane, is that the debate on globalization is a strangely narrow one, which largely leaves out the place and role of *labour* (the people doing the running). It is invariably a debate focused on, and restricted to, discussions of *capital* mobility, especially the mobility of financial capital. The impotence of states is explained (as we have just seen) by the emergence of truly global capital markets, by the size of the capital flows involved in those markets and by the speed with which – via modern technology – capital in the form of money can move from national economy to national economy. It is ultimately a 'bankers ramp' argument, whose emergence has rather pushed into second place the older (that is, the 1970s) 'transfer payments' and 'investment strike' arguments about the power of transnational industrial corporations, the emergence of global production systems and the inability of national governments to control national economic activity when the key players have their own global structures, production priorities and overseas resources. That older set of arguments is still there in the globalization literature, but the current emphasis is clearly on the mobility of financial capital.

Isolating capital mobility in the discussion of globalization in this way is misleading. It is misleading partly because (and to the degree that) it creates the impression that capitalism was without a global dimension until the rise of transnational corporations and IT-linked financial centres. This is clearly false, as many critics of globalization have rightly said (particularly Radice, 1999). If the global parameters surrounding state action are now qualitatively different, that has to be because of developments in a system which has always been global; and if certain capitalist models are now constrained by the increased scale of economic flows across their boundaries, those constraints are largely of their own making, a direct product of the export-led dynamic which fuelled capitalist growth in the postwar 'golden age'. But the narrow conception of globalization is misleading in an even more profound sense (and one which is not much commented upon in the literature) in that it invites us to think of capital in a fetishized form. It predisposes commentators to treat capital as a 'thing' rather than as a 'social relationship', and in consequence not to spot the degree to which capital's ability to realize itself on a global scale is itself dependent on the creation of real production processes on that same global scale. For underneath the movements of capital lies the world of global labour; and beneath the global circuits of financial capital lie circuits of industrial production itself. Capital is not suddenly globally mobile simply because of an IT revolution, as many of the cruder versions of the globalization thesis imply. Technological change in information and communication systems facilitates (and thereby amplifies) capital mobility; but it does not create or trigger that mobility. The enhanced global mobility of capital in the past three decades has social rather than technical roots. Capital is more geographically mobile than it was in the past because it now has more proletariats on which to land.

Accordingly, its mobility has to be charted not just on a geographical map but also on a *social* one. As capital moves, the relative power of different kinds of capitalist alters: industrial capitalists, financial capitalists, capitalists whose profits depend on investment in one economy, capitalists whose profits depend on investments in many. And as capital moves, it may temporarily settle in other forms of capital (in existing stocks and shares, in property, in speculative commodities); but it ultimately has to return, to enhance its value, to the commodities made by real workers in real places. It has to return to employ new strata of workers in established capitalisms (particularly, since the Second World War, in core capitalisms, women workers, rural workers and immigrants); and it has to create whole new proletariats where once stood only subsistence peasantries excluded entirely from commodity production and capitalist wage-labour systems. Capital, that is, as it moves, does more than constrain the policy options of national governments: it actually alters the balance and character of social classes, and does so increasingly on a global scale. Globalization in its modern form is a process based less on the proliferation of computers than on the proliferation of proletariats. The growth in the size of the world proletariat and the change in its geographical centres of gravity – and not simply the enhanced mobility of capital – are among the defining features of the current phase of global capitalism. Prior to 1973, the bulk of the world proletariat resided in North America, Western Europe and Japan, surrounded then by subordinated peasantries in the old colonial empires, sealed off by the Iron Curtain from the wage-labour forces of the communist bloc, and underpinned by pockets of industrial proletariats in Central and South America, South Africa, Australia and parts of the Indian subcontinent. But that is not the shape of the contemporary global proletariat. The past thirty years have seen a vast expansion of proletarian numbers in East (and South) Asia, and in South America; and they have seen the Iron Curtain, sealing off Western proletariats from commodities manufactured by workers in the communist bloc, largely disappear (totally and physically disappear in Europe, more partially but equally potently disappear in China). In effect, at currently 3 billion people (one-third of whom are, according to the ILO, now unemployed or underemployed!) the world proletariat has doubled in size in a generation.

Once globalization is understood in this wider sense, as encompassing labour as well as capital and involving social as well as technical change, it becomes possible to understand more accurately its impact on the viability of models and the politics of the Left. It becomes possible to recognize that the particular capitalist models with which we have been concerned here were all what Kotz and others have called *social structures of accumulation*, structures which had at their core particular settlements between different social classes (Kotz et al., 1994). The form which the combined and uneven development of capitalism as a world system took after 1945 left space – for at least a generation – for the consolidation of strong industrial bourgeoisies and well-unionized working classes in a string of core capitalisms; and indeed those capitalisms flourished precisely to the degree to which such industrial bourgeoisies did actually consolidate themselves. (Each model, you will remember, depended for its high-growth period on large-scale capital investment in locally based manufacturing industry, around which – for a generation – was fused a strong set of shared interests between national industrial capital and organized labour.) That consolidation of classes and fusion of interests then went through two phases: initially (for all but the US) one of technological convergence with US capital, through reconstruction and catch-up based on investing locally in American-style technologies; and later, particularly for Japan and Germany, survival by moving up-market, redeploying low-technology production into new proletariats (at home and especially abroad) while using existing stocks of capital and skills in the core economies to produce higher-value-added products. By its nature, however, each phase could only be temporary. Technological convergence was a once-and-for-all phenomenon, which, once achieved, left competitiveness dependent on the different labour and social costs associated with various social structures of accumulation. Japanese industrial capital caught up with US industrial capital both by copying technology and by working Japanese labour longer and harder than US labour; and both survived thereafter only by bringing their SSAs progressively into line, by cutting US real wages and by inflating Japanese ones. And the 'new international division of labour' which shifted low-technology production to new economies (with new industrial bourgeoisies and new proletariats) was equally short-lived, because as those economies consolidated similar capital stocks and skills – as their social capability (in Abramovitz's terms) grew – then their catch-up left more and more high-quality markets vulnerable to competition on the basis of the costs of SSAs. Increases in the speed of technology diffusion then reduced ever more quickly the space for more generous SSAs protected by technologically induced productivity differentials, to leave labour costs (both wage costs and social costs) as *the* territory upon which current struggles for competitiveness are increasingly being fought.

Karel Williams's extraordinarily important work on the global car industry provides critical supporting data here. He and his colleagues have looked closely at the crisis of cost recovery now besetting core manufacturing industries in advanced capitalist economies, and have established three clear things. The first is that between the 1940s and the 1980s major car companies (based as they were in North America, Western Europe and Japan) competed between each other without major structural crisis, because each was embedded in an economy with a broadly similar (and high) social settlement, each of which 'involved some combination of high wages, short hours and a high mark up for social charges' (Williams et al., 1995: 74). Japan was the exception for most of that period, but as its technological congruence with the rest grew, so its social settlement came into line also. The second is that, in the car industry at least, technological congruence is now bringing production processes into line in *all* the major car producers,

Table 8.2   Build hours per vehicle in the US, German, Japanese and South Korean motor vehicle manufacturing industry

	1972	1975	1980	1985	1988
US	169	174	202	155	174
Germany	268	279	318	258	256
Japan	217	176	135	139	132
South Korea	3,033	1,475	1,255	572	352

Source: Williams et al., 1995: 78

including the new ones in East Asia, and is doing so at precisely the moment when the saturation of the global car market is inducing price cutting across the industry as a whole. (Table 8.2 shows that the technological gap between North American car producers and those of South Korea is now shrinking fast.) The third is that the social settlement surrounding these new producers is significantly lower than that into which the old ones are embedded, and that in particular (as we noted earlier) agreements made on hours worked and wages paid are far less generous to South Korean workers than they are to workers in Europe and the US. In the original core capitalisms, labour costs per employee in manufacturing were still three times higher than in South Korea in the 1980s, a time when Korean workers put in virtually *twice* as many hours each year as did workers in Sweden. In the context of an increasingly shared technology and still divergent social settlements, the precariousness of the class accords negotiated in easier times in Western Europe and even in North America and Japan is obvious. As Williams and his colleagues have it, 'enterprises which are disadvantaged by their social settlement will either run down production or transfer production elsewhere if the values of key variables within their native settlement cannot be changed', so ensuring that 'competition between social settlements where the structural variables have different values' will be 'seriously threatening for workers in high wage, relatively privileged settlements' (Williams et al., 1995: 73, 72).

In general it is now clear that once the postwar processes of convergence and catch-up were complete, the logics of over-production and credit creation endemic to this stage of global capitalism became unstoppable. With falling returns to industrial investment held at bay only by demand inflation, industrial and financial circuits of capital progressively diverged, the systematic retreat of marginal capital from industrial production into financial speculation intensified, and the rate of global capital mobility quickened, as remaining holders of industrial capital sought progressively lower social structures of accumulation in which to embed themselves. As the technology gap narrowed between production processes controlled by different national bourgeoisies, the pressure of lower labour and social costs elsewhere began to erode the stability of working-class rights extracted in core capitalisms, while ensuring that the newly emerging proletariats never got within sight of such rights themselves. The competitive process between national capitalisms began a *racheting down* of social settlements: both by intensifying the wage–effort bargain (lowering wages, quickening and elongating work) and by eroding welfare provision. In the process, sections of industrial capital progressively relocated abroad, in the process slowly converting their owners from a national to an international bourgeoisie. The 'golden age' of national class accords between national labour movements and local industrial classes is coming to an end, as the national sections of the industrial bourgeoisies of advanced capitalist economies lose their centrality in the dominant power blocs to more internationally dependent bourgeois strata, and as the national bourgeoisies that remain face increasing competition in both home and overseas markets from foreign counterparts able to extract more commodities at lower cost from proletariats less well organized and entrenched than their own (Panitch, 1994: 87). Across the advanced capitalist world as a whole, national industrial bourgeoisies have taken their bat home. They will no longer play ball with local labour movements seeking to combine employment security with industrial and social rights. For industrial capital as a whole, the new game in town is the ratcheting down of labour costs, and with it the de-construction of the non-liberal capitalist models in which some of them have hitherto been obliged to participate.

The new politics of the Left

It is perhaps now clear that there is an element of truth in each of the polarized positions within the globalization debate. It is undoubtedly the case that the range of institutional structures consolidated in the various capitalist models over the last fifty years will remain in place, and will affect how a broadly shared set of competitive pressures will be mediated within different national capitalisms. Path dependency will remain. There has been (and there is still) too much investment in particular institutional structures to expect them to vanish overnight (Zysman, 1996: 177–8). In particular the density of institutional linkages between sections of capital that have been such a feature of the Japanese and German modes of economic governance are likely to thin only slowly. There is already evidence of the tenacity of those linkages (Baker, 1996: 13), evidence quite compatible with the emergence of a degree of thinning: a degree both of internally generated separation between banks and industry in the German case and (in the Japanese banking system) of institutional reform which has been largely externally triggered. It is even conceivable that the structures of corporatist intermediation between capital and labour will also survive, although the evidence is stronger of a more common pattern of nascent employer withdrawal from national systems of wage determination. For what globalization has done to the various capitalist models with which we have been concerned is less to obliterate their differences than to 'freeze' in space and time the pattern of the high and low growth trajectories they have created. The enhanced global mobility of capital and the international legal and regulatory structures which now protect it have significantly reduced the space within which new developmental state growth trajectories might be forged by emerging national bourgeoisies in economies which are not yet extensively industrialized; and the space has surely vanished for any new corporatist-induced example of rapid economic growth. The new world order is one in which a neo-liberal specification of capitalist governance is firmly embedded; and unless market mechanisms are more capable of facilitating major changes in the growth trajectories of individual economies than has been argued here, it seems self-evident that the ranking of economies in international league tables of competitiveness bequeathed to us from the 1980s is unlikely to change very much in the period to come.

But *continuity of institutions* is less important than *discontinuity of outcomes*; and here it is clear that the changing balance of global social forces is producing a convergence of effects. The architecture of institutional arrangements may not be changing, but what that architecture delivers (especially for workers) definitely is. In particular, the social settlements achieved by strong labour movements in advanced capitalist economies in that postwar 'golden age' when the size (and geographical location) of the global proletariat was largely fixed are now being eroded. They are being eroded by employers' offensives which are themselves triggered by intensified competition between capitalist enterprises in the context of a far larger pool of available wage labour. If corporatist structures remain, then as with the Garrett and Lange argument on Sweden, they are simply being used to ratchet down wages and labour rights in a slower and more negotiated way than would be effected by the slash-and-burn employment policies dominant in more liberally based capitalist models. This may be a more civilized way of proceeding, but it is still ratcheting down; and because it is, we have to recognize that although the institutional structures of 'trust-based' capitalisms may remain in place, their substance will not. In the burgeoning literature on which capitalist model will 'win through' in the next phase of intensified competition, it is rarely noted that the list of possible winners is restricted to those who own capital. In the uncertainties surrounding the precise victors, the certainty that labour will lose is rarely mentioned. It is rarely conceded, that is, that though the form of the models may stay, the substantive differences they once represented for the rights and rewards of workers are beginning to evaporate.

For unfortunately, we seem again to be entering an era in which the private ownership of the means of production cannot be relied upon to guarantee living standards and job security even to core workers, one in which the defence of established wages and rights requires in consequence more than the pursuit of new class accords with local employing classes of the kind that sufficed for this purpose a generation ago. In each generation, the defence of workers' rights always requires an appreciation of the class formations and institutional structures available for that defence; and in the new global order key classes and institutions available to the Centre-Left in the past have already succumbed to anti-proletarian pressures. Certainly national industrial bourgeoisies and national state apparatuses in core capitalisms seem less available for the negotiation of new capital–labour accords than they were before 1973. For in the broadest terms it is now clear that locally based employers are now less and less likely to agree even to the maintenance of existing workers' rights and rewards (let alone to their growth) because those employers either are themselves already going off-shore or, if remaining committed to local investment and employment, are increasingly vulnerable to foreign competition from firms less burdened by high wages and entrenched labour rights. In the broadest terms too, it is clear that leading elements within the national state structures of a series of advanced capitalisms, far from experiencing globalization as an externally generated problem, have in truth actively participated in the construction of the legal and institutional frameworks within which this global capital mobility has developed. They have competed with each other to lower exchange controls, attract foreign direct investment and contain labour costs; and they have done so with enthusiasm, in a determined attempt to meet their own internally generated set of short-term electoral require-ments (Panitch, 1994: 72–3; 1998: 14; Watson, 1999: 74). Now, of course, since globalization has been politically constructed in this way, by that very token it can in principle be de-constructed; but this time such a de-construction will clearly require a politics of the Left that is sufficiently radical and self-confident successfully to confront (and to transcend) the fusion of state policy and capitalist interests which stand at the heart of the contemporary global assault on workers' rights. The existence of that fusion means that if those rights are to be defended then, in the broadest sense, workers are going to have to defend them on their own.

In fact, the emerging economic difficulties of one capitalist model after another have already had one general political effect which is ostensibly of assistance to that defence. It has put governments of the Centre-Left back into power across most of Western Europe and (on a very generous definition of the Centre-Left) in the US as well. It certainly, for the moment at least, has taken the wind out of the political sails of the European neo-liberal Centre-Right, putting ostensibly left-wing governments into power simultaneously in the UK, France, Sweden and (most recently) Germany itself, and bringing to fifteen the total of socialist or social democratic gov-ernments currently in power in Western Europe. Here then is a moment – one of 'a rare degree of intellectual homogeneity', to quote the French finance minister Dominique Strauss-Kahn (*Financial Times*, 10 November 1998: 3) – at which a bloc of major states could, in principle, unite to reassert a degree of political control over the global movement of capital, and begin to de-construct some of the supra-national institutional arrangements and policies facilitating the unregulated movement of goods, finance, investment and corporate ownership across national boundaries. But what is clear already is that this moment will not be seized by these governments for this purpose. Instead, and at best, the policy shift that will be triggered will be one from Greg Albo's 'competitive austerity' to his 'progressive competitiveness': that is from policies seeking competitive advantage by directly cutting workers' rights to one based on the state funding of labour re-skilling. What will not happen on any scale is any orchestrated state-led attempt to control capital movements directly. Or at least, it will not if the Centre-Left's new 'third way' is given the neo-liberal interpretation canvassed so stridently by the UK's Tony Blair. From the many examples of that stridency, this exchange between Blair and the BBC interviewer John Humphrys on 'the Tobin tax' will suffice to make the point.

JH: . . . There's something else you can do about them and that is impose some sort of tax, some speculation tax.
TB: No, I would say that is the wrong thing to do too, because you actually want people to be able to move money very, very quickly.
JH: Even if all they are doing is gambling with it and threatening to wreck a whole currency?
TB: Well, we've got to be careful of this because I mean it's easy to say at a rhetorical level . . . but actually behind this there are people making investment decisions about economies and if we retreat as a world into protectionism then . . .
JH: But why would that have to be protectionist, taxing the speculators?
TB: If you ended up effectively saying to people, well, 'we are going to tax you for moving your money around', and if we ended up saying, well 'we will consider reintroducing exchange controls', I think it's a very short step from that to countries saying well 'we'll put up import controls'. Now my view is that the global market, in the end, is a good thing for us . . . and the way to handle its consequences is to prepare and equip ourselves for the future. Not to try and resist it or ward it off or say it shouldn't exist. *(cited in Held, 1998: 26)*

If this Blairite orientation does prevail across European social democracy as a whole, then, with greater or lesser degrees of enthusiasm, the new 'third way' governments will – behind a rhetoric of radicalism, modernization and common purpose, and within a policy mixture that will contain vestiges of Keynesian demand management – erode the rights and claims on resources of their labour forces. They will do this to attract globally mobile capital and to restore competitive advantage to nationally based firms of whatever ownership, and they will do it in order to solve their unemployment problem by, in essence, exporting it to others. In the end, of course, if the evidence and arguments of this study are any guide, they will succeed only in ratcheting down the playing field on which the next round of the competitive struggle will then be played out, and in further alienating electorates already highly sceptical about mainstream politics. Those governments are likely then quite rapidly to pay a heavy electoral price, and in the process to leave a gaping political space which, if not filled by a credible (and more radical) form of left-wing politics, will soon be colonized by a protectionist, nationalist Right of the kind foreshadowed by Buchanan in the US and perhaps by Le Pen in France. That would be a democratic and progressive disaster of epochal proportions, which is why the formulation and dissemination of a clear, convincing, progressive and radical alternative to 'progressive competitiveness' is now so vital and urgent a task for the contemporary Left.

The fact that the dominant political response to the emerging difficulties of contemporary capitalism – in the north of the global system if not in the south – is currently restricted to a pale version of old-fashioned social democracy is indicative of the enormous problems of *agency* which beset the Left as the new millennium begins. The social forces and political programmes required for the defence of workers' rights are everywhere weakening under the impact of capitalist recession, and the immediate energies of the remaining institutions of the labour movement – certainly in northern Europe – are currently entirely focused on the defence of welfare capitalism in the face of its salami-like de-construction by political forces of both the Centre-Right and the Centre-Left. That defensive task is vital, but of course will not of itself be enough (or indeed in the end succeed) without the parallel creation of clear alternative answers to the drip-by-drip assertion that globalization leaves us no choice but to retreat to liberal capitalism, and without the emergence of strong cross-national and global forces of resistance to the intensification of the labour process and the diminution of labour rewards and rights.

The intensification of pressure on wages, working conditions and job security is increasingly triggering workers' protests across this new global capitalism, and building a base of shared experiences and interests between workers who were hitherto geographically and culturally scattered (Moody, 1997). What it has not triggered as yet is any effective linkage between those protests, or even the embryo of the formal global structures that labour will require to shadow and counter those already in place orchestrating international trade to a neo-liberal agenda. Nor has it yet triggered a sufficiently extensive debate on the Left on the content of the alternative economic strategies that global labour will need to pursue through those structures. The findings of this study suggest that central to those strategies must be the establishment of a dynamic (in the relationship between national economies) that *ratchets up* wages, working conditions and labour rights rather than, as now, ratchets those wages and rights down. The findings also suggest that the establishment of such a dynamic requires a sharp break with the contemporary drift of economic policy, through the reimposition of tight controls over the movement of capital and the reassertion of democratic and social controls over the economic activities of those who currently own and manage investment funds and productive assets. On the side of labour that ratcheting up will require at the very least the drafting and enforcing of universal labour standards, to apply both to the production of commodities for local consumption and to those released into foreign trade (Sengenberger and Wilkinson, 1995). More likely it will require a fundamental resetting of the structure, distribution and rewarding of paid work (Albo, 1994: 165–7; 1997: 34–7). On the side of capital, that ratcheting up will require at the very least the taxation of speculative capital, the democratization of financial institutions (Pollin, 1995) and the reimposition of capital controls (Crotty and Epstein, 1996). More likely it will require a move back towards more locally self-sufficient production and state-directed manufacturing investment (Albo, 1994: 163–4; 1997: 30–2; Burden et al., 1990).

Whether in the end either moderate or radical resettings are necessary on both the labour and capital sides of the economic equation, the findings and argument of this study suggest that a successful left-wing alternative to current capitalist models will definitely require the development of new institutions of democratic control, new commitments to social equality and a renewed confidence in the capacity of people to arrive by calm and collective discussion at social ends which are superior to those generated through market exchange and the clash of individual self-interests. Left-wing confidence in that capacity, and in the availability of qualitatively new ways of running complex economies, has of course been seriously weakened in the last half-century by the failure of another model not discussed here – Soviet-style central planning – so that we enter the new millennium with a highly developed sense of models that will not work. But the need to find a model that *will* work in ways that capitalist models do not is as strong as ever; and in that sense the task of the Left in the next century remains what it has been throughout the last: to realize the potential for a society of plenty released by the capitalist development of the forces of production, by devising forms of economic governance which are free of the distorting impact on social life of the private ownership of the means of production, distribution and exchange. In the parts of the world system governed by the Christian calendar we may now be entering a new millennium; but the socialists among us are doing so still charged with the completion of the unfinished business of the old one.

Appendix
Theories of Growth

As was mentioned briefly in chapter 1, the contemporary academic debate about the causes of economic growth has its own powerful centre of gravity, its own dominant neo-classical orthodoxy. It is an orthodoxy built around a view of markets as optimal economic and social allocators. It is also an orthodoxy which produces a particular mind-set, one which understands economic activity as the coming together of discrete actors and factors in a linked set of markets (commodity markets, labour markets, product markets). It conceives of the central relationships at play in those markets as being organized in distinct production functions. And it understands the process of growth as a combination of two different kinds of movement: movement along a production function (by intensifying labour processes, exploiting economies of scale, and replacing labour by capital, all in the context of a given stock of knowledge, a given technology), and movements of whole production functions (as the stock of knowledge increases and technical progress ensues). In such a conceptual universe, different growth patterns are seen as the necessary consequence of differences in the workings of such production functions: as the consequence of differences in either the quantity of factors deployed or in the quality of their interaction. And the broad thrust of this approach is one that treats the untrammelled interplay of market forces as the best guarantor of both economic growth *and* the convergence of growth paths between economies, such that, if growth and convergence do not occur, analysis has to focus on inadequacies in market performance. It has to focus on the location of inadequacies in

For a fuller treatment of the themes raised in this Appendix, see Coates, 1999b.

either the supply or the quality of factors of production, or on the existence
of barriers or blockages to their free and unregulated interplay.

Such an approach, although long dominant in professional economic
circles, has never been without challenge. Its central premises have regularly been questioned from within the profession: by Schumpeterians and
post-Keynesians, and now by the 'new growth theories' of (among others)
Lucas, Romer and Scott. Each of these approaches, in its different way,
questions whether the interplay of unregulated market forces automatically
creates an optimal distribution of resources or eventually pulls economies
to similar growth paths and levels. Neo-liberal orthodoxies have also been
challenged – largely from outside the ranks of professional economists – by
two other broad literatures as well. They have been challenged by a
centre/centre-left literature which insists on treating markets as social institutions and which is convinced that capitalism works best – that its growth
rates will be highest – when liberal institutions are tempered by processes
of social cooperation and cohesion that more conventionally trained economists would invariably treat as barriers to growth. And they have been challenged too by a Marxist-inspired literature which explains different growth
performances as the product of different class relationships and underlying
structural contradictions within capitalist modes of production, and which
expects neither the convergence of growth paths nor the existence of prolonged and unbroken periods of economic growth.

The debate around neo-classical growth theory

A central reference point in the recent debate on the causes of economic
growth has been the work of the American economist Robert Solow, who,
with others, formulated in the 1950s what is now widely referred to as 'old
growth theory' or 'the neo-classical growth model'. Solow later described
his writings in the mid-1950s as an attempt to improve on the then dominant Harrod-Domar model of economic growth. Harrod-Domar had
explained economic growth as the consequence of the interplay of three
variables – the savings rate, the rate of growth of the labour force, and the
capital–output ratio – which were all givens or constants: the first a matter
of preferences, the second a matter of social demography, the third a matter
of technology (Solow, 1988: 307). Dissatisfied with such a view, not least
with its implication that growth could come by increasing the savings ratio
alone, Solow replaced the notion of a capital–output ratio with what he later
termed 'a richer and more realistic representation of technology', by distinguishing just three factors: 'straight labor, straight capital, and residual
technical change' (Solow, 1988: 308, 314). Against Harrod-Domar, his
model argued that the equilibrium growth rate of an economy was a function not of its savings and investment rate but 'of the rate of technological
progress in the broadest sense' (ibid.: 309), so that each economy had 'a
unique and stable growth path determined by the growth of the labour force

and of technical progress, with the latter usually assumed to expand at a regular, if unobserved, rate' (Boltho and Holtham, 1992: 2). In the original Solow model, as Nick Crafts later described it, 'growth is independent of the investment rate. . . . policies to promote investment' will necessarily 'run into diminishing returns', and the growth in long-term per capita income requires 'improvements in technology, which are not determined within the model'. In the original Solow model, that is, 'growth is exogenous rather than endogenous' (Crafts, 1996: 31).

Robert Solow's work has had an immense impact on the recent debate on why growth rates differ; but ultimately his original model was (and is) weak. It provided no explanation of its key variable, technical progress. Nor was its assumption of convergence triggered by diminishing returns to capital sustained by the available evidence. Its original formulation inspired the development of a whole set of *growth accountants*, keen to isolate the various factors shaping growth and to reduce the scope of Solow's residual technical variable (see in particular Dennison, 1962; 1967; 1979; 1985; Maddison, 1995a); and its persistent weaknesses stimulated the production of a range of alternative explanations of economic growth which are now widely discussed in the relevant specialist literature under the general label of 'new growth theory' or more accurately – 'post-neo-classical endogenous growth theory'. These new writings tend to depart from the assumptions and approaches of neo-classical economics only cautiously and to a limited degree, but to do so none the less by criticizing the absence of a link, in Solow's original model, between investment rates and growth rates. By abandoning the assumption that the investment ratio will not affect the trend rate of growth (because of diminishing returns to capital which raise the capital–output ratio) a string of new growth theorists have been able to produce models or explanations of economic growth which have 'the effect of permitting an increase in the investment ratio to increase the trend growth rate, because the productivity of investment is not reduced' (McCombie and Thirlwall, 1994: 149).

Each new growth theorist has his or her own growth model, but the approach as a whole shares a general tendency to define capital more widely than was normal in the neo-classical model and to emphasize endogenous sources of improved economic growth. So Lucas, in one of the formative articles triggering the new approach, emphasized the importance of investment in human capital as a trigger to growth (Lucas, 1988), while Romer, in another formative piece, emphasized instead the way in which capital accumulation triggers learning, which then necessarily spills out (beyond the initial investing company) to raise efficiency across the economy as a whole (Romer, 1986). In this way, competitiveness and growth are not treated as something which is 'given' to the economy by exogenously generated technical progress but as something stimulated 'internally' by investments – in knowledge and in people, to the point at which, indeed, in the writings of Maurice Scott, the technical progress that Solow treated as an exogenous cause of economic growth is entirely subsumed within the notion of investment, so that when demographic change is allowed for, 'all growth must result from investment' with 'no room left for some third, quite separate, factor called "technical progress"' (Scott, 1989: 15).

For our purposes here, the writings of the new growth theorists contain two strong messages of significance. One is that even between advanced capitalist economies, growth trajectories can differ permanently. Since technical progress can be created internally and endogenously, there are no automatic diminishing returns and no necessary convergence between growth paths – even in core capitalisms. The second message coming from the new growth theory is that state policy has a role to play in determining whether growth paths continue to diverge or to narrow. There is none of neo-classical theory's principled antipathy to state action in the new growth theory. Since 'a general implication of the new growth economics is that institutions and policy may have stronger effects on the growth rate than would have been predicted using the traditional neo-classical growth model' (Crafts, 1996: 41), a case can be made from within new growth theory 'for subsidies, or other policy interventions, to raise investment or R&D or human capital (or perhaps all together)' (Boltho and Holtham, 1992: 11). The new growth theorists recognize the possibility of what is often termed 'path dependency': that economies, once set on a particular growth path, will be held to it by the resulting pattern of interaction between their own internal resources, and that institutions specific to that economy will be critical to sustaining that particular growth path over time. Indeed the arguments of new growth theorists in professional economics and a range of 'new institutional' arguments in political science (the latter best represented, for our field of enquiry, by the work of such analysts as J. Rogers Hollingsworth and Wolfgang Streeck) share similar intellectual territory – as is evident in the main chapters of this book – by recognizing the manner in which economies are embedded in particular matrices of institutions, and perform differently because of the different economic logics those institutions then trigger.

Schumpeterian and post-Keynesian theories of growth

The new growth theorists are not alone in their unease with neo-classical growth theory; nor are their writings the only source of policy prescriptions available to policy-makers keen to encourage better growth performance. Mainstream economics also has space for – among others – both Schumpeterian and post-Keynesian theories of growth.

The economic writings of Joseph Schumpeter do not provide a fully worked through theory of growth, and certainly do not contain a fully worked through answer to the question of why growth rates differ. Nor, of course, are Schumpeter's writings in any way a response to those of Solow, since they predate them by a generation. But Schumpeter's 1911 study, *The*

Theory of Economic Development, and his 1942 study of *Capitalism, Social-ism and Democracy* do give some powerful pointers to how best to explain and enhance capitalist patterns of growth. Three dimensions of Schum-peter's writings in particular figure prominently in the literatures examined in part 1 of this book.

One is that Schumpeterian economics posits a definition of efficiency quite different to that dominant in neo-classical economics circles. In neo-classical economics, the benchmark against which to judge economic activ-ity – Pareto-optimality – is normally applied in a static and short-term manner. This will not do for Schumpeterians, for whom the test of an economy's efficiency has to be more dynamic and long term than that. Schumpeterian judgements of modes of resource allocation turn on the contribution each makes to the long-run stimulation of wealth creation through technical change, and not on its immediate effect on wealth pro-duction under existing technological conditions. This difference in per-spective is a critical one, with considerable ramifications for the study of why growth rates differ. For, as we shall see next, it generates a qualitatively different understanding of the role of markets and competition in the stimulation of long-term growth from that prevalent in neo-classical eco-nomics, and permits a quite different set of understandings of what con-stitute barriers to growth. Neo-classical economics triggers a mind-set that makes large companies (and trade unions and big government) self-evident barriers to growth. Schumpeterian growth theory has no such tunnel vision.

Second, and as just mentioned, there is a considerable gap between the attitude of Schumpeterians and neo-classical growth theorists (both old and new) to the role of competition in the generation of technological change. Schumpeter famously characterized competitive relationships between capitalist firms as a perpetual struggle for monopoly position, the pursuit of market advantage being the spur to technological innovation and the trigger to capitalism's 'gale of creative destruction'. In a Schumpeterian growth model, therefore, it is not competitive pressures *per se* but the pos-sibility of temporarily replacing competitive relationships with oligopolis-tic ones, which 'provides the bait that lures capital on to untried trails' (Lazonick, 1991: 123) and which is, in consequence, the key endogenous source of technical progress. And for Schumpeterians it is invariably the large company that these days is the institutional focus for such entrepre-neurial or innovative behaviour.

Thirdly, in such a model, the key to successful economic growth – and by implication to differences in patterns of growth – is risk-taking or entre-preneurship. At the heart of a Schumpeterian explanation of growth lies the distinction between two kinds of capitalist activity: enterprise and man-agement. It is entrepreneurial behaviour of an innovative kind that, for Schumpeter, drives the growth process: entrepreneurial behaviour that is qualitatively different from the managerial adaptation of existing stocks of knowledge. Innovation and adaptation are thus crucial concepts in the Schumpeterian canon, and, because they are, the agenda of issues relevant to the understanding of the causes of economic growth stretches out far beyond the restricted terrain of neo-classical growth models. It stretches out, at the very least, to the study of institutional structures likely to generate innovation, and even to the social determinants of technology diffusion and transfer.

To that supply-side list of growth determinants, post-Keynesian economics then adds issues of demand, pointing out that while neo-classical views of growth are – in a trivial sense – true (that output is a function of input) the basic question remains of why resources are differentially inputted (both in time and place). Land may be fixed, but labour is not; and its mobilization and that of capital (including land), have to be triggered. In a world where uncertainty is unavoidable (and therefore expectations are crucial to economic outcomes), and where economic and political institutions play a significant role in shaping economic events, post-Keynesians, in contra-distinction to neo-classical economists, give prominence in their explanations of economic growth to the role of demand, to increasing returns (and associated cumulative causation), and to dynamic differences between sectors of the economy. The important intellectual source of post-Keynesian economic growth theory has been the writings of Nicholas Kaldor. His writings on growth (1957; 1961) placed heavy emphasis on the special role of the manufacturing sector as 'the engine of growth' and on the tendency of 'a fast rate of growth of exports and output . . . to set up a cumulative process, or virtuous circuit of growth, through the link between output growth and productivity growth' (Thirlwall, 1987: 185–6). In this way, post-Keynesian growth theory became highly sensitive to the possibilities of self-sustaining as well as endogenously generated economic growth, became sensitive, that is, both to the way in which a fast growth of demand, translated into a fast growth of supply, could bring a rapid growth of productivity (and thus increasing returns to scale in many sectors of the economy, particularly manufacturing) and to the way the rate of technical progress could be affected by the action of firms (via their rates of investment) and by the rate of growth in general (through learning-by-doing).

At the heart of a post-Keynesian understanding of economic growth stand notions of cumulative causation and unequal exchange. To post-Keynesians, economies, once weakened and if left to themselves, weaken further still. For their poor profit levels generate low investment, low investment produces diminished competitiveness, diminished competitiveness guarantees poor profits; and the cycle begins again. The resulting balance of payments deficits require high interest rates, to hold in foreign capital; and high interest rates deter domestic investment, eventually to produce further balance of payments deficits of a progressively more serious kind. In this argument, and quite contrary to neo-classical growth theory, market forces on their own will not break cumulatively self-sustaining cycles of underperformance and, therefore, will not automatically trigger either eco-

nomic growth or economic convergence. And if this is so, then the adequacy
of Solow's growth model is much in doubt. Those doubts may rest slightly
in new growth theory's tentative explorations of internal sources of technological change, and more robustly in the self-confident Schumpeterian
specification of large companies as that indigenous source. What post-
Keynesians then add is the importance – in triggering growth and preventing cumulative decline – of favourable conditions in the product markets of
those innovating corporate giants, so raising issues about the realization of
profits also missing from the original Solow model. And by this point we
are on territory long familiar to Marxist critiques of capitalist growth performance, critiques which combine assertions about the necessary conditions surrounding capital accumulation (of the sort explored by new growth
theorists and by Schumpeterians) with assertions about the conditions necessary for the realization of profit (of a post-Keynesian kind).

Marxist theories of economic growth

There is no single Marxist theory of growth any more than there is a single
neo-classical growth theory; but as with neo-classical growth theory, it is legitimate to speak of the existence of a general Marxist approach to the question of capitalist growth. It is an approach that breaks with the language of
neo-classical economics and departs from its preoccupation with the production function, by talking instead of capital and its accumulation, and by
conceptualizing economic growth as the extended reproduction of circuits
of capital.

Marxists understand the origins of economic growth to lie not in the *technical* interplay of discrete factors of production but in the *social* interaction
of producing classes. If the central category of neo-classical economics is
'the market' and the critical analytical tool is 'the production function', for
Marxists the central conceptual category is 'mode of production' and the
critical analytical device is 'the circuit of capital'. For Marxists capitalism is
a particular way of organizing productive activity which is different in kind
(and inner logic) both from earlier modes of production such as feudalism
and from later modes such as communism. Like any mode of production,
capitalism is a fusion of two things: the forces of production and the social
relationships within which those forces are mobilized and deployed. These
social relationships, for Marxists, invariably take a class form. Certainly in
all modes of production prior to communism, they take the form of a relationship of exploitation between an owning class and a propertyless class,
between a class that labours and a class that expropriates the products of
that labour as its own personal property. In a capitalist mode of production,
where commodity production is general and labour power has itself become
a commodity ('wage labour'), the basic classes in play are capitalists and pro-
letarians; and growth occurs (in Marxist terms, the forces of production are

developed) through the systematic expropriation by the capitalist class of the surplus product of proletarian labour, a surplus realized by capitalists in the form of profits and held in the form of capital.

It is conventional in Marxist economics to distinguish types of capital and to specify the different circuits of production and exchange within which each operates. It is conventional to distinguish merchant capital, industrial capital and financial capital, and to conceptualize the existence of distinct circuits of commercial, industrial and financial activity. Merchant capital – historically the earliest major form of capital – was and is accumulated by buying cheap and selling dear, initially by linking emerging capitalist markets to the surpluses generated in non-capitalist modes of production, and subsequently by exploiting the uneven development of capitalism itself. Financial capital – historically the last of the three types to move to dominance – began life as a lubricant to the buying and exchange of commodities – and is accumulated essentially as a rent extracted from the surpluses created in the circuit of industrial capital. Industrial capitalists buy labour power and raw materials, organize them in productive processes that generate commodities, and realize the profits of their endeavour by the subsequent sale of those commodities. The source of that profit is the gap between the price paid for labour power as a commodity and the revenue gained by the sale of the commodities produced by labour power so employed. On a Marxist understanding of the origins of economic growth, profits are *realized* in the sphere of exchange but are *created* in the sphere of production; and demand and supply are but moments in a single circuit of economic activity whose reproduction depends on the systematic extraction of surplus value.

In such a system, growth is triggered by the struggle to generate and realize profits. This growth struggle is necessarily, perpetually and simultaneously played out on two class fronts: through a competitive battle between capitalists for market advantage and in a class confrontation between capital and labour over surplus extraction. The competition between capitalists alters the relative weight of types of capital over time, normally shifting centres of gravity of whole capitalist classes initially from trade to industry and eventually from industry to finance. It also builds in a tendency to monopoly – a tendency to what Marxists term the centralization and concentration of capital – as winners swallow losers in the rise and fall of business cycles. At the same time, the class struggle between capital and labour stimulates enhanced productivity and eventually technical innovation, as capitalism's inability to extend indefinitely the working day and intensify the work process eventually obliges individual capitalists to invest in new machinery – in Marxist terms, to shift from processes of capital accumulation based on the appropriation of absolute surplus value to those based on the appropriation of relative surplus value, by altering the organic composition of capital. On this understanding, economic growth then comes in waves, as new technology first drastically increases labour productivity and surplus extraction and so increases the rate of profit, before eventually undermining that rate of profit (and slowing capital accumulation) as the productivity gains of the new technology are fully realized, and the rate of increase of surplus extraction no longer keeps pace with the growth rate of the stock of capital (in processes that Marxists refer to as 'the changing organic composition of capital').

In classic Marxist theory, the pursuit of economic growth produces qualitatively distinct stages of capitalism, as the concentration and centralization of capital moves liberal capitalism on to monopoly capitalism and to imperialism, and as the associated rise of labour movements creates new social structures of accumulation in which the state and welfare provision play an increasingly important stabilizing role. And in classic Marxist theory too, economic growth is never unbroken and is at best wave-like in its patterning, as the system's inexorable tension between the rate of exploitation of labour by capital and the changing organic composition of capital itself eventually pulls profit rates down and slows renewed accumulation – at least until class relationships shift, new technologies emerge, and a new spurt of labour productivity can be triggered. Different Marxist edifices are then built on (or even away from) this classical base – variously long-wave theorists (Mandel, 1979), world-system theorists (Shannon, 1992) or regulation theorists (Aglietta, 1979) – but all of them share a common origin in a broadly Marxist discourse that understands economic growth as ultimately a question of capital accumulation achieved through market competition between capitalists as they collectively dominate and subordinate labour.

References

Abe, E. (1997), 'The state as the "third hand": MITI and Japanese industrial development after 1945', in E. Abe and T. Gourvish (eds), *Japanese Success? British Failure? Comparisons in business performance since 1945*, Oxford University Press, pp. 17–44.

Abel, J. D. (1990), 'Defence spending and unemployment rates: an empirical analysis disaggregated by race', *Cambridge Journal of Economics*, vol. 14, pp. 405–19.

Abramovitz, M. (1962), 'Economic growth in the United States: a review article', *American Economic Review*, vol. 52, no. 4, pp. 762–82.

Abramovitz, M. (1986), 'Catching up, forging ahead and falling behind', *Journal of Economic History*, vol. 46, no. 2, pp. 385–406.

Abramovitz, M. (1989), *Thinking About Growth*, Cambridge University Press.

Abramovitz, M. (1993), 'The search for the sources of growth: areas of ignorance, old and new', *Journal of Economic History*, vol. 53, no. 2, pp. 217–43.

Abramovitz, M. (1994a), 'Catch up and convergence in the postwar growth boom and after', in W. Baumol et al. (eds), *Convergence of Productivity*, pp. 86–125.

Abramovitz, M. (1994b), 'The origins of the postwar catch-up and convergence boom', in J. Fagerberg, B. Verspagen and N. von Tunzelmann (eds), *The Dynamics of Technology, Trade and Growth*, Edward Elgar, pp. 21–53.

Abramovitz, M. and David, P. (1996), 'Convergence and deferred catch-up: productivity leadership and the waning of American exceptionalism', in R. Landau, T. Taylor and G. Wright (eds), *The Mosaic of Economic Growth*, Cambridge University Press, pp. 21–62.

Abromeit, H. (1990), 'Government–industry relations in West Germany', in M. Chick (ed.), *Governments, Industries and Markets*, Edward Elgar, pp. 61–83.

Adams, G. (1982), *The Politics of Defense Contracting: the iron triangle*, Transaction Books.

Aglietta, M. (1979), *A Theory of Capitalist Regulation: the US experience*, New Left Books.

Albert, M. (1993), *Capitalism Against Capitalism*, Whurr Publishers.

Albert, M. and Gonenc, R. (1996), 'The failure of Rhenish capitalism', *Political Quarterly*, vol. 67, no. 3, pp. 184–93.

Albo, G. (1994), 'Competitive austerity and the impasses of capitalist employment policy', in R. Miliband and L. Panitch (eds), *The Socialist Register 1994*, Merlin Press, pp. 144–70.

Albo, G. (1997), 'A world market of opportunities? Capitalist obstacles and Left economic policy', in L. Panitch (ed.), *The Socialist Register 1997*, Merlin Press, pp. 1–43.

Aldcroft, D. H. (1982), 'Britain's economic decline 1870–1980', in G. Roderick and M. Stephens (eds), *The British Malaise*, Falmer Press, pp. 31–61.

Aldcroft, D. H. (1992), *Education, Training and Economic Performance 1944–1990*, Manchester University Press.

Allen, C. S. (1989), 'The underdevelopment of Keynesianism in the Federal Republic of Germany', in P. Hall (ed.), *The Political Power of Economic Ideas: Keynesianism across nations*, Princeton University Press, pp. 263–90.

Alvarez, R. M., Garrett, G. and Lange, P. (1991), 'Government partisanship, labor organisation and macro-economic performance', *American Political Science Review*, vol. 85, no. 2, pp. 539–56.

Amsden, A. H. (1989), *Asia's Next Giant: South Korea and late industrialization*, Oxford University Press.

Amsden, A. H. (1990), 'Third world industrialization: "global fordism" or a new model', *New Left Review*, 182, pp. 5–32.

Anchordoguy, M. (1988), 'Mastering the market: Japanese government targeting of the computer industry', *International Organization*, vol. 42, no. 3, pp. 509–43.

Anderson, P. (1987), 'The figures of descent', *New Left Review*, 161, pp. 20–77.

Anglo-German Foundation (1994), *Regional-level Development Initiatives in Germany*, Anglo-German Foundation.

Aoki, M. (1994), 'The firm as a system of attributes: a survey and research agenda', in M. Aoki and R. Dore (eds), *The Japanese Firm: the sources of competitive strength*, Oxford University Press, pp. 11–40.

Arrighi, G. (1982), 'A crisis of hegemony', in S. Amin et al. (eds), *Dynamics of Global Crisis*, Macmillan, pp. 55–108.

Arrighi, G. (1994), *The Long Twentieth Century: money, power and the origins of our times*, Verso.

Ashton, D. and Green, F. (1996), *Education, Training and the Global Economy*, Edward Elgar.

Atkinson, A. B. (1995), 'Is the welfare state necessarily an obstacle to economic growth?', *European Economic Review*, vol. 39, pp. 723–30.

Baker, G. (1996), 'Japan's limited revolution', *Financial Times*, 20 August, p. 13.

Baker, G. (1997), 'Brave new world?', *Financial Times*, 9 September, p. 19.

Barnett, C. (1986), *The Audit of War: the illusion and reality of Britain as a great nation*, Macmillan.

Barnett, C. (1995), 'The human factor and industrial decline', in D. Coates and J. Hillard (eds), *UK Economic Decline: key texts*, Harvester-Wheatsheaf, pp. 60–72.

Barrell, R. and Pain, N. (1997), 'The growth of foreign direct investment in Europe', *National Institute Economic Review*, April, pp. 63–75.

Bartlett, D. L. and Steele, J. B. (1992), *America: what went wrong?*, Andrews and McMeel.

Batra, R. (1993), *The Pooring of America: competition and the myth of free trade*, Collier Books.

Baumol, W. J. (1986), 'Productivity growth, convergence and welfare: what the long run data show', *American Economic Review*, vol. 76, no. 5, pp. 1072–85.

Baumol, W. J. (1994), 'Multivariate growth patterns: contagion and common forces as possible sources of convergence', in W. J. Baumol, R. R. Nelson and E. N. Wolff (eds), *Convergence of Productivity: cross-national studies and historical evidence*, Oxford University Press, pp. 62–85.

Baumol, W. J., Blackman, S. A. B. and Wolff, E. N. (1991), *Productivity and American Leadership: the long view*, MIT Press.

Baumol, W. J. and McLennan, K. (1985), *Productivity Growth and US Competitiveness*, Oxford University Press.

Baumol, W. J., Nelson, R. R. and Wolff, E. N. (eds) (1994), *Convergence of Productivity: cross-national studies and historical evidence*, Oxford University Press.

Bernstein, M. A. and Adler, D. E. (eds) (1994), *Understanding American Economic Decline*, Cambridge University Press.

Best, M. (1990), *The New Competition: institutions of industrial restructuring*, Polity Press.

Best, M. and Forrant, R. (1996), 'Creating industrial capacity: Pentagon-led versus production-led industrial policies', in J. Michie and J. Grieve Smith (eds), *Creating Industrial Capacity: towards full employment*, Oxford University Press, pp. 225–54.

Bienefeld, M. (1994), 'Capitalism and the nation state in the dog days of the twentieth century?', in R. Miliband and L. Panitch (eds), *The Socialist Register 1994*, Merlin Press, pp. 94–129.

Bienefeld, M. (1996), 'Is a strong national economy a utopian goal at the end of the twentieth century?', in R. Boyer and D. Draiche (eds), *States Against Markets*, Routledge, pp. 415–49.

Blackburn, R. (1999), 'The new collectivism: pension reform, grey capitalism and complex socialism', *New Left Review*, 233, January/February, pp. 3–65.

Blair, T. (1998), 'Foreword' to *Fairness at Work*, Cm 3968, May, HMSO.

Blank, S. (1977), 'Britain: the politics of foreign economic policy, the domestic economy and the problem of pluralistic stagnation', *International Organisation*, vol. 31, pp. 674–721.

Bliss, I. and Garbett, J. (1990), 'Learning lessons from abroad', in P. Summerfield and E. J. Evans (eds), *Technical Education and the State since 1850*, Manchester University Press, pp. 189–216.

Bluestone, B. and Harrison, B. (1982), *The De-industrialisation of America*, Basic Books.

Boltho, A. (1985), 'Was Japan's industrial policy successful?', *Cambridge Journal of Economics*, vol. 9, pp. 187–201.

Boltho, A. and Holtham, G. (1992), 'The assessment: new approaches to economic growth', *Oxford Review of Economic Policy*, vol. 8, no. 4, pp. 1–14.

Booth, A. (1995), *The Economics of the Trade Union*, Cambridge University Press.

Borgos, S. (1991), 'Industrial policy in a federalist polity: micro-corporatism in the United States', in M. D. Hancock, J. Logue and B. Schiller (eds), *Managing Modern Capitalism*, Praeger, pp. 65–94.

Bosch, G. and Lehndorff, S. (1995), 'Working time and the Japanese challenge: the search for a European answer', *International Contributions to Labour Studies*, vol. 5, pp. 1–26.

Boskin, M. and Lau, L. J. (1992), 'Capital, technology and economic growth', in N. Rosenberg, R. Landau and D. C. Mowery (eds), *Technology and the Wealth of Nations*, Stanford University Press, pp. 17–56.

Boswell, J. and Peters, J. (1997), *Capitalism in Contention: business leaders and political economy in modern Britain*, Cambridge University Press.

Botwinick, H. (1993), *Persistent Inequalities: wage disparity under capitalist competition*, Princeton University Press.

Bowles, S. and Edwardes, R. (1993), *Understanding Capitalism*, HarperCollins.

Bowles, S., Gordon, D. and Weisskopf, T. (1984), *Beyond the Wasteland: a democratic alternative to economic decline*, Verso.

Bowles, S., Gordon, D. and Weisskopf, T. (1990), *After the Wasteland: a democratic economics for the year 2000*, M. E. Sharpe.

Boyd, R. (1987), 'Government-industry relations in Japan: access, communication, and competitive collaboration', in S. Wilks and M. Wright (eds), *Comparative Government–Industry Relations: Western Europe, the United States and Japan*, Oxford University Press, pp. 61–90.

Brenner, R. (1998), 'The economics of global turbulence: a special report on the world economy 1950–1998', *New Left Review*, 229, May/June, pp. 1–265.

Brezis, E. S., Krugman, P. R. and Tsiddon, D. (1993), 'Leapfrogging in international competition: a theory of cycles in national technological leadership', *American Economic Review*, vol. 83, no. 2, pp. 1211–19.

Brittan, S. (1997a), 'New role models for old', *Financial Times*, 27 February, p. 24.

Brittan, S. (1997b), 'Asian model R.I.P.', *Financial Times*, 4 December, p. 24.

Britton, A. (ed.) (1992), *Industrial Investment as a Policy Objective*, National Institute of Economic and Social Research.

Broadberry, S. N. (1997), *The Productivity Race: British manufacturing in international perspective, 1850–1990*, Cambridge University Press.

Broadberry, S. N. and Crafts, N. (1990), 'Explaining Anglo-American productivity differences in the mid-twentieth century', *Oxford Bulletin of Economics and Statistics*, vol. 52, pp. 375–402.

Broadberry, S. N. and Wagner, K. (1996), 'Human capital and productivity in manufacturing during the twentieth century: Britain, Germany and the United States', in B. van Ark and N. F. R. Crafts (eds), *Quantitative Aspects of Postwar European Economic Growth*, Cambridge University Press, pp. 244–70.

Brown, K. (1998), 'Scoreboard reveals worrying picture for companies' investment goals', *Financial Times*, 9 November, p. 9.

Brown, W., Deakin, S. and Ryan, P. (1997), 'The effects of British industrial relations legislation 1979–1987', *National Institute Economic Review*, no. 161, July, pp. 69–83.

Brunetta, R. and Dell'Arringa, C. (eds) (1990), *Labour Relations and Economic Performance*, Macmillan.

Brunhoff, S. de. (1978), *The State, Capital and Economic Policy*, Pluto Press.

Buchele, R. and Christiansen, J. (1992), 'Industrial relations and productivity growth: a comparative perspective', *International Contributions to Labour Studies*, vol. 2, pp. 77–97.

Buchele, R. and Christiansen, J. (1998), 'Do employment and income security cause unemployment? A comparative study of the US and the E-4', *Cambridge Journal of Economics*, vol. 22, pp. 117–36.

Burden, T., Breitenbach, H. and Coates, D. (1990), *Features of a Viable Socialism*, Harvester Wheatsheaf.

Burkett, P. and Hart-Landsberg, M. (1996), 'The use and abuse of Japan as a progressive model', in L. Panitch (ed.), *Socialist Register 1996*, Merlin Press, pp. 62–92.

Buttler, F., Franz, W., Schetter, R. and Soskice, D. (1995), *Institutional Frameworks and Labour Market Performance: comparative views on the US and German economies*, Routledge.

Buxton, T. (1998), 'Overview. The foundations of competitiveness: investment and innovation', in T. Buxton, P. Chapman and P. Temple (eds), *Britain's Economic Performance*, 2nd edn, Routledge, pp. 165–86.

Cain, P. and Hopkins, A. (1993a), *British Imperialism: Innovation and Expansion 1688–1914*, Longman.

Cain, P. and Hopkins, A. (1993b), *British Imperialism: crisis and deconstruction 1914–1990*, Longman.

Calder, K. E. (1988), *Crisis and Compensation: public policy and political stability in Japan*, Princeton University Press.

Calder, K. E. (1993), *Strategic Capitalism: private business and public purpose in Japanese industrial finance*, Princeton University Press.

Callon, S. (1995), *Divided Sun: MITI and the breakdown of Japanese high-tech industrial policy 1975–1993*, Stanford University Press.

Cameron, D. (1984), 'Social democracy, corporatism, labour quiescence and the representation of economic interest in advanced capitalist society', in J. Goldthorpe (ed.), *Order and Conflict in Contemporary Capitalism*, Oxford University Press, pp. 143–78.

Cameron, D. (1988), 'Distribution coalitions and other causes of economic stagnation', *International Organisation*, vol. 42, pp. 592–604.

Carling, W. and Soskice, D. (1997), 'Shocks to the system: the German political economy under stress', *National Institute Economic Review*, no. 159, pp. 57–76.

Carnoy, M. (1988), 'The changing world of work in the information age', *New Political Economy*, vol. 3, no. 1, pp. 123–8.

Carr, C. (1992), 'Productivity and skills in vehicle component manufacturers in Britain, Germany, the USA and Japan', *National Institute Economic Review*, no. 139, February, pp. 79–87.

Casson, M. (1993), 'Cultural determinants of economic performance', *Journal of Comparative Economics*, vol. 17, pp. 418–42.

Caves, R. E. (1980), 'Productivity differences among industries', in R. E. Caves and L. B. Krause (eds), *Britain's Economic Performance*, Brookings Institution.

Cerny, P. (1996), 'International finance and the erosion of state policy', in P. Gummett (ed.), *Globaliztion and Public Policy*, Edward Elgar, pp. 83–104.

Chalmers, N. (1989), *Industrial Relations in Japan: the peripheral workforce*, Routledge.

Chandler, A. (1990), *Scale and Scope*, Harvard University Press.

Chandler, M. A. (1986), 'The state and industrial decline: a survey', in A. Blais (ed.), *Industrial Policy*, University of Toronto Press.

Chapman, P. G. (1993), *The Economics of Training*, Harvester Wheatsheaf.

Child-Hill, R. and Fujita, K. (1996), 'Flying geese, swarming sparrows or preying hawk? Perspectives on East Asian industrialization', *Competition and Change*, vol. 1, no. 3, pp. 285–98.

Chote, R. (1998), 'Poverty coming back to East Asia: World Bank Report', *Financial Times*, 28 September, p. 4.

Chowdhury, A. and Iyanet, I. (1993), *The Newly Industrializing Economies of East Asia*, Routledge.

Clegg, S. R., Higgins, W. and Spybey, T. (1990), 'Post-Confucianism, social democracy and economic culture', in S. Clegg et al. (eds), *Capitalism in Contrasting Cultures*, de Gruyter, pp. 31–77.

Clement, W. (1994), 'Social democracy unhinged', *Studies in Political Economy*, vol. 44, Summer, pp. 95–123.

Clinton, B. (1993), *President Clinton's New Beginning: the Clinton–Gore Economic Conference in Little Rock, Arkansas, December 14–15 1992*, Donald I. Fine Inc.

Coates, D. (1980), *Labour in Power? A study of the Labour Government 1974–79*, Longman.

Coates, D. (1983a), 'The political power of trade unions', in D. Coates and G. Johnston (eds), *Socialist Arguments*, Martin Robertson, pp. 55–82.

Coates, D. (1983b), 'The character and origin of Britain's economic decline', in D. Coates and G. Johnston (eds), *Socialist Strategies*, Martin Robertson, pp. 32–63.

Coates, D. (1984), *The Context of British Politics*, Hutchinson.

Coates, D. (1994), *The Question of UK Decline: economy, state and society*, Harvester.

Coates, D. (ed.) (1995a), *Economic and Industrial Performance in Europe*, Edward Elgar.

Coates, D. (1995b), 'UK economic under-performance: causes and cures', *Developments in Economics*, vol. 11, pp. 47–63.

Coates, D. (ed) (1996), *Industrial Policy in Britain*, Macmillan.

Coates, D. (1999a), 'Why growth rates differ', *New Political Economy*, vol. 4, no. 1, pp. 77–96.

Coates, D. (1999b), 'Models of capitalism in the new world order: the British case', *Political Studies*, vol. 47, no. 4, pp. 643–60.

Coates, D. and Wiggen, W. (1995), 'State expenditure and economic performance', in D. Coates (ed.), *Economic and Industrial Performance in Europe*, Edward Elgar, pp. 185–201.

Cohen, D. (1995), *The Misfortunes of Prosperity: an introduction to modern political economy*, MIT Press.

Cohen, S. and Zysman, J. (1987), *Manufacturing Matters: the myth of the post-industrial economy*, Basic Books.

Cohen, S. D. (1995), 'Does the United States have an international competitiveness problem?', in D. P. Rapkin and W. P. Avery (eds), *National Competitiveness in a Global Economy*, Lynne Rienner Publishers, pp. 21–40.

Conservative Government (1994), *Competitiveness: helping business to win*, Cmnd 2563, HMSO.

Conservative Government (1995), *Competitiveness: forging ahead*, Cmnd 2867, HMSO.

Conservative Government (1996), *UK Investment Performance: fact and fantasy*, Cabinet Office.

Cooke, W. and Noble, D. (1998), 'Industrial relations systems and US foreign direct investment abroad', *British Journal of Industrial Relations*, vol. 36, no. 4, pp. 581–609.

Corbett, J. (1994), 'An overview of the Japanese financial system', in N. Dimsdale and M. Prevezer (eds), *Capital Markets and Corporate Governance*, Clarendon Press, pp. 306–24.

Corry, D. and Glyn, A. (1994), 'The macro-economics of equality, stability and growth', in A. Glyn and D. Miliband (eds), *Paying for Inequality: the economic costs of social injustice*, IPPR / Rivers Oram Press, pp. 205–16.

Costello, D. (1993), 'A cross-country, cross-industry comparison of productivity growth', *Journal of Political Economy*, vol. 101, no. 2, pp. 207–22.

Cox, A., Lee, S. and Sanderson, J. (1997), *The Political Economy of Modern Britain*, Edward Elgar.

Crafts, N. (1991), 'Reversing relative economic decline: the 1980s in historical perspective', *Oxford Review of Economic Policy*, vol. 7, no. 3, pp. 81–98.

Crafts, N. (1992), 'Institutions and economic growth: recent British experience in an international context', *West European Politics*, vol. 15, no. 4, pp. 16–38.

Crafts, N. (1993a), *Can De-industrialisation Seriously Damage Your Health? A Review of Why Growth Rates Differ and How to Improve Economic Performance*, Institute of Economic Affairs.

Crafts, N. (1993b), 'Was the Thatcher experiment worth it? British economic growth in a European context', in A. Szirmai, B. van Ark and D. Pilat (eds), *Explaining Economic Growth*, North Holland Publishers, pp. 327–51.

Crafts, N. (1996), 'Post-neo-classical endogenous growth theory: what are its policy implications?', *Oxford Review of Economic Policy*, vol. 12, no. 2, pp. 30–47.

Crafts, N. (1997a), *Britain's Relative Economic Decline 1870–1995: a quantitative perspective*, Social Market Foundation.

Crafts, N. (1997b), 'Economic growth in East Asia and Western Europe since 1950: implications for living standards', *National Institute Economic Review*, no. 162, pp. 75–84.

Crafts, N. (1997c), 'The Human Development Index and changes in standards of living: some historical comparisons', *European Review of Economic History*, vol. 1, part 3, pp. 299–322.

Crafts, N. and Toniolo, G. (eds) (1996), *Economic Growth in Europe since 1945*, Cambridge University Press.

Crepaz, M. M. L. (1992), 'Corporatism in decline? An empirical analysis of the impact of corporatism on macroeconomic performance and industrial disputes in 18 industrialised countries', *Comparative Political Studies*, vol. 25, no. 2, pp. 139–68.

Crotty, J. and Epstein, G. (1996), 'In defence of capital controls', in L. Panitch (ed.), *The Socialist Register 1996*, Merlin Press, pp. 118–49.

Crouch, C. and Streeck, W. (eds) (1997), *Political Economy of Modern Capitalism*, Sage.

Cuomo Commission on Competitiveness (1992), *America's Agenda: rebuilding economic strength*, M. E. Sharpe.

Cusomano, J. (1989), *The Japanese Automobile Industry: technology and management at Nissan and Toyota*, Harvard University Press.

Cutler, T. (1992), 'Vocational training and British economic performance: a further instalment of the British labour problem', *Work, Employment and Society*, vol. 6, no. 2, pp. 161–83.

Daly, A., Hitchens, D. M. W. N. and Wagner, K. (1985), 'Productivity, machinery and skills in a sample of British and German manufacturing plants: results of a pilot enquiry', *National Institute Economic Review*, no. 111, pp. 48–61.

Daniel, W. W. (1987), *Workplace Industrial Relations and Technical Change*, Frances Pinter / Policy Studies Institute.

David, P. A. (1985), 'Understanding the economics of QWERTY: the necessity of history', in B. van Ark (ed.), *Economic Growth in the Long Run*, volume III, Edward Elgar.

Davis, M. (1986), *Prisoners of the American Dream*, Verso.

DeGrasse, R. W. (1983), *Military Expansion, Economic Decline: the impact of military spending on US economic performance*, M. E. Sharpe.

Delsen, L. and van Veem, T. (1992), 'The Swedish model: relevant for other European countries', *British Journal of Industrial Relations*, vol. 30, no. 1, pp. 84–105.

Denison, E. F. (1962), *The Sources of Economic Growth in the United States and the Alternatives Before Us*, Brookings Institution.

Denison, E. F. (1967), *Why Growth Rates Differ: postwar experience in nine western countries*, Brookings Institution.

Denison, E. F. (1979), *Accounting for Slower Economic Growth: the United States in the 1970s*, Brookings Institution.

Denison, E. F. (1985), *Trends in American Economic Growth 1929–1982*, Brookings Institution.

Denison, E. F. and Chung, W. K. (1976), *How Japan's Economy Grew So Fast: the sources of postwar expansion*, Brookings Institution.

Department of Trade and Industry (1998), *Our Competitive Future: building the knowledge-driven economy*, Stationery Office.

Dertouzos, M. L., Lester, R. K. and Solow, R. M. (1989), *Made in America: regaining the productive edge*, MIT Press.

Deyo, F. C. (ed.) (1987), *The Political Economy of the New Asian Industrialism*, Cornell University Press.

Diebold, W. (1982), 'Past and future industrial policy in the United States', in J. Pinder (ed.), *National Industrial Strategies in the World Economy*, Croom Helm, pp. 158–205.

Dimsdale, N. and Prevezer, M. (eds) (1994), *Capital Markets and Corporate Governance*, Clarendon Press.

Dobbin, F. (1994), *Forging Industrial Policy: the United States, Britain and France in the Railway Age*, Cambridge University Press.

Dohse, K., Jurgens, U. and Malsch, T. (1985), 'From "Fordism" to "Toyotism": the social organization of the labor process in the Japanese automobile industry', *Politics and Society*, vol. 14, no. 2, pp. 115–46.

Dollar, D. and Wolff, E. N. (1993), *Competitiveness, Convergence and International Specialization*, MIT Press.

Dore, R. (1973), *British Factory – Japanese Factory: the origins of national diversity in industrial relations*, University of California Press.

Dore, R. (1985), 'Authority or benevolence: the Confucian recipe for industrial success', *Government and Opposition*, vol. 20, no. 2, pp. 196–217.

Dore, R. (1986), *Flexible Rigidities: industrial policy and structural adjustment in the Japanese economy 1970–1980*, Athlone Press.

Dore, R. (1987), *Taking Japan Seriously: a Confucian perspective on leading economic issues*, Athlone Press.

Dore, R. (1988), 'Goodwill and the spirit of market capitalism', in D. Okimoto and T. P. Rohlen (eds), *Inside the Japanese System*, Stanford University Press, pp. 90–9.

Dore, R. (1990), 'Two kinds of rigidity: corporate communities and collectivism', in R. Brunetta and C. Dell'Arringa (eds), *Labour Relations and Economic Performance*, Macmillan, pp. 92–113.

Dore, R. (1993), 'What makes the Japanese different?', in C. Crouch and D. Marquand (eds), *Ethics and Markets: co-operation and competition within capitalist economies*, Blackwell, pp. 66–79.

Dore, R. (1997), 'The distinctiveness of Japan', in C. Crouch and W. Streeck (eds), *Political Economy of Modern Capitalism: mapping convergence and diversity*, Sage, pp. 19–32.

Dosi, G., Tyson, L. D. and Zysman, J. (1989), 'Trade, technologies and development: a framework for discussing Japan', in C. Johnson, L. D. Tyson and J. Zysman (eds), *Politics and Productivity: how Japan's development strategy works*, Harper Business, pp. 3–38.

Dowrick, S. and Nguyen, D. (1989), 'OECD comparative economic growth 1950–85: catch-up and convergence', *American Economic Review*, vol. 79, no. 5, December, pp. 1010–30.

Drucker, P. (1988), 'Economic realities and enterprise strategies', in D. L. Okimoto and T. P. Rohlen (eds), *Inside the Japanese System: readings on contemporary society and political economy*, Stanford University Press, pp. 106–12.

Drysdale, P. and Huang, Y. (1997), 'Technological catch-up and economic growth in East Asia and the Pacific', *Economic Record*, vol. 73, no. 22, September, pp. 201–11.

Dumas, L. J. (1982), *The Political Economy of Arms Reduction: reversing economic decay*, Westview Press.

Dunne, P. (1990), 'The political economy of military expenditure: an introduction', *Cambridge Journal of Economics*, vol. 14, pp. 395–404.

Dyson, K. (1986), 'The state, banks and industry: the West German case', in A. Cox (ed.), *State, Finance and Industry: a comparative analysis of postwar trends in six advanced industrial economies*, Wheatsheaf, pp. 119–41.

Eccleston, B. (1989), *State and Society in Post-War Japan*, Polity Press.

Edelstein, M. (1990), 'What price cold war? Military spending and private investment in the US, 1946–1979', *Cambridge Journal of Economics*, vol. 14, pp. 421–37.

Edgerton, D. (1991a), 'Liberal militarism and the British State', *New Left Review*, 185, pp. 138–69.

Edgerton, D. (1991b), *England and the Aeroplane: an essay on a militant and technological nation*, Macmillan.

Edwards, J. and Fischer, K. (1994a), *Banks, Finance and Investment in Germany*, Cambridge University Press.

Edwards, J. and Fischer, K. (1994b), 'An overview of the German financial system', in N. Dimsdale and M. Prevezer (eds), *Capital Markets and Corporate Governance*, Clarendon Press, pp. 257–83.

Edwards, P. K. (1994), 'A comparison of internal regimes of labor regulation and the problem of the workplace', in J. Belanger, P. K. Edwards, and L. Haiven (eds), *Workplace Industrial Relations and the Global Challenge*, ILR Press, pp. 23–42.

Eisinger, P. (1990), 'Do the American states do industrial policy?', *British Journal of Political Science*, vol. 20, no. 4, pp. 509–35.

Elbaum, B. and Lazonick, W. (1984), 'The decline of the British economy: an institutional perspective', *Journal of Economic History*, vol. xliv, no. 2, pp. 576–83.

Elliott, L. (1998), 'McKinsey's waste output', *Guardian*, 30 November, p. 19.

Ellsworthy, R. R. (1985), 'Capital markets and competitive decline', *Harvard Business Review*, September–October, pp. 171–83.

Employment Policy Institute (1993), 'Britain's jobs deficit', *Economic Report*, vol. 7, no. 6, Employment Policy Institute.

Employment Policy Institute (1998), *Employment Audit* (in association with the Centre for Economic Performance), Employment Policy Institute.

Ergas, H. (1987), 'The importance of technology policy', in P. Dasgupta and P. Stoneman (eds), *Economic Policy and Technological Performance*, Cambridge University Press, pp. 57–96.

Esping-Andersen, G. (1990), *The Three Worlds of Welfare Capitalism*, Polity Press and Princeton University Press.

Esping-Andersen, G. (1994), 'Welfare states and the economy', in N. J. Smelser and R. Swedberg (eds), *The Handbook of Economic Sociology*, Princeton University Press, pp. 711–32.

Esser, J. (1990), 'Bank power in West Germany revised', *West European Politics*, vol. 13, pp. 17–32.

Fagerberg, J. (1988), 'Why growth rates differ', in G. Dosi, C. Freeman, R. Nelson, G. Silverberg and L. Soete (eds), *Technical Change and Economic Theory*, Pinter, pp. 432–57.

Feinstein, C. (1988), 'Economic growth since 1870: Britain's performance in international perspective', *Oxford Review of Economic Policy*, vol. 4, no. 1, pp. 1–13.

Feinstein, C. (1990), 'Benefits of backwardness and costs of continuity', in A. Graham and A. Seldon (eds), *Government and Economies in the Post-war World: economic policies and comparative performance 1945–85*, Routledge, pp. 284–93.

Feng, Y. (1997), 'Democracy, political stability and economic growth', *British Journal of Political Science*, vol. 27, pp. 391–418.

Fine, B. and Harris, L. (1985), *The Peculiarities of the British Economy*, Lawrence and Wishart.

Finegold, D. and Soskice, D. (1988), 'The failure of training in Britain: analysis and prescription', *Oxford Review of Economic Policy*, vol. 4, no. 3, pp. 21–53.

Fitzgerald, R. (ed.) (1995), *The State and Economic Development: lessons from the Far East*, Frank Cass.

Freeman, C. (1988), 'Japan: a new national system of innovation', in G. Dosi, C. Freeman, R. Nelson, G. Silverberg and L. Soete (eds), *Technical Change and Economic Theory*, Pinter, pp. 329–48.

Freeman, C. (1995), 'The 'national system' of innovation' in historical perspective', *Cambridge Journal of Economics*, vol. 19, pp. 5–24.

Freeman, C. and Perez, C. (1988), 'Structural crises of adjustment: business cycles and investment behaviour', in G. Dosi, C. Freeman, R. Nelson, G. Silverberg and L. Soete (eds), *Technical Change and Economic Theory*, Pinter, pp. 38–66.

Freeman, C. and Soete, L. (1997), *The Economics of Industrial Innovation*, Pinter.

Freeman, R. B. and Medoff, J. L. (1984), *What Do Unions Do?*, Basic Books.

Friedman, D. (1988), *The Misunderstood Miracle: industrial development and political change in Japan*, Cornell University Press.

Froud, J., Haslam, C., Johal, J. and Williams, K. (1996), 'Sinking ships? Liberal theorists on the American economy', *Asia Pacific Business Review*, vol. 3, no. 1, pp. 54–72.

Fruin, M. and Nishigushi, T. (1993). 'Supplying the Toyota Production System: intercorporate organizational evolution and supplier subsystems', in B. Kogut (ed.), *Country Competitiveness: technology and the organizing of work*, Oxford University Press, pp. 225–48.

Fruin, W. M. (1992), *The Japanese Enterprise System: competitive strategies and cooperative structures*, Clarendon Press.

Fukuyama, F. (1995), *Trust: the social virtues and the creation of prosperity*, Free Press.

Fulcher, J. (1987), 'Labour movement theory versus corporatism: social democracy in Sweden', *Sociology*, vol. 21, no. 2, pp. 232–52.

Galbraith, J. K. and Calmon, P. du P. (1994), 'Industries, trade and wages', in M. Bernstein and D. Adler (eds), *Understanding American Economic Decline*, Cambridge University Press, pp. 161–98.

Garrett, G. (1998), *Partisan Politics in the Global Economy*, Cambridge University Press.

Garrett, G. and Lange, P. (1986), 'Performance in a hostile world: economic growth in capitalist democracies 1974–1982', *World Politics*, vol. xxxviii, July, pp. 517–45.

Gerlach, M. L. (1989), 'Kieretsu organisation in the Japanese economy: analysis and implications', in C. Johnson, L. Tyson and J. Zysman (eds), *Politics and Productivity: how Japan's development strategy works*, Harper Business, pp. 141–74.

Gerlach, M. L. (1992), *Alliance Capitalism*, University of California Press.

Gerschenkron, A. (1966), *Economic Backwardness in Historical Perspective*, Bellnap Press.

Giersch, H., Paque, K.-H. and Schmieding, H. (1992), *The Fading Miracle: four decades of market economy in Germany*, Cambridge University Press.

Gittleman, M. and Wolff, E. N. (1998), 'R&D activity and cross-country growth comparisons', *Cambridge Journal of Economics*, vol. 19, pp. 189–207.

Glazer, N. (1976), 'Social and cultural factors in Japanese economic growth', in H. Patrick and H. Rosovsky (eds), *Asia's New Giant: how the Japanese economy works*, Brookings Institution, pp. 813–96.

Glyn, A. (1992), 'Corporatism, patterns of employment and access to consumption', in J. Pekkarinen et al. (eds), *Social Corporatism: a superior economic system?*, Oxford University Press, pp. 132–77.

Glyn, A. (1995), 'Social democracy and full employment', *New Left Review*, 211, May/June, pp. 33–55.

Gordon, D. (1994), 'Chickens home to roost: from prosperity to stagnation in the postwar US economy', in M. Bernstein and D. E. Adler (eds), *Understanding American Economic Decline*, pp. 34–76.

Gordon, W. et al. (1994), 'Equality and the Swedish work environment', *Employee Responsibilities and Rights*, vol. 7. no. 2, pp. 141–60.

Gough, I. (1996), 'Social Welfare and Competitiveness', *New Political Economy*, vol. 1, no. 2, pp. 209–32.

Graham, O. (1992), *Losing Time: the industrial policy debate*, Harvard University Press.

Granovetter, M. (1985), 'Economic action and social structure: the problem of embeddedness', *American Journal of Sociology*, vol. 91, pp. 481–510.

Gray, J. (1998), 'When the dream turns into a nightmare', *Financial Times*, 23 March, p. 22.

Green, F. (1988), 'Neoclassical and Marxian conceptions of production', *Cambridge Journal of Economics*, vol. 12, pp. 299–312.

Green, F. (1998), 'Securing commitment to skill formation policies', *New Political Economy*, vol. 3, no. 1, pp. 134–8.

Haggard, S. (1990), *Pathways from the Periphery: the politics of growth in the newly industrializing countries*, Cornell University Press.

Hajime, O. (1988), 'Productivity changes in Japan, 1960–1980', in D. L. Okimoto and T. P. Rohlen (eds), *Inside the Japanese System: readings on contemporary society and political economy*, Stanford University Press, pp. 144–9.

Hall, P. (1986), *Governing the Economy: the politics of state intervention in Britain and France*, Polity Press.

Hall, R. E. and Jones, C. I. (1997), 'What have we learnt from recent empirical growth research', *American Economic Review*, vol. 87, no. 2, pp. 173–7.

Hamilton, G. G. (1997), 'Organisation and market processes in Taiwan's capitalist economy', in M. Orru, N. W. Biggart and G. G. Hamilton (eds), *The Economic Organisation of East Asian Capitalism*, Sage, pp. 237–96.

Hampden-Turner, C. and Trompenaars, F. (1993), *The Seven Cultures of Capitalism*, Piatkus.

Handy, C. (1987), *The Making of Managers*, MSC/NEDC/BIM.

Harrison, L. E. (1992), *Who Prospers? How cultural values shape economic and political success*, Basic Books.

Hart, J. A. (1992a), *Rival Capitalists: international competitiveness in the United States, Japan and Western Europe*, Cornell University Press.

Hart, J. A. (1992b), 'The effects of state-societal arrangements on international competitiveness: steel, motor vehicles and semi-conductors in the United States, Japan and Western Europe', *British Journal of Political Science*, vol. 22, part 3, pp. 255–300.

Hart, J. A. (1994), 'A comparative analysis of the sources of America's economic decline', in M. A. Bernstein and D. E. Adler (eds), *Understanding American Economic Decline*, Cambridge University Press, pp. 199–240.

Hayes, R. H. and Abernathy, W. J. (1980), 'Managing our way to economic decline', *Harvard Business Review*, July/August, pp. 67–77.

Held, D. (1998), 'Globalization: the timid tendency', *Marxism Today*, November/December, pp. 24–7.

Helliwell, J. F. (1994), 'Empirical linkages between democracy and economic growth', *British Journal of Political Science*, vol. 24, part 2, pp. 225–48.

Henderson, D. (1990), 'Comparative economic performance of the OECD countries 1950–1987: a summary of the evidence', in A. Graham and A. Seldon (eds), *Governments and Economies in the Post-war World: economic policies and comparative performance*, Routledge, pp. 273–83.

Henderson, J. (1993a), 'Against the economic orthodoxy: on the making of the East Asian miracle', *Economy and Society*, vol. 22, no. 2, pp. 200–17.

Henderson, J. (1993b), 'The role of the state in the economic transformation of East Asia', in C. Dixon and D. Drakakis-Smith (eds), *Economic and Social Developments in Pacific Asia*, Routledge, pp. 83–114.

Henderson, J. and Appelbaum, R. P. (1992), 'Situating the state in the East Asian development process', in R. P. Appelbaum and J. Henderson (eds), *States and Development in the Asia Pacific Rim*, Sage, pp. 1–26.

Henley, A. and Tsakalotos, E. (1993), *Corporatism and Economic Performance*, Edward Elgar.

Henrekson, M., Jonung, L. and Stymme, J. (1996), 'Economic growth and the Swedish model', in N. Crafts and G. Toniolo (eds), *Economic Growth in Europe since 1945*, Cambridge University Press, pp. 240–89.

Henzler, H. A. (1992), 'The new era of Eurocapitalism', in K. Ohmae (ed.), *The Evolving Global Economy*, Harvard Business Review Books, pp. 3–18.

Heseltine, M. (1996), 'Investment in progress', *Financial Times*, 12 June, p. 22.

Hicks, A. (1988), 'Social democratic corporatism and growth', *Journal of Politics*, vol. 50, no. 4, pp. 677–704.

Hidaka, C. (1997), 'A re-examination of Japan's postwar financing system', in E. Abe and T. Gourvish (eds), *Japanese Success? British Failure? Comparisons in Business Performance since 1945*, Oxford University Press, pp. 141–70.

Hiroshi, O. (1988), 'The closed nature of Japanese intercorporate relations', in D. L. Okimoto and T. P. Rohlen (eds), *Inside the Japanese System: readings on contemporary society and political economy*, Stanford University Press, pp. 81–3.

Hirsch, B. T. and Addison, J. (1986), *The Economic Analysis of Unions: new evidence and approaches*, Allen and Unwin.

Hirst, P. and Thompson, G. (1996), *Globalisation in Question*, Polity Press.

Hobday, M. (1995), *Innovation in East Asia: the challenge to Japan*, Edward Elgar.

Hobsbawm, E. (1968), *Industry and Empire*, Pantheon.

Hollingsworth, J. R. (1997a), 'The institutional embeddedness of American capitalism', in C. Crouch and W. Streeck (eds), *Political Economy of Modern Capitalism*, Sage, pp. 133–47.

Hollingsworth, J. R. (1997b), 'Continuities and changes in social systems of production: the cases of Japan, Germany and the United States', in J. R. Hollingsworth and R. Boyer (eds), *Contemporary Capitalism: the embeddedness of institutions*, Cambridge University Press, pp. 265–317.

Hollingsworth, J. R. and Boyer, R. (1997), 'Co-ordination of economic actors and social systems of production', in J. R. Hollingsworth and R. Boyer (eds), *Contemporary Capitalism: the embeddedness of institutions*, Cambridge University Press, pp. 1–48.

Hollingsworth, J. R., Schmitter, P. and Streeck, W. (eds) (1994), *Governing Capitalist Economies: performance and control of economic sectors*, Oxford University Press.

Hollingsworth, J. R. and Streeck, W. (1994), 'Countries and sectors: concluding remarks on performance, convergence and competitiveness', in J. R. Hollingsworth, P. Schmitter and W. Streeck (eds), *Governing Capitalist Economies: performance and control of economic sectors*, Oxford University Press, pp. 270–300.

Hook, G. (1990), 'The rise of the Pentagon and US state building: the defense program as industrial policy', *American Journal of Sociology*, vol. 96, no. 2, pp. 358–404.

House of Lords Select Committee on Overseas Trade (1985), *Report*, Command Paper 238–1.

Howell, C. (1992), *Regulating Labor: the state and industrial relations reform in France*, Princeton University Press.

Howells, J. and Neary, I. (1991), 'Science and technology policy in Japan: the pharmaceuticals industry and new technology', in S. Wilks and M. Wright (eds), *The Promotion and Regulation of Industry in Japan*, Macmillan, pp. 81–109.

Hudson Report (1974), *The United Kingdom to 1980*, Associated Business Programmes.

Hutton, W. (1994), *The State We're In*, Cape.

Hutton, W. (1997), 'Let's dig deeper behind this black propaganda', *Observer*, 26 January, p. 28.

Imai, K.-I. (1992), 'The Japanese pattern of innovation and its evolution', in N. Rosenberg, R. Landau and D. C. Mowery (eds), *Technology and the Wealth of Nations*, Stanford University Press, pp. 225–46.

IPPR, Commission on Public Policy and British Business (1997), *Promoting Prosperity: a business agenda for Britain*, Vintage Books (for the Institute for Public Policy Research).

Israel, J. (1978), 'Swedish socialism and big business', *Acta Sociologica*, vol. 21, no. 4, pp. 341–53.

Itoh, M. (1990), *The World Economic Crisis and Japanese Capitalism*, Macmillan.

Iversen, T. (1998), 'The choices for Scandinavian Social Democracy in comparative perspective', *Oxford Review of Economic Policy*, vol. 14, no. 1, pp. 59–75.

Iwaki, I. (1996), 'Labour market mechanisms in Japan', in J. Michie and J. Grieve Smith (eds), *Creating Industrial Capacity*, Oxford University Press, pp. 143–64.

Jackson, T. (1998), 'The eclipse of manufacturing', *Financial Times*, 15 December, p. 15.

Johnson, C. (1982), *MITI and the Japanese Miracle: the growth of industrial policy 1925–1975*, Stanford University Press.

Johnson, C. (ed.) (1984), *The Industrial Policy Debate*, University of California Press.

Johnson, C. (1986), 'The institutional foundations of Japan's industrial policy', in C. E. Barfield and W. A. Schambra (eds), *The Politics of Industrial Policy*, American Enterprise Institute, pp. 187–205.

Johnson, C. (1995), *Japan: who governs? The rise of the developmental state*, W. W. Norton.

Johnson, C., Tyson, L. D'A., and Zysman, J. (eds) (1989), *Politics and Productivity: how Japan's development strategy works*, Harper Business.

Joseph, Sir Keith (1979), *Solving the Union Problem is the Key to Britain's Recovery*, Conservative Party Central Office.

Kaldor, M., Sharp, M. and Walker, W. (1986), 'Industrial competitiveness and Britain's defence', *Lloyds Bank Review*, October, pp. 31–49.

Kaldor, N. (1957), 'A model of economic growth', *Economic Journal*, vol. 57, pp. 591–624.

Kaldor, N. (1961), 'Capital accumulation and economic growth', in F Lutz (ed.), *The Theory of Capital*, Macmillan, pp. 177–222.

Kaldor, N. (1966), *Causes of the Slow Rate of Economic Growth of the United Kingdom*, Cambridge University Press.

Katzenstein, P. (1985), *Small States in World Markets*, Cornell University Press.

Kay, J. (1998), 'Crisis: what crisis?', *Financial Times*, 25 November, p. 17.

Keeble, S. P. (1992), *The Ability to Manage: a study of British management 1890–1990*, Manchester University Press.

Keep, E. and Mayhew, K. (1988), 'The assessment: education, training and economic performance', *Oxford Review of Economic Policy*, vol. 4, no. 3, pp. i–xv.

Keep, E. and Mayhew, K. (1998), 'Vocational education and training and economic performance', in T. Buxton, P. Chapman and P. Temple (eds), *Britain's Economic Performance*, 2nd edn, pp. 367–95.

Kendrick, J. W. (1993), 'How much does capital explain?', in A. Szirmai, B. van Ark and D. Pilat (eds), *Explaining Economic Growth*, Elsevier Science Publishers B.V., pp. 129–45.

Kenney, M. and Florida, R. (1993), *Beyond Mass Production: the Japanese system and its transfer to the US*, Oxford University Press.

Kenworthy, L. (1995), *In Search of National Economic Success: balancing competition and cooperation*, Sage.

Keynes, J. M. (1936), *The General Theory of Employment, Interest and Money*, Macmillan.

Kitson, M. and Michie, J. (1995), 'Britain's industrial performance since 1960', Bulletin no. 9, Centre for Industrial Policy and Performance, University of Leeds, pp. 1–3.

Kitson, M. and Michie, J. (1996a), 'Britain's industrial performance since 1960: under-investment and relative decline', *Economic Journal*, vol. 106, no. 434, pp. 196–213.

Kitson, M. and Michie, J. (1996b), 'Manufacturing capacity, investment and employment', in J. Michie and J. Grieve Smith (eds), *Creating Industrial Capacity: towards full employment*, Oxford University Press, pp. 24–51.

Kitson, M. and Michie, J. (1996c), 'Incredible shrinking Britain', *Observer*, 21 January.

Kittel, B. (1998), 'The impact of trade unions on economic performance: theoretical elegance and empirical ambiguity', paper to the Political Studies Association, University of Keele.

Knoke, D. (1996), *Comparing Policy Networks: labour politics in the US, Germany and Japan*, Cambridge University Press.

Kogut, B. (ed.) (1993), *Country Competitiveness: technology and the organization of work*, Oxford University Press.

Korpi, W. (1985), 'Economic growth and the welfare state: a comparative study of 18 OECD countries', *Industrial and Labor Relations Review*, vol. 38, no. 2, pp. 195–209.

Korpi, W. (1992), 'Strategies of reformist socialist parties in a mixed economy: the Swedish model', *Socialism of the Future*, vol. 1, no. 1, pp. 101–9.

Kosonen, K. (1992), 'Saving and economic growth from a Nordic perspective', in J. Pekkarinen et al. (eds), *Social Corporatism*, Oxford University Press, pp. 178–209.

Kotz, D. (1994), 'The regulation theory and the social structure of accumulation approach', in D. Kotz, T. McDonough and M. Reich (eds), *Social Structures of Accumulation: the political economy of growth and crisis*, Cambridge University Press, pp. 85–98.

Kotz, D., McDonough, T. and Reich, M. (eds) (1994), *Social Structures of Accumulation: the political economy of growth and crisis*, Cambridge University Press.

Krauss, E. S. (1992), 'Political economy: policy-making and industrial policy in Japan', *Political Science and Politics*, vol. XXV, no. 1, pp. 44–57.

Krugman, P. (1994a), 'Competitiveness: a dangerous obsession', *Foreign Affairs*, March/April, pp. 28–44.

Krugman, P. (1994b), 'The myth of Asia's miracle', *Foreign Affairs*, November/December, pp. 62–78.

Krugman, P. (1996a), 'Making sense of the competitiveness debate', *Oxford Review of Economic Policy*, vol. 12, no. 3, pp. 17–25.

Krugman, P. (1996b), *Pop Internationalism*, MIT Press.

Kyong-Dong, K. (1994), 'Confucianism and capitalist development in East Asia', in L. Sklair (ed.), *Capitalism and Development*, Routledge, pp. 87–106.

Kyotani, E. (1996), 'Sociological foundations of inter-firm co-operation: the case of Sakaki, a manufacturing town in Japan', paper to the 14th International Labour Process Conference, Birmingham.

Landesmann, M. (1992), 'Industrial policies and social corporatism', in J. Pekkarinen et al. (eds), *Social Corporatism*, Oxford University Press, pp. 242–79.

Lane, C. (1989), *Management and Labour in Europe: the industrial enterprise in Germany, Britain and France*, Edward Elgar.

Lane, C. (1990), 'Vocational training and new production concepts in Germany: some lessons for Britain', *Industrial Relations Journal*, vol. 21, no. 3, pp. 247–59.

Lane, C. (1992), 'European business systems: Britain and Germany compared', in R. Whitley (ed.), *European Business Systems*, Sage, pp. 64–97.

Lane, C. (1995), *Industry and Society in Europe: stability and change in Britain, Germany and France*, Edward Elgar.

Lange, P. (1984), 'Unions, workers and wage regulation: the rational bases of consent', in J. Goldthorpe (ed.), *Order and Conflict in Contemporary Capitalism*, Oxford University Press, pp. 98–123.

Lange, P. and Garrett, G. (1985), 'The politics of growth: strategic interaction and economic performance in the advanced industrial democracies, 1974–1980', *Journal of Politics*, vol. 47, no. 5, pp. 792–827.

Lansbury, M. and Mayes, D. (1996), 'Productivity growth in the 1980s', in D. Mayes (ed.), *Sources of Productivity Growth*, Cambridge University Press, pp. 20–51.

Lash, S. and Urry, J. (1987), *The End of Organised Capitalism*, Polity Press.

Lash, S. and Urry, J. (1994), *Economies of Signs and Space*, Polity Press.

Laverack, D. (1996), 'British banks have changed', in S. Milner (ed.), *Could Finance do More for British Business?*, Institute for Public Policy Research, pp. 55–8.

Lawrence, R. Z. (1984), *Can America Compete?*, Brookings Institution.

Lawrence, R. Z. (1987), 'Is de-industrialisation a myth?', in P. D. Staudohar and H. E. Brown (eds), *De-industrialisation and Plant Closure*, Lexington Books, pp. 25–40.

Lazonick, W. (1991a), *Business Organisation and the Myth of the Market Economy*, Cambridge University Press.

Lazonick, W. (1991b), 'Organisations and markets in capitalist development', in B. Gustafsson (ed.), *Power and Economic Institutions*, Edward Elgar, pp. 253–301.

Lazonick, W. (1992), 'Business organisation and competitive advantage: capitalist transformations in the twentieth century', in G. Dosi, R. Giannetti and P. A. Toninelli (eds), *Technology and Enterprise in a Historical Perspective*, Oxford University Press, pp. 119–63.

Lazonick, W. (1994a), 'Social organisation and technological leadership', in W. Baumol, R. Nelson and E. Wolff (eds), *Convergence of Productivity*, Oxford University Press, pp. 164–96.

Lazonick, W. (1994b), 'Creating and extracting value: corporate investment behaviour and American economic performance', in M. A. Bernstein and D. E. Adler (eds), *Understanding American Economic Decline*, Cambridge University Press, pp. 79–113.

Lazonick, W. (1995), 'Co-operative employment relations and Japanese economic growth', in J. Schor and J.-I. You (eds), *Capital, the State and Labour: a global perspective*, Edward Elgar, pp. 70–110.

Lee, S. (1997a), 'Industrial policy and British decline', in A. Cox, S. Lee and J. Sanderson, *The Political Economy of Modern Britain*, Edward Elgar, pp. 108–65.

Lee, S. (1997b), 'The city and British decline', in A. Cox, S. Lee and J. Sanderson, *The Political Economy of Modern Britain*, Edward Elgar, pp. 206–53.

Lester, R. (1998), *The Productive Edge: how US industries are pointing the way to a new era of economic growth*, W. W. Norton.

Levitas, R. and Guy, W. (eds) (1996), *Interpreting Official Statistics*, Routledge.

Leyshon, A. (1994), 'Under pressure: finance, geo-economic competition and the rise and fall of Japan's postwar growth economy', in S. Corbridge, N. Thrift and R. Martin (eds), *Money, Space and Power*, Blackwell, pp. 116–45.

Lincoln, J. R. (1993), 'Work organization in Japan and the United States', in B. Kogut (ed.), *Country Competitiveness: technology and the organizing of work*, Oxford University Press, pp. 54–74.

Lincoln, J. R., Gerlach. M. and Takahashi, P. (1992), 'Kieretsu networks in the Japanese economy: a dyad analysis of intercorporate ties', *American Sociological Review*, vol. 57, no. 3, pp. 561–85.

Lindbeck, A. (1980), 'Consequences of the advanced welfare state', *The World Economy*, vol. 11, no. 1, pp. 19–38.

Lindbeck, A. (1985), 'What is wrong with the West European economies', *The World Economy*, vol. 8, no. 2, pp. 153–70.

Lindbeck, A. et al. (1994), *Turning Sweden Round*, MIT Press.

Lindberg, L. N. and Campbell, J. L. (1991), 'The state and economic governance', in J. L. Campbell, J. R. Hollingsworth and L. N. Lindberg (eds), *Governance of the US Economy*, Cambridge University Press, pp. 356–95.

Lipietz, A. (1989), *Towards a New Economic Order: post-fordism, ecology and democracy*, Polity Press.

Lipset, S. M. (1959), 'Some social requisites of democracy: economic development and political legitimacy', *American Political Science Review*, vol. 53, pp. 69–105.

Lipset, S. M. (1996), *American Exceptionalism: a double-edged sword*, W. W. Norton.

Lodge, G. C. (1986), *The American Disease*, New York University Press.

Lodge, G. C. and Vogel, E. F. (1987), *Ideology and National Competitiveness*, Harvard Business School Press.

Looker, R. J. and Coates, D. (1986), 'The state and the working class in nineteenth century Europe', in J. Anderson (ed.), *The Rise of the Modern State*, Harvester Press, pp. 91–114.

Lucas, R. E. (1988), 'On the mechanics of economic development', *Journal of Monetary Economics*, vol. 22, pp. 3–42.

Lundberg, E. (1985), 'The rise and fall of the Swedish model', *Journal of Economic Literature*, vol. xxiii, pp. 1–36.

Lundvall, B. (1988), *National Systems of Innovation: towards a theory of innovation and interactive learning*, Pinter.

McCombie, J. S. L. and Thirlwall, A. P. (1994), *Economic Growth and the Balance of Payments Constraint*, Macmillan.

McKinsey Global Institute (1998), *Driving Productivity and Growth in the UK Economy*, McKinsey and Co.

Maddison, A. (1994), 'Explaining the economic performance of nations 1820–1989', in W. Baumol et al. (eds), *Convergence of Productivity*, Oxford University Press, pp. 20–61.

Maddison, A. (1995a), *Explaining the Economic Performance of Nations: essays in time and space*, Edward Elgar.

Maddison, A. (1995b), *Monitoring the World Economy*, OECD.

Maddison, A. (1996), 'Macroeconomic accounts for European countries', in B. van Ark and N. Crafts (eds), *Quantitative Aspects of Post-war European Economic Growth*, Cambridge University Press, pp. 27–83.

Madrick, J. (1995), *The End of Affluence: the causes and consequences of America's economic dilemma*, Random House.

Magaziner, I. C. and Reich, R. B. (1982), *Minding America's Business: the decline and rise of the American economy*, Harcourt Brace Jovanovich.

Mahnkopf, B. (1999), 'Between the devil and the deep blue sea: the German model under the pressure of globalization', in L. Panitch and C. Leys (eds), *The Socialist Register 1999*, Merlin Press, pp. 142–77.

Mandel, E. (1979), *Late Capitalism*, Verso.

Mankiw, N. G., Romer, D. and Weil, D. (1992), 'A contribution to the empirics of economic growth', *Quarterly Journal of Economics*, vol. 107, no. 2, pp. 407–37.

Mann, M. (1988), 'The decline of Great Britain', in M. Mann, *State, Wars and Capitalism: studies in political sociology*, Blackwell, pp. 210–327.

Markusen, A. and Yudken, J. (1992), *Dismantling the Cold War Economy*, Basic Books.

Marquand, D. (1988), *The Unprincipled Society*, Cape.

Marquand, D. (1996), 'Introduction' in P. Hirst and G. Thompson, *Globalization in Question*, Polity Press.

Marsh, P. (1997), 'Manufacturers must try harder: an OECD study of productivity', *Financial Times*, 17 April, p. 4.

Mason, G., van Ark, B. and Wagner, K. (1996), 'Workforce skills, product quality and economic performance', in A. L. Booth and D. J. Snower (eds), *Acquiring Skills: market failures, their symptoms and policy responses*, Cambridge University Press, pp. 175–98.

Masuyama, S. (1994), 'Role of Japanese capital markets: the effect of cross-shareholdings on corporate accountability', in N. Dimsdale and M. Prevezer (eds), *Capital Markets and Corporate Governance*, Oxford University Press, pp. 325–42.

Mathieson, M. and Bernbaum, G. (1988), 'The British disease: a British tradition?', *British Journal of Educational Studies*, vol. XXVI, no. 2, pp. 126–74.

Matthews, R. C. O., Feinstein, C. H. and Odling-Smee, J. C. (1982), *British Economic Growth 1856–1973*, Stanford University Press.

Maurice, M., Sellier, F. and Silvestre, J.-J. (1986), *The Social Foundations of Industrial Power*, MIT Press.

Meidner, R. (1992), 'The rise and fall of the Swedish model', *Studies in Political Economy*, vol. 39, pp. 159–71.

Meidner, R. (1993), 'Why did the Swedish model fail?', in R. Miliband and L. Panitch (eds), *The Socialist Register 1993*, Merlin Press, pp. 211–28.

Metcalf, D. (1989), 'Water notes dry up: the impact of the Donovan reform proposals and Thatcherism at work on labour productivity in British manufacturing industry', *British Journal of Industrial Relations*, vol. 27, no. 1, pp. 1–31.

Metcalf, D. (1990a), 'Union presence and labour productivity in British manufacturing industry: a reply to Nolan and Marginson', *British Journal of Industrial Relations*, vol. 28, no. 2, pp. 249–66.

Metcalf, D. (1990b), 'Trade unions and economic performance: the British evidence', in R. Brunetta and C. Dell'Arringa (eds), *Labour Relations and Economic Performance*, Macmillan, pp. 283–303.

Metcalf, D. (1993), 'Industrial relations and economic performance', *British Journal of Industrial Relations*, vol. 31, no. 2, pp. 255–83.

Metcalf, D. (1994), 'Transformation of British industrial relations? Institutions, conduct and outcomes, 1980–1990', in R. Barrell (ed.), *The UK Labour Market*, Cambridge University Press, pp. 126–57.

Midland Bank (1994), *The Mittelstand. the German model and the UK*, Midland Bank.

Minkin, L. (1991), *The Contentious Alliance: Trade unions and the Labour Party*, Edinburgh University Press.

Mintz, A. (1992), 'Guns vs butter: a disaggregated analysis', in A. Mintz (ed.), *The Political Economy of Military Spending in the United States*, Routledge, pp. 185–95.

Mishel, L., Bernstein, J. and Schmitt, J. (1997), *The State of Working America 1996–97*, M. E. Sharpe.

Mishel, L., Bernstein, J. and Schmit-, J. (1999), *The State of Working America 1998–9*, Cornell University Press.

Mishel, L. and Voos, P. B. (eds) (1992), *Unions and Economic Competitiveness*, M. E. Sharpe.

Mishra, R. (1990), *The Welfare State in Capitalist Society*, Harvester Wheatsheaf.

Miwa, Y. (1996), *Firms and Industrial Organisation in Japan*, Macmillan.

Moody, K. (1997), *Workers in a Lean World*, Verso.

Moore, B. (1966), *The Social Origins of Dictatorship and Democracy*, Beacon Press.

Morishima, M. (1982), *Why Has Japan Succeeded? Western technology and the Japanese ethos*, Cambridge University Press.

Mowery, D. C. and Rosenberg, N. (1993), 'The US national innovation system', in R. Nelson (eds), *National Innovation Systems: a comparative analysis*, Oxford University Press, pp. 29–76.

Mutel, J. (1988), 'The modernization of Japan: why has Japan succeeded in its modernization?', in J. Baechler, J A. Hall and M. Mann (eds), *Europe and the Rise of Capitalism*, Blackwell, pp. 136–58.

Nakatani, I. (1995), 'Sources of competitive asymmetries between the United States and Japan', in D. P. Rapkin and W. P. Avery (eds), *National Competitiveness in a Global Economy*, Lynne Rienner, pp. 41–54.

Nau, H. R. (1990), *The Myth of America's Decline: leading the world economy into the 1990s*, Oxford University Press.

Nelson, R. R. (ed.) (1993), *National Innovation Systems: a comparative analysis*, Oxford University Press.

Nelson, R. R. and Wright, G. (1994), 'The erosion of US technological leadership as a factor in postwar economic convergence', in W. Baumol et al. (eds), *Convergence of Productivity*, pp. 129–6?.

Newman, K. (1992), 'Uncertain seas: cultural turmoil and the domestic eonomy', in A. Wolfe (ed.), *America at Century's End*, University of California Press, pp. 112–30.

Newman, K. (1994), 'Troubled times: the cultural dimensions of economic decline', in M. Bernstein and D. Adler (eds), *Understanding American Economic Decline*, Cambridge University Press, pp. 330–58.

Nichols, T. (1986), *The British Worker Question: a new look at workers and productivity in manufacturing*, Routledge and Kegan Paul.

Nickell, S., Wadhwani, S. and Wall, M. (1989), *Union and Productivity Growth in Britain 1974–1986*, Centre for Labour Economics Discussion Paper 353, London School of Economics.

Nishizawa, T. (1997), 'Education, change and in-firm training in postwar Japan', in E. Abe and T. Gourvish (eds), *Japanese Success? British Failure? Comparisons in business performance since 1945*, Oxford University Press, pp. 107–20.

Noguchi, Y. (1994), 'The "bubble" and economic policies in the 1980s', *Journal of Japanese Studies*, vol. 20, no. 2, pp. 291–329.

Nolan, P. (1994), 'Labour market institutions, industrial restructuring and unemployment in Europe', in J. Michie and J. Grieve Smith (eds), *Unemployment in Europe*, Academic Press, pp. 61–71.

Nolan, P. (1995), 'Trade unions and productivity', in D. Coates and J. Hillard (eds), *UK Economic Decline: key texts*, Harvester Wheatsheaf, pp. 122–36.

Nolan, P. and Marginson, P. (1990), 'Skating on thin ice: David Metcalfe on trade unions and productivity', *British Journal of Industrial Relations*, vol. 28, no. 2, pp. 227–47.

Norman, P. (1998), 'Germany looks out', *Financial Times*, 24 August, p. 20.

Norman, P. (1999), 'Working up to change', *Financial Times*, 8 March 1999, p. 18.

North, D. C. (1990), *Institutions, Institutional Change and Economic Performance*, Cambridge University Press.

Norton-Taylor, R. (1998), 'Arms sales leap to record post-cold war levels', *Guardian*, 23 October, p. 16.

Ohmae, K. (ed.) (1995), *The Evolving Global Economy: making sense of the new world order*, Harvard Business Review Books.

Okimoto, D. (1989), *Between MITI and the Market: Japanese industrial policy for high technology*, Stanford University Press.

Olson, M. (1982), *The Rise and Decline of Nations: economic growth, stagflation and social rigidities*, Yale University Press.

O'Mahoney, M. (1992), 'Productivity levels in British and German manufacturing', *National Institute Economic Review*, February, pp. 46–63.

O'Mahoney, M. (1994/5), 'Relative productivity in British and German manufacturing industry', *Signal*, Winter, p. 12.

O'Mahoney, M. and Wagner, K. (1996), 'Anglo–American productivity performance since 1973', in D. Mayes (ed.), *Sources of Productivity Growth*, Cambridge University Press, pp. 141–63.

Omerod, P. (1994), *The Death of Economics*, London, Faber and Faber.

Omerod, P. (1996), 'National competitiveness and state intervention', *New Political Economy*, vol. 1, no. 1, pp. 119–28.

Oulton, N. (1994), 'Labour productivity and unit labour costs in manufacturing: the UK and its competitors', *National Institute Economic Review*, no. 148, May, pp. 49–60.

Oulton, N. (1995), 'Supply side reform and UK economic growth: what happened to the miracle', *National Institute Economic Review*, no. 154, November, pp. 53–70.

Oulton, N. (1996), 'Workforce skills and export competitiveness', in A. L. Booth and D. J. Snower (eds), *Acquiring Skills: market failures, their symptoms and policy responses*, Cambridge University Press, pp. 199–230.

Ozaki, R. (1991), *Human Capitalism: the Japanese enterprise system as world model*, Penguin.

Pain, N. (1998), 'Prospects for the world economy', *National Institute Economic Review*, no. 166, pp. 28–35.

Panitch, L. (1994), 'Globalization and the state', in R. Miliband and L. Panitch (eds), *The Socialist Register 1994*, Merlin Press, pp. 60–93.

Panitch, L. (1998), '"The state in a changing world": social democratizing global capitalism?', *Monthly Review*, vol. 50, no. 5, pp. 11–22.

Pascale, R. and Rohlen, T. (1988), 'The Mazda turnaround', in D. L. Okimoto and T. P. Rohlen (eds), *Inside the Japanese System: readings on contemporary society and political economy*, Stanford University Press, pp. 149–70.

Patrick, H. and Rosovsky, H. (eds) (1976), *Asia's New Giant: how the Japanese economy works*, Brookings Institution.

Peck, J. and Miyamachi, Y. (1994), 'Regulating Japan? Regulation theory versus the Japanese experience', *Environment and Planning D; Society and Space*, vol. 12, pp. 639–74.

Pekkarinen, J., Pohjala, M. and Rowthorn, B. (eds) (1992), *Social Corporatism: a superior economic system?*, Oxford University Press.

Pempel, T. J. (1998), *Regime Shift: comparative dynamics of the Japanese political economy*, Cornell University Press.

Perkin, H. (1997), 'The third revolution', in G. Kelly, D. Kelly and A. Gamble (eds), *Stakeholder Capitalism*, Macmillan, pp. 35–48.

Perraton, J. (1998), 'Education and growth: introduction', *New Political Economy*, vol. 3, no. 1, pp. 121–3.

Perraton, J., Goldblatt, D., Held, D. and McGrew, A. (1997), 'The globalization of economic activity', *New Political Economy*, vol. 2, no. 2, pp. 257–78.

Persand, A. (1998), 'Don't blame Japan', *Financial Times*, 21 August, p. 20.

Pfaller, A. (1991), 'The United States', in A. Pfaller, I. Gough and G. Therborn, *Can the Welfare State Compete?*, Macmillan, pp. 45–99.

Pfaller, A., Gough, I. and Therborn. T. (1991), *Can the Welfare State Compete? A comparative study of five advanced capitalist countries*, Macmillan.

Pianta, M. (1995), 'Technology growth in OECD countries 1970–1990', *Cambridge Journal of Economics*, vol. 19, pp. 175–87.

Pilat, D. (1994), *The Economics of Rapid Growth: the experience of Japan and Korea*, Edward Elgar.

Piore, M. J. and Sabel, C. F. (1984), *The Second Industrial Divide: possibilities for prosperity*, Basic Books.

Pollard, S. (1992), *The Development of the British Economy, 1914–1990*, Edward Arnold.

Pollin, R. (1995), 'Financial structures and egalitarian economic policy', *New Left Review*, 214, pp. 26–61.

Pollin, R. (1996), 'Saving and finance: real and illusory constraints on full employment policy', in J. Michie and J. Grieve Smith (eds), *Creating Industrial Capacity*, Oxford University Press, pp. 255–88.

Pontusson, J. (1987), 'Radicalization and retreat in Swedish social democracy', *New Left Review*, 165, pp. 5–33.

Pontusson, J. (1992), 'At the end of the third road: Swedish social democracy in crisis', *Politics and Society*, vol. 20, no. 3, pp. 305–22.

Porter, M. (1990), *The Competitive Advantage of Nations*, Macmillan.

Porter, M. (1995), 'Capital disadvantage: America's failing capital investment system', in K. Ohmae (ed.), *The Evolving Global Economy*, Harvard Business Review Books, pp. 33–66.

Prais, S. J. (1987), 'Educating for productivity: comparisons of Japanese and English schooling and vocational preparation', *National Institute Economic Review*, no. 119, February, pp. 40–55.

Prais, S. J. (1988), 'Qualified manpower in engineering', *National Institute Economic Review*, no. 123, February, pp. 76–83.

Prais, S. J. (1995), *Productivity, Education and Training: an international perspective*, National Institute of Economic and Social Research, Occasional Paper XLVIII.

Prais, S. J. (1997), 'How did English schools and pupils *really* perform in the 1995 international comparison in mathematics?', *National Institute Economic Review*, no. 161, July, pp. 53–68.

Pratten, C. (1976), *Labour Productivity Differentials Within International Companies*, Cambridge University Press.

Prevezer, M. (1994), 'Overview. Capital and control: city–industry relations', in T. Buxton, P. Chapman and P. Temple (eds), *Britain's Economic Performance*, Routledge, pp. 193–214.

Prevezer, M. and Ricketts, M. (1994), 'Corporate governance: the UK compared with Germany and Japan', in N. Dimsdale and M. Prevezer (eds), *Capital Markets and Corporate Governance*, Oxford University Press, pp. 237–56.

Price, J. (1997), *How Japan Works: power and paradox in postwar industrial relations*, Cornell University Press.

Quilley, S., Tickell, A. and Coates, D. (1996), *Corporate Relocation in the European Union*, European Parliament Directorate-General for Research, Working Paper Series, Social Affairs Series.

Radice, H. (1995), 'Britain in the world economy: national decline, capitalist success?', in D. Coates and J. Hillard (eds), *UK Economic Decline: key texts*, Harvester, pp. 233–49.

Radice, H. (1999), 'Taking globalization seriously', in L. Panitch and C. Leys (eds), *The Socialist Register 1999*, Merlin Press, pp. 1–28.

Randlesome, C. (1994), *The Business Culture in Germany: portrait of a power house*, Butterworth-Heinemann.

Rapkin, D. P. and Avery, W. P. (eds) (1995), *National Competitiveness in a Global Economy*, Lynne Rienner.

Ray, G. F. (1987), 'Labour costs in manufacturing', *National Institute Economic Review*, no. 120, May, pp. 71–4.

Reeder, D. (1980), 'A recurring debate: education and industry', in G. Bernbaum (ed.), *Schooling in Decline*, Macmillan, pp. 115–48.

Reich, R. (1983), *The Next American Frontier*, Penguin.

Reich, S. (1990), *The Fruits of Fascism: postwar prosperity in historical perspective*, Cornell University Press.

Reich, S. (1995), 'Ideology and competitiveness: the basis for US and Japanese economic policies', in D. P. Rapkin and W. P. Avery (eds), *National Competitiveness in a Global Economy*, Lynne Rienner, pp. 55–102.

Reynolds, P. and Coates, D. (1996), 'Conclusion', in D. Coates (ed.), *Industrial Policy in Britain*, Macmillan, pp. 241–68.

Romer, P. M. (1986), 'Increasing returns and long-run growth', *Journal of Political Economy*, vol. 94, no. 5, pp. 1002–37.

Rose, M. B. (1997), 'Education and industrial experience: influences on British experience since 1945', in E. Abe and T. Gourvish (eds), *Japanese Success? British Failure? Comparisons in business performance since 1945*, Oxford University Press, pp. 121–38.

Rostow, W. W. (1960), *The Stages of Economic Growth: a non-communist manifesto*, Cambridge University Press.

Rothstein, B. (1985), 'The success of Swedish labour market policy: the organisational connection to policy', *European Journal of Political Research*, vol. 13, pp. 153–65.

Rothstein, B. (1990), 'Marxism, institutional analysis and working class power: the Swedish case', *Politics and Society*, vol. 18, no. 3, pp. 317–46.

Rowthorn, B. and Wells, J. (1987), *Deindustrialisation and Foreign Trade*, Cambridge University Press.

Rubery, J. (1994), 'The British production regime: a societal specific system?', *Economy and Society*, vol. 23, no. 3, pp. 334–54.

Rubinson, R. and Browne, I. (1994), 'Education and the economy', in N. Smelser and R. Swedberg (eds), *The Handbook of Economic Sociology*, Princeton University Press, pp. 581–99.

Rubinstein, W. D. (1993), *Capitalism, Culture and Decline in Britain*, Routledge.

Rueschemeyer, R., Stephens, E. H. and Stephens, J. D. (1994), *Capitalist Development and Democracy*, Polity Press.

Ryner, M. (1994), 'Economic policy in the 1980s: the 'Third Way', the Swedish model and the transition from Fordism to post-Fordism', in W. Clement and R. Mahon (eds), *Swedish Social Democracy: a model in transition*, Toronto, Canadian Scholars' Press, pp. 245–84.

Sako, M. and Dore, R. (1988), 'Teaching or testing: the role of the state in Japan', *Oxford Review of Economic Policy*, vol. 4, no. 3, pp. 72–81.

Samuels, R. (1987), *The Business of the Japanese State: energy markets in comparative and historical perspective*, Cornell University Press.

Samuels, R. (1990), 'The business of the Japanese state', in N. Chick (eds), *Governments, Industries and Markets*, Edward Elgar, pp. 36–57.

Sanderson, M. (1986), 'Education and economic decline, 1980–1980s', *Oxford Review of Economic Policy*, vol. 4, no. 1, pp. 38–49.

Sandler, T. and Hartley, K. (1995), *The Economics of Defense*, Cambridge University Press.

Saxonhouse, G. (1983), 'What is all this about 'industrial targeting' in Japan?', *World Economy*, vol. 6, no. 3, pp. 253–73.

Schlossstein, S. (1989), *The End of the American Century*, Congdon and Weed.

Schneider-Lenne, E. R. (1994), 'The role of the German capital markets and the universal banks, supervisory boards, and interlocking directorships', in N. Dimsdale and M. Prevezer (eds), *Capital Markets and Corporate Governance*, Oxford University Press, pp. 284–305.

Schor, J. (1992), *The Overworked American: the unexpected decline of leisure*, Basic Books.

Scott, B. and Lodge, G. C. (eds) (1986), *US Competitiveness in the World Economy*, Harvard Business School Press.

Scott, J. (1997), *Corporate Business and Capitalist Classes*, Oxford University Press.

Scott, M. (1989), *A New View of Economic Growth*, Oxford University Press.

Select Committee on Trade and Industry (1994), *Competitiveness of UK Manufacturing: second report*, HMSO.

Sengenberger, W. and Wilkinson, F. (1995), 'Globalization and labour standards', in J. Michie and J. Grieve Smith (eds), *Managing the Global Economy*, Oxford University Press, pp. 111–34.

Shackleton, J. R. (1995), *Training for Employment in Western Europe and the United States*, Edward Elgar.

Shaikh, A. M. and Tonak, E. A. (1994), *Measuring the Wealth of Nations: the political economy of national accounts*, Cambridge University Press.

Shannon, T. R. (1992), *An Introduction to the World-System Perspective*, Westview Press.

Sharp, M. and Pavitt, K. (1993), 'Technology policy in the 1990s: old themes and new realities', DRC Discussion Paper no. 89, Science Policy Research Unit, University of Sussex.

Sheard, P. (1994), 'Interlocking shareholdings and corporate governance', in A. Aoki and R. Dore (eds), *The Japanese Firm: sources of competitive strength*, Oxford University Press, pp. 310–49.

Sheridan, K. (1993), *Governing the Japanese Economy*, Polity Press.

Shin, J.-S. (1996), *The Economics of the Latecomers: catching-up, technology transfer and institutions in Germany, Japan and South Korea*, Routledge.

Shonfield, A. (1965), *Modern Capitalism*, Oxford University Press.

Sierman, C. L. J. (1998), *Politics, Institutions and the Economic Performance of Nations*, Edward Elgar.

Singh, A. (1993), 'Asian economic success and Latin American failure in the 1980s:

new analyses and future policy implications', *International Review of Applied Economics*, vol. 7, no. 3, pp. 267–89.

Singh, A. J. (1977), 'UK industry and the world economy: a case of deindustrialisation', *Cambridge Journal of Economics*, vol. 1, p. 113–36.

Sirowy, L. and Inkeles, A. (1990), 'The effects of democracy on economic growth and inequality: a review', *Studies in Comparative International Development*, vol. 25, pp. 126–57.

Smith, R. P. (1977), 'Military expenditure and capitalism', *Cambridge Journal of Economics*, vol. 1, pp. 61–76.

Solow, R. (1988), 'Growth theory and after', *American Economic Review*, vol. 78, no. 3, August, pp. 307–17.

Solow, R. (1990), *The Labor Market as a Social Institution*, Blackwell.

Solvell, O., Zander, I. and Porter, M. (1992), *Advantage Sweden*, Norstedts.

Sorge, A. (1991), 'Interpreting cross-national comparisons of technology, organisation and human resources', *Organization Studies*, vol. 12, no. 2, pp. 161–90.

Sorge, A. (1993), 'IV: Introduction', in D. Foray and C. Freeman (eds), *Technology and the Wealth of Nations*, Pinter, pp. 271–6.

Sorge, A. and Warner, M. (1986), *Comparative Factory Organization: an Anglo-German comparison of management and manpower in manufacturing*, Gower.

Soskice, D. (1990), 'Reinterpreting corporatism and explaining unemployment: co-ordinated and non-co-ordinated market economies', in R. Brunetta and C. Dell'Arringa (eds), *Labour Relations and Economic Performance*, Macmillan, pp. 170–211.

Soskice, D. (1991), 'The institutional infrastructure for international competitiveness: a comparative analysis of the UK and Germany', in A. B. Atkinson and R. Brunetta (ed.), *Economics for the New Europe*, Macmillan, pp. 45–66.

Soskice, D. (1993), 'Social skills from mass higher education: rethinking the company-based initial training paradigm', *Oxford Review of Economic Policy*, vol. 9, no. 3, pp. 101–13.

Soskice, D. (1997), 'Stakeholding yes: the German model no', in G. Kelly, D. Kelly and A. Gamble (eds), *Stakeholder Capitalism*, Macmillan, pp. 219–25.

Spulber, N. (1995), *The American Economy: the struggle for supremacy in the twenty-first century*, Cambridge University Press.

Standing, G. (1988), 'Training, flexibility and Swedish full employment', *Oxford Review of Economic Policy*, vol. 4, no. 3, pp. 94–107.

Staudohar, P. D. and Brown, H. E. (eds) (1987), *De-industrialisation and Plant Closure*, Lexington Books.

Steedman, H. and Wagner, K. (1987), 'A second look at productivity, machinery and skills in Britain and Germany', *National Institute Economic Review*, no. 122, November, pp. 84–95.

Strath, B. (1996), *The Organisation of Labour Markets: modernity, culture and governance in Germany, Sweden, Britain and Japan*, Routledge.

Streeck, W. (1989), 'Skills and limits of neo-liberalism: the enterprise of the future as a place of learning', *Work, Employment and Society*, vol. 3, no. 1, pp. 89–104.

Streeck, W. (1992), *Social Institutions and Economic Performance*, Sage.

Streeck, W. (1997a), 'German capitalism: does it exist? Can it survive?', *New Political Economy*, vol. 2, no. 2, pp. 237–56.

Streeck, W. (1997b), 'German capitalism: does it exist? Can it survive?', in C. Crouch and W. Streeck (eds), *Political Economy of Modern Capitalism: mapping convergence and diversity*, Sage, pp. 33–54.

Streeck, W. (1997c), 'Beneficial constraints: on the economic limits of rational voluntarism', in J. R. Hollingsworth and R. Boyer (eds), *Contemporary Capitalism; the embeddedness of institutions*, Cambridge University Press, pp. 197–219.

Swenson, P. (1991), 'Bringing capital back in, or social democracy reconsidered', *World Politics*, vol. 43, July, pp. 513–44.

Tabb, W. K. (1995), *The Postwar Japanese System: cultural economy and economic transformation*, Oxford University Press.

Taylor, R. (1995), 'Work culture that brings no satisfaction', *Financial Times*, 23 August, p. 8.

Therborn, G. (1977), 'The rule of capital and the rise of democracy', *New Left Review*, 103, pp. 3–42.

Therborn, G. (1987), 'Does corporatism really matter: the economic crisis and issues of political theory', *Journal of Public Policy*, vol. 7, pp. 259–84.

Therborn, G. (1991), 'Sweden', in A. Pfaller et al. (eds), *Can the Welfare State Compete?*, Macmillan, pp. 229–69.

Therborn, G. (1992), 'Lessons from 'corporatist'' theorising', in J. Pekkarinen et al., (eds), *Social Corporatism: a superior economic system?*, Oxford University Press, pp. 24–43.

Thirlwall, A. and Sanna, G. (1996), 'The macro determinants of growth and "new" growth theory: an evaluation and some new evidence', in P. Arestis (ed.), *Employment, Economic Growth and the Tyranny of the Market*, Edward Elgar, pp. 131–56.

Thirlwall, A. P. (1987), *Nicholas Kaldor*, Edward Elgar.

Thompson, G. (1989), *Industrial Policy: USA and UK Debates*, Routledge.

Thompson, G. (1991), 'Why wasn't there a Keynesian revolution in economic policy everywhere?', *Economy and Society*, vol. 20, no. 1, pp. 103–19.

Thurow, L. (1992), *Head to Head: the coming economic battle among Japan, Europe and America*, William Morrow.

Thurow, L. (1996), *The Future of Capitalism*, Nicholas Brealey Publishing.

Tolliday, S. and Zeitlin, J. (eds) (1986), *The Automobile Industry and its Workers: between Fordism and flexibility*, Polity Press.

Tomlinson, J. (1997), 'British industrial policy through a Japanese mirror: why no MITI in Britain', in E. Abe and T. Gourvish (eds), *Japanese Success? British Failure? Comparisons in business performance since 1945*, Oxford University Press, pp. 45–60.

Trompenaars, F. (1993), *Riding the Waves of Culture: understanding cultural diversity in business*, The Economist Books.

Tyson, L. and Zysman, J. (1983), 'American industry in international competition', in J. Zysman and L. Tyson (eds, *American Industry in International Competition: government policies and corporate strategies*, Cornell University Press, pp. 15–59.

Tyson, L. and Zysman, J. (1989), 'Developmental strategy and production innovation in Japan', in C. Johnson, L.D. Tyson and J. Zysman (eds), *Politics and Productivity: how Japan's development strategy works*, Harper Business, pp. 59–140.

Tyson, L. D'A. (1992), *Who's Bashing Whom? Trade conflict in high-technology industries*, International Institute for Economics.

van Ark, B. (1992), 'Comparative productivity in British and American manufacturing', *National Institute Economic Review*, no. 142, November, pp. 62–73.

van Ark, B. and Crafts, N. (1996), 'Catch-up, convergence and the sources of postwar European growth: introduction and review', in B. van Ark and N. Crafts (eds), *Quantitative Aspects of Post-War European Economic Growth*, Cambridge University Press, pp. 1–27.

Verspagen, B. (1996), 'Technology indicators and economic growth in the European area: some empirical evidence', in B. van Ark and N. Crafts (eds), *Quantitative Aspects of Post-War European Economic Growth*, Cambridge University Press, pp. 215–43.

Vitois, S. (1997), *German Industrial Policy: an overview*, European Network on

Industrial Policy: Working Papers in European Industrial Policy, no. 9, Department of Commerce, University of Birmingham.

Vogel, D. (1987), 'Government–industry relations in the United States: an overview', in S. Wilks and M. Wright (eds), *Comparative Government–Industry Relations: Western Europe, the United States, and Japan*, Clarendon Press, pp. 91–116.

Vogel, E. F. (1987), 'Conclusion', in G. C. Lodge and E. F. Vogel (eds), *Ideology and National Competitiveness*, Harvard Business School Press, pp. 327–42.

von Tunzelmann, G. (1995), *Technology and Industrial Progress: the foundations of economic growth*, Edward Elgar.

Wade, R. (1988), 'The role of government in overcoming market failure: Taiwan, Republic of Korea and Japan', in H. Hughes (ed.), *Achieving Industrialization in East Asia*, Cambridge University Press, pp. 129–63.

Wade, R. (1990), *Governing the Market: economic theory and the role of government in East Asian industrialisation*, Princeton University Press.

Wade, R. (1992), 'Review article: East Asia's economic success: conflicting perspectives, partial insights, shakey evidence', *World Politics*, vol. 44, no. 2, pp. 270–320.

Wade, R. (1996), 'Globalization and its limits: reports of the death of the national economy are greatly exaggerated', in S. Berger and R. Dore (eds), *National Diversity and Global Capitalism*, Cornell University Press, pp. 60–88.

Wadhwani, S. (1990), 'The effect of unions on productivity growth, investment and employment: a report on some recent work', *British Journal of Industrial Relations*, vol. 28, no. 3, pp. 371–85.

Wakiyama, T. (1987), 'The implementation and effectiveness of MITI's administrative guidance', in S. Wilks and M. Wright (eds), *Comparative Government–Industry Relations: Western Europe, the United States and Japan*, Oxford University Press, pp. 211–32.

Walker, M. (1993), 'National innovation systems: Britain', in R. R. Nelson (ed.), *National Innovation Systems: a comparative analysis*, Oxford University Press, pp. 158–91.

Warwick, P. (1985), 'Did Britain change? An enquiry into the causes of national decline', *Journal of Contemporary History*, vol. 20, pp. 99–133.

Watson, M. (1999), 'Rethinking capital mobility', *New Political Economy*, vol. 4, no. 1, pp. 55–76.

Watson, M. and Hay, C. (1998), 'In the dedicated pursuit of dedicated capital: restoring an indigenous investment ethic to British capitalism', *New Political Economy*, vol. 3, no. 3, pp. 407–26.

Weidenbaum, M. L. and Athey, M. J. (1984), 'What is the rust belt's problem?', in C. Johnson (ed.), *The Industrial Policy Debate*, University of California Press, pp. 117–32.

Weiner, M. (1981), *English Culture and the Decline of the Industrial Spirit 1850–1980*, Cambridge University Press.

Weiss, L. (1993), 'War, the state and the origins of the Japanese employment system', *Politics and Society*, vol. 21, no. 3, pp. 325–54.

Weiss, L. (1997), 'Globalization and the myth of the powerless state', *New Left Review*, 225, September/October, pp. 3–27.

Weiss, L. (1998), *The Myth of the Powerless State: governing the economy in a global era*, Polity.

Weiss, L. and Hobson, J. (1995), *States and Economic Development: a comparative historical analysis*, Polity.

Westney, E. (1993), 'Country patterns in R&D organization: the United States and

Japan', in B. Kogut (ed.), *Country Competitiveness: technology and the organizing of work*, Oxford University Press, pp. 36–53.

Wever, K. and Allen, C. S. (1991), 'The financial system and corporate governance in Germany: institutions and the diffusion of innovations', *Journal of Public Policy*, vol. 13, no. 2, pp. 183–202.

Wever, K. and Berg, P. (1993), 'Human resource development in the United States and Germany', *International Contribution to Labour Studies*, vol. 3, pp. 31–49.

Whitley, R. (1992a), *Business Systems in East Asia: firms, markets and societies*, Sage.

Whitley, R. (1992b), *European Business Systems: firms and markets in their national contexts*, Sage.

Wilkinson, F. (1991), 'Industrial organisation, collective bargaining and economic efficiency', *International Contributions to Labour Studies*, vol. 1, pp. 1–25.

Wilks, S. (1990), 'The embodiment of industrial culture in bureaucracy and management', in S. Clegg, S. G. Redding and M. Cartner (eds), *Capitalism in Contrasting Cultures*, Walter de Gruyter, pp. 131–52.

Wilks, S. (1996), 'Class compromise and the international economy: the rise and fall of Swedish social democracy', *Capital and Class*, no. 58, pp. 89–111.

Wilks, S. and Wright, M. (1991), 'Part 1: Context', in S. Wilks and M. Wright (eds), *The Promotion and Regulation of Industry in Japan*, Macmillan, pp. 11–50.

Williams, K., Cutler, T., Williams, J. and Haslam, C. (1987), 'The end of mass production?', *Economy and Society*, vol. 16, no. 3, August, pp. 405–39.

Williams, K., Haslam, C., Williams, J. and Cutler, T. (1992), 'Against lean production', *Economy and Society*, vol. 21, no. 3, August, pp. 321–54.

Williams, K., Haslam, C., Williams, J., Johal, J., Adcroft, A. and Willis, R. (1995), 'The crisis of cost recovery and the waste of the industrialised nations', *Competition and Change*, vol. 1, no. 1, pp. 67–93.

Williams, K., Thomas, D. and Williams, J. (1983), *Why are the British Bad at Manufacturing?*, Routledge and Kegan Paul.

Williams, K., Williams, J. and Haslam, C. (1989), 'Do labour costs really matter?', *Work, Employment and Society*, vol. 3, no. 3, pp. 281–305.

Williams, K., Williams, J. and Haslam, C. (1990), 'The hollowing out of British manufacturing', *Economy and Society*, vol. 19, pp. 456–90.

Williams, K., Williams, J., Haslam, C. and Wardlow, A. (1989), 'Facing up to manufacturing failure', in P. Hirst and J. Zeitlin (eds), *Reversing Industrial Decline*, Berg, pp. 71–93.

Wolf, M. (1996a), 'No answer in Germany', *Financial Times*, 16 April, p. 18.

Wolf, M. (1996b), 'The ills of manufacturing', *Financial Times*, 14 May, p. 18.

Wolf, M. (1996c), 'End of relative decline', *Financial Times*, 12 June, p. II.

Wolf, M. (1998), 'The equity puzzle', *Financial Times*, 16 December, p. 21.

Wolff, E. N. (1994), 'Technology, capital accumulation, and long-run growth', in J. Fagerberg, B. Verspagen and N. von Tunzelmann (eds), *The Dynamics of Technology, Trade and Growth*, Edward Elgar, pp. 53–74.

Wolff, E. N. and Gittelman, M. (1993), 'The role of education in productivity convergence: does higher education matter?', in A. Szirmai, B. van Ark and D. Pilat (eds), *Explaining Economic Growth*, North Holland, pp. 147–67.

Womack, J. P., Jones, D. T. and Roos, D. (1990), *The Machine that Changed the World*, Rawson Associates.

Yoshitomi, M. (1996), 'On the changing international competitiveness of Japanese manufacturing since 1985', *Oxford Review of Economic Policy*, vol. 12, no. 3, pp. 61–73.

Young, A. (1995), 'The tyranny of numbers: confronting the statistical realities of the East Asian growth experience', *Quarterly Journal of Economics*, vol. CX, August, pp. 641–80.

Young, G. (1992), 'Industrial investment and economic policy', in A. Britton (ed.), *Industrial Investment as a Policy Objective*, National Institute of Economic and Social Research, Report Series no. 3, pp. 1–36.

Young, M. K. (1991), 'Structural adjustment of mature industries in Japan: legal institutions, industry associations and bargaining', in S. Wilks and M. Wright (eds), *The Promotion and Regulation of Industry in Japan*, Macmillan, pp. 135–66.

Zysman, J. (1983), *Governments, Markets and Growth*, Cornell University Press.

Zysman, J. (1996), 'The myth of a "global economy": enduring national foundations and emerging regional realities', *New Political Economy*, vol. 1, no. 2, pp. 157–84.

Zysman, J. and Cohen, S. (1986), 'The international experience', in D. Obey and P. Sarbanes (eds), *The Changing American Economy*, Blackwell, pp. 41–55.

Zysman, J. and Tyson, L. (eds) (1983), *American Industry in International Competition*, Cornell University Press.

Index